THE IMPERIAL WAR MUSEUM BOOK OF

THE WAR IN ITALY 1943–1945

Michael Carver, born in 1915, was commissioned into the Royal Tank Corps in January 1935 and was serving with 1st Royal Tank Regiment in Egypt at the outbreak of the Second World War. Thereafter he served in armoured formations throughout the desert campaign of North Africa, towards the end of which he assumed command of the regiment, which he continued to do in Italy in 1943 and in the landings of Normandy in 1944. There at the age of twenty-nine, he was promoted to command 4th Armoured Brigade, finishing the war with them on the shores of the Baltic.

Carver held important command and staff appointments, at home and abroad, culminating in the posts of Chief of General Staff and, as Field Marshal in 1973, Chief of Defence Staff. He was created a life peer in 1977.

He wrote fifteen books and edited two others, mostly of twentieth-century military history, as well as numerous articles and book reviews. Lord Carver died in 2002.

Second to None: The Royal Scots Greys 1918–1945

El Alamein

Tobruk

The War Lords (ed.)

Harding of Petherton

The Apostles of Mobility

War Since 1945

A Policy of Peace

The Seven Ages of the British Army

Dilemmas of the Desert War

Twentieth Century Warriors: The Development
of the Armed Forces of the Major Military Nations
in the Twentieth Century

Out of Step: Memoirs of a Field Marshal

Tightrope Walking: British Defence Policy Since 1945

Letters of a Victorian Army Officer:
Edward Wellesley 1840–1854 (ed.)

Britain's Army in the Twentieth Century

The National Army Museum Book of the Boer War

THE IMPERIAL WAR MUSEUM BOOK OF

THE WAR IN ITALY
1943–1945

A VITAL CONTRIBUTION TO VICTORY IN EUROPE

Field Marshal Lord Carver

GCB, CBE, DSO, MC

PAN BOOKS
in association with
The Imperial War Museum

First published 2001 by Sidgwick & Jackson

This edition published 2002 by Pan Books
an imprint of Pan Macmillan Ltd
Pan Macmillan, 20 New Wharf Road, London N1 9RR
Basingstoke and Oxford
Associated companies throughout the world
www.panmacmillan.com

ISBN 0 330 48230 0

3 5 7 9 8 6 4 2

A CIP catalogue record for this book is available from
the British Library.

Typeset by SetSystems Ltd, Saffron Walden, Essex
Printed and bound in Great Britain by
Mackays of Chatham plc, Chatham, Kent

Acknowledgements

I wish to express my thanks to the Director-General, Robert Crawford, and the staff of the Imperial War Museum, in particular to Dr Christopher Dowling, Keeper of Museum Services; to Roderick Suddaby and Simon Robbins of the Department of Documents; and to David Parry and Hilary Roberts of the Photograph Archive. Throughout they have given me every encouragement and help, with courtesy and enthusiasm. I am also greatly indebted to William Armstrong, Nicholas Blake and Charlie Mounter of Sidgwick and Jackson, with whom it has once again been a great pleasure to work. As on so many previous occasions, I must express my appreciation to the Librarian, Timothy Ward, and the staff of the Prince Consort's Army Library at Aldershot. Their kindness and help have, as always, been invaluable. I am grateful, once again, to Bruce Hunter, my agent, for his encouragement and help at every stage. Finally I must express my thanks to the contributors, or their copyright holders, from whose papers I have quoted extracts, listed in the Index of Contributors.

Preface

This book does not claim to be a comprehensive and evenly balanced history of the Allied campaign in Italy from 1943 to 1945. That campaign was waged by two armies, the Fifth US and the Eighth British, supported by the US and Royal Navies and the United States Army and Royal Air Forces. The Fifth US Army always contained British troops, a complete corps except in the advance from Rome to Florence and in the final stage. It also included a French corps until July 1944 and a Brazilian division in the later stages.

Eighth Army was very much a Commonwealth one, with a Canadian corps until the end of 1944, a New Zealand division, three Indian divisions and a South African armoured division, until the latter was transferred to the Fifth US Army from Florence onwards. Eighth Army also included a Polish corps, a Jewish brigade, and an Italian contingent. Canadian and South African Air Force squadrons served with the RAF, while some ships and many individuals from the Commonwealth served in and with the Royal Navy. But all the excerpts from personal papers, letters and diaries that are quoted in the pages that follow are taken from those deposited with the Documents Department of the Imperial War Museum, almost all of them from men or women from the United Kingdom: two are from Canadians, two from Australians, one from a New Zealander, and one from a South African. Although some are from British soldiers serving in Indian Army divisions, there are no contributions from Indians themselves, nor from Poles, Frenchmen or Americans. The picture presented therefore is almost exclusively that seen through the eyes of those who came from the British Isles, most of them soldiers, although there are personal accounts also from sailors and, fewer, from airmen.

Within these limits I have tried to achieve a balance between different arms, services and experiences, concentrating however on those of the front line. I have found the experience of reading a large number – many more than those here published – very moving, none more so than when a letter has been a man's last. The sense of duty, of courage or resignation in face of danger, hardship and disappointment of every kind, compensated for by the strength of comradeship, inspiring leadership and wry humour, are all impressive. That did not surprise me. It is what experience of the British army in war, and reading and writing its history, have led me to expect. I hope that readers will also be impressed. Much of the story is a grim one. War in Italy from 1943 to 1945 in many ways resembled that of 1914–1918. But it was not all grim. The beauty of Italy, both in town and countryside, and the friendship of the Italians, especially that of the poor in remote places, was welcomed and appreciated by many. It was a tragedy for Italy that Mussolini's ambitions involved his people in Hitler's even greater ones, so that, when his successors managed to extricate their nation from the Axis partnership, their country became a battleground, fought over bitterly and bombed to destruction.

Contents

List of Illustrations

Section One

1. General Alexander conferring with Generals Montgomery and Patton. (NA5015)
2. General Montgomery handing cigarettes to men of the 51st (Highland) Division. (NA 5004)
3. 51st (Highland) Division passing through Vizzini. (NA4854)
4. 252 Field Company Royal Engineers building a bridge near Catania. (NA4904)
5. Sherman of 44th Royal Tank Regiment landing in Sicily from a pontoon. (NA4548)
6. Bren-gun carriers landing from an LST at Salerno. (NA6622)
7. Carriers of 46th Division being ferried across the River Volturno by 272 Field Company Royal Engineers. (NA7762)
8. A Sherman tank of 4th County of London Yeomanry fording the Volturno. 17 October 1943. (NA7860)
9. 6th Cheshires moving up to Monte Camino. 6 November 1943. (NA8484)
10. 17-pounders of 65th Anti-tank Regiment Royal Artillery (Norfolk Yeomanry) moving through Scarfati. 29 September 1943. (NA7455)
11. A 5.5in medium gun of 99 Battery, 74th Regiment Royal Artillery, in mud near Monte Camino. 19 November 1943. (NA8787)
12. RAF Spitfire ready for action. (NA7830)
13. Stretcher bearers bring casualties down the side of Monte Camino. 3–4 December 1943. (NA9367)
14. Sister M. W. Sampson QAIMNS treating casualties at 21 Casualty Clearing Station. 10 January 1944. (NA10718)
15. General Eisenhower with Generals McCreery and Mark Clark on his farewell visit to Fifth US Army. 23 December 1943. (NA10077)
16. The River Trigno beyond Termoli. (NA8601)

Section Two

Section Three

Glossary

AVREs Armoured Vehicle Royal Engineers. Various types on a tank chassis.

Bde Brigade.

Bn Battalion.

Bofors 40mm light anti-aircraft gun.

Bren-gun carrier Small tracked and lightly armoured infantry vehicle.

Coy Company.

DD tank Duplex Drive amphibious tank.

Dingo Daimler wheeled armoured two-man scout car.

DUKW Amphibious wheeled truck.

folboat Collapsible canoe, usually launched from a submarine.

groupement French army term for a collection of units under one command, not forming a regular established formation.

Jaeger German army name for certain units who had originally been light infantry: literally 'hunter'. British army rifle and light infantry regiments were formed on their pattern for service in the American War of Independence.

LO Liaison Officer.

LCA Landing Craft Assault.

LCI Landing Craft Infantry.

LCT Landing Craft Tank.

LST Landing Ship Tank.

Mark IV Panzer   The original German Mark IV (P(an)z(er)k(ampf)w(agen)) was designed as a close infantry support tank, equipped with a comparatively low-velocity 75mm gun to fire high explosive shells in support of the Mark III, equipped with an armour-piercing gun, 37mm and later 50mm. In 1942 the Mark IV(F) carried a high-velocity armour-piercing 75mm gun.

Mark V Panzer (Panther)   Introduced in 1943, this was the most effective German tank of the war. With a thick, sharply angled front plate, it carried an improved 75mm armour-piercing gun, and was more mobile than the Mark VI, the Tiger.

MDS   Main Dressing Station. The stages of casualty evacuation were from Regimental Aid Post (RAP) to Forward Dressing Station (FDS), usually one per brigade, to MDS, one per division, thence to Casualty Clearing Station (CCS), from which the casualty would be evacuated by road, rail, air or hospital ship to a field or base hospital.

Nebelwerfer   Multi-barrelled mortar, originally designed to project chemi-cal-warfare shells. The projectiles made a banshee-like sound in flight, provoking its nickname 'Moaning Minnie'.

No. 36 grenade   Grenade fired from a rifle.

OKW   Oberkommando Wehrmacht. The High Command of the German armed forces.

PIAT   Projector Infantry Anti-Tank. Fired a hollow-charge warhead from the shoulder.

QAIMNS   Queen Alexandra's Imperial Military Nursing Service.

RAP   Regimental Aid Post. See MDS, above.

Spandau   The British name for the German army machine gun.

stonk   A concentration of artillery fire.

TAC   Tactical, sometimes used as an abbreviation for Tac HQ, Tactical or Forward Headquarters.

Tiger German Mark VI tank. Introduced in 1943. A heavy (56 ton), thickly armoured tank, carrying a shortened version of the 88mm anti-tank gun.

Tirailleurs Sharpshooters. Many French colonial infantry regiments were named *Tirailleurs*.

wadi Arabic for a dried-up river bed, sometimes used for any dry ravine.

Maps

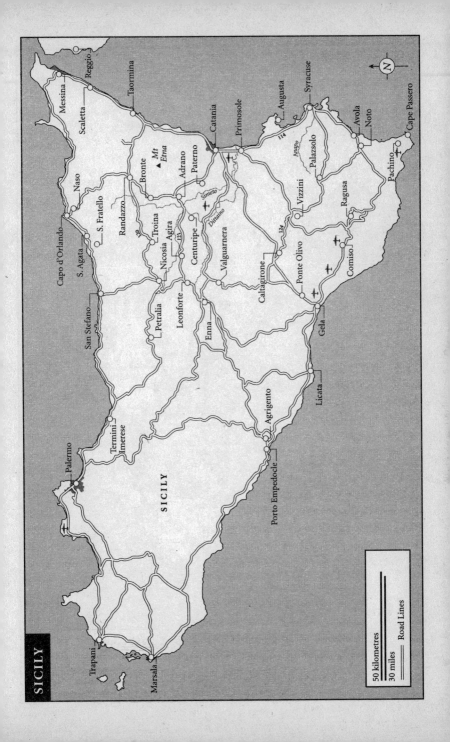

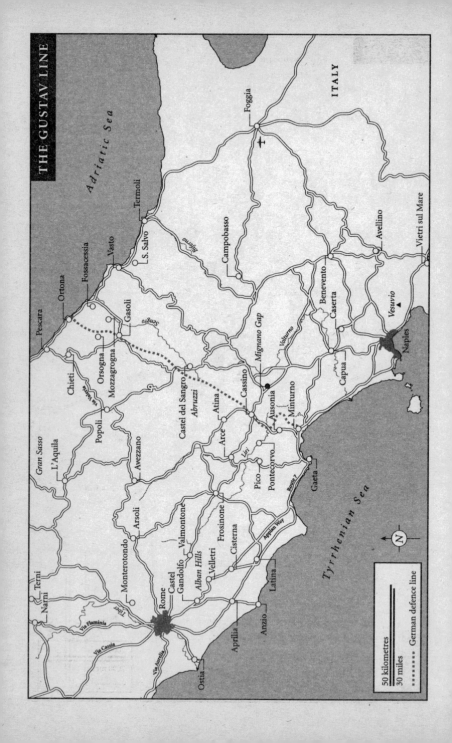

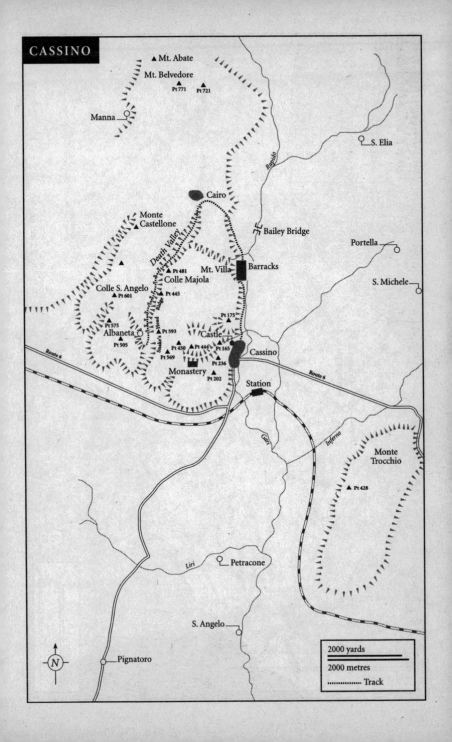

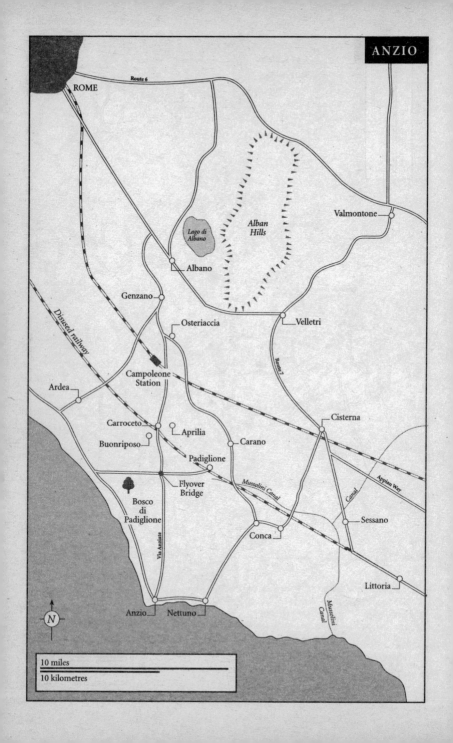

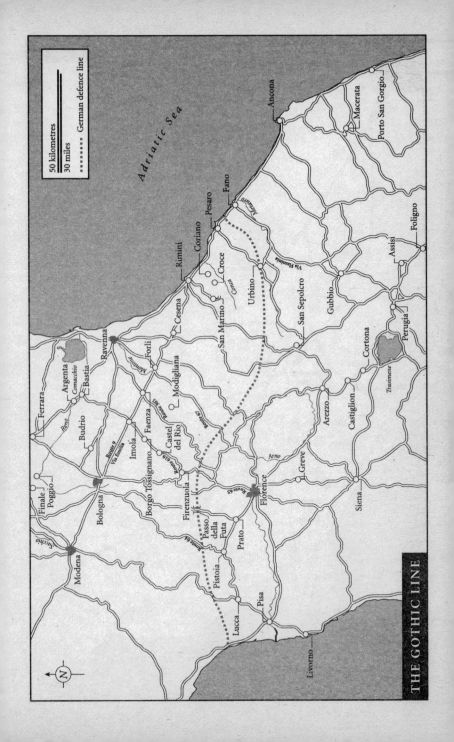

THE GOTHIC LINE

1

Campaign Strategy

The purpose of the campaign in Italy from July 1943 to May 1945 and its conduct were matters of dispute between the Allies at the time, and have been between historians and others since. It is not a straightforward story. As the defence of France collapsed at the beginning of June 1940, Mussolini slid off the fence to join Germany, and Britain found herself facing superior numbers of Italian forces both on the Libyan frontier of Egypt and on the borders of Italian-occupied Abyssinia in the Sudan, Somaliland and Kenya. The only region in which it was possible for Britain to engage the Axis powers with any prospect of success was the eastern Mediterranean and the Middle East, the latter being vital to her as a source of oil. Hopes, slender as it was to prove, were placed on forming a Balkan alliance designed to weaken Italy, which invaded Greece from Albania in 1940, and Germany by depriving her of the natural resources of the area, notably oil from Romania. If successful, it might even earn the support of Turkey. These hopes were undermined by defeat of the expeditionary force sent to Greece in April 1941, by which time the Germans had intervened in Libya to save their Italian allies, who had been soundly trounced by General O'Connor. The gloomy prospect which these developments produced was fundamentally changed by two events of that year: Hitler's invasion of Russia in June and the Japanese attack on the US fleet in Pearl Harbor in December, bringing Britain two powerful allies.

Immediately after the latter, Winston Churchill went to Washington to coordinate strategy with President Franklin Roosevelt. That which he proposed was based on a paper prepared by his Joint Planning Staff which stated:

> We hope that the offensive against Germany will take the form of large-scale land operations on the Russian front, large-scale bombing operations supplemented by amphibious raids of increasing weight

from the United Kingdom and a gradual tightening of the ring round
Axis-controlled Europe by the occupation of strategic points in the
Atlantic Islands, North and West Africa, Tripoli and Turkey. Every
opportunity will be taken to try and knock out Italy as an active
partner in the war. These operations will be followed in the final
phase by simultaneous land operations against Germany itself, from
the West by the British, from the South by the United States and
from the East by the Russians.*

At that time General Auchinleck had just launched Operation CRU-
SADER in Libya, which relieved the siege of Tobruk and drove Rommel
and the Italian army out of Cyrenaica, the eastern province of Libya.
Churchill succeeded in persuading Roosevelt that the defeat of Germany
should take priority over that of Japan, but the US Chiefs of Staff did
not approve the indirect strategy which the British favoured, nor that
the main American effort should be in the Mediterranean. They insisted
on a direct strategy, building up a strong US force in Britain to cross the
Channel and take the shortest route to Berlin. They looked scornfully at
any diversion of effort into the Mediterranean, which they suspected as
being motivated by Britain's concern to protect her imperial interests
and by her reluctance to face the hazards of a direct confrontation with
Germany across the Channel.

This divergence of view over strategy was to persist for the rest of the
war and directly affect the campaign which was eventually waged in Italy
itself. The first test of it soon arose when the Americans had to decide
what their army was to do in 1942. Brigadier-General Dwight D.
Eisenhower, Chief of the US Army's Operations and Planning Staff,
wrote on 22 January 1942:

> We've got to go to Europe and fight – and we've got to quit wasting
> resources all over the world – and still worse – wasting time. If we're
> to keep Russia in, save the Middle East, India and Burma, we've got
> to begin slugging with air at West Europe; to be followed by a land
> attack as soon as possible.†

---

* Michael Howard, *The Mediterranean Strategy in the Second World War* (London:
  Weidenfeld & Nicolson, 1968), p. 16.
† Howard, p. 22.

He prepared a plan (Operation BOLERO) to build up a force of 48 divisions and 5,800 aircraft in Britain, most of which would be American, to launch a cross-Channel operation in April 1943 (Operation ROUNDUP), at the same time making provision to use a smaller force (4 divisions and 700 aircraft) for the same purpose in the summer of 1942 (Operation SLEDGEHAMMER) if a Russian collapse seemed imminent. The British planners were rightly opposed to the latter, but the Chiefs of Staff accepted a commitment to the former, although remaining convinced that it would be disastrous to attempt it until German forces that could oppose it had been sufficiently weakened or distracted by operations elsewhere.

But President Roosevelt was keen to see the US Army in action elsewhere than in the Pacific before the end of the year, and his Chief of Army Staff, General George C. Marshall, reluctantly agreed to an operation to occupy French North Africa in the hope of bringing the French forces there into the Allied camp. He argued against it as undermining BOLERO and thereby prejudicing ROUNDUP, and, when forced to accept it, hoped to limit it to landings on the Atlantic coast of Morocco and occupation of Morocco and Algeria only. However, pressure from Churchill forced him to extend it to landings within the Mediterranean with Tunis as a final objective.

This operation (TORCH) was launched under Eisenhower's command immediately after Montgomery's victory at El Alamein at the beginning of November 1942, and very nearly reached Tunis before rapid German reinforcement stopped General Anderson's British First Army only fifteen miles from the city towards the end of the month. Five months were to pass before (First Army having been joined by Montgomery's Eighth) Bizerte and Tunis were occupied and all German and Italian forces in North Africa surrendered.

Argument about what Allied forces were to do when that happened had been going on even before Operation TORCH was launched. General Marshall had intended that active operations in the Mediterranean should be closed down in favour of establishing a 'defensive encircling line' and all British and American effort should be concentrated in Britain for ROUNDUP; but by the time that Roosevelt and Churchill and their staffs met at Casablanca in January 1943, it was clear that TORCH was not going to be completed until the spring and that ROUNDUP in 1943 would not be possible. In addition, Marshall's naval and air force colleagues saw advantage in ensuring that the Mediterranean could be opened for shipping, replacing the long roundabout Cape route, and that bombers attacking Germany could be based in Sicily or southern Italy.

British views about where to strike next in the Mediterranean had been divided. Churchill and General Alan Brooke had been inclined to think of the Balkans, while making feints elsewhere, but Lord Louis Mountbatten's Combined Operations planners, with bitter memories of Dieppe, shrank from the risk of a major amphibious operation in an area which the Germans could reinforce by land more rapidly than the Allies could build up their forces by sea, and favoured Corsica and Sardinia. President Roosevelt's influence was decisive. He wanted to keep US troops in action in the European theatre in 1943 and was attracted by the idea of eliminating Italy from the war. Churchill readily agreed that the next step would be the invasion of Sicily (Operation HUSKY) in the hope that it would divert German effort from the Russian front and wear down her strength generally, and force the collapse or surrender of Italy, which Germany would then be forced to occupy. The British Chiefs of Staff at that stage did not want to embark on the invasion of the Italian mainland, but, with the strong support of Churchill, had their eyes on fomenting trouble for the Germans in the Balkans, which an Italian collapse would compel them to reinforce. No decision was made about what should be the next step after Sicily. That was to be taken at the next summit meeting, in Washington in May 1943.

Planning for the invasion of Sicily was immediately set in hand. General Eisenhower was to remain in Supreme Command, with General Alexander, as his deputy, responsible for the detailed planning of the land force operations. Admiral Sir Andrew Cunningham, the British naval Commander-in-Chief Mediterranean, and Air Chief Marshal Sir Arthur Tedder, the British Commander-in-Chief of the Allied Air Forces Mediterranean, would also continue to command the naval and air forces involved. As they and their staffs were still fully involved in the conduct of the operations in North Africa, a special planning staff was established at Eisenhower's headquarters in Algiers under the British Major-General C. H. Gairdner. His task was complicated by the wide dispersion of the forces involved. The British land forces were to include one corps (30th) taken from the troops already fighting in North Africa in both First and Eighth Armies, another (13th) from troops based in or near Egypt, and the 1st Canadian Division, sailing direct from Britain, while one of the US divisions would sail direct from the USA. The target date for the operation was the most favourable period of the moon in July, which meant in the first two weeks, assuming that operations in North Africa would have come to an end by 1 May.

It was difficult for the planners to assess with any confidence what would be the state of either the Allied or the Axis forces which had been engaged, and even more difficult to forecast what German and Italian opposition in Sicily itself would be. That was least difficult in the case of the navy. The Italian fleet had not put to sea since the middle of 1942, and the naval threat was virtually confined to that of submarines. The principal naval concerns were the actual assault landings and the ability to deliver reinforcements and supplies thereafter, and the potential air threat to both. The air forces also were confident that they could dominate the skies over the invasion itself, but were anxious to acquire landing grounds ashore as soon as possible, to give cover and support to the troops after they had landed. Until they were available, fighter aircraft would be operating at extreme range from North Africa and Malta. Both these concerns led the planners to place emphasis on the need to capture ports and airfields at an early stage. Sicily's only major ports were Messina, in the north-east corner, and Palermo, in the north-west. The other ports on the east and south coasts could offer very limited capacity. Messina was clearly too well protected to be an early objective, but Palermo could be captured early on. The airfield complexes were near Catania on the east coast, between Ponte Olivo and Comiso inland of Gela at the eastern end of the south coast, and at the western end of the island, near Castelvetrano, south-west of Palermo. These considerations led the planners to propose two separate task forces, a western one, which would most conveniently be American, one division of which would land on the southern side of the western corner, followed by another division assaulting Palermo directly a few days later; and a larger eastern one, primarily British, which, with three divisions, would first seize the airfield complex and ports of the south-eastern corner, and, once fighter aircraft were based ashore there, would advance north to seize the airfield complex and port of Catania, reinforced by another division landing in that area. A force of eleven divisions, including two airborne, should be ashore by D+7 and should be adequate to deal with German and Italian forces likely to be opposing them. The eastern task force would then advance to Messina, while the western one protected its left flank.

Alexander's first reaction to this plan was dislike of the wide separation of the two task forces, but Gairdner persuaded him that the ports of the south-eastern corner would not be capable of supporting concentration of the whole force there. On 13 March Gairdner's plan was accepted by Eisenhower, Alexander, Cunningham and Tedder; but, when General Sir Bernard Montgomery, the commander of Eighth Army, who had been chosen to command the eastern task force, studied it, he objected to the wide dispersion of the three landing areas selected for his force, and suggested abandoning the western one near Gela. This was opposed by Cunningham and Tedder, leading Alexander to propose a compromise by which the US division from the western task force, of which Lieutenant-General George S. Patton, commander of the US 2nd Corps, had been selected as the commander, should be diverted from its objective, the airfield complex round Castelvetrano, to Gela. The one assault division left to Patton would thus have to land near Palermo while the nearby airfield complex had not been attacked except from the air. It is not surprising that the Americans objected. The British Chiefs of Staff solved the problem by providing another division from the Middle East and staging it through Malta.

This did not satisfy Montgomery, who, on 23 April, flew to Cairo to see Lieutenant-General M. C. Dempsey, whose 13th Corps was to play a leading part in the assault. He had also been acting as chief of staff of the eastern task force, but Montgomery had, a few days before, sent his own chief of staff, Major-General F. de Guingand, back to Cairo to study the plan in detail and take over as chief of staff of the force.

Dempsey and de Guingand supported Montgomery's view that a greater concentration of strength was needed in the south-eastern corner if opposition of the nature that First and Eighth Armies had been meeting in North Africa were to be overcome. As a result Montgomery sent a tactless, almost insubordinate signal to Alexander dictating his terms and stating that he had given orders that the planning of the task force's assault was going to be based on the abandonment of the landings near Gela and Pozzallo. His only landing on the south coast would be at the south-eastern tip at Pachino. He ended his signal with the words: '. . . the operation will NOT be possible with the resources available if

Sicily is developed before July into a heavily defended island strongly held by German troops.'

This naturally caused consternation in Algiers. Alexander found Montgomery's revision of the plan acceptable, but Cunningham and Tedder did not. Montgomery now came up with another suggestion: that Patton's operation at the western end of the island should be cancelled and that his force should land between Gela and Pozzallo. In the face of the misgivings of Tedder, because it left two of the three airfield complexes to be attacked only from the air, and of Cunningham for the same reason and because it reduced the spread of the assault areas, Eisenhower accepted the proposal on 3 May, and it was approved by the Combined Chiefs of Staff as they assembled, on 12 May, for the TRIDENT conference in Washington, the day on which the German and Italian forces in North Africa surrendered.

That conference saw a repetition of the arguments that had taken place at Casablanca between General Marshall's opposition to anything that could weaken or delay ROUNDUP and British ambitions in the Balkans, including their hope of bringing Turkey in on the Allied side. The British Chiefs of Staff proposed that success in Sicily should be immediately followed by landings in Calabria, the southern mainland, from where the anti-German Communist resistance movements in Greece and Yugoslavia should be supported. If the Italians were to cease fighting actively alongside the Germans, Italy should be occupied as far north as Rome, forces landed to support Tito in Yugoslavia, the Dodecanese islands in the eastern Mediterranean occupied, and increased pressure applied to Turkey to join the Allies. This would be more effective, by diverting German forces, in paving the way for a successful ROUNDUP in 1944, than transferring US and British forces in the Mediterranean back to Britain.

General Marshall reluctantly went halfway to accepting this argument, but insisted that a firm date – May 1944 – must be fixed for ROUNDUP, now renamed OVERLORD, and specific forces committed to it, including the transfer of seven experienced divisions, four American and three British, from the Mediterranean to Britain in time to take part in it. That having been agreed, he accepted that Eisenhower should 'mount such operations in exploitation of HUSKY as are best calculated to eliminate Italy from the war and to contain the maximum number of German forces.' Argument about what that should be began as soon as the conference ended. Some favoured no more than occupation of Sardinia and Corsica. Previous British reluctance to invade the mainland had now disappeared, and, urged on by Churchill, the Chiefs of Staff set their eyes firmly on Rome; but nothing had been decided when Montgomery's and Patton's soldiers landed in Sicily on 10 July.

Strategic arguments had also been going on on the other side of the hill. The Italians, from Mussolini downwards, had been hoping to bring the war to an end, or at least their part in it, since the Battle of El Alamein, and the Germans realized this. Three different groups were involved: dissident Fascists, led by Counts Ciano and Grandi, Mussolini's son-in-law and his former ambassador in London; the underground anti-Fascist parties; and a group of senior officers in the High Command (Comando Supremo), headed since February 1943 by the anti-German General Ambrosio. All saw Mussolini himself as an obstacle, although he was as keen as they were to end the war, having suggested, in vain, to Hitler that he should make peace with the Russians, so that they could turn their combined strength against the Anglo-American Allies. Ambrosio correctly guessed that the next Allied move, after North Africa, would be to Sicily and perhaps also to Corsica and Sardinia.

The Germans in Italy were officially under Italian overall command, but actually under the orders of Field Marshal Kesselring. His advice to the German High Command (OKW) and Hitler was to offer reinforcements to Italy and generally encourage them to fight for their homeland. He wanted to make use of them as long as he could, and in any case to force the Allies to fight for every mountain and valley. Being an airman, he recognized the importance of keeping Allied bomber bases as far away from Germany as possible. He also appreciated the defensive possibilities of the terrain, especially in winter, and believed that forcing the Allies to attack would mean that a German defence could contain and cause severe losses to a much larger Allied force, which might otherwise be made available for a more direct attack on Germany.

The opposite view was put forward by Field Marshal Rommel, whose experience of serving with the Italians gave him a low opinion of them. His advice was to abandon them to their fate and concentrate German strength to hold the Apennines north of the line Pisa–Rimini. Hitler prevaricated, but, for the time being, inclined to Kesselring's view, authorizing the latter to offer a total of five divisions as reinforcements. On 12 May Mussolini, acting on the recommendation of Ambrosio, turned the offer down. As a result OKW prepared a contingency plan, codenamed ALARICH, for Rommel to command an army group (B), with his headquarters at Munich, which would be built up to a strength of fourteen divisions to hold the northern Apennines, to which, in the event of an Italian collapse or defection, all German troops in Italy would withdraw. However, when Kesselring visited Sicily in early May, he was shocked by the poor state of the defences. In the light of his criticisms, Ambrosio agreed to accept more German divisions, bringing the total in Italy to six, two of which, Hermann Goering Panzer and 15th Panzer Grenadier, were sent to Sicily, as well as a significant increase in German air force deployment to Italy.

2

Sicily

July 1943

The Italian troops defending Sicily formed their Sixth Army, commanded by the sixty-six-year-old General Alfredo Guzzoni, brought back from retirement to replace the younger and more efficient General Mario Roatta, whose forceful attempts to galvanize the defence of the island had annoyed its inhabitants. The coastal defences were manned by the equivalent of six divisions, most of the soldiers being Sicilians, under two corps, the 12th in the west and the 16th in the east, both of which also had two mobile divisions in reserve. The German 15th Panzer Grenadier Division was deployed in support of the 12th and the Hermann Goering Panzer Division of the 16th, in theory under their command but in fact taking their orders from Lieutenant-General Frido von Senger und Etterlin, the German liaison officer with Guzzoni. Neither of them had much faith in the coastal divisions, which they expected to do little more than report and impose a slight delay on any landing. They wanted the Italian mobile divisions to be held well back from the coast, ready to be deployed to contain any landings and try to push them back, while the two German divisions were concentrated in the centre of the island, ready to launch a counter-attack. Kesselring disagreed and, foreshadowing the arguments about German deployment to oppose OVERLORD, insisted that both the German and the Italian mobile divisions should be deployed well forward to try and push an Allied landing back into the sea before it could be well established ashore. He foresaw serious difficulty in moving these divisions any distance on the narrow Sicilian roads in the face of Allied air attack. Guzzoni gave in to him, having no confidence that the island could be held for long anyway.

Alexander's plan for the invasion was complicated by the wide dispersion of the areas from it was launched. In Eighth Army, Lieuten-

ant-General Miles Dempsey's 13th Corps, sailing from Suez, was to land
south of Syracuse with Major-General H. P. M. Berney-Ficklin's 5th
Division on the right near Cassibile and Major-General S. C. Kirkman's
50th Division on the left near Avola, while 1st Airlanding Brigade of
Major-General G. F. Hopkinson's 1st Airborne Division landed to seize
the Ponte Grande Bridge over the River Anapo just south of Syracuse.
The corps was then to advance to capture Syracuse and Augusta, and
eventually Catania, with 2nd Parachute Brigade seizing the crossings of
the River Mulinello west of Augusta and 1st Parachute Brigade the
Primosole Bridge over the River Simeto south of Catania.

Lieutenant-General Sir Oliver Leese's 30th Corps was to land on the
Pachino peninsula with Major-General Douglas Wimberley's 51st
(Highland) Division, sailing from Tunisia and Malta, and 231st Infantry
Brigade, sailing from Suez, landing at the tip and on the northern side,
while Major-General G. G. Simonds's 1st Canadian Division, sailing
from Britain, landed on the southern side. The corps was to secure
Pachino airfield and then advance north-westwards, the Highland Division to Palazzolo Acreide and the Canadians to Ragusa, linking up with
the Americans. When Montgomery's proposal that Patton's 2nd US
Corps should land round Gela was accepted, he had urged that it be
placed under his command. This was predictably rejected by the Americans, who, in order to make certain it could not happen, decided to
upgrade Patton's command to that of an army, designated the Seventh.
Under him 2nd Corps, now under Lieutenant-General Omar N. Bradley,
was to land on a frontage of some forty miles on either side of Gela,
Major-General Troy H. Middleton's 45th US Division, sailing from the
USA, staging at Oran in Algeria, on the right to seize the airfields near
Comiso and contact the British in the area of Ragusa; Major-General
Terry Allen's 1st US Division ('The Big Red One'), sailing from Algiers
and Tunis, in the centre to take Gela and Ponte Olivo airfields, and
Major-General Lucian K. Truscott's 3rd US Division, sailing from
Bizerte, to land at Licata to take the port and airfield there. At the same
time 505th Parachute Regimental Combat Team of Major-General
Matthew B. Ridgway's 82nd Airborne Division, flying from Kairouan in
Tunisia, was to seize the area east of Ponte Olivo and block the routes
which the enemy might use to move against the beachhead. The 2nd US
Armored Division was embarked at Oran as a floating reserve.

All the convoys concentrated in the area round Malta on 9 July. The timing of the landing on 10 July, just after midnight for the first airborne drop and 2.45 a.m.* for the touchdown of the first assault craft, was a compromise between the need of the airborne troops for moonlight to help both the pilots and navigators of the aircraft and their own operations, and that of the sailors for darkness to conceal their approach. Deception measures were initiated to try and mislead the enemy as to where the actual landings would take place. Lieutenant R. Aitchison RNVR was First Lieutenant of Vosper Motor Torpedo Boat 84 which was sent on a mission for this purpose, and describes the action:

> A week or so before the landings on Sicily took place, and before any of us knew what was afoot, our curiosity was aroused when two of the Vospers had fitted on their foredeck, a great big box mounted on a turntable. No-one would admit to knowing what they were for, if the crews themselves knew, or guessed, they kept the secret very well. It turned out that they were very powerful loudspeakers, soon to be christened Rumble Rumble machines, and were to go to a bit of coast well to the north of the bit where the landings were actually to take place, and make loud invasion noises; whatever they were. It's now well known history that an unseasonal storm blew up on the night of the invasion. We were part of a group detailed to patrol to the north of the landing, hopefully to intercept any enemy vessels that might attempt to interfere from that direction. Although the prevailing weather would normally have kept us in harbour, we sailed late in the afternoon well before dusk, and began battling our way northward. Several times the group had to reduce speed or stop while one of the boats corrected some defect and we began to get alarmingly behind schedule. The wind showed no sign of abating, the darkness and flying spray was making station keeping difficult enough anyway, but then the coxswain began to find it difficult to turn the wheel and soon couldn't prevent the boat from sheering off to port as it jammed completely when he tried to correct by turning to starboard. A signal to the S.O. [Senior Officer] brought the group to a halt once more and he had no choice but to press on with the other boats and leave us to sort out our troubles as best we could.

Lieutenant Aitchison's crew managed to cure the defect and take the boat back to Malta. His account continues:

---

* All timings were B time, i.e. two hours after Greenwich Mean Time.

Three days later we left Malta at 12.45, heading north once again. This time to patrol in the Straits of Messina as tail-end Charlie of a group of three boats, the others were 81 and 77, with Lieutenant Chris Dreyer aboard 81 as S.O. At dusk we were approaching the Straits, some 20 miles wide at their mouth, reduced speed and continued slowly on before stopping some 4 or 5 miles south of Messina to await developments. It was then about 10.00 pm on a clear, calm night with good visibility.

We had started up and were under way when I was called and emerged through the charthouse door onto the bridge. Looking forward I could clearly see, fine on our port bow, two submarines steaming towards us, more or less on a reciprocal course. They were in line ahead and both had navigational lights burning. 81 and 77 were very close to the first sub and appeared to be trying desperately to back off and manoeuvre themselves into a firing position. We were still some way away and our C.O. had a little more time to assess the situation. He took us round in a 270 degree turn to starboard, which brought us back ahead of the first sub and in an excellent firing position. As we ran in, near enough at the ideal 90 degrees to our target's course, an ear-splitting crash shattered the silence and a vivid flash lit the area like daylight. In that instant of brilliant light I saw the second sub, broken in half and, some 20 or 30 feet above the water, the entrails of the stern half revealed in glowing red. Seconds later our boat lurched as her torpedoes left the tubes. We could see that the first sub had begun to dive and the tracks of our torpedoes would pass well ahead of it. The C.O. shouted to get the depth charges and we continued on the same course, passing as close over the submerging sub that I felt sure our propellers would foul his jumping wire as we dropped the depth charges almost on top of him. But it was clear that he would be far enough away to escape much damage by the time they had sunk to the set depth.

Our three boats regrouped and 81 went off to look for survivors as shouts had been heard from the water, ordering us to stay and keep watch where we were. 77 still had her torpedoes, both tubes having misfired when she made her attack. When 81 returned we re-formed in line ahead and continued our slow and silent passage northwards, very soon observing a spirited battle going on behind us and near to the Italian coast.

For the main assault itself, both sailors and soldiers naturally hoped for clear, calm weather; but during 9 July a fresh north-west wind blew up, raising a choppy sea, slowing down the landing craft and tending to blow them off course. It died down before dawn, leaving a strong swell; but by this time the soldiers, who had been on board for twelve hours or more, were seasick, cold, and cramped and many of them were soaking wet.

Able Seaman K. G. Oakley was serving in Fox 1 Naval Beach Commando, given the task of landing first on the beach through which 151st Brigade of the 50th Division was to land, in order to set up the beach control organization. He wrote:

At midnight of the 9th July we lay at anchor eight miles from Avola, our immediate objective. After a good meal we donned our equipment and manned the assault boats. I was sitting right in the stern of the boat and spent some time making myself comfortable. At last the order came "Lower Boats" and we were away, the sea was rough and our boat was thrown against the parent ship. "Crash!", away went the two-inch mortar, swept over the side of the hook of the boats falls. "It's time they supplied us with umbrellas", said one soldier, as another great sea swept over us.

Now came that very trying time between ship and shore when one wonders if he will survive the unknown that lies ahead. The boats were tossed all over the ocean and all the soldiers were sea-sick but they had cardboard boxes to vomit into and this helped them a lot.

Suddenly a flare burst above us and surprise was lost, when we still had about a mile to go. The formations split up and began to make for their own landing places, with fire from enemy machine guns passing over them. Tat-Tat-Tat-Tat, Bren guns began to speak and then "Crunch", "Down Door" and we were there. A sapper began to cry, plead and cling to the floor-boards, swearing he would not move. We left him (his nerve was gone) and dived into about three feet of water to wade fifty yards to the shore. The shrill whine of bullets speeded us on and at last we went to earth at the water's edge. Bren guns engaged the enemy machine-guns and we began to take our bearings. We had landed in almost exactly the right place and so it did not take us long to set up our lights and call in the second flight. We then waded out along the length of the beach, to find the best landing places. These were marked and the Assistant Beach Master and myself proceeded to find the Beach Master. By this time the enemy M.G's had been silenced but we could not find the B.M. I was detailed to find him and make the report, so off I went towards the Marina d'Avola. I joined up with four more B. Commando's but could not find the B.M.

We were approaching the Marina tower when a sniper opened fire at us. We took cover and replied as best we could. Our cover was a ledge towards the top of a small cliff and to regain the beach, we had to cross a lot of open ground. We had decided to make a dash for it when one of our destroyers, H.M.S. Tartar, opened fire at the tower. The situation became sticky. Tartar's shells fell short and were too close for comfort. I decided to make a run for it when the sniper opened up again at a man coming from our beach. This man appeared to be hit for he rolled in the water and floated away (However we found out later that it was the A.B.M. and he was playing "possum"). A while later we made a run for it and regained our beach safely. No other B. Commando's had landed and the B.M. had not appeared so we did our best getting the craft in and directing the avalanche of men ashore. It was about this time, nearly an hour after H. hour that a battery in the hills began to shell us. A landing craft carrying about two hundred and fifty men was the target. It was beached and the men were pouring off down two ladders, but near misses and one hit were making things hot. I waded out and told the men to jump for it as the water was not very deep. A few jumped and I steadied them as they fell and then it came. A terrific explosion and I felt myself fading away into oblivion. I came too [sic] under the water I felt numb and shocked, had I been wounded? or maybe some limbs were missing? I could not tell and then I felt someone clutch my legs and drag me down again. I lost my reason and kicked like mad until I was free and shot to the surface. A body floated by, it's limbs still kicking. It must have been the man who clutched me. The water had become a sea of blood and limbs, remains of once grand fighting men who would never be identified.

I staggered through all this to the water's edge and then looked dazedly around. My comrades were fleeing for cover and in the water were men crying for help. I went into the water again to fetch a man whose arm was hanging on by a few bits of cloth and flesh. He cried; "My arm! look, it's hit me!" I said nothing, but managed to get him to the beach and lay him down. I then collapsed, exhausted and still those shells came down far too close for comfort. I rose again to see a man sitting on the ladder of the landing craft crying "Help me, oh help". I went and goodness knows how I got him to the beach as he was hit all over his body and was a dead weight with shattered legs dragging in the water. I shall never forget how he thanked me as I lay there almost sobbing at such terrible sights; so this was War!

By this time the cruiser supporting us had silenced the batteries and I had time to look around. The Landing Craft had been hit almost directly above where I was standing at the time of the explosion. How did I get away with it? A man or his remains lay splattered over the side of the L.C.

A few more B. Commando's had landed by this time but the B.M. had not turned up and only one A.B.M was there to take charge. Craft were coming in all the time and I could always find something to do. At about H plus four hours, the B.M. turned up and it was about this time that we had a calamity. An L.C.I. [Landing Craft Infantry] had beached some distance from the shore and the men were ordered to disembark. At once they were up to their necks with full equipment on and it looked serious. I went out to give a hand and was swept off my feet by the receding tide. I caught hold of one soldier and tried to get him ashore but discovered that my boots and tin helmet were pulling me down. I was forced to release the soldier and had to fight for my own life as the tide was taking me out and under. I struggled desperately but it was no use. I threw away my tin hat and tried again. Twice I went under and I had almost given up when I saw a boat coming along picking soldiers up. I hailed it with what little breath I had left and they threw me a line, which I missed. So I was left until they had picked up two soldiers and then they threw me a life-belt and towed me to the beach, where I collapsed again.

I came to and swilled my mouth out with fresh water, for I felt as if I had swallowed half of the Med. In the meantime a lifeline had been passed to the L.C.I., and I hung on to that and assisted soldiers to get ashore. All visible signs of enemy had now disappeared and our troops and equipment were pouring ashore. At dusk came the enemy bombers and this became their practice for the next few days. During the machine-gun air attack on the beach (which took place on the second day) one A/B and Sub.-Lt of the B.Commando's were injured.

Lieutenant D. F. Brown RNVR was in command of the 51st Flotilla of Landing Craft Assault, launched from the Landing Ship Infantry *Orontes* a few miles off shore. The troops he was carrying were Durham Light Infantry of 151st Brigade of the 50th Division, whose objective was Avola. He describes his experience:

Having embarked our assaulting infantry, all boats were lowered into the blackness and the heaving seas below. Now my problems started. Although I did not know it then, the ships were at least six miles further off the coast than they should have been. Then, instead of the two LSIs being in line abreast with their bows heading towards the distant land, as they should have been, the wind and the heavy sea had swung them into line ahead, and beam on to the land. The two flotillas of LCAs both started to get into some confusion, with the M.L. [motor launch] – our navigational leader – in the middle of it all. For some inexplicable reason our M.L. moved away to get clear (fair enough) only to seaward and not towards the shore. Oh dear whatever could she be doing? and what was I supposed to do now? Nothing like this had been envisaged in the planning, or, indeed, in any of my own anticipations. The inside of my mouth suddenly felt dry, terribly dry. I could hardly go back on board to try to sort it all out in a conference room! I was on my own. Oh boy, was I on my own. The ball was squarely in my court. So – I had to take a snap decision. It was dark, very dark; I decided that I must follow that M.L.: on no account must I lose it, and I must avoid getting mixed up with the 54th Flotilla. Oh dear what on earth had I done to deserve all this, and I had gone to such a lot of trouble to get it right. I shall never know whether or not I took the right decision. I believe that I did, because having taken her wide sweep to seaward and then set her course towards the shore our M.L. just kept going. There was no waiting to ensure that she had her 'brood' safely in station behind her, she just belted on on her designated course and speed. This, now, was the start of where all the hours, days, weeks, yes even months of training was to really tell. My officers and coxswains knew exactly what they had to do. Basically this was to catch up and then to keep station on me, and after a lot of dreadful apprehension and tension on my part, they all eventually made it. We, both flotillas, were in station on that M.L. and on our way. I heaved a small sigh of relief, and permitted myself to relax a little.

At that point Brown believed himself to be only about ten minutes behind schedule, but 'the sea was pretty foul, we were shipping it green over the bows'. At 0230, as he passed two marker submarines twenty-five minutes late, the ML ceased to guide them and he had to head straight for his allotted beach with five other LCAs to form the first wave of the infantry assault. After half an hour, on his final approach, he was due to pick up a small light forming the letter 'J', displayed to seaward by a folboat (collapsible canoe); but he could not see it. Eventually he was able to make out the coastline and guessed that he was a little to the south of where he should have been, when, at last, he spotted it. During this run in he 'heard many desperate cries for help from the water', but, as he was already over an hour late, he had to harden his heart and ignore them. Making a last-minute change of course to avoid some rocks, he drove his craft ashore: 'And so, 90 minutes late, my troops were ashore. Late, and slightly out of position, but at least on the right beach and in the right order'.

The cries which Lieutenant Brown heard were almost certainly from soldiers of 1st Airlanding Brigade. A combination of the weather, the inexperience of the American aircrew towing the gliders, who had only been trained in daylight operations, and the anxiety of some of the pilots when they encountered anti-aircraft fire, some of which came from our own ships, caused 47 of the 134 gliders to be prematurely released over the sea with fatal consequences, and only 12 to reach the objective area. However the 73 men dropped there succeeded in holding intact the Ponte Grande bridge south of Syracuse, until the leading troops of the 5th Division reached them next day. G. R. Brown, a non-commissioned officer of the 2nd Battalion The South Staffordshire Regiment, was in one of the gliders and lucky to survive. This is his account:

We sat tight – staring across at each other – unseeingly in the darkness. I linked arms with my companions on either side – ready to 'take the strain' of the landing. We'd no idea where we'd land – top of a tree – through the front door of a house – we just hoped for the best. Suddenly – I heard a noise up the front. The lights suddenly came on. Someone – Lieut. Barratt was smashing away at the roof with a hand-axe. Someone else was yelling "Prepare for ditching" (the R.A.F. term ditching is used when a plane is crashing or making a forced landing in the sea). The lights went out again. I don't know how I felt

– I can't remember. I *do* remember slipping off my equipment in record time and howling to everybody in general "How the hell does this thing open?" ('This' being a panel in the roof that was to be used for escape if ever we *did* crash into the sea). Thank God Sgt. Colclough came round sufficiently to tell me what to do, though I'm pretty sure I didn't open it the 'correct' way – even then. I ripped and tore at it – swung on it – and grappled with it, until it eventually came away, leaving a hole some two feet square – or maybe less. We were still gliding along. Then – I heard a rather calm voice say "Don't take off your equipment – we might make land yet." I think it was the voice of Major Lane – my Company Commander – who was doing the trip in my glider. I breathed again. I didn't fancy coming down in the sea – I couldn't swim! I could tell we were losing height rapidly – and knew it wasn't far away – the land – or the sea. I didn't know which to expect. Anyway, I started to put on my equipment. Didn't mean to be left behind if we *did* land in the right place. I could see the stars shining – through the escape hole – just above my head.

Suddenly – someone yelled "Hold tight". I flung my equipment off and sat down quickly. I grabbed hold of someone on either side and waited for it – land or sea. "Land – please" I prayed. "Crash!" – we pulled up with a jolt. I could feel myself being flung forward. I expected getting a "black-out". I thought we'd made the land – then I realised that the sea was pouring in. "Hell – we've had it." I pulled myself to my feet and made for the hole I'd just made. Everybody seemed to be going for that hole (though I discovered later *four* holes had been made altogether). It was a deadly business. Somehow I got there – and found myself half in and half out. Somebody who was already out grabbed me and heaved me up. I could scarcely realise that I'd made it. I was now standing on one of the wings. Pulling myself together, I started blowing up my rubber life-jacket (which we all wore, deflated round our chests during the trip, and which, though not guaranteed to keep a man afloat, are a great help to anyone who makes an effort to swim). It was then I noticed how close we were to the land. "Must be Sicily", I thought. "And only a mile or two away". Right on the enemy's doorstep.

Brown then realized that some of his comrades were struggling in the water and he helped to pull them out and gave one of them artificial respiration. His account continues:

I noticed then, that the wings weren't so far out of the water as they *had* been. The old wreck was going down. For the tenth time since the take-off, I prayed. All our weapons and equipment were lost. We had to take our boots off – as she was still sinking – and it looked like we'd have to get wet. Oh – if only I could swim – I prayed again. My shorts were ripped. I still had socks, hose-tops,* shorts and shirt on. I had my red beret on when I came through the hole – but it had gone. I still had my paybook – with razor-blades, a couple of photos and a 10/- B.M.A. note tucked inside. I'd a handkerchief, a cig. case (containing three soaked Woodbines), a Field Dressing – and, in the big pocket I'd stitched on to my shorts, I'd a Mills Grenade and 15 rounds of 'buckshee' ammunition. I threw the grenade and ammunition into the sea. Someone looked at his watch – Sgt. Williams it was. It had stopped at 10.32 pm. Probably the time we hit the water. So we'd been about two and three-quarter hours in the air.

Suddenly, a big searchlight on the beach switched on and swung round in a big half circle – as though searching the waves for us. Then – rat-a-tat. Three bursts of machine-gun fire whistled round us. We were spotted! But the light swung round and left us in the dark again. It swung round several times. Each time we lay flat on the wings – lying very still – hoping it would pass by. Each time – I watched the approaching beam – it seemed to linger on us – only to carry on its sweep. It was a bit of a nerve-racking affair. I expected 'getting it' any minute. But no – I decided that the Iti's were just getting jittery and were having a go at anything. We weren't fired on again. One of the officers decided on a roll-call. There should be 32. Only 30 answered the names. Two must have been drowned. We scanned the sea – shouted – but no reply. Company Sgt. Major Woolhouse and a Sgt. of the Engineers were missing. There was a silence.

I saw four or five gliders go sailing overhead – like great silent hawks. One flew very low. I *knew* he'd hit the hill in front – he did! With a crash. A few minutes later, there was a crash and the whole place was lit up. To my surprise – in the light of the burning glider – I could definitely see a number of figures dash away and disappear

---

* Stockings without feet, worn with socks. They had coloured turnover tops in regimental colours.

into the darkness beyond. They couldn't have hit the deck too badly after all. And they'd evidently set the glider on fire for security reasons. I felt a little better.

Our own 'Horsa' was still going down and the water was washing round our chests.... Major Lane just then decided that *he'd* swim for it – taking with him the other good swimmers. Five went – two officers and three privates. As he, the Major pointed out – with a little less weight on – the wreck might possibly hold up better.... We wished them luck ... It had it's effect. The glider came up slowly – and soon the water was only up to our knees ... The wind was still blowing hard. We all realised that we were getting farther out to sea.

Three more, a sergeant, a lance-corporal and a private, set off to swim to the shore, leaving twenty-two on the wreck, who were eventually rescued, suffering from thirst and cold, by passing Commando assault craft at 4.45 a.m., having been on the wreck for six and a quarter hours.

Lieutenant P. R. Hay was in the destroyer HMS *Tartar*, which escorted and provided fire support to the landings on 'Jig' beach. His ship first had to lead a flotilla of landing craft to a sonar buoy laid by a submarine two or three miles offshore, but their ASDIC failed to locate it and in any case the flotilla they were supposed to be leading had gone astray. When dawn came, he expected to face air attack, but none came 'so we merely contented ourselves firing at shore batteries who were engaged in firing at our own barges on the beaches.' The enemy batteries had ceased firing by 0730 hours, after which things became rather quiet. By 1530 all the larger ships of the first assault convoy had left and not long afterwards the first air attacks began, his ship being narrowly missed by several bombs. The account in his day-book reads:

Another 2 or 3 alerts caused most of us to miss supper, & then came Dusk Action Stations. We laid a smoke screen to seaward of our convoy and then waited. The Hospital ships – 'Talamba, 'Aba' and another 3 funnelled one of the 'Talamba' class – were further out to sea, well lit up with Red Crosses blazing up into the night.

The first night raid started in C. Passaro direction and we watched 'flak' going up for about a ¼ of an hour. It really looked beautiful – the tracer starting white, turning to green and then to red – & of course the yellow & orange of flares & shell bursts and the red glow from bombs – they really formed an attractive sight if you didn't think of the reason for it all.

Then our turn came. Most of the firing was on the port side of the ships – Major Laird [? Lind] took over my port Oerlikon – so I didn't see much. However we did quite well in the tracer & colour line ourselves for 10 minutes or so: then things quietened down a bit.

I looked forward to see what I could & there was 'Talamba' with all her lights except 2 or 3 out. I thought this must be an air raid precaution, but then noticed she was down by the stern. We were closing her all this time and soon could see liferafts in the water & little red merchant navy lifebelt lights: we could also hear shouts.

As we closed the ship, we passed the life boats & could hear a most unearthly noise of Goanese shouting and chattering. Apparently, as always, these Goanese had rushed straight to the boats, lowered them & pushed off immediately the ship had been hit, leaving about 2 boats for the nurses, patients & medical staff – & no hands to lower them!!

We went round to the port side & closed the ship from the port quarter, picking up swimmers on the way. The ship was still upright but her well deck aft was nearly awash. We got alongside – or about 20 feet off – and people swam or paddled across in scores . . . In less than 10 minutes though, the Talamba had listed considerably to starboard & was sinking faster by the stern. Still people swarmed down ropes or lowered injured and still they came across.

Finally, however it was obvious she was about to go, and we had to go astern. The order had hardly been given, when with a cracking, hissing sound her stern went under, her bows reared up and she began to slide under (still 2 or 3 people were jumping off her sides). As she disappeared her 2 after funnels were wrenched from their positions & forced up to the surface again, only to sink a moment later in the boiling, hissing water.

A minute later there was no sign of her save some boats, & some odd wreckage – one large square piece with a red cross & about 12 people on it. We spent the next half hour or so picking up survivors both wounded & well – UGANDA & one or two other ships also helped. We picked up about 200 ourselves, including 12 nurses. Several of these were badly injured – though only 1 nurse was hurt at all. As it was only H2300 we went alongside BULOLO – the HQ ship and transferred all the survivors where they would be more comfortable.

Lieutenant-Commander G. R. Grandage was in command of LST 424 in the 7th LST Flotilla. He was transporting troops of the 51st (Highland) Division, with tanks and other vehicles, from Tunisia. Having arrived offshore punctually at 0600 hours on the 10th, he was told by the Senior Naval Officer to anchor and wait until called forward, and it was not until 1900 that the call came, as he describes:

At 1900 at last we had our orders to beach. I could see it was going to be a difficult beach to make. There was already one L.S.T. [Landing Ship Tank] in discharging her vehicles and two L.C.T.'s [Landing Craft Tank] were beached about 70 feet away from her. I had to beach in between with about 10 feet to spare either side, and furthermore it was essential to run in at a good speed to get the ship as close in as possible in order to reduce the amount of water in which the tanks and vehicles had to wade. Numerous craft lay between us and the beach so that I had to worm my way amongst these. At last I got the ship squared up and headed right and then "Full Speed", 10 knots. There were some hair-raising seconds as the ship took a slight sheer one way or the other[:] at one time it seemed inevitable that we would strike the other L.S.T. and tear our sides open. With too much wheel on she would swing round on to the L.C.T.'s so only the least amount of wheel was required and those seconds taken to swing the right amount seemed interminable. However she cleared very nicely and slid onto the beach and came to a standstill.

The O.C. Troops had been on the bridge with me as we ran in and orders were being passed by microphone to speakers throughout the ship. First an order from me to open the bow doors and then an order from the Major telling his drivers to stand by and so on. We shook hands and he left me to go down into the tank space and mount his tank. I followed him after a few minutes when I was satisfied there was nothing more to be done on the bridge. It was a grand sight watching these 13 Sherman tanks go down the ramp and into 5 feet 6 inches of water. Just the turret was showing above the water with an officer or N.C.O. sitting in the cockpit directing the driver, who was below the waterline, by means of a telephone. There seemed a curious expression on their faces, one of grim determination, and confidence in themselves and their machines, intermingled with an expression of delight that they were getting ashore on to enemy territory.

Gunner B. R. Christy of 368 Battery of the 92nd Field Regiment Royal Artillery, with the 5th Division, had the same experience of hanging about all day in his LST before they landed about 4 p.m. He wrote:

"Stand by your vehicles" had come the order as at last our L.S.T. was signalled to the beach and slowly she slid forward to the absurdly small stretch of yellow sand. Truck motors were started up & the roar filled the great space of the hold. The chains holding them were released. As the big door in the bows was lowered we crowded forward between the lines of Sherman tanks, which were to go off before us, to watch the final phase in the Navy's part of the operations. Slowly the L.S.T.'s bows slipped down the coast within yards of the land. The sand shelved steeply & looked soft and treacherous. Would the vehicles make it? At last we grounded & held firm. There was a bare stretch of twenty yards between the lowered prow door & where small waves lapped the beach. The first of the Shermans rumbled out of the hold, through the water with a great cloud of steam & fumes & without pausing, clambered up the beach & was away. The others followed with almost clockwork precision. It gave one a grand feeling to watch them rumble off into action. The first of our vehicles followed, but it could not make the beach. A tractor hauled it out in no time. Soon came 'Y's turn, but we, like the others, stuck & had to be hauled out.

A sailor's helping hand was held out, but it was not needed; the warm water reached only to the thighs of my khaki drill trousers & I squelched ashore. The Command Post truck was soon started again & with quickly spoken instructions from the beach party & a cheery farewell, we were on our way. "Mind the mines & keep to the taped track", they said. We lurched up & down steep slopes in the finely churned dust of an olive orchard, sardined under the truck's canopy or clinging to the back and ducking with gritted teeth as boughs scraped the roof. Dusty-faced comrades from the Battery, out of invasion craft, greeted us at the assembly area, after we had done the essential "dewaterproofing", & now it was a wide straight stretch of tarmac road.

One of the assaulting infantry of 50th Division's 151st Brigade was Private Ernest Kerans of the 9th Durham Light Infantry. He wrote:

There was only two feet of pebbles between the sea and the low cliffs of Avola, where we landed, right on target. The moment I put my foot on land two enemy fighters, their machine-guns blazing away, skimmed overhead. I got awful wet diving under a low over-hanging ledge in the cliff at the same time as a wave. We climbed the bank, cut the wire and ran across a vine-yard to the road. Odd rounds of rifle fire did nothing to slow us down. What slowed me was falling over a couple of vines and my puttee getting wrapped around one of them. The company settled down to a steady trot up a narrow lane that bypassed the village. There were a lot of Italians in the few houses we passed, a lot of them busy changing from their uniform into civies. We could not prove it and hadn't got time to try. A big officer tagged himself on to me. I think he was a press-reporter, and somebody must have told him I was in the Intelligence Section, giving him a totally wrong impression. "What are we going to attack first?" "There is a farm-house on a hill, about a mile ahead, to the right of the lane, we are going to capture it, 'Brew-up', and have some breakfast." "Don't joke, man, what are we on?" "I'm not joking, sir." He left us in disgust, but that is just what did happen. We took the farm without opposition, had a brief rest and a cuppa while Nobby waited for his companies 'Sit-reps' (Situation reports), perused them and talked things over with his officers while we enjoyed our 'Brew'. Then it was down the lane and onto the road for Nota. There was a thick wood to the left of the road and from each tree hung a dead allied paratrooper (Americans I think). It was weird, we could only leave them there. A few yards further on, in a ditch following the road, was a long line of wounded Italians, screaming, weeping and pleading. I had started to leave the column to have a closer look at them when the sergeant major shouted at the top of his voice: "You help that lot and I'll shoot you."

Most of the landings so far described had been in the northern sector, that of Dempsey's 13th Corps of 5th and 50th Divisions. Major C. N. Barker was commanding a company of the 1st Battalion of the Gordon Highlanders in the 51st (Highland) Division, the right-hand division of Leese's 30th Corps, which landed further to the south, near Cape Passero.

They were due to land at 0345, transferring by scrambling nets in the early hours from a large ferry into LCAs, which had been lowered into the rough sea. He wrote:

> With considerable cursing, crashing, and clanking we were loaded and the coxswain pulled away from our parent ship which was silhouetted against the night sky. We felt very small. As soon as we were clear of the leeward side we felt the full force of the rough sea as we pitched and rolled whilst manoeuvring into our assault position. Encaged in steel we sat or squatted steel helmeted in full battle order facing each other with only the stormy sky visible, the only sound the crashing and thumping of waves as we headed towards a hostile rocky shore. As I squatted in the bow awaiting a tap on the shoulder to indicate that we had hit the beach and I was to launch myself into the unknown, I wondered what was passing through the minds of the others! one hoped that they were just blank! For too much imagination in such circumstances can be unhealthy.
>
> The engine revs gradually got slower and the buffeting eased as we sailed into the lee of a small island off Cape Passero the moment was at hand! Suddenly there was a crunch, the ramp went down and out I rushed onto what I imagined would be a flat beach only to find myself in deep water. We had hit a rocky ledge off shore. My ammunition boots steel helmet grenades acted as ballast and down I went until, suddenly my large pack strapped to my back gave me unexpected buoyancy and I struggled to the beach. It was a narrow escape. Once ashore I dashed forward to ensure that some fisherman's huts were empty. I was about to shoot what I took to be an Italian soldier who turned out to be my CO, in his enthusiasm he had landed in the first wave ahead of schedule, he was lucky as my adrenalin was flowing freely.
>
> The very rough weather had assured us of complete surprise, additionally we had landed on a beach considered unlikely to be used on account of its rocky nature. The Italian garrison had been stood down so only an occasional shot was fired at us. I quickly reconnoitred the beach exit during which I had to jump hurriedly over some cactus to avoid a sniper and landed on a sunken road bruising my heel which was painful to walk on for the rest of the campaign. Standing waist deep in the sea I directed the landing craft to the best

landing sites. The assault was highly successful with all the objectives taken by daylight.

Our orders had been to consolidate with all speed and then press on inland and establish depth to our defence. We had hardly any transport so we gathered as opportunity offered mules, donkeys, carts and the odd baby Fiat banger to help carry kit. As we pressed on inland the Hermann Goering Division Reconnaissance kept us under observation. The Italians put up no resistance. We pressed on in searing heat through beautiful country and did not encounter resistance until we reached Vizzini a most impressive town built on the top of a cliff and most formidable and an ideal defensive position which the Germans had not been slow to recognise and now occupied.

The 1st Canadian Division landed on the left of the 51st Highland, preceded by No. 2 Commando, whose task was to destroy the coastal guns and fortifications and form an initial bridgehead within which the Canadians would land. A. E. Hines was a Royal Marine serving in that Commando. He wrote:

We boarded our landing craft about 4 am and were lowered away and formed up to go in. A midget submarine was our marker. We had a choppy sea and wet landing up to our chests in water, There were holes everywhere and when my section waded ashore in the beautiful warm water the chap in front of me disappeared and then came up spluttering and cursing. I was "killing myself", although the situation was serious. His opinion of the Royal Navy could not be printed especially when we found later we had landed on 40 Commando's beach and taken some of their objectives as well as our own. When we got among the sand dunes where we could smell the wild garlic (this causes blindness if eaten) machine gun tracers were just passing over our heads. The Italians were putting up token resistance but we moved fast and took all our objectives. At the last one at Ponta Castalatso, we captured umpteen prisoners. A friend of mine Corporal Bill Murray lost an eye from an Italian "Red Devil" grenade. The Italian that threw it died quickly. Bill was later given the D.C.M. We had been given one decoration and had a conference deciding that as Bill had lost an eye he should have the medal.

No sooner had we signalled our success to the Command Boat we struck inland and formed a defensive perimeter. My section was in a field of melons, Les Stockell another friend of mine went on further and shot up an Italian horse drawn field gun team. Later I wish he hadn't because the smell was appalling. Later that morning the Canadians landed with their tanks and heavy equipment. One lot found a farm with big hogsheads of wine and had more casualties from drunkenness than they did from enemy action. Apart from a few mortar rounds, we were not disturbed very much and we feasted on melons (we regretted it later!).

It was air attack that worried Sapper Richard Eke of the 754th Field Company Royal Engineers, which was engaged in clearing the beaches of mines and other obstructions. He wrote:

The aircraft had vanished in seconds and left behind them a holocaust. The petrol lorry at the cross-roads had exploded into a gigantic ball of flame. The driver could still be seen sitting in his cab as the inferno consumed all the vehicles and trees in a twenty yards radius. The M.P. [military policeman] we were admiring had been blasted from the face of the earth, together with the leading jeep and its occupants. A bulldozer was quickly on the scene to clear the vital cross-roads, pushing the burning remains of the truck to one side, and filling in the crater in the centre.

Exhausted by their beach-clearing activities, they were moved from the beach to an olive grove, where they could get some cover and dig slit-trenches. Eke's account continues:

We had had no food all day except the few hard biscuits and corned beef that was in our packs, and the drink of warm water at midday. Word went round that the platoon cook, wherever he had been hiding all day, was getting a meal ready and brewing tea. It was the best news received yet, and morale was decidedly higher as we sat under the olive trees discussing the day's events. Some thought we should try and find our missing friends down in the sand by the water's edge, but they must be dead by now, and in any case, the heavy traffic was still pouring ashore at that point. The meal was a stew (what else?) of biscuits and corned beef. Just a hot pink pulp, but in a short time nothing was left. The tea was hot strong and sweet, drunk from the same mess tin that contained the stew. A drop was left in the tin to rinse it out ready for the next meal. Although the sun was still high, sleep was in the minds of the renowned sleepers, and some were already rolled up in their blankets. It was the wisest thing to do, as from now on, no sleeping would be guaranteed.

I looked down at the shallow depth of my fox-hole. I had hit a thick root only two feet down, and was too tired to dig any deeper. To give extra protection I had fitted a roof of corrugated iron over the top covered in soil, and resting on short branches as rollers. From inside the trench laying on my back, I could roll the roof completely over the top of my head. Some of the others preferred to spend the night above ground, and settled down in the lee of an overhanging rock. The last air attack of the day came out of the setting sun, a high level attack aimed mainly at the shipping laying off the beach. There were one or two hits, and the rumour spread that the hospital ship containing all the beach casualties had been hit and sunk.

Flight Lieutenant John Carpenter of 92 Squadron RAF, equipped with Spitfires, painted a very different picture of the air situation in the letter he wrote to his parents on 22 July:

I was over the beaches with the squadron at dawn and we had a bird's eye view of the whole operation. Big ships shelling the coastal fortifications and landing craft fussing to & fro from the mother ships to the beaches and back again for more troops. The sun was coming up over the horizon as we returned from our first patrol and we knew the first part had gone off well, Spitfires were over all day from dawn to dusk and they also kept a close watch on the aerodromes to see that nothing took off to interfere with our troops. This patrolling went on for a few days with the odd engagement with some venturous Huns, but mainly our ships were kept free from bombing and strafing. We moved into Sicily soon after and took up our quarters on a landing field that had been left ploughed up by the Italians a few days before, flying all day covering our advancing army; prisoners were brought back and shut up in P.O.W camps in their own country. The Sicilians seemed friendly and frequently gave us the 'V' [victory] signs, tomatoes, grapes, 'mealies', nuts were all given to us and we sampled the proverbial Italian 'Vino'.

Flight Lieutenant G. M. Ball was an Australian serving with 43 Squadron RAF, also equipped with Spitfires. He wrote:

On the first day of the landings I was patrolling over our landing area in the Gulf of Noto (where we could see sunken gliders) with Ted Trenchard-Smith as my No. 2. Ted called me to say that he could see a twin-engined aircraft below, but I could not sight it. I told Ted to go down after it and not to lose sight of it, but for some reason he only continued to direct me to it, so down I went. Suddenly I spotted it. I had been looking along the coast but actually the machine was inland a bit. I recognized it straight away as an 88. The crew must have been very dopey, for I followed and caught it up without it taking any evasive action at all. I had a good overtaking speed and went close in giving it both cannon and machine gun fire. I fancied that I could see strikes on both the right engine and the fuselage, but there was no spectacular explosion nor fire. I climbed steeply to the left and then did a wing-over to the right and caught sight of the JU88 just as it disappeared into the sea. I can only imagine that I must have put the starboard engine out of commission and possibly killed or injured the pilot. Up above, Ted, who was probably more concerned with the danger of us being jumped by enemy fighters, had not seen the JU 88 disappear and told me later that the last time he had seen it was just as I broke away and it seemed still to be undamaged. I made a claim when we returned, but it sounded a bit weak when my own No. 2 could not confirm it.

Four days after the initial landings, we took off as a Squadron for a patrol over Sicily. At the end of the patrol when we would normally be returning to Hal Far, we were told to put down at Comiso, an aerodrome in Sicily. I was one of the first to land and I had the usual guilty feeling as if I shouldn't be there as I made my circuit around the unfamiliar field already well stocked with aircraft – German aircraft! Although we were now in 'American Territory' I was glad to find British Servicing Commandos to welcome us and to direct us to our dispersal points. I was guided to a position just inside the perimeter track. When I dismounted from my Spitfire I noticed a JU87 Stuka Dive Bomber upside down on the other side of the perimeter track. While waiting for the rest of the Squadron to land I walked over to it and was a little taken aback to find that the pilot was still in it – minus his head. His gunner lay alongside it, dead.

It had obviously been a fairly recent crash, so I asked the Commando what had happened. The Commando, who did not attempt to hide his contempt for those concerned, told me that three

Stukas arrived at Comiso apparently still believing it to be in Italian hands. They made normal approaches to land, but as each was about to touch down, the Americans shot at it, killing or injuring the pilot. One had tried to "go around" again but it crashed near the end of the runway and the one I was looking at had opened his throttle but swerved off the runway and hit a gun position, overturned and skidded inverted to the position where I was now looking at it. The Stukas were German but the pilots had been Italian.

The next day when I came down to the aerodrome the burial party were at the crashed Stuka near my Spitfire. They had just dug a shallow, temporary grave and before disposing of the bodies they went through the pockets of the dead men looking for identification papers etc. Things of no value they just discarded. I picked up a couple of photographs taken from the pilot's pockets. If they were of himself, he must have been very young, hardly out of his teens; the picture showed him in civilian clothes. Another picture was of a little boy of about two years. I should have liked to have shown the pictures to his executioners.

It was fortunate that the Italian coastal troops offered little resistance, so that, although many troops landed in the wrong place and not in the right order, and tank landing craft with tanks and artillery were as much as six hours behind schedule, landings in both corps areas were successful, and by the end of the day 13th Corps had taken Syracuse and was in contact with the German Battle Group Schmalz of Hermann Goering Division between there and Augusta. 30th Corps had secured Pachino and begun repairing the airfield.

The Americans, around Gela, had a more difficult time. The swell was worse and the beaches were obstructed by sand bars which caused the assault craft to breach to. The Italians put up a stiffer resistance and German air attacks were more effective. The 1st US Division was counter-attacked early in the day by the Hermann Goering and Italian Livorno Divisions, and was only saved by naval gunfire support. After the failure of this attempt to drive the Allies back into the sea, Guzzoni decided to withdraw to a line running from Augusta in the east through Caltagirone to Porto Empedocle in the west. If he was forced back from that line, he would stand on one from Catania westward to Enna, and then north to San Stefano on the coast. The key to successful withdrawal to that was the firm defence of the road junctions between Enna and

Leonforte. Kesselring, who was visiting him between 12 and 15 July, approved. Meanwhile Hitler ordered the German 1st Parachute Division in France to be got ready for deployment in Sicily.

Patton, however, feared a renewal of counter-attacks and decided to fly in the rest of 82nd US Airborne Division at 10.45 p.m. on the 11th, and every effort was made to warn all anti-aircraft guns, on land and at sea. There had been several air attacks on shipping off the beaches during the day, in one of which an ammunition ship had exploded spectacularly. One came in at 10 p.m. which damaged several ships, and had not long been over when the first flight of paratroopers passed overhead to land successfully beyond the beaches; but, as the second flight approached, a single Allied anti-aircraft gun opened fire, which provoked all the others to open up. Some pilots prudently turned back, but others pressed on, some to be shot down, others to jettison their loads as soon as they could on land or over the sea. 23 aircraft were lost and 37 severely damaged: 81 paratroopers and 60 aircrew died, 132 were wounded and 16 were missing. The culprit who fired the first gun was never traced, and senior naval and air force officers joined in blaming Patton, Bradley and Ridgway for ordering an operation which ran severe risks, particularly if the airdrop coincided with an enemy air raid, and proved to be unnecessary.

The critical situation in the American sector had indeed passed, and during the next two days the 45th and 1st US Divisions began to advance northwards. This led, on 13 July, to a serious Anglo-American clash. Montgomery's plan was for 13th Corps to advance by Route 114, the only road of any capacity along the east coast, north from Augusta, which was not occupied until the 12th, helped by a Commando landing to capture Lentini, and the planned parachute landing at the Primosole Bridge between there and Catania, which took place in the early hours of the 14th. It had been postponed more than once and one of those frustrated by this was Lieutenant P. A. Angier of the 4th Parachute Battalion. He wrote in a letter home:

As we twice got into the aircraft, you can understand these days were a bit of a strain. There are incidents that will remain my memory a long time. It was rather like being part of a stirring and rather terrifying piece of music which suddenly stopped. I was rather glad we did not go the first time as it had been a tiring day getting ready and we were a bit over-wrought. Last night was disappointing as, although no honest man really wants to go into action, we had the job so carefully planned and rehearsed that we could not fail to achieve success. However we await our next call. Don't think for a moment I am looking round for fighting! We shall see plenty of that before the war is over. One's reactions are very queer on these occasions. You have waves of courage and waves of trembling inside. When I was resting I used to curl inside and sweat and be restless and take deep breaths whenever I struck one, as however you try you cannot keep it out of your mind that now is "Der Tag". A look at your watch and the thought, in five hours from now the green light, I wonder what it will be like this time? Everyone has the same reactions from the highest to the lowest. The men were marvellous as, although they feel the same as us, perhaps worse, as they have not so many responsibilities to think of, they were singing and cheering as I have never seen them before. Nothing can compare with the spirit of the British soldier at this moment.

There was no road between Route 114 in 13th Corps's sector and Route 124 through Vizzini that would make it possible for 30th Corps to develop its strength further west to outflank the airfield complex west of Catania. Route 124, from Vizzini north-west through Caltagirone and then north to the key road junction area round Enna and Leonforte, had been allotted in Alexander's plan to the US Seventh Army. Alexander visited Patton on 13 July and restrained him from thrusting his left-hand division, the 3rd, further inland, on the grounds that it would disperse his forces, whose principal task was to protect Montgomery's left flank. He went on to see the latter, who persuaded him to readjust the inter-army boundary and allot Route 124 to him, so that 30th Corps could use it to outflank not only the Catania plain but Mount Etna also, and then thrust up to the north coast, a move which Bradley intended that his corps would make by that route. His 45th Division found the 51st (Highland) Division at Vizzini and using the road when they reached it that day, and it was not until midnight that the order was received from Alexander's headquarters that he had reallocated the route to Eighth Army. Bradley and Patton were furious, reinforcing their suspicion that they were being made to play second fiddle and make it possible for Montgomery to claim the conquest of Sicily as his victory.

The latter's northward drive now began to slow up. The Commando raid on Lentini was a failure and the parachute drop on Primosole Bridge could not be called a success. On their approach flight, the aircraft carrying 1st Parachute Brigade were first fired on by the navy's anti-aircraft guns, two being shot down and nine forced to turn back: the 87 which flew on met heavy anti-aircraft fire from the Catanian airfield complex and dispersed, so that, of the 1,900 men who had set off, only 200, with three anti-tank guns, landed near the bridge. There they were met by the German 3rd Parachute Regiment, who had landed there two days before. Nevertheless they succeeded in capturing and holding the bridge throughout 14 July; but were forced back to the south bank of the river until the leading troops of the 50th Division reached them next day.

Sergeant J. A. Johnstone of the 2nd Parachute Battalion was one of the 200 who landed. This is his account, written some time later:

Before hooking up I checked on the lads, and then stood to the door. The pilot made a 90 degree turn, and I caught a glimpse of beach, white under the moonlight and the outline of the estuary, before the mysterious shadowy shapes of the land were sliding beneath as I peered down. Then suddenly the shadows were enlivened by a regular firework display of flares and tracer streaming up all around us. The red light went on and I stood with hand on the hamper. The green came and I gave a heave on the hamper and with a "good luck" shout to the lads I launched myself after it. I floated down like the fairy queen with my aerial wand in my hand, until I paid it out below me on a length of parachute cord attached to my belt. The flat shadows below loomed close. I clamped my feet together and landed with a breath-taking wallop. I lay for a moment with the radio uncomfortably under my chest, but then eased myself up and felt feverishly for the quick-release box, banged it, and scrambled out of the harness.

I stood upright and almost mechanically assumed that I was physically intact, though in fact I must have landed heavily on my left shoulder, for although I felt nothing then, it was some weeks before I could raise my arm above shoulder height.

Suddenly I felt terribly alone as I looked around and could see no one near me. I don't even remember any sound, for the aircraft had droned away up the DZ, and was in fact hit, or the pilot took evasive action shortly after I went, because I learned later that a violent lurch caused a man to fall, blocking the gangway so that the majority could not get out for a time, and landed well up the DZ.

Johnstone was soon joined by Sergeant Fisher and four or five of his section. Together they set off in the direction in which they believed their forming-up area to be, avoiding some parties of Germans on the way. As he led his men on, he came across the Brigade Major, who told him that Colonel Frost and the 2nd Battalion had gone off up the road he was on to the high ground which was their objective. He continued on and, as it got light, moved his party into the shelter of a vineyard. His account continues:

As we lay tense among the vines it was soon evident that we were in the middle of a nice fire fight, for from the hill above us came the solid thunk of a bren in reply to the spandau cobra hiss. Then we heard the swish and crump of mortars coming from the German side onto what we now know was a handful of "A" Company on Johnny I. I think I remember also identifying the bark of 88s down the valley, but whether they were ranged on Johnny I or the bridge, which, like Arnhem later, had been gained by the brigade only to be lost because of lack of numbers and lightness of armament. [sentence not concluded]

For how long this went on I have no idea, nor had I at the time, but abruptly, as usually happens in war, our situation changed completely, for there was the sound of movement close in the vines and I was startled by an abrupt command in German, "Hande Hoch". I found myself on my knees, hand on sten, and gazing at the back and left side of a stocky little figure whose schmeiser was levelled at the burly form of the C.M.P. sergeant, who later turned out to be "Biff" Whitehead, a professional rugby player of international standing. As I say, the German's back was half turned to me and I started to raise my sten, to be checked by George Fisher's urgent "Not now Johnnie!". I don't know exactly what passed through my mind at that moment. I had never killed a man at close quarters or indeed at all, that I knew of for certain. Did I remember the misfire on the DZ? Certainly I had no appreciation of the tactical situation which I suspect that the sharper witted cockney, George, may have realised that we were about to be enveloped in the advance of German paratroopers up the hill. I saw them moving swiftly and competently each side of the little hide-out a minute or two later. Anyway, I lowered my sten and it was all over.

By this time the two regiments of the German 1st Parachute Division had been reinforced by the rest of the Hermann Goering Division, which had moved eastward from facing the Americans to the western end of the Catania plain. On 16 July 50th Division, supported by 4th Armoured Brigade, launched a major attack to capture and cross the Primosole Bridge. This was to be followed that night by a landing at Catania by two Royal Marine Commandos and 17th Brigade from 5th Division. After that, the rest of 5th Division, passing through the 50th, would join them and continue the advance northwards. In the early hours of 16 July 50th Division succeeded in getting one battalion of 151st Brigade, 8th Durham Light Infantry, with a squadron of 44th Royal Tank Regiment, over the bridge; but attempts to enlarge the bridgehead beyond that were not successful.

Private Kerans of the 9th Durham Light Infantry described his part in this battle:

During the night [14/15 July] two tired and bitter paratroopers came up the road to the battalion. They had captured the bridge but could not hold it any longer. Most of their mates were dead or captured. So deep was their sorrow they tried to talk the I.O. and the C.O. into waking the lads and making the attack right away. There were tears in their eyes and anger in their voices as they talked. To the best of their knowledge they were the only ones left from the battle and it was definite that the bridge was in German hands. They swore they were coming in with us and taking no prisoners.

Kerans then describes an action during the night against Italian commandos who had come up the river in three amphibious vehicles, in which the Italians suffered heavy casualties. He then describes the attack made by his battalion on the 15th:

They started to cross the river then all hell broke loose. On the other side of the river suddenly a row of heads, machine-guns and rifles popped up. Soon the river ran red, literally, with the blood of the Durhams. Some did reach the other side, scamber up the bank and engage the enemy in hand to hand fighting, but there was not enough to hang on to what they had gained. We in H.Q. Company went down to see what we could do to help, there wasn't a lot. We stopped just short of the river and fired at anything that looked Tedescish. One or two of us went into the river to try and rescue some of the wounded. It wasn't easy, bullets buzzed about us like bees. The bloke nearest to me had himself to be rescued. After all these years memory is defective. I seem to remember dragging wounded under a bridge, to keep bullets off us, this would itself be Plimsole [sic] Bridge. Unless there were two bridges? One 100 yards to the left? I went under some bridge to keep bullets off me and my charges. The Padre was there too. (I think it was a stone one too.) What was left of the battalion went back up the hill to have a meal and much needed rest. The 8th Battalion made sure we were not followed.

About 0200 hrs [16 July] the next night the 8th D.L.I. went in. Allied guns had been belting away before that. By dawn the 8th had got most of their men across and gained quite a foothold. However the Germans were Paras, well armed and they knew what to do with them. With both sides it was hand to hand, rifles bayonets and plenty of Spandaus. While we were enjoying our well-earned rest the 8th and the Germans kept the 'Hand to hand' up all day. When night came the weakened 9th had to go back in and take over, there was nobody else. There had been no time for burial parties and there were dead bodies everywhere. A sunken road was paved with them. As usual I went in with the I.O. and the C.O. at the head of H.Q. Company's little column. The first person we met was a German sentry. I me-owed to him to keep quiet, or else. Visher was not so diplomatic, he hissed, "Give him to me." That's the last I saw of either of them for the remainder of that battle. You can't argue with an officer, but you can think.

The rest of us went on, Nobby with us. Down the side of a big farm building where a lot of 8th battalion wallahs were dug-in. To the road. Across it in a mad dash and through a field to a deep ditch that ran 90 degrees to it. With a C.O. with you there are things done more dangerous than with a 2nd Lieut. Now we were in the thick of the bullets and grenades. Some of our carriers had got across and were going up the road towards Catania. They weren't getting very far, like I say there was a lot of opposition. About forty yards from us, just across the road, two enemy dashed out of a farm building and put something that exploded under one of our carriers. Charlie Sollis and self fired at them two or three times. I don't know if we hit them, they gave up the idea. From the other end of our short trench a "Tiger" fired down it. I think it was. I dug myself into the side of the trench until it went away. In a battle like this nobody knows whose who. There were now less than a score of us. Nobby got the men on a carrier to ask for a 'smoke-screen'. This was put down (I think by a carrier) and we ran like the devil the way we had come. We ran back to a deep hollow about 40 yards from the bridge, bomb hole I think. The bridge was still under constant shell-fire. Nobby must have thought I was undestructable, he sent me to the bridge to make a Sit-rep. There were explosions all the way to it and around it and me but I went. The sides were O.K., but the floor across was more 'Holy than Godly'. Suddenly I got a painful 'upper-cut' which floored me. A nose-cap from a shell fell almost into my hand. I lay stunned for a few seconds but as sense returned I realised that this was not the safest place to be and dashed back to rejoin the C.O. and the rest who by now had returned to the other side of the road. It was not a big cut, I wiped the blood off a couple of times and it soon stopped.

The battalion advanced under heavy fire, it was slow going. All day we hung on to half a mile of land every inch of it hard won. When night came we had made some sort of position but had neither food or water. By the moonlight, in No-mans-land, we could see a farm-house. It was less than forty yards ahead. With a Jerry-can and Charlie Sollis 'covering me' the two of us warily made our way towards it. It was a huge barn, the floor 6 inch deep in liquid. We tasted it and found it to be Vino. There, wrecked by the enemy, were huge vats with the bungs knocked out. They were all around the walls but not much left in, we only just managed to half-fill a jerry-can. Suddenly there was what sounded like a loud snore. We dropped the tin and pointed our weapons at a very drunken goat that was staggering around in the corner. We enjoyed a quiet laugh, refilled our can and set off for home. As we did so others were entering from the enemy side. We did not argue with them, we did not do this killing business just for the sake of doing it.

The battalion got organised. The 'I' Section went back to the river-bank. There wasn't much small arms fire but plenty of shelling. The Bridge was getting more than its share. There were still plenty of casualties. One or two Shermans got through and for the first time the Germans began to give themselves up in large numbers. Rumour had it we were to be relieved tomorrow. In theory things were good but Nobby and Big Bill went round with the officers from another Division or the 69th Bde when a salvo of enemy shells got both of them. I'll bet he said "I am not showing them I dive for cover every time a shell explodes." The sort of thing he would do. He was killed instantly, it was like losing a father. When they told us on our river bank I could not help but cry out "If they can kill Nobby, what chance have any of us?" Visher told me to shut up or I'd have everybody bomb-happy.

No Nobby, but the rest of the battalion was relieved and went on a very high plateau, not far from the river behind Plimsole Bridge. We washed and changed ourselves and were reinforced, the latter had to be. The Brigade lost 600 men. When you realise that no battalion had more than three-hundred men to start with, it meant that one in three had gone.

Lieutenant D. J. Fenner was commanding 13 Platoon of C Company of the 6th Durhams, who attacked across the river on the left of the 9th. He wrote:

The whole battalion moved silently in single file to the attack. Rum had been issued before we left and was of some comfort in this limbo period where we had little to do but occupy our thoughts with the grim and inevitable prospect ahead. We reached a dry ditch running towards the river and began moving through a battlefield where our parachutists and the Germans had fought. All around the vegetation had been burnt by phosphorus bombs and tracer bullets. Evidence of the fighting was everywhere. The ditch contained many burnt bodies. One completely blackened sat upright staring sightlessly at each member of the battalion as he struggled past in the moonlight. The only sound came from the burst of harassing fire from the Cheshire machine-gunners and the bull frogs croaking in the reeds. We paused before the leading company entered the river, bayonets were fixed, rifles and machine guns cocked. Ben Dickinson, the platoon runner and oldest soldier in the platoon argued with Connel, the sergeant, about the need to fix bayonets. He said he had never found it necessary to use one. I cannot remember the outcome of this disagreement but I did appreciate the easing of tension it produced amongst us. Then we were on the move to the river, sliding down the bank into chest high water, again in single file, guiding ourselves by hanging onto a wire stretched between the banks for this purpose. Below the far bank the battalion bore left then turned to face the enemy, the three assaulting companies in line. So far all had gone well, our objective, a sunken road, was some 500 yards away through the vineyards. It needed a few more minutes to pass before zero hour when someone said "What are we waiting for?" another voice said "Let's get stuck in." Then followed a general move by all the leading platoons up the bank, through the vineyard towards the sunken road. My recollections of what happened after that are confused. Firing began at isolated Germans seen running away, then from the direction of the road came a murderous fire from the Spandaus located there. The gunners were firing on "fixed lines", they could not see us in the dark. Bursts of tracer swept past at knee height. The line of infantry kept going on in spite of men being hit until we were struck by heavy concentrations of artillery. Some of this was probably enemy DF (defensive fire) but in the opinion of those who had been shelled by our gunners on previous occasions we were in our own. Ben Dickenson [sic] was clear on this point. He shouted "when I get out of this I'll do those bloody gunners". He sounded a bit optimistic, shells were dropping all around, then it stopped, lifted, and groups of men got up, moved on through the cactus hedge into the sunken road. There was a lot of shooting, suddenly it was over and we had taken about 8 prisoners, all but two wounded. Mark organised what remained of the company astride the road. There were elements of two platoons and we started to provide some entrenching tools. The older soldiers acquired the much more efficient German article and were soon digging in at great speed. The place was littered with German equipment, spandau machine guns, belts of ammunition and corpses. Our prisoners were parachutists, one spoke good English and told us that three days ago they had been in the south of France! A fierce battle was in progress to our right where the 9th were going in. Apart from the pop of small arms fire, where we were was comparatively quiet. In the first light of the summer's day we dug while the stretcher bearers attended to the wounded lying thick in the vines.

When Dempsey and Montgomery together visited Kirkman in mid-morning on the 16th, they decided to cancel the landing at Catania. A renewed attempt by 50th Division on the following night to get more troops over succeeded, but strong resistance was still being met and a further attack was launched during the night of the 17/18th, which made a limited advance as far as the Fosso Bottacelo, two and a half miles beyond the bridge. Dempsey now decided that 5th Division, instead of passing through the 50th, should try and get forward on its left.

By this time 30th Corps was making progress further to the left on Route 124. 51st (Highland) Division had had to call on 45th US Division to help clear Vizzini, after which 1st Canadian Division passed through them. The Highlanders then turned north-eastwards, directed to the western end of the Catania plain. This involved them in a tough battle as they tried to cross the River Dittaino as the first step in a thrust towards Paterno. Major Barker describes his part in it:

When we reached the Dittaino river the position changed dramatically. Here the Germans stubbornly defended the river lines as they dominated the flat plain from the Etna foothills and so the battle for Sferro began. The Black Watch were pinned down in the bed of the river and it became clear that a full scale attack would be necessary with fire support. The road to the river was very exposed and heavily shelled so movement forward in daylight was out of the question. We recced from afar and after dark moved forward in file to the area of the bridge which was still intact and took up assault positions in the river bed. At H hour we scrambled up the far side to attack Sferro station. The German response was immediate and deadly, they opened up with spandaus, mortars and artillery, the latter caused a lot of casualties in the river bed and in the open country in front of the station – unfortunately a number of railway wagons in the siding were set on fire which made us easier targets as we stormed the station and quickly consolidated our positions beyond it forming a useful but very exposed bridgehead which was to prove a most unpleasant and dangerous spot for the next ten days. The bridgehead was completely overlooked[:] any movement by day was severely shelled so all adjustments and restocking with food and ammunition was done by night. Bridgeheads are always tough spots as they are in small contained areas aggressively contested. Sferro was no exception.

We had hoped to fight our way out but the plan was changed and we had to endure about ten days in this hot spot being subjected to shelling at the slightest movement. The Command Post was in the station yard behind a stone wall. Wooden sleepers lying in the station were used to give some form of cover over our trenches which were only shallow scrapings in the side of the track. On the last evening before we were relieved a howitzer shell scored a direct hit on the HQ. Dazed and covered with dust and debris I crawled out unharmed to find that the signal centre alongside had received the full impact, the occupants of which Leslie Syme being one were either dead or were dying from terrible wounds from shell splinters and a vast amount of wooden splinters from the railway sleepers – it had clearly been a great mistake using them. Once again one was completely numbed by the shock – this was the horrible reality of war one could only try to forget that but for a few feet it would have been oneself. The doctor gave morphine injections but there was no way of saving their lives that night we moved out a sad Battalion the bridgehead had taken its toll. Leslie was one of the best we all missed him greatly.

The Hermann Goering Division having moved eastwards, the Canadians had a fairly easy run, delayed by demolitions and rearguards, until they reached the important area of road junctions east of Enna on 18 July. Their commander, Guy Simonds, then decided to bypass Enna itself and head due north for Leonforte, causing another Anglo-American row, as Bradley was relying on Leese to occupy Enna in order to protect his right flank as he headed for Caterina. He was partly pacified by a case of champagne from the latter and help in securing the town with his 1st Division. While the Canadian 2nd Brigade attacked Leonforte, their 1st attacked Assoro, a mountain village a few miles to the southeast on 21 July.

Major Lord Tweedsmuir had recently taken over command of the Hastings and Prince Edward Regiment when his commanding officer had been killed. He was the son of the well-known writer John Buchan, who had been ennobled to be Governor-General of Canada, and had died in 1940. Tweedsmuir's regiment led their attack on Assoro and he chose an imaginative plan which began with an assault on the Norman castle on a cliff above the village. In describing the battle, he quotes from the account written by one of his subalterns, Farley Mowat:

All along the cliff edge steel-helmeted heads began to appear. Men hauled themselves up on to the few acres of relatively flat ground which crowned the summit. George Baldwin, leader of another of the assault platoons, saw me and yelled that he would search the castle ruins. I waved agreement, and as soon as the rest of my platoon had crowded up behind me I led them at a run across the plateau, a few yards down the opposite slope to the shelter of some low stone walls. Sure that the firing must have alerted the Germans, I expected them to begin shelling us at any moment. But secure in their belief that Assoro was impregnable, they had posted no troops other than the artillery observation team which had been dealt with.

It was full daylight now. Close below were the huddled roofs of Assoro village with skeins of blue smoke rising from the chimney pots. A quarter of a mile further down the slope a narrow gutted road ran south to the main German positions. On the lip of the massif overlooking the village, to our amazement, we beheld clusters of German soldiers strung out all along this road, gathered round their morning fires, in a scene of cheerful, almost domestic tranquility. Through my binoculars I could see some of them shaving. Others stood stripped to the waist enjoying the first warmth of the sun. A despatch rider puttered lazily along on his motor cycle, waving to some anti-aircraft gunners, who were breakfasting from a steaming portable field kitchen. There was a rumble of heavy engines and the head of a supply convoy appeared out of the north. One, two, a dozen trucks came slowly into view, gears grinding on the steep gradients as they brought forward their loads of rations, water and ammunition. Down beside me Sergeant Bates was fairly wriggling with excitement. Before I could give an order, a Bren gunner in one of the other platoons tightened his trigger finger. Instantly the dozen Brens of the Assault Company went into action, reinforced by several 2″ mortars and three score rifles.

Outpouring of fire from Assoro's crest must have come as a shattering surprise to the Germans down below, and had they been troops of a lesser calibre, a debacle such as had occurred at Valguarnera must have ensued. But the 15th Panzer Grenadiers were old soldiers, toughened in Africa, and they were a fighting breed. Although several trucks were hit, and two or three burst into flames, the surviving drivers flung themselves into the ditches and began to return our fire with their machine pistols. The 26mm anti-aircraft troop leapt to their guns, cranked down their barrels, and were soon hosing us with streams of tracer high explosives. I even saw two cooks abandon their pots and pans to seize rifles and open fire on us. They were a courageous lot, but we had the advantage of surprise, good cover and overwhelming fire power, and one by one their weapons fell silent.

The alarm had reached the Germans manning the forward positions, hidden from our view, half a mile southwards. At once they began sending their front line vehicles back up the road to prevent them from being cut off. Trucks and weapon carriers in groups of two or three came roaring along at full speed, the rifles and machine pistols flaring up at us as they reached the gamut. Some got through but before long the wreckage of those that failed had completely blocked the road. Thereupon, three armoured half tracks veered off on to the verges and ground up the slopes towards us through a tangle of vineyards. Immune to our small arms fire, they were only halted by the increasing steepness of the slope. Once stopped, medium machine gun and 81mm teams leapt out of them, took cover and engaged us fiercely.

The battle was not yet half an hour old and already the Germans were counter-attacking. Worse was soon to come. Several field and medium batteries located just to the north of us, covering the approaches to Leon Forte, swivelled their guns to bear almost point blank range upon Assoro's peak. As at Valguarnera we had sown the wind. Now the whirlwind burst upon us. I had just moved my platoon a little farther down the slope to a more protected position, when the world exploded in an appalling cacophony of sound and fury. The cramped plateau on to which nearly 500 men were now crowded, virtually vanished under the mounting pall of dust and smoke, shot through with malevolent tongues of flame.

. . . The noise, smoke and confusion was so great that I was cut off from everyone except Bates and a couple of men from 9 Platoon, who were huddling behind the same broken wall that sheltered me. I did not know that several members of my assault platoon had been wounded, nor that Sharon and Robinson, a steady and inseparable pair, had been obliterated by a direct hit on their shared slit trench. I only knew our situation was desperate and getting worse.

At this stage Tweedsmuir and his supporting gunner, Kennedy, managed to gain observation of the German gunsites and bring their own supporting artillery to bear. It proved effective and the intensity of the enemy fire slackened off. Mowat continues:

I found I had one man killed and three men wounded from my hybrid platoon, but most of the other platoons had suffered heavy losses. We survivors were slow to recover our wits. The several hundred shells which had fallen within the narrow confines of the Battalion area with such violence, had left us almost comatose. Action was the only effective anecdote. There was not a great deal to distract us once the casualties had been dealt with, except deepen our shallow scrapes of fox-holes in anticipation of renewal of the fury. I was actually grateful when Alex, my Company Commander, sent his runner with a message ordering me to take a patrol into the village and see if it was free of Germans.

As Mowat made his way through the steep, narrow alleyways, he met an Italian officer who told him that the Germans were in strength further down. Soon after that his patrol was subjected to an intense bombardment which he described thus:

The Moaning Minnie* bombardment which followed was well-nigh unendurable. Though I had experienced spasms of fear during the previous few days, what I felt now was undiluted terror. Salvo after salvo screamed into our position and massive explosions and shuddering blast waves poured over me. My whole body grew rigid, muscles knotting so tightly they would no longer obey my orders. Mercifully this new bombardment did not last long. Unable to bring transport forward because of Kennedy's observation of the approach road, and the devastatingly accurate fire of our guns, the Germans were having difficulty replenishing their ammunition and so had to practice some economy. On the other hand, we had, as we had begun the day, only the ammunition which we carried on our backs up Assoro's precipice. We were now literally reduced to counting every round. We had virtually no food; and what muddy water we could obtain from a shallow well near the castle barely sufficed to meet the needs of the increasing number of wounded, let alone the rest of us, lying, parched and baking, on that shard of rock under the pitiless Sicilian sky.

---

* The German multi-barrelled mortar, originally designed to project chemical-warfare shells, and thus named *Nebelwerfer* (cloud-thrower). The projectile in flight made a banshee-like sound, hence its nickname.

Lord Tweedsmuir added his own words:

Every man had a white face with slits for eyes. White from the rock
dust that had blown in clouds from the explosions on that rocky
peak. All men were lying down, trying to get as much cover as they
possibly could from the next lot of shelling they expected. Looking at
these recumbent forms it would seem hard to tell the dead from the
living. One's mind wanders vaguely in those circumstances. I remember thinking I had made quite a discovery when I realised that you
could tell them apart, because the flies walked on the faces of the
dead. The skin of our faces and arms and legs was scorched by the
sun. Our heads were swimming with heat and exhaustion. We lay
and suffered in that heat. The rocks were too hot to touch and so
was the metal of our weapons. We had practically no water, and we
hadn't eaten for more than 30 hours, or slept, other than occasional
nodding and dozing.

I suddenly began to feel that infantry, quite regardless of their
cause or their country, all through history had really been the one
similar sort of man. I crept to the edge of the castle and looked
through my field glasses and heard two men lying in a slit trench,
talking: "There's the old man", said one of them. "Poor old fellow.
How tired he looks." I was 31 years old. Curiously to be called the
old man is a term of affection. I am sure the Roman legionnaires
said the same thing about their centurions.

Every now and then the Germans would fire air burst shells
which exploded just above the ground. I was lying a few feet from a
wireless operator when a great jagged piece of steel landed between
us. I and the signaller looked at it dumbly and, curiously, without
any interest. And so that blazing day reached its climax in the
evening.

Farley Mowat continued:

An hour after sunset we came under another thundering bombardment and, as it ended, a battalion of Panzer Grenadiers attacked
from the north-west. They were met, halted, and broken mainly by
the massed fire of three regiments of our distant guns called down
upon them by Tweedsmuir over that blessed radio set. Twice more
the grenadiers tried to clamber up the slopes. Twice more they were
driven back. After the last attempt, they retreated to the road. Shortly

thereafter we heard an upsurge of vehicle noises. The Germans had given up Assoro and were pulling out from their positions overlooking the Dittaino.

The Anglo-American row over Enna and Leonforte was minor in comparison with the one which blew up as a result of Alexander's orders issued on 16 July. Once Eighth Army had taken Catania and the airfields in the plain, Montgomery was to drive towards Messina on three routes: north up the coast from Catania; east from Leonforte on Route 121 to Adrano; and east from Nicosia, when his troops had reached it, on Route 120 to Randazzo on the northern side of Mount Etna. These thrusts would involve breaching the enemy's main defence line, running southeast from San Stefano round the southern edge of Mount Etna to Catania, withdrawal to which Guzzoni had ordered the day before. Patton's Seventh US Army was told to protect the rear of Eighth Army in two phases: in the first, to secure the area of road junctions round Enna and to the west of it: in the second, to move north from there to Petralia on Route 120, west of Nicosia; and if the advance of his left-hand division, the 3rd, to Agrigento, which Alexander had reluctantly agreed to on 13 July, absorbed too much effort, he was to postpone it until these two tasks had been completed. In fact Truscott had taken Agrigento and Porto Empedocle on the 16th.

Patton and Bradley were furious at this relegation to a purely secondary role, which confirmed their suspicion that Alexander was intent on reserving the principal role for Montgomery. They were supported by Major-General John P. Lucas, who was acting as Eisenhower's liaison officer with Patton. While Patton flew to Tunis to see Alexander, who had returned there, Lucas flew to Algiers, hoping to see Eisenhower and remonstrate with him. Faced with a grim Patton, Alexander gave way, although not to the degree Patton wanted. The former added to his orders that, once Patton had reached Petralia, he should 'take advantage of the situation by pushing north a detachment to cut the coast road' and that the operation must not be started before he was ready to operate from a secure base. Patton was not going to argue about these limitations. He correctly estimated that there was very little threat from the western half of the island, and that, by moving fast to Palermo and the north coast, he could influence events in his favour, while Montgomery was struggling to get round Mount Etna. Leaving

Bradley to carry out the tasks set out in Alexander's orders, he formed a provisional corps under the command of his deputy, Major-General Geoffrey Keyes, consisting of Truscott's 3rd Division, Ridgway's 82nd Airborne, two Ranger battalions and Gaffey's 2nd Armored Division. Truscott's division led the way, starting off on 19 July, and with great dash reached Palermo at the same time as the leading troops of 2nd Armored Division on the 22nd, the Italian garrison offering no resistance. In Bradley's 2nd Corps, 1st US Division reached Petralia next day, and the 45th, further west, reached the north coast at Termini Imerese, halfway between Palermo and San Stefano, on the same day.

Meanwhile Eighth Army was making slow progress. 13th Corps could make no headway towards Catania, and Montgomery decided to make no further major attack on that axis, transferring his main effort to 30th Corps, which was to be reinforced by Major-General Vivian Evelegh's 78th Division, brought over from Tunisia. Leese's principal thrust was to be made on Route 121 to Adrano, leaving Route 120 further north free for the Americans to use. On 25 July Alexander issued fresh orders. The US 2nd Corps, reinforced by Major-General Manton S. Eddy's US 9th Division, was to drive eastward along the coast road and Route 120 to the south of it, while 30th Corps would aim for Adrano, the 51st Division attacking northwards to the east of it. 13th Corps was to keep up pressure towards Catania, but was not to press its attack.

On the following day Mussolini was deposed by his own Grand Council and removed to an island off Naples, and a few days later the Italian General Staff authorized Guzzoni to hand over operational command in Sicily to the German General Hube. The latter then had Major-General Walter Fries's 29th Panzer Grenadier Division and the remains of the Italian Assietta Division on the north coast facing 45th US Division at San Stefano; Major-General Eberhard Rodt's 15th Panzer Grenadier Division, with the 5th Regiment of the Italian Aosta Division, covering Route 120 east of Nicosia and Agira on Route 121; and Major-General Paul Conrath's Hermann Goering Division, with also the 3rd and 4th Parachute Regiments and two Fortress Battalions, covering the whole of Eighth Army's front east of Agira. Although Kesselring, on 27 July, had told Hube that Sicily was to be held at all costs, he started discussing the possibility of evacuation with Hitler and OKW, and both Hube and Guzzoni began considering it; but it was not until 5 August that a firm decision was taken to put it into effect.

In Leese's 30th Corps, 1st Canadian Division lost no time in pressing eastward along Route 121 from Leonforte to Agira, which they reached on 23 July to find it firmly held by 15th Panzer Grenadier Division. After several attacks, some of which failed to reach their objectives, 2nd Canadian Brigade and 231st British Infantry Brigade finally succeeded in capturing vital high ground overlooking the town on 28 July, and the Germans withdrew after the Canadian Division had suffered 438 casualties. 231st Brigade then led the advance to Regalbuto, seven miles further on, which they reached on the 29th. On the following day the division's 3rd Canadian Brigade, further south, attacked and captured Catenanuova on the River Dittaino to secure a start line for 78th Division to attack north from there towards Centuripe. They began that on the night of 30/31 July against the German 3rd Parachute Regiment, who then withdrew to Centuripe, which the leading troops of the division, 36th Brigade, reached on 1 August. The brigade's attack on the town next day, even after it had been reinforced by two battalions from 11th Brigade, failed, and Evelegh, in the late afternoon, committed the 38th (Irish) Brigade to an attack on their right which succeeded in capturing the town by first light on the 3rd. Lieutenant P. Royle, serving with 17th Field Regiment Royal Artillery, was acting as a Forward Observation Officer in support of the Irish Brigade's attack on Centuripe. This is his account:

> As it grew light so we could see the bulk of Etna away to our right front, still smoking and very soon the sun was up and the warm night was changing to hot morning. I was walking a few yards behind the Company Commander and as we approached the crest I found two men out of the leading section lying dead – the first casualties of the day. Having encountered opposition the Battalion started to probe the enemy defences and I moved away to the right and found a suitable spot for an OP, got the wireless working and had soon established contact with the battery. The town of Centuripe lay about 4/500 yards ahead of me connected by a narrow strip of ground possibly a 100 yards wide on either side of which were deep ravines. This strip of ground appeared to be the only possible approach to the town – to attack up the ravines would not only be difficult – it would be sheer madness. The top slopes of the ravines had been cultivated into terraces, but below these the ground sloped away at angles steeper than 45 degrees. It was a very strong defensive position.

My field of vision ran from the town itself to about 120 degrees to my right including the road running eastwards out of the town. The ground at the left of the town as I looked at it was obscured and this was the area being attacked by 36th Brigade ... I suppose I directed several thousands shells into enemy positions that day and two shoots I can remember clearly.

The first was considerable enemy troop movement away to my right just the other side of the ravine and the Company Commander thought it was a counter-attack developing. I considered this important enough to engage with the entire regiment, so I gave the order "Monkey target" (the codeword for a regimental target) and a map reference. A couple of ranging rounds and I was near enough to order "10 rounds gun fire". 240 shells landed in an area not much bigger than a football pitch in the space of 60 seconds. I had the Company Commander by my side while this was going on and he was visibly impressed, so much so that he thought up an excuse for a repeat performance. In my opinion it was not really necessary as the threat of a counter-attack had been broken, but I always worked on the principle that if my infantry asked for anything, they got it. Without more ado I turned to Corbett and said "Repeat" and another 240 rounds whistled over and landed on target.

The second shoot was at enemy movement on the edge of the town. For this I was only firing 10 Battery (8 guns) but I must have hit an ammunition dump or lorry because there was a very loud explosion and a huge mushroom of black smoke.

I was kept busy all day but fortunately there was very little counter artillery or mortar fire from the Germans – it was very much one way but the leading companies were pinned down by small arms fire and it wasn't until late afternoon that the Inniskillings were able to make a real advance into the town. As I wrote in my diary '... the infantry started going forward at 4.30 and at 5 I got hit in the backside and the left wrist by a machine gun ...'.

When the order to advance was received, the Company I was with moved to its left and picked its way in single file over the crest of the strip of land running towards Centuripe and we found ourselves on the terrace amongst the grape vines. Each terrace was about four feet wide and three feet below the one above and I suppose we dropped down about four terraces which meant that we had our right flank protected against enemy fire, but away to our left the other ravine sloped steeply down and up the other side to the only road running into Centuripe from the south and up which 36 Brigade were attacking. We had progressed about 200 yards towards the town when suddenly [a] machine gun opened up on us from across the ravine – the German P/34 unmistakable from its very high rate of fire.

An awful lot seemed to happen during the next five or six seconds and looking back it all happened in apparent slow motion. As the machine gun started firing, the file of infantry in front of me went to ground and I saw the bullets striking the stone wall of the terrace on their right a foot or so above them. Some of the men were lying flat, others had their heads raised looking to their left front to try and pin point the firing. The machine gunner was sweeping the terrace with fire from left to right and the bullets striking the wall were approaching me fast. We were on the bottom terrace and glancing to my left I noticed that two or three feet below me there was a shallow hole – it may have been a hole caused by a shell or mortar. I decided that I would be safer there than lying on the terrace with everybody else so I jumped towards it. As I was in mid air, bullets started to kick up the dust in this very hole and I can remember quite clearly thinking 'that place is no good – I have to get out of it immediately.' I landed and took off in one movement and as I did so I felt a sudden sharp pain in my left buttock – as though someone had jabbed me with a knife. I knew at once that I had been hit and I let out one hell of a shout – not because I had been hurt – I felt nothing after the initial pain – but because I was scared stiff. By this time I was in mid air again and landed five or six feet lower down the ravine, only to take off once more for another six foot leap. I came to rest and instinct and experience made me lie completely still for several seconds until the bullets had stopped flying around.

The bullet had entered the back of his left leg, nine or ten inches above his knee, and emerged from his left buttock, leaving a hole three inches in diameter. He was picked up by two stretcher bearers, but the sides of the ravine were so steep that he found it easier to walk, supported by them, than be carried. Having climbed down and up the other side, he was picked up by an ambulance and taken to the Advanced Dressing Station.

Meanwhile the 1st Canadian Division had attacked Regalbuto, which they secured on the 2nd. Further north, 1st US Division had met strong opposition on Route 120 at Troina, which they did not secure until 6 August, when 15th Panzer Grenadier Division, having suffered heavy casualties, withdrew. 9th US Division then took over the advance. On the coast road 45th US Division captured San Stefano after a sharp battle with 71st Panzer Grenadier Regiment of 29th Panzer Grenadier Division on the night of 30/31 July, after which 3rd US Division passed through them, negotiating many demolitions before coming up against a strong position at San Fratello, twelve miles further on, on 4 August. There the division had as tough a battle with 29th Panzer Grenadier Division as the 1st Division had faced against the 15th at Troina, and it was not until 8 August that they succeeded in forcing the enemy out of it.

By now Patton was bursting with impatience to reach Messina, as he was determined to do before Montgomery, who had conceded, in meetings with him on 26 July and at Palermo on the 29th, that Patton's was the main thrust to Messina. At Palermo Montgomery was lucky to survive a hazardous landing as the runway was too short for his aircraft, the Flying Fortress he had acquired from Eisenhower as a result of a wager. He had abandoned any major attempt to force a way to Messina from Catania with 13th Corps, which he was now preparing for a crossing of the Straits to the mainland. All his hopes rested on Leese taking Adrano and advancing north from there, west of Mount Etna, through Bronte to Randazzo, to which 9th US Division was also directed from Troina.

On the night of 6/7 August 78th Division entered Adrano, whence the Germans had withdrawn, as they had also by that time from the whole of the Catania plain. On the 5th von Senger had told Guzzoni that withdrawal to a line north of Mount Etna was inevitable, and within the next few days both Germans and Italians began openly preparing to transfer their troops to the mainland. However, when 78th Division advanced north from Adrano, they met strong resistance on 8 August at Bronte, and at Maletto, seven miles short of Randazzo. The former was taken by the division's 11th Brigade on that day, while 36th Brigade passed through, clearing Mount Rivolia. 38th Brigade then took up the running, clearing Maletto on the 12th and entering Randazzo next day. Further advance from there was to be left to the Americans, Eighth Army's effort being limited to that being carried out east of Mount Etna by 50th Division along the coast road and by first the 5th and then the

51st on a minor road on the mountainside. The Reverend W. J. Hill, a
Methodist, was the Chaplain with the 1st Battalion the King's Own
Yorkshire Light Infantry in the 5th Division. His diary reads:

6.8.43. This morning the C.O. asked me to go back & find out
definitely who were the men in the German-made grave. He expected
I should find the particulars in a tin or a bottle near the surface. The
information we had was not sufficient to really establish identity.
Well I didn't find the tin, so I had to uncover the bodies! They had
been buried 16 days in hot ground & the job wasn't very pleasant.
That didn't matter, what did matter was that the first body I looked
at was that of a company commander who we had felt fairly confident
was a prisoner in enemy hands. He was a grand fellow with a very
nice wife and youngster, a county rugger wing three-quarter, too. I
identified the other two, entered their particulars on a label, buried it
with them, in a tin, read the service, erected a nice cross my boys
had made & on which I had their names, then we rejoined the unit
in time for the march forward again.

7.8.43. ... We moved up and took over the positions as darkness
was falling. We had a few British and German wounded to collect &
tend. I stayed with two bad cases (one of my own platoon commanders & a German Panzer-Grenadier) in the roadside until round
midnight waiting for an ambulance to take them back ... The QM
[Quartermaster] got up the hot meal some time after that. What time
I ate I can't say. I had gone to sleep again; sometime during the night
is as near as I could put it.
   ... We spent the afternoon burying two more Germans. They
were part of a machine-gun crew which had been attacked by the
laddie who had too much to drink the day before. I had wondered
how much truth & how much alcohol had been mixed up in his
ravings. I found there was more truth than I expected, he was a
carrier-driver & had driven slap into the enemy positions. This
particular machine-gun post had been constructed 50 yds back from
the road side & had a good field of fire. The carrier-tracks went
straight for it, circled it at close quarters & then returned to the road
leaving two of the gun crew dead, one dying & the other badly
wounded. One of the dead was a mere boy. He looked 15 & couldn't
have been more than 17. His pay book was badly soaked with blood
& I couldn't see his age. I could see that he had joined the army in

May this year. There was a little paper cross among his collection of photographs which gave me a greater feeling of reality as I read the burial service than I usually have when giving Christian burial to Germans. I always give them Christian burial, but mostly I wonder whether it is what they would have asked for. After some of the pronouncements of official Nazism it seems rather out of place to commit the bodies of their warriors to the ground 'in sure and certain hope of the resurrection to eternal life through the Lord Jesus Christ'. They *may* be Christians is the feeling I always have & since the actual 'committal' is prefaced by 'Blessed are the dead which die in the Lord' I feel that to be some sort of apology for giving Christian burial to a possible avowed pagan. I have of course no such doubts about the prayer for the consolation of their relatives.

On the north coast Patton meanwhile tried to hasten progress by amphibious landings behind the positions of 29th Panzer Grenadier Division. Truscott's 3rd Division was having difficulty forcing them out of the San Fratello position, and a battalion group, which was all that there was landing craft for, was landed east of San Agata on the night of 7/8 August. It landed unopposed, but soon had to beat off a counter-attack, inflicting heavy casualties on the enemy in the process. However, the latter were already withdrawing to a line behind the River Zappula at Naso and Capo d'Orlando, where Truscott prepared to attack them on 10 August, Patton insisting on another amphibious landing two miles east of Capo d'Orlando. When Truscott proposed a twenty-four-hour postponement of his attack on the German line, Patton lost his temper and insisted that the landing go forward as planned. It was nearly a disaster, Truscott's forward troops, after some fierce fighting, arriving just in time to save it on 12 August. During the night 13/14 August Hube broke contact everywhere and began his withdrawal to the main-land, which he had completed by the morning of the 16th. Late that day a patrol from 3rd US Division entered Messina unopposed.

Ten miles to the south the British Lieutenant-Colonel J. M. T. F. Churchill's 2 Commando, with half a squadron of tanks from the 3rd County of London Yeomanry, and detachments of the Royal Engineers and Royal Artillery, all under the command of Brigadier J. C. Currie, commander of 4th Armoured Brigade, had landed in the early hours of the 16th and made their way to Messina, arriving there the following morning just before General Patton made his own entry, annoyed to

find British bagpipes already playing, although the Highland Division
had got no further north than Taormina. Lieutenant Joseph Nicholl was
serving with 2 Commando. He refers to himself in the third person as
'Joe' and describes what happened after they had landed:

So in single file they moved along the top of the embankment
towards the village. The danger now was that they would bump into
their own men just as much as meet the enemy. Feeling terribly sky-
lined as the ground dropped away on both sides, Joe tried to think
what he would do if a machine gun opened up on them now.
Hearing a loud explosion behind them, they instinctively turned
round. It was certainly louder than any noise our weapons could
have made. Someone said they'd heard a lorry a moment before
and a shout. There was no deciding what had happened, so they
moved on.

A low culvert ran under the railway. Dickie decided to use it to
get up on to the street, which was quite close now. Joe sent Cpl.
Watt and Sgt. Heery down into a garden to get them to cover the
movement up the culvert. But as they were slipping down the slopes
of the embankment, a gun of some sort fired straight down it. The
echo was trebled in that narrow gully. Dickie yelled, "Fix bayonets.
Charge!" and raced off, without waiting for anyone to complete the
first operation. This meant that the only ones capable of following
him were those with Colt .45 pistols, Frank and Sgt. Prescott.
Together they disappeared round the corner.

In the meantime, the gun fired twice again. The first shot forced
Joe into a doorway. He battered at the woodwork, but was unable to
make the slightest impression. There was no handle and no lock – it
must have had a great beam locked into position on the other side.
Joe was unable to get a fraction of cover and look over his left
shoulder to fire his automatic. With his second round, the gun fired
again. He felt a sharp biff in the back. Realising that nothing hurt, he
paid no more attention to it. It was only afterwards, when he took
off his small pack, that he noticed two small holes in it. On the top
was a Bren magazine, which now had a large dent in it. The round
inside the magazine was bent. Joe realised that he had had a rather
remarkable escape. The jagged piece of metal would in normal
circumstances have passed through the pack and cut a nasty hole in
the back of his neck: instead it had ricocheted off. The spare Bren

magazine had come in useful. Meanwhile Dickie & Co. had captured the machine gun post in the street, but Dickie had received a nasty thigh wound and Sgt. Prescott had also been wounded. Sgt. Heery and Cpl. Watt instead of being able to provide covering fire had met with a packet. Sgt. Heery had been wounded and Cpl. Watt had been killed.

The attack had begun at 0415, and it was now rapidly growing lighter. The situation, too, began to take shape. No one knew quite what had been happening on the right, but Dickie was convinced that they should move off to the left to ensure that there were no enemy positions on that side. It was fairly obvious that they had only bumped into a German rearguard, and there would be nothing in that direction. But they had to make certain and so down the road they went. Dickie was finding it painfully difficult to keep up. Frank and Joe told him to get his leg attended to, but Dickie was as stubborn as a mule and insisted on staggering on. The ever-resourceful Smith, his batman, came to the rescue. Diving into a backyard he discovered just the thing – an Italian bath chair. So, with two scouts in front, with his moustache bristling and looking as he might on the front at Brighton or the Pantiles at Tunbridge Wells, Dickie followed, pushed by the smirking Smith.

Rounding the first headland after the village, they were faced by the most complete and systematic demolition imaginable. At a point on the road where a steep cliff became a precipice dropping straight down to the sea beneath, the road had been cratered. It was just possible for men in single file to make a path for themselves in the side of the cliff. A bath chair was out of the question. Faced with this, Dickie accepted the inevitable. They turned round and re-entered the village. Here they discovered some Priests (105mm guns mounted in the chassis of a Sherman tank) in the Piazza, and all too soon realised they were being mortared. They moved rapidly away. The baptism by that sort of fire is never pleasant, and particularly so in an enclosed space. The Troop was quickly given the job of combing the hillside for the O.P. which was bringing fire so accurately onto the guns. Dickie had been taken off and Frank was in command. Joe set off for the woods, looking for what he did not exactly know. He had vague ideas of a little house in the trees or a rocky eyrie hidden in some crag. But wherever it was, it wasn't to be seen. As nightfall settled in, he returned. Frank had come back earlier to attend the simple funeral of Cpl. Watt, Sgt. Duffy and, really tragically, of John Jeffreys. In the fracas in the early hours of the morning, a lorry was heard. As it approached, the driver was ordered to halt. Instead a shot rang out. This was met by a rattle of tommy gun fire, which hit the contents of the lorry and caused the explosion. The occupants were killed and it was seen that the cargo had been a collection of mines and demolition material. But in the melee, Sgt. Duffy had been shot, and, beside him, John mortally wounded. 'Frankie and Johnnie' had been their theme song, and they had been really inseparable. John, the dashing cavalier, and Frank, the quick-witted fighter, each typified one aspect of the compleat Commando soldier. Frank took the separation very hardly and he was never quite the same person again. He lost his capacity for jollity.

When Frank got back, the Troop were having a hot meal from hay boxes under awkward conditions. Some parts of the road and hillside were being plastered by mortars, and it was a question of finding the right spot. With darkness the mortaring ceased. By about midnight Brigadier Currie, commanding the 4th Armoured Brigade, of which the Comamndo was now a part, rightly assessed that the Germans were moving out. Probing forward through the newly laid minefield, he soon had the whole force creeping along behind the slowly advancing Engineers with their mine-detectors, some on jeeps, some on foot, and some in DWKs [DUKWs: amphibious trucks]. Painfully slowly, in the face of this menace, along those eight miles into Messina the party wended its way. As they got closer and closer to the town, the locals began to come out. Cautiously at first, but then with ever increasing violence they proceeded to hurl their favours at their conquering liberators. Sometimes it was only blown kisses, sometimes flower petals, but later it was fruit of all sorts. A bunch of grapes even cracked the windscreen of a jeep, much to the fury of the driver who threw it back at the crowd, who by this time were making a monster fiesta of it and solemnly clapping their hands.

By 1000 hrs Messina was entered, but much to the impotent anger of the Commando, the Americans were there first, having come along the North coast road. Messina was not very healthy. The bombing of the town and port had been severe. Now the coastal guns on the other side of the strait, at Reggio, were beginning to open up, to add to the Chaos. The town was to be in the American zone, and so the Commando was conveyed back to Scaletta by 8 o'clock in the evening, and from there back to Catania the next day.

Hube's withdrawal had been a masterpiece of careful planning and efficient execution. Neither Cunningham's naval nor Tedder's air forces had done anything effective to interfere with it. Between 1 and 16 August he succeeded in transferring to the mainland 39,650 men, including casualties, 9,185 vehicles, which included all his heavy weapons, and 11,855 tons of stores.

3

Salerno to the GUSTAV Line

September to December 1943

While Alexander had been rather vaguely supervising the activities of Montgomery and Patton in Sicily, Eisenhower had been discussing with the American and British Chiefs of Staff where to go next and how. Views on this had been changing on both sides of the Atlantic. General Marshall now favoured an amphibious operation to capture Naples, followed by a rapid advance to Rome. He saw it as the best way of knocking Italy out of the war and turning the Mediterranean into an even greater liability to the Germans. Churchill had much more ambitious ideas. He did not want to stop at Rome, but press on into the valley of the Po and then decide whether to turn left into southern France or right towards Vienna. He did not really believe that OVERLORD could succeed. Plans were complicated by tentative approaches from the Italian government, headed by Marshal Badoglio, after Mussolini had been removed.

After much discussion, Eisenhower decided to leave the occupation of Sardinia and Corsica to General Giraud's French troops and planned that Lieutenant-General Mark W. Clark's Fifth US Army should land in the heel of Italy, between Taranto and Bari, while Montgomery's Eighth crossed the Straits of Messina into the toe. The two armies would form 15th Army Group, commanded by General Alexander. A direct assault on Naples was rejected as being beyond the cover of land-based fighter aircraft. Success in Sicily and the prospect of Italian surrender, however, persuaded Eisenhower to adopt a more ambitious plan for Mark Clark's army, consisting of 6th US Corps (Major-General E. J. Dawley) and 10th British Corps (Lieutenant-General Richard McCreery). It would land in the bay of Salerno, thirty miles south-east of Naples, a week after Montgomery had crossed the Straits of Messina. Firm decisions on this plan were complicated by the dilemma which the Italians faced: they hesitated to surrender until a sufficiently strong Allied force was estab-lished on the mainland to protect them against the Germans. They proposed that an armoured division should land at the mouth of the Tiber while an airborne one landed round Rome. The first was clearly impracticable. Serious consideration was given to the second, and senior officers from the 82nd US Airborne Division were secretly sent to confer with the Italians in Rome; but it was rejected when they realized that the Italian proposal somehow to disarm the German anti-aircraft defences was unrealistic.

Meanwhile the Germans were making their plans. Hitler prevaricated between the rival views of Kesselring and Rommel, finally deciding on a compromise, influenced by his fear of southern defensive positions being outflanked by amphibious landings. He ordered a staged withdrawal to the northern Apennines, based on a succession of well-prepared defence lines, the first main one, the GUSTAV line, running from south-east of Pescara in the east to the Rivers Rapido and Garigliano on the western side of the Apennine watershed halfway between Naples and Rome.

Italy's surrender and realignment with the Allies was announced on the evening of 8 September, nine hours before the first Allied troops landed on the beaches east of Salerno, 10th British Corps on the left and 6th US Corps, with 36th and 45th US Divisions, on the right of the River Sele. In 10th Corps, 56th Division (Major-General D. A. H. Graham) was on the right and 46th Division (Major-General J. L. I. Hawkesworth) on the left. The follow-up division, 7th Armoured (Major-General G. W. E. J. Erskine), was not due to begin to land until 15 September. The Italian surrender had made it possible to send 1st Airborne Division (Major-General G. F. Hopkinson) in cruisers and destroyers to land unopposed at Taranto on the same day. Lieutenant-Commander J. Whitton RN, commanding HM Submarine *Unshaken*, had had an interesting encounter with an Italian submarine in that area the previous day. He had been operating in the Adriatic when he was recalled to Malta with the news of the Italian surrender and that 'all Italian ships at sea were to proceed to Allied Ports forthwith, ships failing to comply with this order would be treated as hostile'. As he was passing through the Straits of Otranto, his hydrophone operator reported the noise of 'high-speed revs'. The noise turned out to be an Italian submarine steaming northwards on the surface about 1,500 yards away, with an unusually large number of people on the bridge. As she was in

no position to make a quick dive, Whitton decided to take the risk of
boarding her. He describes the action:

The enemy, oblivious of what was happening on her starboard bow,
was some 1000 yards away. 'Surface'. UNSHAKEN sped to the surface
– 'Open the Hatch' whistle signal given by 'Percy' intently watching
the Depth Gauge. I followed 'Feet's feet, behind the somewhat
drenched gun crew through the upper hatch, arriving in time to see
the gun fire and see the 'round' splash some 100 yards ahead of the
Italian. UNSHAKEN then turned 'hard-a-port' to swing round on
the enemy's starboard side ready to turn again 'hard-a-starboard' in
preparation to lay alongside the enemy's starboard bow and board.
I had no intention of crossing her bows or stern which would give
them the opportunity to use their bow or stern tubes on me. The
manoeuvre was going fine, thanks to the 'Chief Plumber', my Chief
Engineer, 'Sam' Evans – getting both main engines to full power
immediately on surfacing.

The Italian's reaction to the shot across his bows and sighting
UNSHAKEN, due, I suppose, to surprise, was slow – however a burst
of some automatic weapon in our direction was quickly silenced by
a return of machine-gun fire into the water near him, and he, seeing
our 3 inch, now quite close, following him as we manoeuvred round,
stopped further firing. I suppose they, and now there were even more
chaps on the bridge than before, had come up to see what was 'going
on', were wondering what the hell was going to happen. By this time
the UNSHAKEN was alongside stopped, with our bows against the
Italian's bow and the boarding party, led by 'Shaver' brandishing a
'45', jumping over and racing along the forward casing, climbing up
the enemy's conning tower with the main object to secure the
conning tower hatch to stop them diving and subdue any further
resistance.

The boarding party, led by 'Shaver', consisted of one E.R.A.
[Engine Room Artificer], a Leading Seaman and a stoker, the latter –
Stoker Greenhalgh – was a hefty grizzly bearded chap who, before
joining the Navy, fought in the Spanish Civil War on the republican
side and had had the misfortune to be taken prisoner by an Italian
contingent and had been badly beaten up by them. It was for this
reason I selected him from volunteers as a member of the boarding
party. I managed to warn 'Shaver' who, after all, was a guest and not

familiar with the ship's company, to keep an eye on one of his team who hated Italians, but, as things turned out, he was a good man for the job.

At this juncture, the Captain of the Italian submarine was ordered to proceed to Malta and that UNSHAKEN would escort him there: this was a verbal communication over the intervening space of about 20 feet from bridge to bridge and could be done without shouting and in a mixture of broken English and shocking Italian. The Italian Captain was a bit of an excitable fellow and a somewhat heated exchange followed – he shouting that he wanted to go to Brindisi and me shouting 'Malta' – this went on for short period – Brindisi – Malta. The argument was settled quite quickly by one of two things: 'Percy' had sent up my uniform cap, possibly to give the proceedings a little more dignity or authority, which I put on; also the 3 inch gun, still manned and ready for action, was ordered to 'load one round of high explosive'. The loading number, a seaman, with some personal initiative, held up the 3 inch high explosive shell and displayed it rather like a music hall conjuror, to a very impressed Italian audience, he then slipped the round 'home' into the gun, slamming the breach shut; the muzzle of the gun was trained on the Italian captain's stomach at a range of about 13 feet. 'Shaver' – who was standing close to him – was asked to stand aside. With a shrug of the shoulders and hands in the air, the Italian agreed – Malta.

The British 13th Corps (Lieutenant-General M. C. Dempsey), in Montgomery's Eighth Army, had already crossed the Messina Straits on 3 September after a massive bombardment which proved unnecessary as the Germans had already withdrawn and the few Italian soldiers in the area offered no resistance.

In spite of the absence of opposition, Eighth Army's progress northwards was slow, as the German General Herr's 76th Panzer Corps (26th Panzer and 29th Panzer Grenadier Divisions) carried out a skilful withdrawal, making full use of mines and demolitions on the few roads leading through the mountains of Calabria.

Mark Clark's Fifth Army got ashore successfully at Salerno on 9 September, but soon ran into trouble, especially in the American sector, as the German General von Vietinghoff, commanding their Tenth Army, ordered Hube's 14th Panzer Corps, responsible for the Naples area, to take the troops which had been in reserve to deal with the possibility of landings further north (the 15th Panzer Grenadier and Hermann Goering Divisions), and drive Clark's troops back into the sea. He was to be joined by Herr's 76th Panzer Corps, which was to break off from holding up Montgomery.

Initially the main German effort was made against the British 10th Corps, as posing the greater threat to Naples. Both Hube's divisions were involved in attacks against 56th Division, trying to reach Mount Eboli from Battipaglia, and 46th holding Salerno itself. In spite of some critical moments, including one near Battipaglia when a battalion was surrounded and most of it had to surrender, both divisions, with the help of air and naval gunfire support, managed to hold their ground. The American divisions were having a more difficult time, particularly the 45th on the left.

Engine Room Artificer C. Simkin was serving in the destroyer HMS *Lauderdale*, which was providing gunfire support to the American sector. He wrote:

> The Americans had two heavy cruisers, several destroyers and about half a dozen salvage vessels at this beach head. These salvage vessels were something the British Navy did not have, but within a few days they had a job to do.
>
> I was on watch in the engine room, when one of our stokers came down to tell us that we had just come to rest near one of the Yank cruisers and our Captain was having a shouting conversation with the American captain then I did something I should not have done, I went up the ladder to have a look at the cruiser at close quarters, then I spotted an aircraft above, saw it was an enemy plane and it had just dropped a wireless-controlled bomb and my feet did not touch the steps as I slid down the ladder to the engine room plates and as I landed the engine room telegraph moved to full ahead both and as I whipped open the engine throttles the ship jumped into action, it just lurched forward, unfortunately the American cruiser did not move fast enough and the bomb hit her on B turret and passed through the shell room below. This bomb plus the subsequent flooding of the magazine killed 215 Americans on that cruiser.
>
> When this happened those salvage ships rushed in to help the stricken cruiser and were able to get her back to Malta, and days

later I saw her dead stacked up on two lighters being taken away for burial.

The wireless-controlled bomb was easy to identify in daylight because it had wings and a tail just like a small aircraft and once it was launched from its parent aircraft the pilot of that plane could control its pitch, direction and fall. To answer this weapon we immediately used to go full ahead so we could manoeuvre at high speed and switch on the ship's wireless altering the frequency in an attempt to take over control of the bomb away from the pilot.

Another provider of gunfire support was the monitor HMS *Roberts*, in which Lieutenant P. J. Cardale was the navigating officer. He wrote:

On the 4th of September, "Roberts" sailed from Bizerta to join up with the assault convoys leaving for the landings in the Gulf of Salerno. The evening before the landings, news was received of the capitulation of the Italians. We wondered what effect this would have on the landings, but in the event, it had virtually none, as the Italians had been replaced by Germans. The landings were made without preliminary air or naval bombardment, very early on the 9th of September. "Roberts" was assigned to the Northern Sector in support of the British 10th Corps, whilst the American 6th Corps, landed on the South of the Bay. Although the landings were successful, the Germans were soon counter-attacking and bringing in reinforcements of armour. The troops were hard-pressed and I believe that at one time the Americans were preparing to withdraw. Several of the F.O.B's [Forward Observation Bodies] became casualties, which sometimes delayed calls for fire. Bombardment reinforcements in the form of the battleships "Warspite" and "Valiant" and some cruisers, were brought in, and there is no doubt that Naval bombardment played a crucial part in saving the day, and certainly in "Roberts" we were arrogant enough to think that there was no other bombarding ship as effective as we were, and that the battleships were amateurs! We were bombed on most days, and "Warspite" among others, was hit. "Roberts" was unscathed and managed to shoot down at least one enemy plane. "Abercrombie", our sister ship, who was supporting the American sector, struck a mine and had to retire on the first day.

One diversion caused me personally some anxiety. My intrepid Captain was incensed to see some landing craft, lying at anchor about half a mile off the beach, come unexpectedly under heavy fire, probably from tanks not far inland, although we could not in fact see the source of the fire. We had not had a call for fire for some time, and so the Captain immediately invited me to put the ship between the landing craft and the beach. There appeared to be barely enough room, and this was hardly the role of a heavy bombarding ship. However, the sight of a ship with large guns coming straight towards them, must have persuaded the tanks (or whatever they were) to retire. There was no more trouble, and we managed to get back to our bombardment area without beaching!

On the left of McCreery's 10th Corps, Brigadier Robert Laycock's 2nd Special Service Brigade was given the task of capturing Vietri, a small port on the northern flank of the bay, immediately west of the town of Salerno, where the road and railway to Naples left the coast and struck northwards through the hills, and where it was thought there was a coast defence gun position. 2 Commando led the assault, landing without difficulty. 'Joe' Nicholl was still with them and picks up the tale:

The sea was so calm and the silence so complete, that the men in his craft asked Joe if they could smoke. They were approaching the little beach at Vietri sul Mare. The reply came in a splash in the water in front of them. "Those perishing destroyers dropping short", said someone. But another in the sea just behind them meant they were the target. The coxswain put on full speed. The German mortar bombs landed in the sea all around them. They went into that beach very hard, rapidly the soldiers ran ashore. But the sailors, instead of unloading the stores of food and ammunition, pulled out as fast as they could, and took back garbled accounts of the incident. This later caused a frantic order from the Divisional Commander on the main beaches to Brigadier Bob Laycock to clear the town of Vietri, which they were at that moment quietly occupying. It also caused a serious lack of supplies for the Commando at what might have proved a serious point in the battle.

In the meantime, Joe and his men rushed up the cobbled, terraced street, protected for the moment by the high buildings on either side. Up in a school overlooking the bay, Joe found Jack Churchill with 10 or 12 German prisoners. He explained very simply that the gun batteries had been captured, and 6 Troop would be in reserve while isolated pockets of Germans were being mopped up. The mortaring had stopped, and Joe took his Section into a house reported free of the enemy. Here he found a remarkably fat Italian changing rapidly into civilian clothes. He turned out to be the Naval Officer commanding the port of Salerno. He obligingly gave Joe one of his bars of medal ribbons which could be press-studded onto any of the Admiral's shirts, though not, apparently, onto his pyjamas!

2 and 5 troops were threatening Salerno and Joe was told to protect the two 6-pdr anti-tank guns. Not a very inviting job. He got the Brens sited to cover the maximum amount of the road below and himself moved forward with the riflemen. They had not been in position long before they could see them moving round on the high ground to their left. Then, as they moved out of sight, a Tiger tank came slowly out of Salerno just below them. The anti-tank gun fired first, with a near miss, and though the tank received 2 direct hits at 900 yds from a 6 pdr, the second Tiger, from a hull-down position, fired back. The shots exploded behind Joe. He moved back to see what the damage was, and found one of the shots had landed in the tree just above the Bren and knocked out most of the crew. Barnes, Basire and Williams had been wounded. Williams caught it in the throat, but, cheerful cockney that he was, he wrote to one of his buddies later from hospital, "I talk now like what Nat Gonella sings!" Further back Peter Lea, the Intelligence Officer, who had already won the George Medal, was killed outright. Tragically he was hit in the head when not wearing a steel helmet. Another young officer who would have done brilliantly if he had had the chance.

Pat Henderson, with 1 Troop, had succeeded in getting down to the road just in front of the Tiger tank. He lay behind the low brickwork in front of the house, with a P.I.A.T. [Projector Infantry Anti-Tank]. Fitting the unfamiliar bomb into the cradle, he looked through the sight. How far away was that tank? About 100 yds. He squeezed the trigger. Slowly the bulky round seemed to describe [words missing?] through the air. It landed short. Quickly reloading, he fired again. This was more successful. It hit the side of the tank, but failed to explode. He continued firing. Not unnaturally the tank occupants took umbrage; but they couldn't depress the gun low enough, and had to be content with battering away at the house behind him. Bits of masonry and shrapnel spattered the ground around him, but he eventually got a hit on the turret of the Tiger, which retired into Salerno. 1 and 3 Troops had been sent up to White Cross Hill and 4 prisoners had been captured by 3 Troop at the point of the bayonet. Behind him in Marina and Vietri there had been heavy mortaring during the day. Five German tanks had been seen in Cava coming down from the North, so with only two anti-tank guns, the two Commandos [the other was 41 RM Commando] were hemmed in on the only roads leading from their position. But Pat Henderson's effort had had its effect, because that evening a Squadron of the 44th Reconnaissance Regiment were able to get through Salerno from the main beaches. And that first night was quiet.

To the right of the Commandos, 46th Division's assault had been led by its 128th Brigade, of three battalions of the Hampshire Regiment, which had landed successfully to the east of Salerno. It was followed by the 138th, which moved through them towards Salerno itself and into the hills to the north. N. Wray was the Company Clerk of A Company of the 6th York and Lancasters and wrote an account of the first few days:

Midday approached and it was 138 Brigade's turn to land. The beaches (code named Red and Green) were under fire from 88s in the surrounding hills, and from self propelled guns moving towards the beaches protected by counter attacking infantry. The Jerrys attacked at many points in the Divisional area. The 6th Battalion York and Lancaster Regiment were moving slowly across the water towards the landing beaches. Confusion on shore as beach masters struggled to order vehicles up the exit tracks and inland. Lines of infantry waded through the water, up the shingle and into the Assembly Areas. Some of these were still occupied by the enemy and had to be cleared. Shells were dropping over the beaches and behind, causing casualties.

A Company's L.S.T. 116 turn came. We were dressed for the assault, with all the weapons and ammo. described earlier. The renewal of these items over the next few days was uncertain. We were told to leave nothing behind. Once more we were ordered below to await orders for landing. A few of us crept up the companion way to have a quick look. Ducking behind the manned Oerlikon on the bows I could see a line of shingly beaches. Towards the Salerno end, vehicles and buildings were burning as shells landed.

A few miles back I could see, through the mist, a ring of mountains. On these slopes German observers were directing fire. We were heading for Green Beach. As we came within a thousand yards, a destroyer moved ahead of us, laying a smoke screen. Shells began plopping in the water, in front and on either side. One whistled overhead and landed behind us. To our left, peering through gaps in our protective smoke screen, white shell bursts showed up against the green shore line. The angry whine of the shells that landed behind us made us less detached and we toppled terror stricken down the companion way back into the hold. The ship's engines slowed down. We waited below. The dim lights seemed dimmer. Muffled explosions were taking place. We expected the loud speakers to tell us to disembark. The engines started up in earnest, and we were told to "Stand down".

When we were once more allowed on deck, the ship was in the middle of the Gulf of Salerno. We could see the whole of the Sorrento Peninsula. The mountains rose behind Salerno and the beaches were a thin line miles away. I leant on the rails. The sea was covered with many anchored vessels waiting to unload. Warships lay further out to sea. On our craft loud speakers were relaying orders to our crew. Warnings of enemy air attacks were wirelessed round the convoys. Raids were pressed home in other areas, but to us on L.S.T. 116 everything was quiet. Ominous patches of wreckage drifted past us on the water. Why we had turned tail as we came to land on the beach I will never know.

The rest of the battalion had landed and moved forward to the outskirts of Salerno and thence along the road to Avellino, a few miles up which they met the enemy, their C Company suffering heavy casualties. A Company disembarked after dark and reached Salerno on the 10th. Wray's account continues:

We reached the outskirts of Salerno by mid morning. Some runners were sent up the road towards Avellino to find B.H.Q. We halted by some railway sidings. Looting was taking place by the Ittis among the trucks. Some of us were sent to stop them. The trucks contained thousands of phials and hyperdemic syringes. Box after box were strewn around and smashed. Many trucks had been broken into and their contents emptied on the rail side.

Orders came to move. Up the first of many hills we struggled during the next few days. The platoons were deployed on the summits facing inland. We in Company H.Q. scratched shallow holes in the hillside for protection against shell fire. Being Company Clerk I made out casualty returns on blokes who reported sick for some reason. After a few hours in this "Back Up" position the tramping of heavy boots turned the dry ground to a fine dust which got into everything. Somewhere in front of us a German patrol was aiming M.G. fire in our direction. We lay in the dust. In front the platoons were sheltering in the rocks and hiding in the undergrowth. Soon the firing died down and the battalion concentrated near the lateral road. 139 Brigade had landed and moved through the Hampshires who were dug in round the beaches. They continued their march to take over the Avellino road area. We passed through Salerno to defend the hills immediately behind the town. Later it was planned to strike north and join the Commandos.

Lieutenant Duncan Raikes was commanding a troop of the 325th Battery of 46th Division's Anti-Tank Regiment, Royal Artillery, the 58th. He was supporting one of the Hampshire battalions on the right flank, in the area in which, on the first day, the 5th Battalion had lost 40 men killed and 300 wounded or captured. He describes his experience a few days later near Pontecagnano:

About evening, I began to be slightly worried – the infantry in front of us were little more than a token, & did not seem to be getting reinforced, which suggested that, if anything, as they say, 'developed' during the night, it might be a bit awkward. I was hardly reassured when the handful of infantry there still were in front of me moved about 400 yards to the right. The fact that their new positions were tactically sounder was cold comfort. However, at dusk, I was delighted to see a few Armoured Cars of the Recce Regiment roll up & park in the grove a short way behind us & their occupants dismount, & still more to see that their officer was an old friend of mine, Monckton, whom I had known well. His boys had come to act as infantry in our area, which was a great relief.

It was a night of continued alarms & excursions, of periods of intense quiet, when there mightn't have been a soul for miles, & then some one would send up a Verey light, or let off a Tommy gun for no particular reason & every firearm in the valley would open up, the tracer would fly across from one side to the other. Monckton's boys & mine would loose off with no particular object in view, with the rather vague intention of giving the impression that there were more of us than was the case. I don't for a minute believe it would have mattered anyway, but at the time it seemed rather a good idea. A house a bit to the right of us was set on fire, but otherwise no damage was done. As far as I can make out, there were in fact no patrols or any other activity of any kind on foot the whole night, and all the random & extremely nerve-racking firing was chiefly the result of nervous tension – on both sides. Monckton & I spent most of the night in my troop H.Q., where, since it was completely under cover, my batman was able to brew tea practically continuously, or else we would wander up & down his little sector & occasionally go into my O.P.

The next morning was quiet. His account continues:

About 1400 hrs, the fun started once more. It lasted about 3 or 4 hours, & during the whole I don't think anybody had the faintest idea of what was happening. All we could make out from various sources were that a fair number of small parties of Bosche were trying to infiltrate down the valley. Bear in mind that because of the vineyards & oranges, our maximum vision at ground level was about 100 yds. You would look through the stalks of the vines & the stakes which supported them, & it was like looking through a wood of saplings or young birches in England. You know how it is, you see a bit of movement between the trees, but you have no means of telling how far away it was, or even in which direction it was going. Well it was rather like that here so that whenever anybody saw anything, they would open up & the chaps next door would say 'What the hell are you firing at?' and the answer would be 'I thought I saw something over there.'

    I spent most of the time in the 'O.P.', where the view of the immediate neighbourhood, being from above looking down through the vines, was no better than from the ground, but we had a good view of the general scene, & the road. The Bosche was supporting his little attack with heavy but very inaccurate M.G. fire, & there was a continual 'pewt-pewt-pewt' over our heads & an occasional 'ping-ping-ping' on the wall behind me. He was also sending over plenty of mortar bombs etc, though none very near the house.

General Alexander conferring with Generals Montgomery and Patton.

General Montgomery handing cigarettes to men of the 51st (Highland) Division.

51st (Highland) Division passing through Vizzini.

252 Field Company Royal Engineers building a bridge near Catania.

A Sherman of 44th Royal Tank Regiment landing in Sicily from a pontoon.

Bren-gun carriers landing from an LST at Salerno.

Carriers of 46th Division being ferried across the River Volturno
by 272 Field Company Royal Engineers.

A Sherman tank of 4th County of London Yeomanry fording the Volturno. 17 October 1943.

6th Cheshires moving up to Monte Camino. 6 November 1943.

17-pounders of 65th Anti-tank Regiment Royal Artillery
(Norfolk Yeomanry) moving through Scarfati. 29 September 1943.

A 5.5in medium gun of 99 Battery, 74th Regiment Royal Artillery, in mud near Monte Camino. 19 November 1943.

RAF Spitfire ready for action.

Stretcher bearers bring casualties down the side of
Monte Camino. 3–4 December 1943.

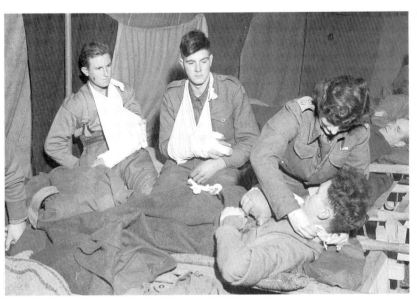

Sister M. W. Sampson QAIMNS treating casualties at
21 Casualty Clearing Station. 10 January 1944.

General Eisenhower with Generals McCreery and Mark Clark
on his farewell visit to Fifth US Army. 23 December 1943.

The River Trigno beyond Termoli.

Raikes and his men were shelled and mortared but not directly attacked. Fighting seemed to be going on almost all round them, but the road was still open. He was much relieved when, late in the day, some infantry came and took up a position in front of him. There were outbreaks of firing during the night, which kept everyone on the alert, but no attack. His account continues:

Came, at last, the dawn. After it was fully light, I got down to a short sleep, till breakfast was ready, but was disturbed by my Battery Commander, whom I hadn't seen for 24 hours, he having been extremely busy since then elsewhere. He stayed for a cup of tea & a chat, & pushed off. We had breakfast about 0700 hrs, after which I began to notice signs of something brewing up on the hill on the right. I knew one of our other troops was up there, so I was naturally interested in what was going on, so I went into the farmyard, from which I could get a good view (the O.P. not being any good except for looking to the front). There was certainly a lot going on on the right hand hillside. I saw quite a number of Bosche advancing along the slope & coming under very heavy fire. They tried to put down smoke, but the wind was wrong, & they were sending over a lot of mortar & Arty shells. They didn't seem to be making much headway, & had mostly gone to ground – remember I said that that hillside was partly open & partly wooded? well, they seemed to be lying low near one of the edges of the woods & were drawing a lot of M.G. fire. I was absolutely fascinated by all this, and was watching intently through my field glasses, kneeling on one knee by the farmyard fence, when all of a sudden somebody lifted me up & threw me about 3 yards backwards, at the same time giving me a colossal clout on the right-hand with a two-foot rule, & being extremely noisy about the whole business. More indignant than hurt, I looked round, a trifle dazed, to see who had perpetrated this outrage, & could only see a large hole in the ground a few yards away. I then realised that there were others dropping in the neighbourhood, so I got into the hole. It was then that I realised there was a certain amount of good Raikes blood about the place, & also that my right hand was not behaving as it should. When things quietened down, I got out of my hole, & walked to my T.H.Q., where I found my batman extremely distressed, he seemed to think (a) that I had about 5 minutes to live, & (b) that it was all his fault & started fussing around with field dressings etc

for all he was worth. He soon fixed me up, & using my field glasses
as a sling, I took a quick look round, gave a few instructions to my
Troop Sgt., summoned my driver & set off back to the R.A.P. where
the M.O. bandaged me up proper, gave me some hitherto unsus-
pected 3-star French brandy, & took me down to the nearest Main
Dressing Station. Here I sat in a tent till I went in & had the hand
tidied up, & redressed. They were not particularly busy there, & there
was an extremely nice M.O. who was a pipe smoker. At my request
he fished my pipe & baccy out of my right-hand trouser pocket &
filled the pipe.

Having waited on a stretcher in an orchard near the dressing station
for over twenty-four hours, he was evacuated by landing craft to a
hospital ship.

On 12 September pressure increased against the American sector. On
the right, 36th US Division lost some key high ground, and on the
following day 16th Panzer and 29th Panzer Grenadier Divisions, withdrawn from facing Eighth Army, drove a wedge into 45th US Division's
positions on the east bank of the River Sele and got within two miles of
the beach, forcing Dawley to withdraw the perimeter of his defences.
This also threatened McCreery's right-hand division, the 56th, especially
its right-hand brigade, the 167th. Sergeant P. J. Hyland was serving in
254 Battery of the 64th Field Regiment Royal Artillery, which supported
that brigade. He describes his experiences since landing on the 9th:

As soon as it came the turn of our command post trucks to leave the
ship they duly rumbled down the sloping lowered bows and we
followed on foot moving off to a rendezvous forty or fifty yards to
the left but still on the beach and hidden from view of the enemy on
the ground by a somewhat elevated road which I imagine served both
as a highway and a protection against the sea for the nearby farmland.
By this time our signallers, in the back of one of the trucks, were
receiving a coded message giving us instructions from the assault
party that had gone in close behind the infantry. It was whilst my
lieutenant and I were decoding it that we were suddenly attacked by
a dive bomber that released its bombs overhead. They went off with
an ear splitting explosion but exactly where I never did know because
everybody, myself included, was face downward in the sand. Unfortunately both my officer and I hung on to the decoding sheet of

paper which was ripped into two halves. After that little bit of excitement we worked out exactly where we had to go and then moved forward off the beach and along the road. On the way, during one of the several halts, we came upon a very large field of those large plum shaped tomatoes for which Italy is so well known. Needless to say we helped ourselves to a few and they were delicious.

Well quite soon we reached and occupied our battery area and had to start digging our command post. This took several hours as usual as we had to take turns about either to dig or to deal with the gunnery side. The battery had already received some casualties having lost a captain and a gunner killed and several men wounded. One of my two officers had already been evacuated from the beachhead with suspected jaundice and the other was ordered up to one of the battery observation posts later in the day leaving me in charge for a few hours until a replacement officer was sent over. Curiously the officer sent to the OP said to me: 'carry on sergeant, I'll see you in the morning!'. Unfortunately he and his OP party was captured and oddly enough I next saw him several years later, long after the war had ended, in the morning, on a train travelling up to Manchester.

After that first night we were kept busy firing in defence of our infantry and so far as we in the command post were concerned it was a case of snatching a few hours sleep in turn during the quiet periods which do of course occur.

The next morning a reconnaissance party went off to select a new battery position closer to the now established front line and we all had to move later in the afternoon to what seemed a good site for our command post. This entailed a lot of work in abandoning the old dug-out, digging a new one and transporting and installing all our equipment and the signallers as well. And while this was going on we had to remain in action and do everything we were called upon to do. Two of our officers and several other ranks at the OP's were reported missing and for most of the day and all through the night we were called upon for gunfire in support of our infantry the 9th Royal Fusiliers who were having to fight off fierce counterattacks in and around the small but strategically important town of Battipaglia from four battalions of German infantry with supporting armour. In fact the area around this town had been earmarked by the enemy for their attempted breakthrough to the sea and the hoped for destruction of the beachhead.

One typical incident that happened at the OP on this second day of the invasion was when it went in with an infantry attack on the German positions. Suddenly four enemy soldiers jumped out of a dug out and surrendered to the signaller who was loaded down with equipment and carrying a Tommy gun. He sent them running back to our lines and then there was an outburst of enemy artillery and mortar fire. The signaller dived into a small farmhouse and found his officer waiting for him. A salvo of shells fell around the house, a haystack and barn beside it went up in flames and they were in some danger of cremation. The officer yelled out orders through the 'phone for supporting fire from our guns which gave them a respite and the chance to smoke a cigarette while awaiting the next crisis.

On the following three days they were constantly in action and were subjected to both enemy counter-battery fire and an air raid. On 12 September they fired a programme in support of the 45th US Division on their right, whose position was critical.

Clark was seriously alarmed at this threat to the US 45th Division and even contemplated withdrawing one corps and transferring it to the sector of the other, a proposal his naval advisers declared to be impractical. The situation was saved by dropping two Regimental Combat Teams of the 82nd US Airborne Division into the American sector and by intensifying air and naval gunfire support. On this occasion control of anti-aircraft fire was effective and one Regimental Combat Team landed successfully in the US sector on the night of 13/14 September. Additional air and naval gunfire support was also provided and seaborne reinforcements, including the British 7th Armoured Division, began to land on 14 and 15 September. Among the reinforcements was a draft of infantrymen to replace casualties. Private R. H. Day, from the 1/6th East Surreys in the 78th Division in Sicily, was in one of these drafts, sent to reinforce the battalions of the Queen's Royal (West Surrey) Regiment in 169 Brigade on the left of the 56th Division. He wrote:

We were split up into twos as soon as we had dropped our kit and told to dig slit trenches. The company sergeant major said shells were dropping periodically, so we got to work. Tired as we were, we dug and this soon became as natural as breathing or eating. The mosquitoes were out in their droves now and I could not dig for more than a few seconds before having the urge to slap my face and hands and legs. We still had the shorts we wore in Algeria and the pests took advantage of this and attacked with all they had. It was very dark and I could barely see my digging partner and his pick occasionally struck the earth uncomfortably close to my head.

Suddenly a voice rang out in the still air. It was the C.S.M. calling out names. Sixteen of them he called and mine was among them. We were wanted for one of the companies tonight. My stomach felt empty despite the big supper a few minutes ago. We were packed into a 30cwt. truck and were off, along the tree-lined roads and lanes with their sharp bends and rough surfaces. Not many of us talked in that truck. What was there to say? Frivolous conversation was out of place; each man was wrapped in his own thoughts. The truck rumbled on, halting now and then for the driver to give his password to a lone sentry. The mountains loomed as massive, dark shapes and we were aiming for them. After endless moments the truck reached its destination and we silently got out. The creaking of crickets and the buzzing of mosquitoes was all that could be heard.

A guide, armed with a rifle and bandolier, greeted the lance-corporal in charge of us and we followed him in single file. It was hard going now across the rough ground and several times I stumbled in an unseen ditch or furrow. Silently we trudged on for more than a mile, then: 'Halt, New York,' someone challenged. 'Giants,' was the reply in a low voice. 'O.K., come along, Jim,' said a cheery Cockney voice, and we began to go up a slight slope. An ambulance loomed and two medical orderlies smiled at us. 'Quiet tonight, eh, Jim,' said one. Jim took us a little farther, to a small house lying in a valley between two steep hills. There a bedraggled figure with unshaven face and wearing a cap comforter and spotted scarf took us over from the guide. He was a full corporal and he led us up a winding track, bordered by white tape. We had to clamber through prickly shrubs and eventually we halted, a few feet from the crest of a hill.

Here a young, lanky lieutenant greeted us with the words: 'Good evening, chaps. I'll show you your positions.' He added: 'You're lucky tonight. Four slitters are already dug for you. I've sent a section out on standing patrol and you can sleep in theirs.' Very welcome words, I thought. I was dead tired after a hot and dusty day and was quite ready to sleep in any position. I had not taken into account my turn of guard, but here again I and the other newcomers were lucky because, since there was a forward section on standing patrol, there was no need for us to do any guard duties that night. We sixteen had been divided to strengthen three platoons in the 2nd/6th Battalion. Nine, including myself, had joined Mr Curtis, the lieutenant who welcomed us. He commanded No. 7 platoon.

I could not get comfortable that night. I tried the slit trench and curled up but soon got violent cramp in my leg muscles. I then lay alongside the trench, wrapped in my only cover, the gas cape. Our positions were on one side of the hill and my body was lying at an angle of 40 degrees. Try as I did I could not prevent myself from gradually slipping inch by inch. So I altered my position again and lay with my feet against a small tree. My slipping stopped but before long a stone was biting into my left hip. I shifted once more and finally dozed off despite the incessant drone and the bites of the despicable insects.

I was woken while it was still dark but there were not so many mosquitoes about. The time had come for 'Stand-to.' I rose stiffly, feeling cold now, and stood up inside the trench, gazing outwards with tired eyes. When the dawn broke and the visibility became clear I saw a wonderful sight. Opposite our line of hills there was another range extending to the east where it was lost against the background of mountains. Below there was a lovely, rolling valley and overlooking it on the other side there was a cluster of white buildings tucked among the hills. This village did not look real from where I stood and I doubted whether many people remained there. Three miles to the left, across flat, orchard country, so flat it looked like a sand-table model, there was the sea. A vast fleet of ships littered the bay.

Again the sun burned ruthlessly from a cloudless sky and the scarcity of water was a constant trial. There was only one bottleful for 24 hours for each man, and this supply was brought up on the carrier with the other rations at about 7.30 each night. Four of us were detailed to go to the bottom of the hill, which was known as Hill 60, to fetch the containers with the hot stew and the fruit or treacle pudding, the regular supper. Also the tea and two cans of water. It was a difficult and strenuous job, feeling our way down the rocky track, getting ourselves caught up in the shrubs and struggling to keep our balance as we made the return journey, with neither arm free to catch hold of branches to help our climb. All that guided us in the dark was a white tape laid out by the signallers. In the morning while it was still dark another four men would make the return trip for the breakfast meal which was tinned bacon or sausages and biscuits and margarine and tea. At midday we had bully beef or sardines or cheese and biscuits with a little jam sometimes and tea again, in powder form, each man using his own 'tommy' cooker to boil the water. We were on compo rations, so each man had a bar of chocolate, several boiled sweets and seven cigarettes a day, but of the V brand which were very poor indeed.

After Stand-down a long hot day lay ahead of us. There was nothing for us to do but lie in what shade we could find or sit and chat or try to write a letter. There was one man on the observation post all the time. Shellfire was quite fierce at times and once we had an excellent view of our shells smashing down on enemy positions in that village opposite. The houses were hidden by the clouds of smoke and dust sent up by the bursting shells. It seemed impossible that anyone could live after that deluge of fire and after the shelling had ceased an eerie silence and deathly pallor lay over the village. Several times during the day an 88mm shell burst in the valley below but usually at a fairly good distance from our positions. The German artillery fire was spasmodic compared with ours. During the first two days of the landings it had been very fierce and consistent but now, after a week, a lot of their guns must have been withdrawn.

On the 16th the leading troops of Eighth Army made contact from the south. Also on that day von Vietinghoff told Kesselring that the Allies were too firmly established ashore to be ejected, and he began withdrawal towards the River Volturno, north of Naples, in the west and the River Biferno in the east, the VIKTOR line, which Kesselring told him to hold until 15 October, while the main defensive line for the winter, the GUSTAV line, was being prepared. The Allied approach to it was to be made as difficult and expensive as possible.

As the Germans began to withdraw, Alexander gave Montgomery and Clark their orders for the next phase. The former, joining hands with 1st Airborne Division, which had been reinforced by the 5th British Corps (Lieutenant-General C. W. Allfrey), would secure Bari and then advance along the east coast to capture the airfields round Foggia, with two corps, the 13th, comprising 1st Canadian Division (Major-General G. G. Simonds) and 78th Division (Major-General V. Evelegh), and the 5th, comprising 1st Airborne Division (now Major-General E. E. Down), 5th British Division (Major-General G. C. Bucknall) and 8th Indian

Division (Major-General D. Russell). The time needed to build up logistic support, using the ports of Taranto, Bari and Brindisi, meant that Montgomery could not begin his advance until 1 October. He expected to reach Termoli and the Biferno, fifty miles beyond Foggia, two days later, but logistic problems would prevent him from moving his main force beyond there until 15 or even perhaps 20 October. He optimistically and unrealistically forecast that, while waiting on that line, he would be able to operate light forces as far as Pescara, and that, in about ten days from the time he began to move his main force forward from the Biferno, he would be in Rome. While Montgomery was securing the Foggia airfields, Clark was to capture Naples and open its port. The next step for both armies was to advance to Rome and Terni, fifty miles north of the holy city. A more distant objective was the port of Leghorn (Livorno) and the cities of Florence and Arezzo. These ambitious projects took little account of the fact that Alexander's land forces were not much larger than those which the Germans could produce to oppose them, if they decided to stand and fight, or of the advantages to the defence provided by the terrain and the winter weather.

McCreery's 10th Corps in Fifth Army reached the Volturno by 5 October without much difficulty, but met strong resistance from 15th Panzer Grenadier and Hermann Goering Divisions between Capua and the coast, as did the 34th and 36th Divisions of the US 6th Corps (now commanded by Major-General J. P. Lucas) on their right, when they attempted to cross the river on 12 October. Private N. Wray of the 6th York and Lancasters took part in 46th Division's attack across the lower reaches of the river.

> Slowly and silently we edged towards the river bank. Well hidden we awaited nightfall. By 01.00 hours on the 13th of October the battalion crossed without interference from the enemy. B Company crossed first, followed by A and D Companies, Battalion H.Q. and C Company last of all.
>
> As A Company approached the crossing point I dimly discerned the far bank and dark water swirling swiftly past. The banks, about three feet high, were muddy and fell steeply into the water. Stretched to the enemy side were two ropes. A line of 'squaddies' struggled across in the darkness. With both feet on one rope and grasping the higher one in a tight grip, we slithered into the water. Gingerly we

moved towards the opposite bank. Some of our own Pioneer Platoon were in the water helping, giving instructions and encouraging us to 'get a move on'. Quickly the water got deeper and I could feel it eddying round me. The current strained to pull me off the bottom rope. Further into the river, water climbed past my thighs. In midstream the lower rope was above the river bed and the water was round my chest, just missing wetting my Africa Star ribbon. We had orders to keep our rifles dry but they trailed over our shoulders. The three 2 inch mortars in their case were under water as I struggled to keep hold of the rope. Completely soaked we reached the enemy side where our pioneers and many helping hands pulled us up the bank. Sodden but relieved we formed up in a soaked, shivering long line. The enemy had left us alone.

The operation arosss the River Volturno started the day before. At the estuary was 128 Brigade, with 139 Brigade further inland. Our battalion was put under the command of 139 Brigade for the crossing, to fill a space between the two units. A few tanks landed on the enemy side to give support cover in case of counter attacks. We were in the line between the Hampshire Regiment and the Leicester Regiment. On our right the Sherwoods had crossed the river near Cancello, where some enemy tanks had countered the thrust, causing many infantry casualties, in a nearby wood.

With B Company leading on the left and us in A Company, we moved off to the plain. We squelched towards a canal which was a barrier across our front. As we stumbled along in the dark we were stopped by a heavy burst of tracer bullets. First a bright line punctured the darkness on our left. It slowly traversed the plain and came towards us. It passed us. Then they were firing on our right. Repeatedly they swept back and forth across us. No one in 8 platoon was hit. In the confusion we dived into a very wet ditch. We were drenched already so lying in the shallow ditch didn't trouble us. I heard Sergeant Gill shouting encouraging advice, 'Keep your head down and keep your arse down as well'. More than one weapon was firing. Lines of tracers came towards us whipping and whining, seeming only a few inches above our heads, cracking as they shot past. A little further up the ditch Sergeant Gill shouted, warning us that there were several ordinary bullets between the pink tracers. Men in other companies also shouted warnings to each other across the open spaces.

Daylight broke and we scurried back towards the river bank not wanting to be left in the open during the daytime. This was where 'Bingley the Boogie Woogie Mortar Man,' did a bunk, and went to live with his girl in Naples for the rest of the campaign.

The battalion moved back to dig in behind the river stop banks which were a few hundred yards from the river. We talked about Bingley and wondered whether he had been wounded and whether to go back and find him. The suggestion was not carried out as he was behind me during the firing and had buggered off when the machine guns stopped. It was broad daylight and any movement in the fields would be in full view of Jerry. The battalion spent the day there.

Fusilier Gilbert Allnutt was serving in the 8th Battalion of The Royal Fusiliers in 56th Division further up the river near Capua. His morale was also at a low point, as he explains:

The German reputation for regularity was well confirmed on the Volterno [sic] and if one had a watch one could have put it right by the regularity of the mortar bomb attacks that fell on us. It was on the banks of this river and later at Anzio, that I felt a true sense of understanding and sharing the privations of the soldiers of the 1914–1918 War. It was on the Volterno that I plumbed the depths of misery.

In early October 1943 'Sunny Italy' changed its face and it began to rain. A steady drenching rain which, in no time, produced inches of water in the bottom of the slit trenches. Somehow, despite this continual rain, we managed, with our limited supply of Tommy Cooker fuel, to brew up a mug of tea for the two occupants of the slit trench. My comrade performed the almost impossible feat of eating cold meat and vegetable stew but for me biscuits and a tin of cheese sufficed. I had little appetite in the line. As the rain continued to fall the message was passed from Captain Goldstone from trench to trench by word of mouth: 'try to keep your rifles dry'. So we sat in our trenches getting wetter and wetter in a continuous state of misery punctuated by occasional mortar attacks with moments of danger and terror. I recollect it as a period of inactivity with our role to hold the river bank against attack, until the main assault over the river took place. In this attack we would have a supporting role with our old comrades The Queen's Royal Regiment making the crossing in our sector.

Sitting in a trench where the water had built up to nearly a foot and which one dare not leave was my fate for several days. The misery nearly came to an end one day during one of the regular mortar bomb attacks. We could virtually sit and watch this neat and methodical pattern of bombs as they fell around us. Then came the bomb which seemed clearly to have my name on it as it came screaming down. I commended my soul to God. There was a shattering explosion, the earth trembled and shook, earth flew and my comrade yelled out. The next bomb fell a little further away and the neat pattern continued for the usual number of rounds. Shaken, with a ringing in my ears and the smell of cordite in my nostrils, I realised that somehow I had survived. I looked cautiously over the edge of the trench and, there only a foot away I saw a shell hole. My small pack with my eating irons and mess tin was not in sight. I picked my rifle up and the woodwork fell off. My comrade had shrapnel in his leg but I seemed to have got off scot free. Captain Goldstone broke his no movement order to come over and see how we were and we went back with him to Company Headquarters. He saw the shell hole and its proximity to our trench. I still remember the concern he showed and his disbelief that I was still in one piece.

The US 45th Division, in the river's upper reaches in the mountains, was more fortunate and turned Hube's left flank, the Germans withdrawing on the 16th and the whole river line being in Mark Clark's hands by the 19th.

The army was not alone in feeling the effects of the bad weather. O. V. Cox of the RAFVR was a Sergeant in 18 Squadron RAF, equipped with Bisley bombers, operating from Sicily in support of the Fifth Army. He describes the operation in which he took part on 2 October:

The weather forecast that – 'we may run into light rain or drizzle' – who was kidding who? We had not left the coast very long before we ran into an extremely violent electrical storm and it was necessary to get up over twelve thousand feet before we could get above it. Our normal operating altitude was about seven or eight thousand feet and more often than not we just wore a high necked pullover under our battle dress tunic, however, getting up to this extra height proved to be very uncomfortable and we were glad when we left the storm

behind us so that we could drop down to our normal operating
height in order to thaw out. Our flight proved to be very uneventful.
We had not crossed the Italian coast until we were well north of
Naples and the target was well out into the country. I doubt if
anyone below would think that any enemy aircraft would be flying
considering the weather conditions we had encountered. We did
arrive at the target area and dropped two of our four bombs, Jack
scoring direct hits on one of the bridges. We did another 'run in' on
one of the other bridges and as far as I can remember they were near
misses and probably did very little damage. Nevertheless we were
very pleased with our efforts thinking that the other two bridges
would be destroyed by one or the other of the eighteen aircraft which
had taken off at intervals behind us.

Through having to climb to over twelve thousand feet with a full
bomb load on our outward journey we had used far more fuel than
we would normally have done and were now hoping we would be
able to miss the storm on the return flight, unfortunately this was
not to be. The only chance of us being able to reach base was by
flying the very shortest route which meant that we would have to fly
through the storm, this time it was out of the question that it could
be avoided by climbing to twelve thousand feet or more. Mac did his
best to avoid the centre of the storm but we were suddenly struck by
lightning which completely put our radio and intercom. equipment
out of order. We were not so much concerned about the wireless
being u/s but the intercom was a different matter as it was extremely
difficult for anyone to hear what anyone said and at times hearing
was non-existent. Here again this was not really important as far as
Jock and I were concerned as we were together, but it was certainly
important for Mac to hear what Jack was saying when he was given
a bearing to fly. I am afraid shortly after this we realised we were off
course and although we were flying in the right direction we had lost
our way. I would stress that this was not anyone's fault, just the luck
of the draw. As far as I can remember one figure of a bearing given
had been misheard although it had been repeated several times, you
can tell the great difficulty Mac and Jack were having. Eventually we
saw Stromboli, a volcanic island off the north coast of Sicily and at
the same time we more or less regained contact, although very
indistinctly, one with the other.

Mac informed us that we were very low of fuel and it was certain that we would not be able to get back to base. We therefore had two choices, the first was to bale out and the second was to ditch. He put the choices to us all but I told him that as I was the 'spare' member I was agreeable to fall in with what ever the others chose, it also gave the opportunity of a majority vote with only three members to choose, as it turned out it was unanimously to ditch. It was decided to get as near the north coast of Sicily as we could and then ditch. It was considered that if we baled out we would be spread out over a very large area of the sea in darkness and very bad weather, whereas if we were all together in one dingy the chances were that we would be found quicker.

We all immediately went about our ditching drill which for me meant stowing the Vickers gun and battening down the hatch in the floor. This done I decided to retrieve the Veary Pistol and all the cartridges and stuffed the lot inside my tunic (I thought that if they did not get wet they could prove to be very useful). The next thing I did was to undo my monkey strap as it was not a means of support when ditching and could prove to be a very great hindrance. Jock above me had switched the IFF [Identification Friend or Foe] on to distress and reeled out his trailing aerial to its full extent, this aerial droops down about twenty five feet below the aircraft and if the Wop/Ag (Jock) puts his finger on the line he feels a tug and the pilot knows he is then approximately twenty feet above the water. The only trouble we had at the back was that Jock could not jettison his guns (rusted in?) and this meant that the escape route for us was rather restricted. I told him I was not inflating my May West in order that I would not be too bulky to get past his guns. I was on the floor facing backwards with my back resting against Jock's legs, and hands laced behind my head, this was the best support I could find. Everyone was ready and when Mac saw the land far ahead he started the descent. He warned us that it would be very bumpy as the sea was bound to be rough. For me it was a question of waiting and I thought this was an opportune moment to say the Lord's Prayer and pray for everyone's safety. Jock had his hand on the wire of the trailing aerial and suddenly shouted that it had hit.

I wonder what happened next. The next thing I knew was that I was floating around in the sea by myself. I tried to shout but only managed what seemed to me to be very weak cries. I tried to blow

my whistle but could not get enough breath to do so. I heard voices
and thought that the rest had got into the dingy and were looking
for me so I gave a few more weak calls and then I was suddenly
grabbed and I shouted with pain as I was hauled aboard a boat.
Oblivion once more.

The next thing I knew was that I was in a warm bed.

He had been found and brought ashore by Sicilian fishermen and
taken to a British army hospital, where, to his dismay, he discovered that
he was the only survivor of the crew. He had suffered three fractures of
the spine and all but three of his ribs were broken or fractured: he was
suffering from severe concussion, had temporarily lost his sight and
often lost consciousness. He was initially paralysed from the waist down,
but gradually recovered. He was full of praise for the hospital and wrote:
'What a marvellous hospital this is with wonderful staff led by Major
Gavin Cleland who was assuredly responsible for me being able to tell
this tale today.'

On the other side of the mountains to McCreery, Dempsey's 13th
Corps led Eighth Army's advance to the VIKTOR line, with 78th Division along the coast and 1st Canadian making for Campobasso and
the headwaters of the Biferno in the mountains. Two of Evelegh's
brigades, with the two Commandos (3 and 40 RM) and the Special
Raiding Squadron of the Special Service Brigade, landed north of the
river mouth at Termoli on 3 October, as his 11th Brigade struggled
across the river below the town. After three days of fierce fighting,
during which 4th Armoured Brigade succeeded in getting its tanks
across the river to support the infantry, the high ground north of it
was in British hands and the German 16th Panzer Division withdrew
ten miles to their next temporary defensive line, named BARBARA,
which ran just north of the River Trigno south-westwards to the headwaters of the Volturno, close to the GUSTAV line. The critical day at
Termoli was 5 October.

Lieutenant-Colonel K. G. V. Chavasse was commanding 56th
Reconnaissance Regiment in the 78th Division. He described his unit's
part in the action:

The next Divisional objective was the town of Termoli on the East
coast. The River Biferno had to be crossed and the bridges were all
blown. 11 Brigade got across by scrambling and wading and the

Sappers made a pontoon bridge by which the R.H.Q. and B squadron got across. Then it started to pour with rain and all cross country approaches became almost impossible, and no tanks had been able to cross.

B squadron pushed on up the road running North-west of Termoli. No 3 [Army] Commando had landed and dug in to defend the town, soon augmented by the other brigade (36 Bde). B squadron captured a German motorcyclist. It was found he was from 16 Panzer Division thought to be on the West Coast! Termoli was only lightly held by garrison troops, but 7 miles up the road B squadron bumped into the forward elements of 16 Panzer and found itself in action against German Mark 4 tanks and a considerable force of enemy infantry. 11 Bde had been advancing on the left of the road and also soon encountered this unexpected opposition. B squadron withdrew to a brickworks on the left of the road and on 11 Brigade's right. I was given command of a mixed force consisting of B squadron, No 3 Commando, an SRS [Special Raiding Squadron] troop that had landed with the Commando and a battery of anti-tank guns with orders to hold the high ground west of Termoli, and defend this position against the advancing Panzer Division.

The Germans launched a heavy attack with tanks and artillery; most of the anti-tank guns were wiped out, and B squadron lost touch with R.H.Q. as its link wireless vehicle had been destroyed by a shell. Following confused mortar and machine gun fire, R.H.Q. moved forwards to an olive grove on the east of the road, where B squadron had parked its vehicles, as it was now defending the brickworks on foot. No 3 Commando was also there, and the grove dominated the surrounding countryside.

October 5 dawned in a drizzle to find the Argyles [sic (on the left of B Sqn) in the open, holding tanks and infantry with no tank support. So the Brigadier* ordered the Argyles to withdraw and their C.O. contacted Marcus Mahon (commanding B Squadron) and advised his withdrawal (as he had no means of contacting me) which he did, in conjunction with the Argyles. During the afternoon the enemy advance on Termoli continued, and tanks and infantry approached the olive grove. I ordered the evacuation of all vehicles except L.R.C.s of R.H.Q. and it soon became clear that R.H.Q. and

* Brigadier B. Howlett.

No 3 Commando was being encircled. It has been alleged – elsewhere – that when this became obvious I was reported as having said 'Splendid, we now have an all round shoot!' I can't remember this myself.

It was now getting dark, and we could hear the voices of the enemy infantry, through the shelling. The order to withdraw came to me from Divisional H.Q. I remember walking through the olive grove with bullets whistling to contact the C.O. of the Commando to tell him to withdraw. Then came the problem of getting our vehicles out. I got on to Division, over the air, and asked for as much *noise* as possible, so that the enemy would not hear vehicles starting up. I remember having to talk in a soft tone, as if I could hear their voices in the dark they could hear mine! I also remember the gunner saying to me that he had never been asked for 'noise' before! Anyway they gave it and plenty of it too and we slipped away unnoticed to behind the firmer line that had been established behind us. The withdrawal was completed by 0245 hours in the morning of 6th October. By this time the Irish Brigade were landing at Termoli. Later that morning an Irish Brigade attack, supported by Canadian tanks, pushed the Germans out of the Termoli area, taking the next ridge to the North and thus clearing the way for a further advance. Later on I was notified that I had been given a 'bar to my gong' [his DSO] for the action at Termoli.

One of those landing with the Irish Brigade was Major B. H. Westcott, commanding a company of the 2nd London Irish Rifles. He records his brief experience before he was wounded, and his subsequent medical evacuation:

When we landed at last the town was being shelled and it was difficult in the dark and confusion to find our assembly area. We were told to expect a German attack at dawn. The London Irish Rifles were to defend the inner perimeter of the town. At dawn we were heavily shelled and even attacked from the air by Stukas which because of their howling bombs was more scary than it appeared. H company suffered no casualties at this stage and the Germans did not put in a ground attack.

Eventually I was called to attend an 'O' [Orders] Group in the top of a warehouse where we could see some of the country to the north of Termoli. H Company's objective was the cemetery and a hill just beyond. It was during this 'O' group that I bumped into an old friend from Hale, Arthur Komrower. Then a captain, later a lieutenant-colonel, he was in command of No 3 Commando which had landed in Termoli a couple of days before. He was at the 'O' group to help us with our plans of attack as he had some knowledge of the terrain and enemy positions. H Company were to attack through No 3 Commando who were holding a line just south of the cemetery.

Having made my plans for our attack I had my own 'O' group with the platoon commanders and we got into position near some of the units of No 3 Commando.

So into the attack we went and received little opposition initially. I was standing up trying to direct operations when I was spun round and knocked down – or that's what it felt like, just as though I had been hit with a sledgehammer. A German sniper who had been left behind in the cemetery had concealed himself behind the tombstones and had shot me from about twenty-five yards range. The bullet entered my left shoulder and then into my chest, deflating my left lung. It then hit my rib-cage (four ribs were broken) ricocheted off my ribs and exited from the middle of my back about ¼″ from my spine.

The date of my wounding was 6th October 1943, which was Val's birthday – so for all the wrong reasons I was one of the few husbands who never forgot his wife's birthday.

The company stretcher-bearers loaded me onto the top of my jeep (which was modified to take stretchers) and whisked me off to the Battalion first aid post. By this time I had managed to take my own issue of morphine tablets and had my forehead pencilled with an 'M'. They were pretty useless and when our own MO examined me he gave me an injection of morphia which was much more effective in killing the pain. An ambulance took me to a casualty clearing station where I was laid on the floor on my stretcher waiting to be examined in the operating theatre. I suddenly realised that on the other side of the row of stretchers was Wilson, my batman. I asked him about his wounds and he replied that when the bullet came through me it had nicked the bridge of his nose. Two birds with one shot! I did not see him again as I was moved back and back by ambulance until admitted to a field hospital in Bari and put into a small ward of about 4–6 other wounded officers. Here the medical officers decided to put my chest into plaster, which apparently was the worst thing they could have done. What with my broken ribs, one collapsed lung, and the pressure of the plaster cast, I could hardly breathe at all and it was extremely painful. I can remember waking in the middle of the night in agony and clawing at the plaster to try and tear it off. The MO on duty gave me a real dressing-down. Fortunately I was only there for two nights as I was then moved to a general hospital which the 8th Army had taken over in Taranto. The journey was horrendous – the field ambulances of those days were very badly sprung and the stretchers were hard. It was also extremely hot and I had to ask the ambulance driver to stop so I could be given a drink of water. It was a great relief to arrive and be admitted to a proper bed in a large, airy ward. On the second afternoon I was in and out of consciousness and suddenly realised my bed was surrounded by red hats who were inspecting the hospital and visiting the injured. In a daze, I heard the sister say of me that I was very seriously wounded and that my prospects of recovery were not good. I can remember a fury welling up inside and a determination to survive.

Shortly after this visitation from the brass hats I was moved to a private room and a Harley Street chest specialist examined me. He quickly established the problems and had the plaster removed. The next day he had me turned over onto my stomach so that he could put a large needle into my damaged lung. He joined a pump to the needle and sucked all the gunge out dispelling each pumping operation into a large basin. It was excruciating and obviously not a pretty sight as one of the nurses fainted. This was the beginning of my recovery. Although I could only breathe through one lung and my ribs were very sore, I knew that my left lung would recover eventually.

After three weeks in Taranto, he went by hospital ship to Bône in Algeria and thence in a very hot, poorly manned hospital train for 250 miles, taking all day, to a hospital near Algiers airfield. This proved a welcome contrast to his previous experience, as he describes:

The nursing here was fantastic and I was given wonderful physio treatment for my lung. A rather pretty physio used to get on top of my bed and kneel on my good lung and say 'Now breathe'. To start with I could hardly breathe at all and it was very painful but gradually

I was taught to stop using my right lung (the good one) whilst continuing to breathe and expand my damaged lung. I was soon transferred to a convalescent home in Algiers where we awaited discharge and in my case a return to 'Blighty'.

The Canadians meanwhile were pushing through the mountains in pouring rain, and on 14 October occupied Campobasso, from which the Germans had withdrawn.

In Mark Clark's sector two roads ran from Capua to Rome: No. 7 along the coast, crossing the Garigliano near Minturno and then following the coast through Gaeta and the Pontine Marshes; and No. 6 crossing the River Rapido at Cassino, just north of its junction with the Liri, and then following the valley of the latter north of the Aurunci Mountains to the Alban Hills. In Montgomery's sector, he had to reach Pescara, twenty-five miles beyond the River Sangro, before he could take the Via Valeria to Rome through Avezzano. Alexander hoped that he could exert pressure on one flank to draw German strength there and thus weaken resistance on the other sufficiently to make a breakthrough. The immediate task, however, was to reach the GUSTAV line before breaching it. On the left flank, the coastal route offered poor prospects. The River Garigliano could only be approached over a flat wet plain, everywhere overlooked by the mountains to the west: all bridges had been demolished and mines laid extensively on both banks. Even if a crossing succeeded, Route 7 lay close between the seashore and the mountains. 7th Armoured Division reached the river there on 2 November, before it was withdrawn to hand over its equipment to the 5th Canadian Armoured Division and sail for Britain. Clark planned to concentrate his strength to clear the approaches to the mouth of the Liri valley, which was guarded by a series of large hills or 'Monte'(s) on either side of Route 6: to the south, in succession, Montes Mattone, San Croce and Camino, and to the north, Maggiore, Monaco and Cesima, with Camino and Cesima forming the side walls of the Mignano Gap sixteen miles south-east of Cassino. Another temporary German defensive line, the BERNHARDT, ran from the southern end of the BARBARA line at Colli a Volturno across the Mignano Gap to the Garigliano between Montes San Croce and Camino. Mark Clark gave 6th US Corps the task of advancing along Route 6 and the Volturno valley to the north of it, while McCreery cleared the Montes on the left flank with 56th Division (now Major-General G. W. R. Templer) on the right and the 46th on the left. On 3 November both corps came up against the BERNHARDT line east of the Mignano Gap, strongly defended by 14th Panzer Corps, now commanded by Lieutenant-General von Senger und Etterlin. On the 6th, 56th Division attacked Monte Camino from the south while 3rd US Division did so from the east. Both attacks failed and, after renewed attempts to break through the Gap also failed, Clark (with Alexander's approval) decided that a pause was needed, as his troops, fighting in harsh terrain in filthy weather, were totally exhausted. Since crossing the Volturno the Americans in his army had suffered 7,000 and the British 3,000 casualties.

Montgomery's progress was affected by logistic difficulties. The build-up of logistic resources for a further advance had been affected by the demands of the Allied air forces for tonnage to support the establishment of air force bases in the area of Foggia, not only for the air support of Alexander's forces, but for strategic bombers to attack targets in southern Germany and central Europe and transport aircraft to deliver supplies to resistance movements in the Balkans and as far away as Poland. The establishment of these bases had been the principal reason why the air forces had supported the decision to invade Italy.

Once satisfied that his logistic resources would be able to support an advance as far as Pescara, Montgomery reorganized his army for his next push, 5th Corps taking over the coastal sector with 78th and 8th Indian Divisions, supported by 4th Armoured Brigade, and 13th Corps, with 5th and 1st Canadian Divisions, supported by 1st Canadian Army Tank Brigade, inland. 5th Corps's attack was postponed by rain until the night of 1/2 November, when 8th Indian Division was to cross the River Trigno ten miles upstream from 78th Division's attack over the river by the coastal road and railway. Fighting was fierce, but, when 78th Division reached San Salvo, three miles beyond the river, on 3 November, the commander of 16th Panzer Division, Major-General Sieckenius, decided to withdraw to the BERNHARDT line behind the River Sangro, which covered the GUSTAV line ten miles further back behind the River Moro. 78th Division reached the Sangro on 8 November.

Signalman H. A. Wilson of the Royal Corps of Signals was with 8th Indian Division, serving as cipher operator at the divisional headquarters. His diary for 1 November reads:

Left for San Felice, encamping south-west of the town and facing the river Trigo [sic]. This time we are right up in front of the artillery. This positioning of Div (and other) Hqrs very near the front line is one of Montgomery's innovations. He believes in close contact with the brigades and battalions. Jerry is entrenched behind the river and we can easily see the ridges he occupies.

We should never have arrived. We should have been killed on the road which was extremely treacherous, and we certainly would have been if the back wheels of the lorry hadn't been equipped with skid chains. Before the start of the journey Squithy warned us about the road, stating that an acting Provost Marshall [sic] had been killed at a certain point when his jeep ran over the edge. So did a tank and two soldiers in it were injured. 'Angels and ministers of Grace, defend us!' declaimed Heales, with his eyes on the driver. Squithy took a swig out of his whisky bottle.

Our convoy, all equipped with skid chains, was held up several times while vehicles were pulled out of ditches and off embankments. At the spot mentioned by Squithy our driver kept insanely hugging the edge of the cliff, and I and Spiers, peering anxiously out of the back, suddenly saw a void under our right-hand wheel as the truck leaped a culvert. 'Jesus wept!' cried Spiers, white as a ghost. The name of Christ is sacred to me but I thought its use justified on this occasion.

But as well as danger there was beauty in the Appenines, especially when the sun broke through the clouds to light up the woods of oak and saplings, the grassy glades on the hill slopes and the quaint little rustic dwellings.

Arrived San Felice 3.30 p.m. Cloth-head (Capt. McClaran) directed us to allotted places. Everyone began to dig in. Squithy came looking for his revolver. 'They tell me I have to wear the damn thing. The Germans might send out patrols in the night. However our guns will be putting down a barrage to keep them quiet.[']

Hardly any work. Spiers and I bedded down in the truck.

Tuesday 2:- Got a frightful start at 4 a.m. when the guns opened up from behind. This was the first time they've been so near and my first experience of shells whizzing over my head. They soughed through the air making a noise like a train steaming through a tunnel. The din was appalling and the echoes added to it. Spiers and I smoked for a while, then we got used to it and went asleep again. I reckon you get used to anything in this world.

At dawn the guns woke us up again. Now I know why early-morning tea is called 'gunfire'.

During the morning our medium bombers attacked Jerry's ridge. Spitfires followed them their cannon guns blazing. Then our 25 pounders opened up again. All day long these attacks continued in the same sequence – barrage, bombers, Spitfires, barrage – with half hour lulls between each. During one of these the Angelus rang comfortingly in San Felice on the hill.

Cpl Kenison (Ken for short) now keeps his hen in the cipher truck, It gets no fatter though he gorges it on American biscuits. This afternoon it began cackling when Spiers and I were on duty. 'I've never heard it cackle before', I remarked, 'It must be the shells', for they were whining over at the time. 'It didn't mind the barrage this morning', replied Spiers, Suddenly he cocked an ear. '"Wait a moment!', he exclaimed. 'Those shells are coming *our* way. The bally hen's right. Jerry's having a pot at us – look!' and he pointed to clouds of smoke rising among the trees midway between us and the batteries. This was the first time either of us had been at the receiving end of shell fire. I looked around hoping to see everybody in Hqrs running for shelter but nobody seemed disturbed so we carried on working. But I felt as insecure as an earth-bound fly under a poised swat. Sgt. Fisher, who yesterday pooh-poohed the idea of digging in his bivvy, worked like a navvy at it this evening.

Hitherto Alexander had allowed each army commander to time his own operations, trusting to chance to keep the pressure up on both flanks simultaneously. Now he decided to take a more direct hand in the strategy himself and time their respective operations so that one might strike when the other's attack had drawn enemy reserves to his front. His plan was for Montgomery to strike first by crossing the Sangro on 20 November, while Mark Clark waited until the end of the month to attack astride the Mignano gap to seize the mouth of the Liri valley at Cassino. Meanwhile Kesselring had persuaded Hitler to abandon his fall-back position of the Rommel strategy and to release resources to strengthen the GUSTAV line. Rommel's Army Group B was abolished and his headquarters converted into that of Fourteenth Army, the command of which went to General von Mackensen, who became responsible for the area of Rome and for dealing with any amphibious landing behind von Vietinghoff's Tenth Army.

Montgomery, whose Eighth Army had been reinforced by the 2nd New Zealand Division (Lieutenant-General Sir Bernard Freyberg), gave the task of assaulting across the Sangro near the coast to 5th Corps, with 78th and 8th Indian Divisions, while the New Zealanders advanced through the mountains fifteen miles upstream, aiming for Casoli and eventually Chieti, twenty-five miles beyond on the Via Valeria west of Pescara. 13th Corps, with 5th British and 1st Canadian Divisions, was to carry out a diversionary attack twenty-five miles further south towards the headwaters of the Sangro. Heavy rain raised the level of the river and caused postponement of the start of the attack until 27 November, by which time 76th Panzer Corps had been reinforced by two divisions, so that 5th Corps faced three German divisions, 65th Infantry, 90th Panzer Grenadier and 26th Panzer, while the New Zealanders faced 16th Panzer and 13th Corps faced 1st Parachute Division. After fierce fighting over several days, the attacks were successful and the Germans withdrew to the main defences of the GUSTAV line behind the River Moro, only fifteen miles from Pescara. Bombardier [?] R. F. Coltman was a signaller in Q Battery of the 52nd Field Regiment Royal Artillery. His diary describes 8th Indian Division's part in the operations:

On the night of 27th/28th November the attack went in. The 1/5th Battalion, the Royal Gurkha Rifles captured Mozzagrogna but supporting arms were unable to reach them. The enemy counter attacked with flame-throwers and tanks and the Gurkhas were driven out. Whilst they remained in the strongly built houses the Gurkhas lost few men, but on being ordered to withdraw, and having to come into the open streets they suffered heavily in casualties. There was the danger of the Battalion being lost but the Royal Fusiliers of the same Brigade, the 17th, attacked and enabled the remnants of the Gurkhas to withdraw to our own lines. The attack was made again the following night. Very heavy fighting followed, but Mozzagrogna, the king-pin of the German winter line, was captured; and in the following three days San Maria and Fossacesia fell to our troops. The 78 Division were again advancing up the coastal road. The Regiment had fired 16,000 rounds in those three days. The 1 Canadian Division were now moving into the line to relieve 78 Division.

On the 8 Indian Division front, 21 Brigade had passed through 17 Brigade with the capture of Mozzagrogna, and were pushing towards Romanoli. The Battery was giving direct support to the Royal

West Kents with whom it had an O.P., and the B.C. was with Battalion H.Q. Communication between O.P. and command post was a terrific problem and over forty signallers were engaged on that one task. Over fourteen miles of cable connected the O.P. with the command post and the line was frequently going out. Direct communication was impossible and relay stations both for line and wireless were imperative.

On the day before the attack on Romanoli, the Battery suffered its first fatal battle casualties. A call on the line from Battalion H.Q. asked for the duty officer to speak. The message was 'It was feared that the B.C. and two signallers had been killed.' Later in the afternoon the Commander of 'D' Troop, who was acting O.P. officer with the Royal West Kents, confirmed the news, he having identified the bodies. The line from Battalion H.Q. to the O.P. had been cut and the B.C. decided to go forward to the O.P., despite heavy German shelling on route. He took two signallers with him and it was whilst they were on their way to the O.P. that they met their deaths.

A gloom settled over the battery but I was somewhat concerned that all feeling of sympathy was, especially among the officers, mainly conferred upon the B.C. I should have thought that the same sympathy and feeling should have been shown towards the two signallers who were killed with him. Surely their lives had as much value; their desire to live was as great as that of the B.C. My own thoughts and sympathies turned to those at home. To the B.C's widow and child; to the widow of one signaller well known to me – he was married just before the Regiment left England; and to the relatives of the other signaller who I did not know.

Montgomery now decided that 78th Division had borne the main burden long enough and moved it over to his left flank to relieve 13th Corps, which took over responsibility for the thrust towards Chieti, bringing 5th Division with it and handing over 1st Canadian to 5th Corps to lead the advance along the coast road. The Canadians launched their attack over the River Moro on 8 December, and by the 20th had patrols into Ortona; but it was another week, after a fierce struggle against 90th Panzer Grenadier Division, before they were through the town. During these operations they had been supported by the British 4th Armoured Brigade, one of its units being 44th Royal Tank Regiment, a Territorial Army unit from Bristol, in which Sergeant C. E. S. Tirbutt was serving. His diary records:

Tuesday 7th Dec. On night of 5th was hauled out from playing cards in the truck at 2100 hrs and hastily collected minimum kit and in company with Jack Ayrie was taken by jeep to what remained of the Sangro river bridge. It was on its side practically submerged and we had to walk along a very narrow iron structure aided by a rope which ceased half way across. River not too deep but very swift flowing and must admit this was one of the worst moments of my life as since my mastoid operation my balance has been a little suspect. The portion without the rope was a nightmare. Probably the dark helped as we could never see the full extent of the rushing water. Had to leave our bedrolls behind as we should never have made it with them. However we got across and calling in on B1 I collected a ground sheet and two blankets. Caught up with the tanks at midnight and found I was to be Tug Wilson's operator/loader and what a day we had. Moved off in the dark at 0530 hrs following the Moro river for some time until we found a suitable crossing place. Then up a very steep slope to the village and only six tanks made it. Major Forster [actually Foster] was grand going forward on foot repeatedly for personal recce. We threaded our way through the village meeting only one badly frightened Hun who crept out of a building with his hands up. Canadian infantry very glad to see us. We halted at the far end of the village and fanned out hull down to watch and wait. Suddenly the peace was shattered by Gray Boyce's voice over the air saying vehicles had been heard from the road, and next moment a Mark IV danced into view. Hell for leather, actions automatic, load, fire, reload. Hit it with probably third shot and pumped in a few more until it brewed up. Tug was bloody good, a trifle excited but did not let it affect his judgement. Pleased as a schoolboy. Having disposed of one we were at once fired on by another, and had to scuttle behind a house. Observation bad and we could only see A.P. [Armour Piercing] and Browning [machine gun] flashing back and forth between two invisible opponents. We thought he was behind a haystack so we waited with the gun pointing over the rear of the tank. He moved out and we fired together and felt a thud and the engines cut out. Driver reported engines refused to start again so we were sitting meat. Baled out and nipped behind cover as there was plenty of dirt flying about. We did not find out till much later that our first shot had knocked out the Mark IV. Tug had his Tommy Gun and ordered me to take the crew to safety. I took them into the village and left them in a building and rushed back to Tug borrowing a couple of grenades en route from the Canadians. Tug not there so tried engines but failed to start. A great deal of small arms flak around so took shelter in doorway of a house. Through window I could see two dirty big Mark IVs stationary and both still alive. I tried to get Dusty Miller in the nearest tank to fire through the window but the angle was too great. Suggested brewing up a haystack to use as a smoke screen but we eventually decided not feasible. Remained there for some time spotting for Dusty Miller then Tug turned up and we immobilised the guns on our tank. While Tug went looking for an ambulance for Capt. Hunniball and Hugh Bishop I tried the engines again and this time one responded. The Major turned up and together we went over and looked at Graham Boyce's tank. One shot through the bottom of the driver's compartment and one through his headspace and the gun mounting badly knocking about jamming the gun solid. Feeling pretty low we climbed up to look into the tank wondering what kind of horrible sight we should find but were relieved and amazed to find nothing. Apparently all crew had managed to get out. Inspected the Mark IVs. Our first shot must have killed the co-driver, the other two smashed the track and bogies. We reorganised and left a guard tank and leaguered at the top of track up which we had climbed from the valley. The Major held a short pow-pow and congratulated us all on a bloody good show and we retired to bed but were heavily shelled all night and got little sleep.

Meanwhile the New Zealanders and 5th Division had reached Orsogna, defended by the German 1st Parachute Division, but could not get beyond it. Serving with the New Zealanders was the 2nd Parachute Brigade, which the seventeen-year-old Fusilier E. W. Brown had just joined. He describes his experience:

Well now I was off again to join my new regiment which was the Second Independent Parachute Brigade. There were three battalions, the fourth, fifth and sixth battalions and I was in the Sixth Royal Welsh Fusiliers Parachute Battalion. After joining them we were then sent up to the front line to a place called Pedi Peti Demonti. We took over some empty houses and used them for our billets for the time we were there. The Germans were about two miles away but all we got were shells coming over and some German patrols. The patrols did come a bit close some times but that was to try and find out where we were after all that is the main idea of having patrols. Well we were doing patrols as well mostly at night and nearly every night. There was an Italian there who used to bring eggs to the house most days, but on one of these visits he came late at night and then said he didn't want to go back home on his own. Well for me he could have stayed and slept on the floor but the Sergeant had other ideas. Right he said we'll draw straws. Yes he meant straws. He said the one who draws the short straw would be the one to take the man home. We all thought that this was fair, and to this day I don't know if it was fixed or not, but yes I got the short straw. Trying not to look too worried I said come on then lets get it over with and picking up a Tommy gun off we went. He lived about three miles away sort of one mile down and one mile across which meant we were getting very close to the Germans. It also could have been a put up job to get one of us to the Germans but I wasn't too worried I kept my finger on the trigger of the tommy gun. I thought if it was going to be them or me it wasn't going to be me not if I could help it anyway. To take him home we had to go through a lot of trees, it was a nice moonlight night with quite a lot of wind on. As the wind blew all the trees would move and make a lot of shadows and it was hard to tell if they were trees or people. We stopped a few times to make sure but I wasn't worried as I still had my finger on the trigger of the gun. The going wasn't too bad. I did have a bit of company and after a few more stops we arrived at his home. He thanked me very much in Italian and I set off back for the billet. The way back seemed a lot further than what it had been going there and the trees were all blowing about. There seemed to be more shadows than trees, I could have been wrong but I wasn't going to take any chances so I stopped and got behind some trees just off the road. I just waited until the shadows got nearer and they did passing about ten yards away from me. It was a German patrol with about ten or more men in it. I was still ready with my finger on that trigger but my heart was beating like a big drum it was a wonder the Germans didn't hear it. I was a bit worried though even so because there was a lot more of them and only me on my own. All I could do was keep quiet and wait for them to go by. I waited for quite some time after them had passed by just in case there were any more of them on the way. When all seemed to be quiet I set off again for the billet. Arriving there I gave the password and went into the house. The Sergeant asked me was everything right and I said yes, there was a German patrol coming this way but apart from that everything was O.K. The Sergeant then said, with what I thought was a sort of smile on his face, well then this must have been your lucky day then. Why was that I asked. He then said look at your gun. I looked at my gun and to my surprise I realized I had taken the gun but no ammunition. Well blow me I said or something like that after all, I was back now and I could be brave and make a joke of it. I wouldn't have felt so brave if I had found out sooner that I had no ammunition with me.

Mines were one of the worst hazards of the battlefield. Sapper Eke's 754 Field Company Royal Engineers was involved in clearing them in 78th Division's sector higher up in the mountains, as he relates:

We drove out, heading up the road towards Roccaraso. The job facing us soon became obvious. For almost half a mile the straight road in front of us was blocked by fallen trees. It must have once been a beautiful avenue of tall poplars, but the thoroughness of the German demolition teams had felled every tree directly across the roads as precisely as if they had been placed there. Only infantry patrols could get past against the German rearguards well dug in at the end of the road.

Our officer had already surveyed the road from the air from a Lysander spotter plane, and the heavy equipment required to move the trees was already under cover just off the road. We were warned that during the daytime we would be under observation from the German rearguards on the high ground in front of us, and in range of their mortars. The news did nothing to raise our morale, and reluctantly we walked slowly towards the trees, our eyes scanning the road surface immediately in front of us. The disturbed patches on the road soon appeared, and the mine sweeping teams were called forward. Our two bren-gun crews were despatched through the undergrowth on either side of the road to forward positions, as protection for the road clearing squad. In front of us hopefully, the British infantry were patrolling still further ahead.

We were in the same mine-sweeping squads as we had been on

the beach, and now all thoughts of food were forgotten [they had missed breakfast] as we concentrated on the effort of staying alive. We swept the whole width of the road and verges towards the first tree. Anti-tank 'Teller' mine positions could be seen in the roadway, and the deadly hidden prongs of the anti-personnel 'S' mines were in the verges. The 'Teller' mines were cautiously uncovered, and we were startled to find that instead of the dull black metal casing, they were made of smooth concrete. This was the first one of this type that had been found, and we willingly retreated out of range while the platoon sergeant removed it from the ground. The disarming of the mines was treacherous, and we were making very slow progress.

The invisible prongs of the 'S' mines covered in grass and leaves, could only just be detected on the mine-detectors, and our eyes covered every inch of grass in search of the three deadly half inch long wires. Every studded boot was placed gently down, knowing that any false step would be our last. Section by section we moved slowly forwards silent except for the hoarse choked word of 'Mine' from the discoverer.

The first tree was reached without mishap, and the bulldozer was called forward as we wrapped chains around the trunk. The whole platoon moved fifty yards back, and the tree was dragged down the road to a cleared space. It was midday and at last we had our breakfast of hunks of dry bread and jam and mess tins of tea. The drill was repeated for every tree, each one taking almost an hour. It was almost nine p.m. and the light was failing. The sighting of the tell-tale clues of mine positions had become almost impossible when the next break was called. As we fell back on the grass we were suddenly aware of our tiredness and hunger. We had spent a sleepless night on the trucks, and had worked all day with hardly any food.

Minesweeping of a very different kind was being undertaken far away on the other side of Italy by MMS 172, in which A. Rigby was serving as a telegraphist. He wrote:

On return to Maddalena we heard that the Fleet Sweeper 'Felixstowe' had sunk after hitting a mine – thankfully no hands lost. I felt part of this tragic loss of a ship because as the ship was going down I responded to a radio signal from the ship's wireless operator which said 'Request immediate tow'. I replied but they did not need our help. Christmas was rapidly approaching but it brought only sadness to Sam Bedall, our leading seaman from Barmouth who heard his wife had died leaving him with two young children. We wondered how our families were, perhaps preparing for Christmas with decorations on the tree tying up parcels and stretching rations to provide celebratory meals.

Daylight on 24 December found us terribly close to the Isle of Elba, still occupied by the Germans. It was just sixteen miles away and in the distance we could faintly see the Italian mainland where, far to the south, the Eighth and Fifth Allied armies were advancing slowly but surely. Allied commanders were figuring out how to overcome enemy resistance at Monte Cassino and making elaborate plans for the landings at Anzio. At 18.30 hours we anchored in the harbour at Bastia – the most advanced base in the Mediterranean and not long evacuated by the Germans. A familiar sight greeted us – destruction, devastation – again the aftermath of Allied raids. Another minesweeper, MMS 118 and a motor launch joined us in the harbour early on Christmas morning and I rowed over to the 118 to collect mail and a bag of Christmas fare which included a turkey, ham, pork, sausages, mincemeat Christmas puddings to add to the chickens I had bought from the Sardinian farmers a few days earlier. We supplemented the food with wine from a Corsican wine bar, blissfully unaware of another tragedy on its way.

I was sitting reading quietly when I heard a loud groan from the afterdeck; hurrying along the deck I saw George Spratt, our gunner, writhing in agony from a self-inflicted gunshot wound. The bullet had entered his stomach; for what reason we shall never know but he was foolishly examining a newly-acquired pistol when the gun went off. George died in hospital a few days later. Christmas Day ended with further drama as two stokers from MMS 118 drifted out into the open sea in a small boat. In the darkness, we searched for them way past the harbour boom and the stiff breeze made the sea choppy. Eventually we found their boat on a beach – they were safe. As if this was not enough we had to contend with our tipsy skipper, Gerry Laybourne, who sobered up when he fell fully clothed into the icy waters of the harbour at two o'clock in the morning.

We started minesweeping out of Bastia immediately after Christmas Day but paused for a morning to bring George aboard ship, along with the Padre and a Naval Chaplain. At 09.10 in a position N70E we held a service on deck and laid our shipmate to rest in the deep. I manned the wheel and reflected that a burial at sea is an experience most poignant and heart rending. Before I completed my sea-time I would be present at many such services. On the day George was buried and on succeeding days we spent hours and hours searching for and destroying mines. But New Year's Day was another day to remember! At 11am I casually tuned in my W/T to hear distress signals from the 'Polman' a Fleet Sweeper urging help for an American Landing Ship Tank which was sinking in heavy seas close to the rugged Corsican coast. We put out to sea, battled against the rough seas and got close enough to the LST which was listing over on the jagged rocks to be able to throw a rope across to two American GIs, the only ones left aboard. The rope fell on the deck close to the men but they were too badly shaken to do anything with it and they looked disconsolate as we went full astern just in time to avoid a nasty collision. As we turned away we saw life jackets, a carley float and a small boat floating by. Two unexploded mines floated perilously near: we steered clear of them and as we did so, between bouts of seasickness, I sent a signal back to our base radio station. We found no other survivors – the LST drifted further on to the beach later. The two Americans were not in any great danger, we reassured ourselves, if they remained on deck until the weather abated.

Christmas for most of the soldiers in the front line was not a particularly happy one, but most tried to celebrate it in some suitable way. The Reverend E. N. Downing was chaplain with the 4th Parachute Battalion. After a few verses of doggerel about what he called the 'Mad Mile', which he described as 'the crazy road to hell', he wrote:

That position seemed particularly allergic to Padres. There were four of us [with the brigade], two C of E, one C of S and one RC. While 5th Battalion was in occupation the RC., Fr. Gerry Bankes, a first-class man, went up to visit them, and as he was walking in to Battalion HQ, a shell landed near and he was badly wounded. (It was, in fact, some twenty years later before the last piece of shrapnel was dug out of him, though he was able to soldier on with a Regular Commission till about 1970). On the very next day dear John Robertson, the 'Jock's' own Padre, was conducting a Funeral when the same thing happened. His wounds left him very lame, and he had to be invalided out. (He ended up as Minister of a Church in the Edinburgh district of Pilrig, where he died some years ago). Two good men lost to us. Fifty per cent casualties among the Padres in two days. The next day again I was ordered to go up and finish off the interrupted Funeral. Along the Mad Mile we could not drive very fast, because of the potholes and also because the turning was not easy to find. We had a little way still to go, when a shell whistled over us and landed not many yards to our left, but on soft ground giving us a splattering of clods only. So we just didn't make it seventy per cent casualties in our Department in three days. A very slight lowering of range this time, and ... But the Devil looks after his own, doesn't he?

4th Battalion's turn to go forward came a few days before Christmas. We were waiting a few miles back in the little town of Casoli (a hill-top town, like so many in southern Italy) and I had developed a most tiresome boil on the side of the neck which made me quite feverish. On the day when we were to move up, the boil had become really bad and I felt rather ill. I asked Philip, our MO, if he couldn't do something to hurry it up. (Silly question, because I knew that it was impossible). He sent me to George Wells, in command of the Regimental Aid Post, along the road, who put me to bed and dosed me with 'M & B', the sulphur drug, which was the best before penicillin came in.

I thought of the Colonel's remark about the Padre who went sick when anything unpleasant was looming, and wondered what he would say when he knew I had done the same. However, I was let loose in three or four days. George had eventually lanced the thing, and told me it was a carbuncle. The Colonel never said a word; I still wonder if he did know, or what he said if he did.

Christmas came a few days after we had moved up. Troops noticed with some wonder that the Germans celebrated 'Heiligenacht' by ringing the Church bells on their side of the valley. For myself I had felt at something of a loss, for we clearly could not assemble any large number of men for a Service when we were under fire. My final decision, after consultation, was to have one Service, Holy Communion, at Battalion HQ, and then to go round with the Reserved Sacrament to every position. The only suitable time for the Service was midnight, and I celebrated a real Midnight Mass in a real Stable, with a real Manger for Altar. The whole situation, with the Manger and the danger, stranger than I had ever known, made it the most real and poignant Christmas I ever experienced.

I spent the morning and afternoon going round giving Communion in seven different places. 'B' Company was particularly easy to find, since, possessing an artist, they painted and erected an Inn sign, proclaiming their headquarters as the 'Duck and Scramble'. From there it was on to 'A' Company where, after the little Service, I was constrained to eat an enormous Christmas dinner of pork and plum pudding in the Company cookhouse. That made it a heavy business to set out for the afternoon calls.

While we were holding this position, a party had to go out every night and occupy forward trenches. There was a night when one of the men refused to go down into the trench, and I was told to talk to him next morning. I learned that he was a Londoner, who some time before, in one of the heavy London air-raids, had been buried, and now had an apparently unsurmountable phobia. It was decided to give him another chance that night, and I attempted some advice, which proved totally unpractical, and next day I saw him being taken away under guard. He gave me a sad look, and I knew I had been a dismal failure.

Montgomery now realized that he had not the strength to force his way to Pescara and then, through the winter, down the Via Valeria towards Rome. He therefore recommended to Alexander that Eighth Army's offensive should be halted. Alexander agreed, but told him to keep up sufficient activity to prevent troops from 76th Panzer Corps being transferred across the mountains to the 14th. A few days later, on 30 December, Montgomery left Italy to assume command of 21st Army Group in Britain and prepare for ROUNDUP, taking Dempsey, Bucknall and many of his staff with him. He was glad to go, both to escape from what he thought was a dead-end and at the prospect of the great challenge before him. His place was taken by Lieutenant-General Sir Oliver Leese, whose 30th Corps Headquarters had been transferred to Britain after Sicily. Eisenhower also left to command OVERLORD, as ROUNDUP had been renamed, and was replaced by General Sir Henry Maitland Wilson, British Commander-in-Chief Middle East, his former command being absorbed into Allied Forces Mediterranean, as Allied Forces North Africa was renamed.

Fifth Army's assault on the BERNHARDT line towards Cassino was planned to include the landing of one division in amphibious craft in the area of Anzio, twenty-six miles south of Rome (Operation SHIN-GLE); but there were strict limitations on that. At the QUADRANT summit conference at Quebec in September it had been decided that 80 per cent of the British and American landing ships in the Mediterranean would be transferred to Britain by mid-December, which would leave the capacity for landing of only one brigade. Eisenhower pleaded for the retention of enough to land a division, and, after considerable discussion between the American and British Chiefs of Staff, it was agreed that fifty-six British and twelve American could stay until 15 December. However, the Chief of the Imperial General Staff, General Sir Alan Brooke, told Alexander to plan on being able to keep them until 15 January. This limitation of time, as well as military realities, demanded that the Anzio landing should not take place until it was certain that Clark's troops, advancing by land, could soon join them: they must be within thirty miles. Clark's plan was to attack the BERN-HARDT line from its southern end. First, the British 10th Corps and the US 2nd (the latter with 3rd and 36th US Divisions and the Special Service Brigade) would renew the assault on Monte Camino, which 10th Corps would then hold while 2nd US Corps cleared the rest of the hills covering the Mignano Gap. Meanwhile 6th US Corps, with 34th and 45th US Divisions, would execute a diversionary attack further north. When this phase was complete, a direct attack on the mouth of the Liri valley would be mounted. The operation was originally planned to start on 30 November, but the bad weather, which had delayed Montgomery's attack on the Sangro, made Alexander suggest to Clark that it should be deferred to 12 December; but the latter thought that this could prejudice the chances of launching SHINGLE, and decided to start on 2 December.

Fighting for Monte Camino, held by 15th Panzer Grenadier Division, was fierce and prolonged, and it was not until 10 December that it was finally all in Allied hands, 46th and 56th Divisions in 10th Corps having suffered 1,000 casualties. 2nd US Corps then faced further tough fighting against 29th Panzer Grenadier Division before it secured the western exits from the Mignano Gap on 17 December. Further north 6th US Corps made little progress in the mountains, until they were reinforced by the French General Alphonse Juin's 2nd Moroccan Division, which forced the Germans there back to the GUSTAV line. However there were still further defences between the line and the leading troops of 2nd US and 10th Corps, and Mark Clark realized that SHINGLE had to be cancelled and that his exhausted troops had to be given a rest before he launched a further attack to reach Cassino.

4

First Assaults on the GUSTAV Line

January 1944

The deliberate pace of the steps of Alexander's armies towards the GUSTAV line made both the American and the British Chiefs of Staff realize that the chances of a rapid advance to Rome, which had been assumed when they met at Quebec, had greatly diminished. Both Marshall's hope of a major switch of effort to Britain by the end of the year and Churchill's of an exploitation to the Po valley were doomed to disappointment. The next summit meeting, SEXTANT, was to be held at the end of December, in Cairo with Chiang Kai-Shek and in Teheran with Stalin. In preparation for it, the British Chiefs of Staff suggested to their American colleagues that pressure must be kept up on the Germans in the Mediterranean, even at the expense of delaying the planned date (1 May 1944) of OVERLORD if necessary; Alexander should not stop at Rome, but continue to the Pisa–Rimini line, 150 miles north; support to partisans in the Balkans should be intensified; and more pressure should be applied to Turkey to join the Allies. The Americans were not enthusiastic and suspected the approach as yet another British attempt to wriggle out of OVERLORD. Churchill still had doubts about it and was also influenced by other motives. In spite of the failure of an operation to occupy the Dodecanese islands of Cos and Leros in October, he hankered after the capture of Rhodes and a general campaign to 'set the Balkans alight'; and, as American predominance increased, he wanted to keep the spotlight on Italy, where most of the Allied troops came from the British Commonwealth and were commanded by his favourite general, Alexander. Brooke was more realistic. He was genuinely and firmly committed to OVERLORD, but fearful of embarking on it unless substantial German forces could be held away from France. Although he was a firm believer in support to Tito in Yugoslavia, he had no time for Churchill's Aegean fantasies. He saw continued pressure on the Germans in Italy as the best method, other than Russian pressure, of diverting their forces from France. He was not however such a fervent admirer of Alexander as Churchill. In his *Notes on my Life*, he wrote of him:

He held some of the highest qualities of a Commander, unbounded courage, never ruffled or upset, great charm and a composure that inspired confidence in those around him. But when it came to working on a higher plane and deciding matters of higher tactics and of strategy he was at once out of his depth; had no ideas of his own and always sought someone to lean on.*

Brooke did not think much either of Alexander's Chief of Staff, Major-General A. A. Richardson, who lacked recent operational experience, and at the end of the year he replaced him with Lieutenant-General A. F. (John) Harding, who had gained a high reputation as both a staff officer and an operational commander in the field throughout the campaign in North Africa, from its earliest days almost to the end, when he had been wounded. Brooke was particularly keen to retain sufficient amphibious shipping in the Mediterranean to be able to land and maintain a significant force behind the German front line.

This conflict of views over strategy was resolved by Stalin in Teheran. First of all he declared that once Germany was defeated, Russia would join in the war against Japan, thus making it less urgent for Roosevelt to placate Chiang Kai-Shek. Secondly, he showed little enthusiasm for greater effort in Italy but strongly supported the American proposal for a landing on France's Mediterranean coast to precede or coincide with OVERLORD. The combination of these factors made it possible to cancel BUCCANEER, the proposed amphibious attack on the Andaman Islands in the Bay of Bengal, and transfer fifty American landing ships to the Mediterranean, where they would be available to support Alexander until they were needed for the landing in southern France (Operation ANVIL), which would be carried out by two divisions, followed up by ten from the USA. It was to take place in May 1944, as was OVERLORD, and the two were to have priority over all other operations. Once Rome was taken, Alexander would continue as far as the Pisa–Rimini line: after that, pressure on the Germans would be maintained, but ANVIL would have priority. Capture of Rhodes was desirable but not essential. The

* David Fraser, *Alanbrooke* (London: Collins, 1982), p. 381.

deadline of 15 January for the transfer of sixty-eight landing ships from the Mediterranean to Britain was confirmed.

On his way back from the conference, Churchill met Eisenhower and Alexander at Carthage, near Tunis, and promptly went down with pneumonia. He exploited his enforced stay there to resuscitate SHINGLE, strengthened to a two-division assault, with two more divisions as follow-up and a capability for maintenance without the necessity of an immediate junction with other forces. This was made possible by the retention of fifty-eight British landing ships until 5 February, by which time fifteen from the Indian Ocean would have arrived. Churchill envisaged the landing force as immediately thrusting inland fifteen miles to the Alban Hills, cutting von Senger's lines of communication on Routes 6 and 7 and forcing him to withdraw from the GUSTAV line.

Alexander immediately began to plan on this basis, the difference from the original SHINGLE being that the attempt to seize Cassino and the mouth of the Liri valley tended to be supplementary to the landing at Anzio, rather than the other way round. He told Clark that the aim of the landing was to 'cut the enemy lines of communication and threaten the rear of the German 14th Corps'. The task was given to Major-General Lucas's 6th US Corps, the assaulting forces being 1st British Division (Major-General W. B. C. Penney) and 2nd Special Service Brigade on the left, seven miles north of the small harbour of Anzio: three US Ranger battalions and one Parachute one at Anzio itself, and 3rd US Division (Major-General L. K. Truscott) and another Parachute battalion five miles further to the east. Only one brigade of 1st Division, the 2nd, would land in the initial assault, followed by the Commando Brigade. The rest of 1st Division would remain afloat as a reserve until the result of the other landings was known.

The area beyond the beaches was flat, reclaimed from marshes, up to the foothills some twelve miles inland, where the railway from Naples to Rome ran from near the small town of Cisterna to that of Osteraccia, there joining the railway from Anzio at Campoleone station. Two roads led inland from Anzio: one to Osteraccia, and thence to Albano, the Via Anziate; the other through Nettuno, a mile to the east, to Cisterna, and thence to Velletri, a branch road to Osteraccia breaking off half-way between Anzio and Cisterna, just south of the Mussolini Canal. Clark was told that the landing should take place between 20 and 30 January, as close to the 20th as possible. Clark's orders to Lucas were to 'seize and secure a beachhead in the vicinity of Anzio' from which he was 'to advance to the Alban Hills'.

The Garigliano Assault

Alexander issued his general orders on 12 January, accompanied by an optimistic intelligence assessment which described the Germans as tired and trying to rest and refit, with only two divisions in reserve. The plan for the rest of Fifth Army involved five phases. In the first, 2nd US Corps was to advance towards the mouth of the Liri valley, capturing the last two positions, Montes Porchio and Trocchio, between the Mignano Gap and the River Rapido. This would be followed by attacks on von Senger's flanks. Juin's French Expeditionary Corps (2nd Moroccan and 3rd Algerian Divisions), which had replaced 6th US Corps to the north, would attack through the mountains towards Atina, while McCreery's 10th British would cross the lower reaches of the Garigliano and advance north-westwards through the Aurunci Mountains. These flanking attacks having drawn von Senger's forces away from his centre, Keyes's 2nd US Corps would cross the Rapido there on 20 January and thrust up the Liri valley. Two days later Lucas would land at Anzio. While Fifth Army was thus advancing towards Rome, Eighth Army was to keep up the pressure on the Adriatic coast, having lost three divisions, the 1st to 6th US Corps, 5th to 10th Corps (replacing 7th Armoured), and the New Zealand Division into Army Group reserve west of the Apennines, ready to exploit the success of Fifth Army's operations, which Alexander had optimistically called 'the Battle for Rome'.

The battle began with the French attack, launched on the night of 11/12 January in filthy weather. Initially it met with encouraging success, bringing them up to the main defences of the GUSTAV line west of the Rapido, the east bank of which 2nd US Corps had reached by the 15th. On their left 10th British Corps, opposed by the German 94th Division, successfully crossed the Garigliano near its mouth on 17 January, with 56th Division on the right and the 5th on the left; but bridge-building was slow, as the crossing area and approaches to it were under enemy observation and subject to accurate artillery fire. The first thirty-ton bridge, capable of taking tanks, was not completed until 20 January, and no bridge could be used in daylight. 10th Corps's ability to expand its bridgehead was therefore limited, and by the time that Kesselring had released 29th and 90th Panzer Grenadier Divisions to von Senger to seal it off, which they did in a series of counter-attacks by 22 January, McCreery's men were left in the foothills in possession of the original GUSTAV line's defences a few miles west of the river on a frontage of some twelve miles. Private S. C. Brooks was serving with the 6th Cheshires, who manned 4.2in mortars and Vickers machine-guns in the 56th Division. His diary covers this period:

Jan. 16. We are getting ready for action again, the big river crossing this time, got life jackets from navy. Pln. moved out, we shall soon. I'm in 8 pln. B Sect this time. Plns move out *Jan.17.* On the *18th* they go in, commandos first of the Polish army, then the Bde., all on boats. We get across dry, all 8 across. Tip, Lou, Jack Deaves and Nob and a carrier move into the battle area 7 miles through Sessa Aurunca, the river is 2½ miles down the road, find a cave to cook in. I make an igloo of 4.2[in] mortar tins, very comfortable. We have a batt. of 7.2s round us, a terrific din every few minutes, can observe strike on hills 1000 yards away, can see shells leave muzzle, horrible cordite smell hangs around all day.

2.0. [p.m.] Jan 18. We are bombed by about a dozen dive-bombers, didn't drop flat much, don't appear to have done any damage, some go for river, everything from heavy A.A. to mess tins go up ... Up to 6.0 all seems to be going well, objectives I believe taken. Plevin and Stelfox go up on a mine, don't know how serious yet, lad brings them back and can't recross river ... Hear that a pln. of C.Coy has been reported missing. Artillery going all day from 7.2s down. Lou and I inspect a 7.2, crikey I wouldn't like to be at the receiving end, shell weighs 200 lbs.

Friday 21 Jan. We get a doing with shells at 2 o'clock, none very near but uncomfortable, one hits chapel 20 yards away, shrapnel whistles round us but no blast. 7 & 9 plns. are now out of action and are in village, 8 still in. Have been attacked four times in one day, must be hot stuff on that road at 7 pln. A tank appeared on the scene and was straight way knocked out with a Sherman. Capt. James goes in dock with jaundice or something, Mr. Gingell takes over command. Situation across the river is reported to be satisfactory. Rumour has it that two Divs. have landed S. of Rome, hope this is true, it will help a lot, said to be 1 Yank and 1 British Divi.

Saturday 22 Jan. They tell me Capt. James has been awarded the M.C. for the valley at Salerno. 8 pln. attacking to the side of Castle Forte. Get in a sticky spot. Burgon goes in dock with blast in the stomach, not too bad, three others also but nothing serious. Our tanks have a go at Castle Forte, but that's all they do, have a go at it. No bridge across the river yet, all troops etc. are rafted, a bad state of affairs. Our pln. come out 12.0 last night and are in action again tonight, have our own views on this. Two lads, Mcnab and Beresford can't be found, that makes 4 altogether from this Coy, I'll say no more. 9 men arrive as reinforcements, the oldest is 20, they are from N. Africa and have done 9 months in the army with a total of two months service abroad, naturally no action. We take them down the field and show them where our shells are landing and where theirs are dropping, they move on to platoons, I wish them every luck. We have a new R.S.M. a man from D.L.I., a big bloke he is and looks very pleasant I don't think, he's after moving somebody's feet already.

Sun. 23 Jan. Appears a little quieter just now, they still shell the river at will but we are getting none. 12 pln of Coy. repeat the performance of Salerno and get cut off . . . My shanty of 4.2 mortar tins is doing well, gunfire has not knocked it down yet.

27 Jan. Big attack, we hold on to back of two tanks, take a few more hills, our blokes are shelled a lot and Sgt. Bowness is killed, very hard luck, all the others seem to come out O.K. During this attack our fellows find C. Coy guns lost on first day. I have spoken to Bennett of that unfortunate first day incident, he tells me Mr. Norton led pln. into action and went 1½ too far, discovering this they were plucky enough to get into action but were in the middle of an infantry concentration and were charged, and it turned into a scramble back in the dark. Tommy Smith, Jack and Bennett dived into a gulley with two more lads and got away. Pln. Comm was killed and J. Broadley and Barrett and a few lads made it to a river bed. Bennett, who got away, said as they came back they saw some Germans in position with spandoes [sic] all ready waiting but they got away with it by pretending to be Germans themselves, good job it was dark. When they got to our lines they were challenged by R.Fs. who said this is 400 yds. bridgehead. Ben said we had pln. 1½ higher up, or at least we had.

Lieutenant D. H. Deane of the 2nd Scots Guards in 201st Guards Brigade in the same division also kept a diary. His read:

18 [January] Tuesday. Early reveille, move off in trucks with our hearts in our mouths. Along dreary roads of deodatia passing very ominous blood waggons coming back the other way. Turn off to debussing area, and wait – wait interminably it seems, no one knows what for. At last move off and march for an equally long period – troops absolutely whacked, cross the Garigliano in sinister silence. A very pretty American girl lashing up coffee to the ambulance drivers – I wonder if we look heroic filing away into the darkness. More marching in all about 10 miles and arrive in a field with damn all to shelter from the cold.

19 Wednesday and 20 Thursday. The fun, so called, started at 0100 hrs this morning when shells arrived every minute. No one had dug in owing to tired men, so we all had to shovel away flopping down at odd moments from the bursts of H.E. In the morning go up and recce our attack with George, Alistair and Neil. I am reserve Pl. and feel nervous, but in a funny way. Came across a lot of Grenadier water carriers crawling on their stomachs, with stuff flying every-where tracer, airburst and 210s. Our attack was cancelled, as we had to form up in a minefield which seemed stupid enough. Came down and brought up 15 Platoon to a little knoll we are to hold. Everything is very noisy still and I am quite bewildered – the enemy seem to be all round. The Hampshires had a bloody time in the night and had to do a daylight attack on San Gemigniagno churchyard. Behind are impregnable mountains, obviously with armies of Boche. Wounded from Hampshires and Dorsets pouring through, to the accompani-ment of spandaus all the time. Poor wretches they have had their share of bloodiness.

21 Friday. The attack seems to have fizzled out and we are here for a bit anyway – much quieter though the Hampshires are to have another go for the churchyard tonight – what good will it do them – little that I can see as vast mountains lie in front, bleak and sinister.

22 Saturday. Went to link up with some gunners in their o.p. and got blown about horribly by mortar stonk which came down very fiercely – There was no room in their trenches so I had to lie in a crack in a rock until it calmed down – I said goodbye to them over my shoulder and flew back to my own small fortress. Large German shell came over and set 4 carriers alight killing 4 from H.Q. Company. What they call a casa shifter.

23 Sunday. Quite a nice Sunday with letters from Jim and Elizabeth. Kept round and with a compass for fun plotted a mortar chart taking sound bearings on the mortars and also some large guns from the Coast giving the Grenadiers horrible stick. I feel secure enough in a German trench send back the information and am very proud to see the Cruisers get to work on the guns. Terrifying sight to see their 8″ guns firing out to sea and then hours after hear the projectile swishing in towards Gaeta.

25 Tuesday. A BLOODY day – very quiet in the morning with nice weather, and then Peter and I are asked to go up to the awful cliff behind us on which Victor G – les [?] got killed and R.F. had to be taken off. Go through Bn HQ & Support to pick up Brodie Clarke. Just before we came down having finished our recce, we were seen and Peter got killed by an 88mm. Brodie and I saved ourselves by jumping into a latrine which was nasty, but P. got it all to himself. I was pretty shaken and had to tell George that he had been killed. We go up there to night.

26 Wednesday. Last night was quite quiet and today we filed down here to a delightful village serving as a rest area, but quite a long march. One or two shells came over but we were all asleep – Meals came up on the Coy. cooker for a change and we can get our beds up very nice. Bde HQ rang up to say that the coastal battery had been reported hit by Spitfires and could go to my credit for spotting for the Navy – feel very bucked. Lost my silver identity bracelet I had made before I came out – always felt that I looked like a suburban bottle of sherry in it.

Gunner J. Gascoigne-Pees's 392 (Surrey Yeomanry) Battery of 98th Field Regiment was supporting the 5th Division in these operations, as he describes:

Wednesday 26th January was a black day for the Surrey Battery. It was a very clear morning and their first warning of trouble was a ranging air-burst plumb over the Battery area. This was ominous and it was soon followed by a few shells straight into the area. The C.P. staff were inside H truck and it seemed as though the shells whizzed just a foot above the hood. Soon the Troops were reporting to C.P. that some gunners had been hit and all spare men from K and Y trucks were used as stretcher bearers to take the wounded to the R.A.P. The shelling eased off for a while and then came on again very heavily. Several enemy guns must have been engaged on bombarding the position and then C Troop reported one ammo dump on fire and later reported it was out of control. Shortly after that D Troop reported the same thing and some guns had to move their position. More and more shells were pumped into the area but throughout the day the Surrey guns kept firing. The situation was reported to R.H.Q. and the CO2 [second-in-command] ordered the Battery to evacuate the position when it became untenable. It was more than untenable and to hang on would have meant all would have been lost. Their own ammo was burning furiously and exploding and the air was alive with shrapnel. The guns pulled out and C.P. made a rush job of packing up H truck and cleared off. They mustered together again by 391 Battery position and it was a very dazed party that was left. 18 of the gunners had been hit out of about 100 men on the gun position. Luckily there were some rations on H truck and they were able to have a brew-up for HQ party. A few more shells came over while they waited until dusk before they moved back to B Echelon where they spent the night. Jack Beeby, who was i/c one of D Troop guns described the day in his diary: 'The wind changed direction and our smoke screen became useless and at the same time the visibility became very clear. Soon after breakfast I was on the gun firing and with a sudden swish a shell burst two yards in front of our Priest [self-propelled 105mm gun]. A minute later another burst right at the side of us putting the gun out of action. Our armour saved us from injury but the shrapnel damaged a great deal of our equipment. From then on we were shelled solidly all day long. We had casualties every few minutes and to make matters worse two of our piles of ammunition were hit and started to explode all over the place. However we continued firing until several more guns were knocked out and then we were given the order to evacuate. Shells were bursting all around us, trees came crashing down and the air was filled with that horrid acrid smell that comes from bursting shells.

2nd US Corps captured Monte Trocchio, one mile east of the Rapido, halfway between Cassino and the village of San Angelo, four miles south of the town, on 15 January. This secured the start line for the assault over the Rapido, which was twenty-five to fifty feet wide and nine feet deep and here ran fast between flood banks. Fording or swimming across was not possible and boats were difficult to handle in the current. The approaches were flat and flooded, the whole area, except for the eastern side of Monte Trocchio, was open to observation from Cassino and the area of the Monastery, so that assault boats and bridging material could not be brought close to the river in daylight. The far bank was defended by 15th Panzer Grenadier Division, which had laid extensive minefields on both sides of the river. The 36th US Division was chosen for the hazardous task of assaulting across the river on either side of San Angelo, north of the junction with the Liri. South of that river, 46th British Division, under 10th Corps, was also to cross to the village of San Ambrogio, providing left-flank protection to 36th Division. When the latter had established a bridgehead, 1st US Armoured Division would pass through and thrust up the valley.

The crossing was to have been made on the night of 18/19 January, but wet weather and the need for more time for preparation led to its postponement until the 20th. Everything then went wrong, the approach to the near bank in slippery mud became chaotic in a thick river mist in the dark under heavy artillery fire, which did not seem to be affected by the American counter-battery programme. On the right, only two companies succeeded in crossing. On the left, a whole battalion managed to get across, but found their position on the far side untenable and came back. Keyes ordered the divisional commander, Major-General Fred L. Walker, to renew the assault in daylight with intensified artillery support. The left-hand regiment managed to get all three of its battalions over in the late afternoon, but when daylight came on the 22nd, they could not hold their positions and were forced back over the river, having lost many men. The right-hand regiment, crossing after dark on the 21st, got the rest of the battalion over to join the two companies already there, and another battalion also; but, by the end of the 22nd, they had all been killed or captured, except for forty men who managed to escape over the river. The assault had totally failed, the division having lost 143 men killed, 663 wounded and 875 missing.

46th British Division, on their left, had fared no better: in fact worse, although suffering much less. They were due to cross on the night of 19/20 January, and the Germans, on that day, opened the sluices of a dam higher upstream on the Liri, so that the Garigliano was higher and flowing faster than predicted. Crossing by assault boat became chaotic, made worse by the mist, and only one company (of 2nd Hampshires) of the only brigade involved (the 128th) succeeded in establishing itself on the far side by dawn on the 20th. The brigade commander then recalled it and cancelled any further attempts. Although the river level had returned to normal, no more were made by his or the other brigades of the division, to the annoyance of the Americans who were trying to cross on their right. That the liaison between 46th Division and the Americans was far from perfect is illustrated by the experience of Lieutenant Michael Glover of the 2/5th Foresters in that division:

> On 15th January I was told to take out an eight-man fighting patrol to discover whether a bridge over the Gari river was intact. That would have been straight-forward enough but for two complications. One was that, for some inscrutable reason, we were to rendezvous with an American patrol at the bridge. The second was that I was not briefed until just before total darkness so that there was no time for a reconnaissance. To make matters worse, I was briefed from an air photograph – the first I had ever seen – which did not agree with the maps. I learned very soon that the ground very often disagreed with Italian maps.
>
> Without too much difficulty I found the bridge which was blown and unguarded but there was no sign of the American patrol so, after hanging about for half an hour, we set off home. This was more complicated since we knew the map was wrong and I had not been permitted to bring the air photo with me. Consequently I got very lost and a substantial battle broke out on a hill some miles away to our right. Moving in the direction I believed to be right, we heard a considerable noise advancing on us from the right rear. Getting rapidly under cover, I was surprised to see a column of troops, company strong, marching noisily towards us, with every man smoking, behaving as if they were returning from a disorderly peacetime exercise. That reassured me that they were not Germans

so I stepped out on to the track in front of them whereupon they stopped, rather than halted. They turned out to be Americans and the major leading them told me that he too was lost but that they were meant to be attacking Monte Trocchio. I suggested that the big hill where they were having a battle might be his objective and he agreed it might. Before giving orders for his men to march off in the new direction, which he did at the top of his voice, he told me that he had passed an American headquarters about a mile back up the track. The column then slouched off, still smoking in the general direction of the firing. They had only gone about a hundred yards when the enemy shelled the area where they had made so much noise and where we still were, although we contrived to get some cover from a convenient stone shed.

After rather less than the promised mile we came to a farm outside which a radio was talking loudly in the complete uninterest of its large American operator who slept on a chair beside it and failed to wake when, leaving my patrol outside, I walked past him and knocked on the farmhouse door. No one answered so I went in to find the entire headquarters of an American battalion asleep, the only man awake being a lieutenant-colonel of the Foresters whom I did not know but turned out to be a rather dim officer whom I had once served under briefly. He roused the American colonel whose first words to me were, 'Why did you shoot that lootenant of mine?' I explained that we had not fired a round all evening but that we had been down to the bridge expecting to meet an American patrol who had not arrived. By this time his staff were awake and tending to be aggresssive since their officer had, they said, been shot by 'some Goddamned Limey' and he was the one who had been meant to meet me. After a time they calmed down, produced coffee for the patrol and showed me my way home on the map.

I learned the story of the lieutenant's death when I got back to the platoon. About an hour after I had set out for the bridge a number of men wearing round helmets approached the rear gate of our farm in a stealthy if unprofessional manner. The sentry challenged but got no response and challenged again. When there was still no answer, he fired a single shot, believing from the shape of their helmets that they were Germans. The American officer was shot through the head and died at once. He was unlucky because the sentry happened to be an elderly lance corporal, the only man in the platoon who could hit anything with a Tommy gun on a single shot. The American sergeant then shouted that they were friends and later remarked that he could not understand why his officer had failed to answer the challenge, which, on both occasions, was quite distinct. It does not seem to have crossed his mind to have replied himself. He could not explain how they came to be arriving from behind our position at a time when they should have been at the bridge a mile or so in front of us.

Anzio

Pressure on the Germans on the Cassino front was therefore slackening off just as 6th US Corps landed at Anzio in the early hours of 22 January, taking the Germans completely by surprise. Generals Clark and Lucas both held a significantly different view of the operation from that of Churchill, who had envisaged a rapid advance to the Alban Hills, cutting Routes 6 and 7. Clark and Lucas's staff were influenced by their experience at Salerno, and, although the Alban Hills was given as the final objective in the orders which both issued, primary emphasis was laid on the need to establish a secure beachhead and make certain that supply over the beaches and through the port of Anzio could be assured. Lucas was replaced a month later as a result of his cautious attitude,* but, given the speed and vigour with which the Germans reacted when they learned of the landing, there is little doubt that he was right.

In the right-hand sector, the three regiments of the 3rd US Division moved quickly inland to their initial objective, the Mussolini Canal, seven miles away, securing the road junction at Le Ferriere. Reconnaissance patrols were ordered to Littorio, Cisterna and as far away as Velletri, twenty miles inland, but never reached their objectives, having run into Germans on the way. The assaulting infantry of 1st British Division's 2nd Brigade, to which 1st Scots Guards had been attached,

---

* Winston Churchill said he had hoped that 'we were hurling a wild cat on the shore, but all we got was a stranded whale.'

were all ashore by 2.45 a.m., having met no enemy. They were followed
by the commandos of 2nd Special Service Brigade and then the rest of
24th Guards Brigade, which was complete ashore by 11.30, the guns of
67 Field Regiment Royal Artillery having been ready for action since
8.30. All three battalions of 2nd Brigade (from left to right, 1st Loyals,
2nd North Staffordshires and 6th Gordon Highlanders) advanced
through the wooded area of the Bosco di Padiglione to their initial
objectives some four miles inland, where they began to dig in, prepared
to meet a counter-attack, although no enemy had yet been met, even by
patrols which went a few miles further on.

Lieutenant G. H. Dormer was serving in the minesweeper *Hornpipe*,
a converted trawler, which swept and marked channels to the beaches,
as he describes in a rather disordered diary:

Thursday [20 January]. Spent in checking up on everyones lifebelts &
tin hats etc: issuing field dressings, checking over guns and lifesaving
equipment organisation and training. C.O. went to a most secret
conference, of which no details will be released until we are actually
under way. We are pretty well ready for anything now, but I'd like to
get cracking, as all this waiting for it is a bit of a strain. Only 4
trawlers are concerned ... we are lucky this time! I wonder if we ·
shall still say 'lucky' by the time it finishes?

Friday. 'Never sail on a Friday' was disregarded this time. Got going
about noon, behind a big convoy of landing craft. Great secrecy ...
no one told until evening what it was all about, then only the Officers
... but Sparks has known since yesterday, as the time and place were
mentioned in his communication orders. So far, 2000, all is well. We
can see flashes from the Minturno area [about fifty-five miles ESE]
and various aircraft are about. I am going 'into battle' in pyjamas as
usual! Appropriately enough I was reading 'King Henry the Fifth'
today ... 'This Story shall the good man tell his son ...' I hope!

Saturday 1100. So far theres practically no story. The night passed
quietly but the landing craft were very difficult to see, and by 3 a.m.
the convoys were in a fair state of confusion. At 5 I began to have
suspicions, as the course seemed wrong and the speed too slow. So
we asked the nearest LCI and discovered that we were with the wrong
convoy entirely. Leaving them we cracked on and arrived at the
seaward end of the channel into Anzio at daybreak. We found our

flotilla of Fleet Sweepers and joined them for a hectic mornings work of picking up dan buoys ... and then an equally hectic afternoon of the same. It is hard work and it took a long time to discover the best way to do it. We got quite good by the end. I did most of the overside work myself.

Things have been very quiet ... a lovely calm sunny day, with almost cloudless blue skies. The multitude of ships lying off the beaches look more like a review than an invasion Armada. The sweepers cut several mines and one damaged the P— which we are now going to take back to Naples in tow of tugs. There are a few columns of smoke rising from the shore and every now and then a dull thud. Sometimes a cruiser does a bit of bombarding, or a few enemy planes approach. There are a constant series of red warnings, but no attacks yet. I'm sorry not to be staying the night, which will no doubt be more exciting, but we shall very likely come back with another convoy ... The night passed quietly, so quietly that one could be heard from one end of the ship to the other without raising the voice. The sea again was mirror-calm and our speed, 4¼ knots, so slow we hardly ruffled the water.

Lieutenant-Commander Grandage, now with his LST 366, set sail in company with some twenty others at 12.45 on Monday 21 January, due to arrive offshore at Anzio two hours after the assault, and was there at 0700 hrs. The beaches were not suitable for LSTs themselves to beach, so he anchored, opened the bow doors and let the eight DUKWs on board swim out. It was not until the following morning that the other vehicles were discharged by a new method: this was to secure a LCT under the bow of the LST with the latter's ramp on the LCT deck. Another LCT then came alongside the first, and the vehicles then drove down the LST ramp and across the deck of the first LCT into the second.

He then returned to Naples and loaded nineteen tanks, sixteen half-tracks, five armoured cars and nineteen other vehicles, with 300 men, and sailed again for Anzio, in company with eighteen others, at 1700 hrs on the 24th. His account follows:

After an uneventful trip we arrived at Anzio at 0915 the next morning and anchored until 1815 when orders were received to enter the harbour. By this time it had got very dark & there were no lights to show where the harbour entrance was. I had no large scale charts of the harbour but having anchored close to the entrance in daylight, I had a fair idea of the direction to go. My First Lieutenant stationed in the bow for entering harbour had a powerful torch which was useful for lighting up the end of the breakwater which we had to pass on our port side. There was a slight swell running on our beam and every time the ship got into the trough I felt her bump but slide on.

On entering the harbour the hard to which we had to go lay 90 degrees on our starboard side meaning we had to go ahead on the port engine and astern on the starboard. Then came a near disaster. While preparing the mooring wires at the stern, part of one wire fell overboard on the port side and became wrapped round the port propeller. Then came an almost impossible task of manoeuvring to the quay with only the starboard engine available. At one time I was able to get a small landing craft to push the ship's bow round so as to head for the quay.

At intervals I kept hearing an explosion with a sound unlike what I had heard before – it was a more cracking sound and I remarked 'What was that?' Someone replied 'Shells bursting' about 200 yards away. I had not had the experience of being shelled on land before. It was not until 2245 that we were secured to the quay and were able to unload. It had taken 4 hours of painstaking manoeuvring from the time we had left the anchorage only about 300 yards away. I left the bridge and retired to my cabin, sat down quite exhausted and shed a few tears.

Unloading was finished by 0130. I felt it most unwise to attempt getting the ship out of the harbour at night with only one engine available. I got permission to wait until daylight. At 0830 the next morning we left the berth and once again I arranged for a small landing craft to push our bow round until we were heading towards the harbour entrance. By this time there was a fresh wind blowing across the entrance causing a heavy swell. As we cleared the entrance the ship rolled so heavily that the suction for the water circulation was lost and the starboard engine stopped – so we had no engines. The ship had a good way on but the heavy surf was driving the ship towards the beach and a submerged wreck on the port bow. The anchor was let go and the ship swung heading into the swell and the rolling stopped. After 5 minutes the starboard engine was going again. The anchor was weighed and the ship was forced through the surf bumping the bottom every time she was in the trough.

The ship was finally anchored at 1005, but did not sail for Naples until 1600, by which time Anzio harbour had undergone a German air attack. Signalman P. J. Lovett, attached to the 46th Royal Tank Regiment which was supporting the 1st Division, wrote in his diary:

22 January. Dawn – whole fleet at anchor a mile or two off the coast – a balloon floated from every boat, a wonderful sight. A mine floated past – corvettes pot at it and sink it. Initial assault seems to have gone well – seems to be a bit of delay landing us. Through field-glasses I could see the beach from which a steep track made the same morning by 'bulldozers', rose up to wooded slopes. At the top of a track a Scammell was waiting with winch ready to assist any vehicle that failed to climb the steep sandy incline, Bofors guns were already in position against expected dive-bombing, but not a plane did we see. DUKWs (steel boats on six road-wheels, that can drive down the beach and straight into the water) were plying to and fro down the track and up to the sides of lighters to collect fuel, stores and ammo, and blokes on the shore were already digging slit-trenches and bivvy-holes. About midday we moved further in, ready to discharge vehicles on to pontoons stretching to the beach, the water being too deep (seven to nine feet) to permit an attempted wet landing. Then the shelling began – German batteries got the range of the beach and sent over air-bursts and shells, most of which whistled over and landed in the water sending up a shower of spray, but some of them were near misses, bursting with an ear-splitting crack near the boat; if you were below on the tank-deck it seemed like inside a huge bell as shrapnel clanged against the hull. Later a plane dived with lightning suddenness – machine-gun bullets spattered on the deck and two bombs dropped in the woods above the beach. Our boat had to have two attempts at ramming its keel over a sand-bar to get up against the pontoons, and finally at 5 pm we crawled slowly over the pontoons; every vehicle was preceded by a tank which pulled and dragged it across the soft wet sand and up the slope, to the wood. A batch of German prisoners stood at the top of the slope silently surveying the scene – tall youths in field-grey and some wearing those grotesque tin hats. In the wood an MDS* was already up and signs pointing to concentration areas were nailed up on road-side.

---

* Main Dressing Station: see Glossary, page xvi.

fences. A wonderfully good piece of organisation all of it. Cruisers of the Navy stood some miles off-shore doing some heavy shelling – every few minutes tongues of flame leapt from their huge guns, tremendous explosions followed and shells screamed across the sky to cause some little trouble on the Appian Way. We halted for the night about a mile and a half inland, and the work of unloading boats went on all night.

Kesselring's headquarters, some thirty miles north of Rome, had learnt of the landings at 4 a.m., alerted by a German Railway Engineer corporal, who was stationed in Anzio, supervising the supply of timber, cut from the Bosco. He set off on his motor-cycle to find the nearest German unit and did not find one before he met an officer on his way to join his unit, who gave the news to the German town commandant of Albano, who telephoned to Kesselring's headquarters. The latter informed the German High Command in Berlin, who, judging it to be the opening of a new front, immediately put into effect a plan to reinforce Italy from Germany and France, leaving Kesselring free to use his own reserves, which he promptly did. Recalling General Schlemm's headquarters of 1st Parachute Corps from the southern end of the GUSTAV line, where it had been sent as a reinforcement, he gave him three battle groups, totalling seven infantry battalions, a reconnaissance battalion and an engineer company, drawn from the area round Rome. On the following day he made General von Mackensen's Fourteenth Army responsible for sealing off the landings and subsequently driving them back into the sea, for which by 26 January von Mackensen had six divisions, with two more on their way.

The effect of this sharp German reaction was felt when patrols of 3rd US Division, probing forward from the Mussolini Canal towards Cisterna on 24 January, were repulsed by troops of the Hermann Goering Panzer Division, and when patrols of 5th Grenadier Guards from 24th Guards Brigade, ordered to Albano, found Carroceto, a village three miles up the road towards Campoleone station, held by 3rd Panzer Grenadier Division.

Lucas, strengthened by the arrival of the first elements of 45th US Division, was now prepared to release 1st British Division from its reserve role, and on 25 January ordered the division to 'probe towards' Albano, while 3rd US Division did the same towards Cisterna. Alexander and Clark visited the beachhead that day, which saw 5th Grenadier Guards capture Carroceto and Aprilia. They and the 1st Irish Guards were counter-attacked there next day, but managed to hold their positions, suffering a fair number of casualties in doing so. Lance-Corporal E. P. Danger was a clerk at Battalion Headquarters of the 5th Grenadiers. His diary for that day records:

Only 19 of 3 Company managed to get back, in a very dazed state. A few more turned up later but it appeared that one whole platoon had been taken prisoner and some had been taken back in tanks so that we could not shoot at them. At Bn HQ the situation was fairly quiet but casualties were heavy and there was plenty for me to do. Rations were coming up OK and the only shortage was mortar ammunition due to the fact that the Germans had bombed the Anzio port area pretty heavily and blown up an ammunition dump. We were on American K rations which were similar to our Compo but which consisted of one box, per man, per meal. Each meal consisted of a number of little things like a tin of ham, biscuits, sugar, cigarettes, some special chocolate and a bag of coffee. They made a change but you soon tired of them and particularly of the biscuits; these tasted to me like chewing gum.

January 27. We had a quiet night but this morning the CO* was wounded in the foot. He did his best to carry on but it is difficult to command a Bn lying on your back. The second in command† had been wounded on 25 January and command devolved on the senior major‡ who had also been slightly wounded. He was a comparatively elderly man and he felt the strain a good deal I think.

January 28. The Brigadier§ came up this morning and ordered the CO to hospital. Then things began to get pretty hectic. We were being very heavily shelled and we had a very busy half hour when our ammunition dump was hit. Fortunately we managed to put out the flames before too much damage was done but the rest had to go underground in a hurry. Tactically the situation was a little easier but still very active and the command post was a milling mass all day. Our artillery support was excellent but the more artillery you have,

* Lieutenant-Colonel Geordie Gordon-Lennox.
† Major John Nelson.
‡ Major 'Eusty' Miller.
§ Brigadier A. S. P. Murray.

the more OPs there have to be and OPs were fair game for the Jerry gunners. They were particularly anxious to knock off the OP in the bell tower and we got the benefit of their efforts. Lack of sleep was beginning to tell a bit; it was impossible to practice by day and by night we were too busy. Shelling became progressively heavier and we were now being shelled with a heavy gun firing 250 lbs shells. We recovered one shell intact and found it to be 170mm calibre, which is big. This gun was very accurate and the shell landed on target practically every time. We found afterwards that it was mounted on a railway truck.

We had moved the command post permanently into the garage and were reasonably safe except from a direct hit. Tea was a great standby and as we had plenty of supplies we had an almost continuous brew up. We also caught some chickens and cooked them in the intervals between the shells falling. The heavy shelling was beginning to shake us up a bit and there were a number of casualties. During the afternoon someone rushed in to say that some ammunition boxes next to a petrol dump were on fire. He dashed out again with a fire extinguisher but at the precise moment a shell landed and took his leg off and by this time things were well ablaze. We ventured out amongst the exploding ammunition and tried to shift as many cans of petrol as we could but most of them had been holed, they leaked and spread the blaze. Before long the whole lot was well alight and we had to beat a hasty retreat. There was a danger that the blazing petrol would spread to our main ammunition dump and blow the whole lot sky high and, with it, a number of men sheltering in the cellars. Fortunately the wind kept the flames in the other direction.

But this troubled day was not yet over. There was a signal that we were to attack that night and the Foresters were to take over our position. The CO took his officers out on a recce and the party ran into the German lines in error with the result that 5 officers were killed. This was a pretty bad blow and it seemed impossible for the Bn to take the position allotted to it, having lost all its Coy Commanders and in the present state of tiredness and bomb happiness. Accordingly the Adjutant dashed off to Bde to try and call off the attack and, by a stroke of luck, a message was received while he was on his way, to the effect that the position was held by 40 German tanks. Had we gone in the Bn would have been annihilated.

In the meantime, of course, plans had to go ahead and we had to be prepared to let the other people move in. Everyone was dashing around like demented beings and by the time we did move, I and everyone else was exhausted. Eventually it was decided that we withdraw slightly for the night and we marched back a few miles to a field which was very cold and damp, but at least a bit of a rest. Bn HQ was in a house which, amazingly, was still occupied by its Italian owners and at 0400 we did get some sleep and did not wake until 0900 on 29 January.

Meanwhile 3rd US Division had made little progress towards Cisterna. During the next few days Alexander urged Clark to get Lucas to advance to Velletri, Clark's reaction being to urge Lucas to capture Cisterna and Campoleone in order to strengthen his beachhead against possible counter-attack. 24th Guards Brigade attacked northwards from Aprilia on the night of 29/30 January and fought their way to within a mile of the railway at Campoleone station. 3rd British Brigade then passed through them and, against increasing opposition, secured a line just short of the railway. On their left, 1st US Armoured Division, which had also arrived by that time, had been ordered to advance north-westwards to the Via Laurentia, leading to Rome between the railway and the coast, but that involved attempting to cross a series of ravines and they made no progress. On the right, 3rd US Division launched a series of attacks towards Cisterna, also against increasing opposition, but were still a mile from the town on 31 January when Alexander again visited the beachhead, staying until 2 February. He realized that a pause was needed before a full-scale attack to press forward again could be launched – 3rd US Division had suffered 3,000 and 1st British 2,100 casualties since landing. Lucas meanwhile ordered both divisions to organize the positions they had gained for defence in order to meet German attacks which he believed, correctly as it turned out, to be imminent. It left 1st British Division with an awkward and potentially vulnerable salient up to Campoleone, held by 3rd and 24th Guards Brigades.

First Battle of Cassino

Meanwhile Clark had resumed the offensive on the main front. The principal effort was made by 2nd US Corps and most of the burden borne by its 34th Division, while the 36th licked its wounds. The division was to cross the Rapido north of the barracks at Monte Villa, a mile north of Cassino town, and swing round along the ridges to outflank the town and the monastery, heading south for Route 6. One regiment from 36th Division, the 142nd, would move wider round the right flank, linking up with the French. The right-hand regiment of the 34th would seize the village of Cairo before turning south along the ridge of Monte Castellone and Colle San Angelo, heading for Albaneta Farm. The attack began on 24 January, and it was some days before the leading regiments, with tanks to support them, were in any strength across the river; but by the 31st Cairo had been taken and all three regiments were ready to start fighting their way southwards towards the monastery. The original German garrison of Cassino, the 44th Division, had been reinforced by part of the 71st, and von Senger, who had succeeded Hube in command of 14th Panzer Corps, brought a battle group from 90th Panzer Grenadier Division up from the Garigliano front opposite 10th Corps to strengthen the defences. Two weeks of extremely tough fighting in atrocious weather brought the 34th Division to the last of the high ground immediately north of the monastery and into the northern outskirts of the town. The right-hand regiment, the 135th, had successfully cleared the ridge of Monte Castellone and reached Colle San Angelo, where the 142nd from 36th Division passed through them to Albaneta Farm, which they reached, but could not hold. But by this time 34th Division had shot its bolt. Casualties since 24 January numbered 318 killed, 1,641 wounded and 392 missing, and those who survived were utterly exhausted.

North of this attack the French Expeditionary Corps had been switched from their thrust towards Atina to an attack on Montes Belvedere and Abate, two miles north of Cairo, in the hope that this would draw off German troops from opposing 2nd US Corps. They secured the former after a fierce action by 27 January and had reached and almost taken the latter by the same time, having beaten off several counter-attacks. A further one threw them off Abate, but Belvedere was held. Casualties were heavy; one regiment, the 4th Tunisian Tirailleurs, which had borne the brunt of the fighting, lost 15 officers and 264 soldiers killed, 800 wounded and 400 (including 6 officers) missing. All the company commanders were casualties. Down in the south McCreery had moved 46th Division into his restricted bridgehead over the Garigliano, and they began to enlarge it, capturing a series of hills which overlooked the river where it turned north; but the bridges over it south-west of that remained under enemy observation and could only be crossed in daylight by a lavish use of smoke. McCreery's hopes of expanding the bridgehead further were dashed by being ordered, on 30 January, to send one brigade from 56th Division to Anzio and the rest of the division on 9 February, after which he reverted to the defensive.

Anzio again

The need for reinforcement at Anzio had been brought about by German attacks on the beachhead. Von Mackensen's plan was to eliminate 1st British Division's salient as a preliminary step to a full-scale attempt to throw the Allies back into the sea, the main thrust of the latter to be on the line of the Via Anziate, on which the salient lay, and his first attack to pinch it off was made on 3 February. At that time 3rd Brigade held positions just south of the railway at Campoleone with 1st Duke of Wellington's and 1st King's Shropshire Light Infantry in the front line and 2nd Sherwood Foresters in reserve. Behind them the left flank of the salient, in broken scrub-covered hills, was held by 24th Guards Brigade (from north to south, 1st Irish Guards, 1st Scots Guards, 5th Grenadier Guards and 2nd North Staffordshires), and the right by 2nd Brigade with 6th Gordons, 1st Reconnaissance Regiment and 1st Loyals. The US 157th Infantry Regiment from 45th US Division had moved in to the left of 1st Division along the Fosso della Moletta down to the coast. The Germans attacked the rear flanks of 3rd Brigade from the east, west and south-west, with a total of six battalions from 3rd Panzer Grenadier and 65th Infantry Divisions. Fighting was fierce and confused, but this very vulnerable position could not be held for long, and, under cover of a counter-attack by 2nd Brigade, reinforced by the 1st London Irish from the newly arrived 168th Infantry Brigade (of 56th Division) and two squadrons of the Sherman tanks of 46th Royal Tank Regiment, 3rd Brigade was withdrawn, leaving 24th Guards Brigade and 2nd Brigade holding Aprilia and Carroceto, where the road and railway crossed a disused railway line. Casualties had been high, totalling 1,400, the Irish Guards being reduced to a strength of only 270.

3rd US Division's sector had also been attacked, but not so strongly, and General Truscott's men held their positions. Morale generally was not improved by General Lucas issuing orders for the preparation of defences back on the line of the original beachhead perimeter, a precaution which was instrumental in leading to his replacement later by Truscott. General Penney's 1st Division was not to enjoy much respite. On 6 February 3rd US Division's front was attacked by troops from 71st Infantry and 26th Panzer Divisions, who threw back Truscott's outposts, but lost almost all the ground they had gained to the latter's counter-attacks. By this time Penney had brought 168th Brigade into the front line immediately east of the Via Anziate, with 1st London Irish holding Aprilia, 10th Berkshires on their right and 1st London Scottish in reserve. 24th Guards Brigade, west of the road, held Carroceto and Buonriposo Ridge, and 2nd Brigade was on the right, linking up with 3rd US Division. The German attack was commanded by General Schlemm's 1st Parachute Corps. He planned to assault the Guards Brigade sector with the 65th Division's two grenadier regiments of six battalions; 168th Brigade's sector with a battle group from 76th Panzer Corps, consisting of two grenadier regiments from 715th Division and 104th Panzer Grenadier Regiment, a total of nine battalions; and 2nd Brigade's sector with a battle group from 71st Division, while the 26th Panzer and Hermann Goering Panzer Divisions made diversionary attacks against 3rd US Division. The attack was launched after dark on 7 February and met with determined resistance, in which Major W. P. Sidney of 5th Grenadier Guards gained a Victoria Cross, and, although Buonriposo Ridge was lost, most of the main positions were held. Von Mackensen reinforced Schlemm with 3rd Panzer Grenadier Division and renewed the attack on the following evening, driving the London Irish out of

Aprilia after a strenuous struggle. A further attack on the next night, 10/11 February, pushed the Scots Guards out of Carroceto, after which Penney withdrew the division's front to the neck of the salient at the Flyover Bridge, two miles south of Carroceto. Lance-Corporal Danger's diary describes his experience (its accuracy is disputed by regimental historians):

February 8. We had had fairly heavy losses, although not yet on the North Africa scale; one whole platoon was taken prisoner and a lot of the wounded were 'shock' cases. Much trouble was caused in the last attack by the virtual collapse of the Gordons [actually 2nd North Staffordshires], which put the Irish Guards in trouble; they were overrun and lost heavily.

February 9. I went back to the line after 24 hours rest and found that Bn HQ had advanced slightly and was now in a disused quarry or gully. Here tents had been set up and a Command Post was in operation, reasonably safe from shelling. I set about looking for a trench and then went to the Command Post to do some work. An attack was expected and we had three days rations in case of emergency. Sure enough, before long the forward companies reported they were being attacked and as night wore on the situation became more and more critical. A call was sent for reinforcements but none was available. 1 and 3 Companies were completely cut off; we were in wireless communication with the latter until the last. The signaller finally reported that the Germans were within a few yards and he was destroying the set. 4 Company gradually withrew under pressure and were presently around Bn HQ with 2 Company on the right; they were isolated but kept going. Then it became clear that 4 Company had been overrun and the enemy was quite close to us. The situation was serious. We had one mortar with us and this fired to great effect for some time but eventually the Germans reached the edge of the quarry and started throwing down hand grenades. This cut us off from our rations and ammunition and from a small party who were defending the Southern end of the gully. We hastily evacuated the quarry at the North end under cover of a smoke screen and took up positions on the Eastern edge of the quarry. At daylight, Jerry could be seen entrenched about 50 yards from us. Here we sat for the whole long day while Jerry fired everything he had at us, including the kitchen sink.

February 10. To make matters worse it started to rain and before long everyone was soaked. We were joined by a detachment of American Rangers who were first class, and quite fearless. As the night drew on we began to fear that we should be overrun if Jerry attacked in force. Just before dusk he put down a particularly heavy barrage and although nothing developed from this, we could see he was moving towards the gully again; we were positioned on the edge of the gully to try to fight them off. On the edge of the gully we were open to fire from every side and, what was worse, to every wind and in our sodden state it was freezing. We received orders to withdraw if we could and everything possible was piled on to a carrier which went away under cover of a smoke screen while we withdrew over the fields back to the embankment that we had left two days before. We had to abandon a good deal of kit . . .

February 11. Back on the embankment, our position was little less precarious as Jerry was now much nearer and in sight of us. However, his guns were still on the wrong side of the embankment and our dug outs were fairly safe although he sprinkled everything around and started sniping from the left. The only thing was to get into a dug out and trust to luck. An unlucky shot killed our new CO (Lt. Col Huntington) but fortunately our original second in command (Major, later Major General E. J. B. Nelson) who had been wounded earlier in the landing and evacuated to Naples, now arrived back and took command. It transpired later that he had skipped from Naples and found his way back as best he could.

That day was again pretty grim and we were thankful to hear that we were to be relieved that evening. Part of the Bn was to remain until relief turned up and the remainder were to go back that night. The party left behind were relieved the following evening and we found that we had 400 men left out of our establishment of 811. Over 300 men were missing. However, we had held up 3 German Divisions and enabled the bridgehead to be held, although things were still very critical.

While these attacks were in progress, the US Chiefs of Staff were becoming concerned that the Italian theatre was turning into a campaign of attrition, and Churchill was badgering Wilson and Alexander with questions about why Lucas's forces were not advancing towards the Alban Hills when nearly 18,000 vehicles had been landed. Signals flashed to and fro, but the only matter on which all were agreed was that Lucas must go. A roundabout way of getting rid of him was used, similar to that which had been employed to get rid of his predecessor, Dawley, after Salerno. Truscott and Evelegh (from 78th British Division) would both be made Deputy Commanders of 6th US Corps. A little later Lucas would be made Deputy Commander to Clark at Fifth Army, and Truscott would replace him in command of 6th Corps while Evelegh would be found another job. This game of musical chairs was put into effect when Truscott replaced Lucas on 22 February. After three weeks at the headquarters of Fifth Army, Lucas left for the USA, where he was given command of an army. Major T. de F. Jago, Royal Artillery, had joined the artillery staff of Lucas's headquarters on 6 February and recorded his impressions:

> At first I found much at Corps HQ of which to be critical – criticisms which I still think are justified. There was no coordination between different branches of the Staff, – they worked in extraordinary watertight compartments, & one branch, such as the arty, did not know what another, such as G3 (ops) were doing. There were far too many senile officers, of the rank of full colonel and above, they were too old, no idea of the technique of modern war & lived in an atmosphere of 1917 warfare. No one seemed to like to make a decision, & the baby used to be passed on & on, with no one ready or willing to hold it, decide something & give the orders. The Corps Comd, Gen Lucas, was far too old a man, who seemed dazed by what was happening. His Chief of Staff, Gen Kaiser, was an unpleasant man. The senior arty officer was now Gen Meyer with whom I'd come up on the LST [on 6 February]. He was another old man, quite ignorant & incapable, knowing nothing of the handling of artillery in mass. He actually stopped me in the middle of 'phoning a map reference to check whether I'd not made a mistake in using the same reference to refer to a 1/50,000 map, as taken from a 1/25,000!
>
> The artillery set up was strange. The U.S. Corps HQ has no equivalent of our CCRA [Commander Corps Royal Artillery] – only an Artillery Staff Officer. Co-ordination of the div artilleries was always a delicate business, with me as either intermediary, or initiator of the orders. I was often in an unenviable position of having myself to translate into orders & give them the ideas and wishes of the

Artillery Officer. Gen Meyer retired sick after a few days & left the beachhead, Just as well. For Col Edmundson was far more capable. He was a nice little man, had the right ideas, & was sound. Furthermore he liked the British. We always got on well.

The younger officers, Major & below, were a very decent crowd. All most friendly & kind; keen as anything & efficient. The fault lay at the top. Indecision, slowness & inexperience were all there. I longed for a British Corps HQ to conduct the battle. The American artillery was good; their material excellent, & except for one or two elderly senior officers were technically v. good. Their shortcomings were (i) undeveloped system of wireless commn – nothing approaching ours (ii) inability to produce concentrations quickly in observed shooting.

General Alexander's headquarters had not been much better organized. He had been reluctant to establish a proper Army Group headquarters and tried to exercise command from an improvised tactical headquarters alongside that of Air Marshal Coningham's 2nd Tactical Air Force. This was back at San Spirito on the east coast near Taranto, while that of Major-General Sir Brian Robertson, responsible for logistics and personnel matters, was at Naples. Alexander and Coningham were intending to exercise command of operations round Cassino and at Anzio from a train near Caserta, where the eighteenth-century palace of the Bourbon Kings of Naples and Sicily had been earmarked for Allied Force Headquarters, which it was planned should eventually move there from Algiers. An example of the informality of Alexander's headquarters is given by Squadron Leader A. R. Thomas, RAF, whose Special Liaison Unit was responsible for handling the very secret ULTRA intelligence. Having described his journey from Sicily to join Alexander's headquarters at San Spirito, he continues:

We established our unit in a large and very knocked about villa on the beach south of San Spirito. General Alexander had taken another villa for his personal use less than 200 yards away. So fortunately he was very close, as most of our signals came through at night. One often got signals which were called 'Eyes only' signals which meant that they had to be seen by the addressees only and it was here that once in the middle of the night I had one such signal which I had to read to Alexander personally. I put some clothes on and set off down the beach and when I got to his villa I couldn't see any sign of sentries at all. I thought that if I made a noise they'd probably come rushing round and have a shot at me, so I decided to go quietly straight in. To my amazement the door was open and I walked in and found him fast asleep in bed. I never saw anybody else there at all. On these occasions when I had to wake up the General he would usually raise himself on one elbow, read the message and if it was something fairly startling he would raise one eyebrow and say, 'Alright, Tommy, I'll deal with that shortly.' On this particular occasion I never saw anybody else in the villa at all. I think possibly he was so careless of personal danger that he may not have had sentries. However, I didn't say anything about it in case I got somebody into trouble.

When Lieutenant-General Harding arrived at the beginning of January to take over from Major-General Richardson as chief of staff, he had some difficulty in persuading Alexander that it was essential for him to have a proper Army Group headquarters which Robertson must join. The obvious place was the Caserta palace. After much discussion with Allied Force Headquarters, the latter agreed that Alexander's staff could move into the top floor, Alexander and Harding themselves occupying a villa nearby. One of the first arrivals at the new headquarters was the lady who later became Mrs K. P. Mannock, then a major in the Auxiliary Territorial Service, as the army's women's service was then called. She was a staff officer on the personnel side and had been working in Robertson's headquarters in Naples. She described the move:

Mark took us to our new office and there laid out on our desks were the files we had left behind us on the previous morning in Naples. We were very impressed. At first we despaired of ever finding our way round this enormous building. The fragmentation of vast rooms by partitions had created a muddling sort of maze through which one wandered trying to imagine what it might have looked like in its original shape. As for work, I regard myself as having been very lucky in my share-out of work. I found it absorbingly interesting and, by the time we reached Caserta, I was very busy indeed. One aspect of the work particularly pleased me; the daily contact with an increasing number of offices. Personal relationship with my opposite number in Branches and Services was of the greatest importance and I enjoyed these friendly – and sometimes not so friendly – comings and goings. Thus, I spent a great deal of time going up and down flights and flights of stairs, crossing courtyards. I am sure it kept me very fit and very soon I could have found my way round the maze of Caserta blindfold . . .

Our new quarters were a very definite improvement on those which we had left behind. Though no more furnished, it was a very light first floor apartment with views of the countryside as a change from the sea. It was in a dusty street but all Caserta seemed dusty. The great attraction was the bathroom. Now, while there was a water supply, there was no way of heating it from within. But there was a balcony outside the window of the bathroom. In next to no time there was a boiler on that balcony, fired with wood which produced cauldrons of delicious hot water morning and evening. Pailsful of this lovely hot water was passed through the window by our faithful maids and we felt like queens with this wonderful new commodity. Though the supply did not allow for lying down baths, we could, at least, stand in it and throw it over our bodies. It was heaven.

Another lady recruit to Caserta was June Watkins, who was a cipher officer in the Women's Auxiliary Air Force. She describes her arrival:

We drove up to Caserta and in through the palace gates to the courtyard. Here I was dumped with my bag, and someone pointed out where the WAAF transport left. There was a truck standing there, so I went up to the back and called out: 'Is this right for the WAAF mess?' 'June!' a dozen voices called out, and a forest of hands reached down to pull me aboard. Inside were A watch who had come off duty at 7.30 that evening, and Winifred Laws. I was among friends. The mess was a commandeered farm house with a row of hutments stretching out behind it into an orange grove. Topsy whom I had not seen since distant TME days took me in charge, found an empty cubicle for me, and led me into the shower room. Three women stood there, stark naked, showering. 'Ma'am, this is Watkins from Nairobi,' Topsy said. I was still wearing my cap and did not know whether to salute a completely naked woman or not. Hastily I pulled it off. 'Quite right, my girl, just what I would have done!' said the group officer. 'Hallo, so it's you', said another of the naked ladies. It was the squadron officer who had recruited me. 'Thank you, Ma'am, for arranging this posting!', I said. The group officer stopped soaping herself and peered round the edge of the partition at her colleague. 'You mean, this one actually asked to come here?' 'Obviously she does not know what she's coming to – and she probably has her reasons.' The squadron officer gave me a knowing wink. 'And who is your reason?' asked Topsy as she led me away. 'The same dishy wing-co?'. 'A Watch, of course!', I replied, but to myself I thought 'Oh, so he's here and been promoted.' 'Liar!' she said.

She was disappointed not to see 'the dishy wing-co', Peter, at breakfast in the officers' mess; but was so intrigued by new developments in deciphering machinery that she had to be reminded to go for a coffee-break:

And the first person I saw as I walked in at the door was Peter; he stood the other side of the room, the light falling on his gold blond hair. He was surrounded by a group of staff officers most of whom I remembered from Haifa. He saw me at once and crossed the room so hurriedly the others started after him. We stood there, staring at each other, we had not met for eighteen months, could not touch each other.

Sadly for her, Peter's affection had cooled. She had a shock some time later when she happened to be on an airfield when he was returning from a flight, which was overdue. She feared the worst, but the aircraft did eventually turn up, to everyone's relief.

Failure to return was only too frequent an event, as the reminiscences of Aircraftman G. C. Tylee relate. He served in the ground crew of a Spitfire squadron, most of the operations of which were in support of Tito's partisans in Yugoslavia. He was based at Foggia in January 1944 and wrote:

It was ground guns, not enemy aircraft, that took its toll of our pilots. One tubby Welsh Sgt. Pilot nicknamed Caacho was flying at number two and was just releasing his bombs from 50 feet when his number one's bombs exploded under him and Caacho dissolved into thin air along with his Spitfire. Another pilot, Sgt. Callaghan was shot down, his chute opening just before he hit the deck. Not knowing which way to run, he was lucky in his choice and ran towards the partisans. Hard pressed by Jerry, they removed some stones from a thick wall and pushed him inside. The stones were replaced, and the partisans, who never fought pitched battles, retreated, leaving him there entombed for 2 days before they came back to release him and start him on his journey back to his Squadron. Other N.C.O. pilots, having a day out in Bari a couple of days later, using a Jeep they had bought from the Yanks for a case of whisky, were astonished to see Callaghan sauntering down the gang plank of a Royal Navy destroyer which had brought him back to Italy. Instead of stopping to congratulate him on his safe return, they had to hurry back to Foggia to return his kit and private possessions which they had 'borrowed', before he returned to camp and found them missing.

Another N.C.O. pilot, Alan Oates, had his glycol tank holed while straffing. Seeing the engine temperature gauge rise alarmingly, he pulled his Spitfire up to 3,000 feet and baled out. First, jettisoning the hood, then opening the door, he slid out over the rear of the port main plane, making a good exit. Another pilot on the same raid had to leave his aircraft rapidly, but he opened his chute too soon and it caught on the tail plane, dragging him to his death, while yet another pilot forgot to jettison his hood before he jumped, and his unopen chute caught on the hood fastener. By the time he had struggled free he was too close to the ground, and crashed with his aircraft. Alan landed safely and made for the hills. Within an hour he was picked up by the partisans, but it took him 6 weeks to return to our Squadron. He and several American airmen were eventually picked up by a Dakota and flown to Italy. He was later commissioned, and being a good football player he became Squadron Sports Officer in his spare time.

Another recruit to Caserta was Lavinia Holland-Hibbert, then a captain in the ATS. She wrote:

The next day was my first day in the office with my G2,* Major Whittle. We were rather shy of each other. I answered all questions about locations which people asked. I have a huge file called 'Order of Battle Italy' in which every unit in the force is listed under its command and that is my Bible. Daily I flick over the pages looking for 21 Field Park Company, No. 2 Mobile Bath Unit or 1st/2nd Buffs. The G1 apparently thinks we are OK as he sent in a report somewhere

---

* G2. General Staff Officer Grade 2, a major; G1, General Staff Officer Grade 1, a lieutenant-colonel.

saying we were highly intelligent and settling down well. He apparently fears we may disrupt the office and gave us a little talk at the conference about how we should be absorbed into the Operational Headquarters as if we were men and no concessions made, which is of course what we want. So far none of the many people who come into the office appear to regard me with any surprise, but the others say that when they announce, 'Staff Captain A here' the people at the other end of the telephone say: 'But may I speak to a *staff* officer, please.'

She was impressed by General Robertson and even more so by his South African ADC. Being well connected – her uncle, Lieutenant-General Sir Bertram Sergison-Brooke, was head of the British Red Cross in Italy – she moved easily in Guards and Cavalry circles, but after a time got bored with going to parties in rest villas or Officers' Clubs most nights of the week, as she wrote:

As time went on these parties always seemed to end in the same way as Jack or Bill or Ralph or whoever who had taken one got lit up on the very cheap wine and made less and less sense and got more and more amorous; we, avoiding drink and going to these parties every day, longed to go to bed and so it ended, 'For God's sake, take me home, why will you never take me home when I want go, I'm bored with you all.' Sometimes I just found a bed and lay down.

Thirty miles to the north-west life was very different for the members of 9 Commando in the 2nd Special Service Brigade. They had got back to base near Naples from Anzio on 26 January, and on the 30th received orders to take part in an operation at the extreme northern sector of 10th Corps's bridgehead over the Garigliano. Its aim was to extend the perimeter in the mountains further in order to deny the Germans observation of the bridges over the river. Les Callf was commanding No. 10 Section in No. 5 Troop, and this is his account of the operation:

About 1900 hrs Wednesday 2nd February, we moved off in agonizing slowness in single file. Order of march was 4 Troop, Adv. H.Q. 2, 1, H.Q., 6, 5 or 6 R.A. personnel, and 5 Troop. We proceeded round the right shoulder of M. Turlito, down into the valley which sheltered Bde H.Q., and where 3 Troop waited in reserve to give us support from M. Tuga [actually Fuga]. A fatigue party had carried stores,

ammo. etc. to the top of M. Tuga the previous day and returned at
18.30 hrs. keeping approx. to the 500 ft. The column slowly wound
its way round the east side of M. Tuga. Artillery fire was falling all
along the column and voices could be heard calling out in the valley
to the East. Spasmodic bursts of T.S.M.G.* and Rifle fire also came
from the valley. An L shaped fire was alight during the whole of our
travels. Artillery fire was falling fairly thickly in the hollow ground
between M. Tuga and M. Ornito but no casualties were maintained.
The path along which we travelled considerably helped the speed of
the column and the moon gave an excellent light for contact. Boots
however were making much noise on the rocks. At approx. the same
height the column moved North along the East side of M. Ornito
while certain of No. 43 [43 RM Commando] turned West up to the
summit of M. Ornito. The Artillery fire increased in accuracy and
strength, and casualties were taken in the valley between M. Ornito
and the feature immediately to the North. Being in the rear Troop,
we were rather out of touch with movement at the head of the
column. The artillery that was missing the forward troops was falling
amongst us at the rear, but owing to our snake formation being
approx. in the direction of the fire, a direct hit was needed to inflict
serious casualties.

Owing to the extreme slowness of the column, I was constantly
moving up to 6 Troop to make certain that continuous contact
was being maintained, and when our position was precarious in
the valley, I contacted Capt. Templeton at Cmdo. H.Q. in order to
ascertain why we were making for different objectives. At the time I
concluded that the enemy had been located on this more Northerly
feature, and that we were clearing same prior to taking Charles (M.
Faito). Sgt. Wade and Pte McGowan (the latter uncertified) were
killed and several wounded in this valley. Our position was now
8660–37 and we proceeded up the valley in approx. westerley [sic]
direction, still under considerable artillery fire. The column now
attacked the feature to the N.W. across the bare saddle and on to
the forward part of 751 feature. Casualties were heavier still and the
Commando prepared to attack M. Faito (our objective) from the
North. We (the whole column) were still under considerable artillery
fire and during the considerable wait on this feature, we prepared

* Thompson sub-machine-gun.

hasty sangers and scraped hollows under the steepest part of the rising slopes. The forward Troop was presumably occupying the summit of the feature. Word came for 5 Troop to move up and take over the lead, so we proceeded past 6 Troop in single file. As we moved off, 6 Troop also started to move up and when we arrived at the summit, the two Troops were mixed together. The moon had now sunk and visibility was extremely difficult as we cursed and shepherded the Troop into position (single file) on the slope facing South, ready to advance on Charles.

After a considerable delay (absolutely unavoidable) No. 10 Section followed by Troop H.Q. & 9 were strung out in single file down the hill. We were ordered to advance 100 yds, and wait and soon after, another 100 yrds. At this moment a very heavy concentration of Mortar and/or Artillery fire fell amongst the Commando. Two L.M.G.'s and about six scattered riflemen had opened fire on the column just previous to the above concentration. Heavy casualties occurred along the whole line and momentary confusion ensued in the darkness. The enemies' L.M.G. positions were approximately 70 yds away, and their positions could be judged owing to their total use of tracers. One position was immediately to our front and the other was in the vicinity of the house slightly to our right. I had with me an assault team of four led by Cpl. Bostock, an L.M.G. team led by Cpl. Dickenson, my section Sgt. and runner, and one man from the mortar team.

We had pushed on down the gulley immediately we were fired on, and the L.M.G. team opened fire on the right position. The assault team spread out and engaged the front L.M.G. and the E.Y. Rifleman* fired three No. 36s on the right L.M.G. (one failed to explode, the other two were good shots and definitely silenced the position for about one or two minutes. Justified my belief in the weapon). I was going to push my other sub-section on to the right hand L.M.G. but they failed to advance with us and were presumably taking cover from the 'stonk' higher up the gulley. (The L.M.G. group under Cpl. Banbury was, I found out later, returning fire from higher up). I shouted for, and then sent a spare man back, to tell them to push on down to us. Mortar fire was still falling thickly and 6 Troop had now sent three flares up. In between the flares we

---

* The rifleman detailed to fire grenades from his rifle.

continued our advance and, sending my runner back to tell 6 Troop to attack right hand L.M.G. by the house. We continued advancing and attacked and over-ran the front enemy position by the light of the third mortar flare.

I left Sgt. Craig and one other to guard the two prisoners taken at the post and pushed forward with L/Cpl. Bostock's team on to the forward slopes of Charles. We could hear 6 Troop behind us and to our right, and I shouted our position to them, telling them to keep to the right of the house which they attacked. They sustained one killed and two injured by a determined enemy armed with a machine pistol, who fired at point blank range and then managed to escape. I called to 6 Troop to form up on our right for advancing up the slopes of Charles, and Sgt. Reace, who led their assault, brought about 5 O.R.s up to our position.

Sgt. Craig was interrogating the prisoners, one of whom spoke fair English, and learned there was a regt. close by to the West, but that Charles was unoccupied. L/Cpl. Bostock and his team pushed forward 300 yds up the hill as advance patrol. We were still out of touch with the remainder of the Troop, but a voice from up the gulley behind us now ordered us to withdraw. I replied that the positions had now been overcome, and we were on the forward slopes of the objective, ready to advance. Capt.Templeton now joined me and was able to communicate back by wireless, and it was confirmed that we were to withdraw to Laycock (Ornito).

With difficulty they managed to make their way back, bringing the wounded with them, and reached a defensive position at 'Laycock' shortly before dawn. The Commandos, both 9th and 43rd RM, were relieved by the 5th Hampshires in 46th Division's 138th Brigade on 3 February. Of the 19 officers and 350 other ranks who had started off, 12 and 170 were casualties. The Hampshires attempted to advance the line by an attack on the night of 7 February and 6th Lincolns twice reached M. Faito but, on both occasions, were forced back to M. Ornito. After that, 10th Corps went over to the defensive, 56th Division having been taken out of the line and transferred to Anzio.

5

Second and Third Cassino Battles

February to March 1944

The critical situation at Anzio, in addition to demands from the US Chiefs of Staff for a greater effort against the GUSTAV line, persuaded Alexander that the attack to open up the entrance to the Liri valley must be urgently pressed. He had already begun to form an army group reserve by transferring first the New Zealand Division and then the 4th Indian from Eighth Army to the Fifth Army sector, forming a New Zealand Corps, commanded by Freyberg, who handed command of his division over to Brigadier H. K. Kippenberger. 78th Division was also to be transferred, but had not yet moved. Alexander's plan was to hand this corps over to Mark Clark's Fifth Army for him to use it in a renewed attempt to open up the Liri valley at Cassino.

When Freyberg first considered the task, he proposed a wider flanking movement than that used by the 2nd US Corps. 4th Indian Division would advance on a broad front through the mountains south of the French, who would also advance. Meanwhile one New Zealand brigade would thrust down from Maiola to Albaneta Farm and Point 593 at the end of Snake's Head Ridge, to the west of the monastery. The other New Zealand infantry brigade and their armoured brigade would be concentrated east of the Rapido below Cassino, ready to force a crossing and thrust up the Liri valley, when operations in the mountains had succeeded.

But this plan, approved of both by the French and by 4th Indian Division's very experienced commander, Major-General Francis Tuker, was abandoned in favour of a much less ambitious one. 4th Indian was to take over the forward positions which 34th US Division had reached, which it was believed included Point 593, capture the area of the monastery and from there descend its southern and eastern slopes to cut Highway 6 and join hands, in the southern outskirts of Cassino, with the

New Zealand Division, which would have crossed the River Rapido by the railway embankment to capture the station. Meanwhile 34th US Division would hold its positions in the northern outskirts of the town. 4th Indian was to start its attack on the monastery from Point 593 on the night of 13/14 February.

Tuker did not like this plan for a direct frontal assault on well-prepared defences; but he was suffering from one of his recurrent bouts of malaria and had to hand over command of his division to his Commander Royal Artillery, Brigadier H. K. Dimoline. However, as he did so, he insisted to Freyberg that the plan should include destruction of the monastery by air attack which, he said, '*must* be used in its *fullest* weight and concentrated and coordinated with artillery and ground small arms'. Freyberg himself had suggested this on 9 February to Clark, who was not in favour. Badgered ceaselessly by Tuker, Freyberg tried again on the evening of 12 February. Clark was away at Anzio and he spoke to the Fifth Army chief of staff, Major-General Alfred M. Gruenther, who, in the absence of Clark, referred it to Alexander through the latter's chief of staff, Harding, explaining that Clark himself was not in favour. That reference was necessary as an agreement had been reached in December 1943 with the Vatican that neither the monastery nor the Pope's summer residence, Castel Gandolfo in the Alban Hills, would be attacked, the Germans having assured the Vatican that they would not occupy either place. However Eisenhower at the time, passing this information on to his subordinates, wrote:

> If we have to choose between destroying a famous building and sacrificing our own men, then our men's lives count infinitely more and the buildings must go. But the choice is not always so clear-cut as that. In many cases the monuments can be spared without any detriment to operational needs. Nothing can stand against the argument of military necessity. That is an accepted principle. But the phrase 'military necessity' is sometimes used where it would be more truthful to speak of military convenience or even of personal convenience. I do not want to cloak slackness or indifference . . .

Part of the estate of Castel Gandolfo had been bombed in error on 1 and 2 February, causing many casualties among the people sheltering there. The sanctity of the monastery at Cassino arose from its connection with the foundation of the Benedictine order. It was established on the hill outside Cassino in AD 529 by the forty-eight-year-old Roman noble known as Benedict. With twelve fellow monks he erected an oratory dedicated to St Martin of Tours, replacing a temple of Apollo, which they destroyed; and there he died in 543 at almost the same time as his twin sister Scholastica, a nun in a nearby convent. This was at a time when Christendom, based on Rome, was at its lowest ebb, what remained of the Western Roman Empire having crumbled away under the attacks of the Vandals. It was not in Rome that its scholarship was to be preserved, but in the monasteries which spread outwards from Benedict's foundation on the mount which overlooked Cassino, former playground of Mark Antony, and the junction of the rivers Liri and Rapido. The destruction of 1944 was not the first. The Lombards sacked the original foundation in 589, the Saracens its successor in 884 and the Normans its replacement in 1030. The building destroyed in 1944 was largely completed between 1649 and 1717.

Alexander's response to Freyberg's request, passed to Gruenther by Harding, was that, if Freyberg regarded it as a military necessity, it should go ahead. Freyberg stuck to his guns, as did Alexander when Clark remonstrated to him on the morning of the 13th. It was finally approved by General Maitland Wilson in Algiers. When the destruction of the monastery gave rise to considerable controversy after the war, Tuker wrote this defence of the line he had taken:

> When 4th Indian first came across from the Adriatic coast late in January the N.Z. Corps was planning more or less to turn the Cassino features by using the first alternative, that is to say, the operation from the north. That was what we wanted. Very soon, however, for some reason, they started planning to capture Cassino itself, i.e. the town and the monastery and Point 593. This, of course, amounted to a major operation rather than one which would achieve the necessary threat only. We argued that to bring this off would require a combination of both the northern attack and the river crossing. We considered this to be a big undertaking, but within the resources of the New Zealand, 4th Indian and 78th Divisions, because the Army artillery would have full play for all natures of gun from heavy to field on the Gari crossing. Strangely, the Fifth Army seems to have turned this down and to have insisted that the Cassino features should be taken by direct attack. We pointed out then that there was only one way of taking these features in this way and that was by

drenching them by heavy air bombardment over a term of days, following up with heavy artillery bombardment at dusk and immediate infantry attack early in the night. But, we pointed out, unless the heavy air bombardment could be guaranteed and the garrison reduced to imbecility, the plan of direct attack on the Monte Cassino features should be abandoned and the first course of the northern and the Gari river attack adopted. I went on arguing this from hospital by letter through my divisional headquarters.

The smallness of the monastery as a target and the proximity of our own troops made clear weather essential for the attack. That was forecast for 15 February, after which it would deteriorate. That morning was therefore selected.

Meanwhile Brigadier O. de T. Lovett's 7th Indian Infantry Brigade, which was to lead the assault, was in difficulties. The track which led from San Michele, crossing the Rapido by a Bailey bridge, to their forward concentration area at the village of Cairo was so bad that only jeeps and mules could be used for transport, and both were in short supply. As it was under enemy observation by day, it could only be used at night. The same applied to the route forward from Cairo to the American position at Point 593, a distance of 4,000 yards, on which not even jeeps could be used. It was no more than a goat track and by then a very slippery one. Almost everything had to be carried forward by soldiers used as porters. To make matters worse, 1st Royal Sussex, the leading battalion, found that the Americans had not reached the crest of Point 593 and were in such an exhausted state that many of them had to be literally carried away. Before the attack on the Monastery Hill could be launched, 593 itself had to be cleared if enemy there were not to enfilade the attackers from that flank. It had originally been planned that the brigade would relieve the Americans on the night of 12/13 February and launch its attack on the following night, but the difficulties mentioned above, added to by a German attack on the American's right flank on 12 February, caused a twenty-four-hour postponement. The unforeseen need to launch a preliminary attack on Point 593 caused Lovett, on 14 February, to ask Dimoline, who in turn asked Freyberg, for a further postponement of the main attack until the night of 16/17 February. Freyberg reluctantly agreed to this, but, when, later in the day, on a visit to Fifth Army headquarters, he learned that the monastery was to be bombed on the 15th, he urged Dimoline to cancel the postponement, but the latter rightly refused.

So it was before even the preliminary attack on Point 593 had been launched that, preceded by leaflets warning anyone who might be sheltering there, and to the surprise of the soldiers in the front line, between 9.25 and 10.05 a.m. on 15 February, 135 Flying Fortresses of the US Army Air Force, flying at heights between 15,000 and 18,000 feet, dropped 257 tons of 500lb bombs and 59 tons of incendiaries accurately onto the monastery, followed by 47 Mitchells and 40 Marauders, dropping 283 1,000lb bombs, leaving the monastery a shattered ruin. The only casualties were some three or four hundred civilians, as there were no German soldiers inside, although there were some within a few hundred yards of it. It was not long before they occupied the ruins, which provided them with better defences than the intact building would have done, and they had nearly two days in which to prepare them before any attempt was made to attack them there.

1st Royal Sussex's attack on Point 593, made, because of lack of space, by only one company, failed at a cost of thirty-four casualties. The commanding officer, Lieutenant-Colonel Jack Glennie, tried again the following night, 16/17 February, with his whole battalion, but met heavy fire and failed again at a cost of seventy more. While these attacks had been in progress, the other battalions of the brigade, 4/16th Punjabis and 1/2nd Gurkhas, had moved up into positions on their flank and rear, and two more battalions, one from 11th Brigade, 4/6th Rajputana Rifles, and one from 5th Brigade, 1/9th Gurkhas, had joined them, all under Lovett's command. B. Smith, of the Royal Corps of Signals, was attached to Battalion Headquarters of 4/16th Punjabis and describes their move up:

A long bar of lemon light still lingered in the western sky as 'A' Company moved off and we tagged in behind not waiting for our turn with H.Q. Company. The trail passed through San Michelle, emerged from the trees, dipped downwards and swung west towards Cassino. Soon it joined a minor road and animals and men picked their way carefully between the water-filled shell holes with many a halt. The night was still and very dark. The column made its own characteristic noises: a mule snorting, the clang of an iron shod hoof on a stone, the jingle of harness, the creak of leather and the soft murmuring of men; and all the time we listened, ears attuned, senses alert even when talking to a comrade, like wild animals alive to danger. Then the quietness was broken by the rumble of approaching trucks and a convoy of big American Macs [trucks] loomed towards us. Once again our awkward brute excelled himself. He had been a nuisance by stepping out of line and trying to pass the mule in front. Cliff said he must have been a born leader. Anyhow he tried to pass again at the wrong moment, his load was given a glancing blow by a passing truck, he was tumbled into the water-filled ditch and the precious wireless set was sent flying. What a melee it was; imagine having to sort that lot out in the dark and the confusion; and all for four bob a day and the glory. But somehow we did it and dripping mud and oaths we joined the column and stumbled down the road. Half a mile short of Cassino we came to a key junction controlled by a military policeman who urged us quietly up the side road towards the hills. His was an unenviable job as that corner was a prime target and was liable to be plastered at any time of the day or night but he protected himself by directing the traffic from his dug-out at the side of the road with only his head and shoulders emerging like a tortoise. We urged the mules on for another half-mile until the hillside loomed ahead and a familiar voice checked us.

'Signals?' It was the Major, second in command of the battalion – the Mad Major we called him. 'H.Q. is in a farmhouse a quarter of a mile past the Cavalry Barracks on the left,' he said. 'The C.O.'s there – report in.' We did as ordered. The ruined building was heavily draped at door and window and the Colonel was busy with maps by the light of a storm lantern. 'Hello, Sigs,' he said. 'Shan't need you tonight, there's a strict wireless silence on. Go outside and get some rest but be near at hand.' We went outside and helped the Cypriot muleteer to unload our gear and then poked around for a hidy hole. A late quarter moon was just rising and we settled ourselves in a couple of shallow slit trenches in the lee of the building, unpacked our sleeping bags and were hopeful of a good night when it happened. A star shell went up, followed by another. As we had expected Jerry had become suspicious and soon a string of flares lit the whole valley with an eerie blue light. The hind part of the battalion was still straggling across the valley floor. They came under a heavy bombardment from guns and mortars and there were some casualties, a euphemism indeed for dead and shattered bodies. Naturally our artillery responded and the night was hideous with the moans, shrieks, whistles and bangs of projectiles in the varying stages of their separate journeys. That night we heard for the first time a new devilish machine of war, blood curdling in the extreme, as frightening as the Stukka [sic] dive bombers. It was a multi-barrel mortar, known I think as a Nebelwerfer, which spewed out six bombs at every firing. We could plainly hear them discharged a mile or so away and then seconds later the wailing began. The bombs were each fitted with a sound device that gave an unearthly warbling noise before they exploded in rapid succession. It was truly demoralising, an invention of the Devil. Gradually the din subsided, the last to go to bed being a barking dog of a twentyfiver over by Cervaro. A brooding silence descended and men rested in preparation for the ritual hate of the next day. I fell asleep in my slit trench with the smell of the damp earth in my nose, was wakened by the dawn 'stand-to' and then submerged for another hour.

Smith's signal section was due to continue its way forward next night, but had difficulty obtaining a suitable mule. Eventually they had to leave their charging set to be brought up later and to rely on two porters to help them carry their radio set and spare batteries. His account continues:

It was turned midnight and moonrise was due when our small party of four shambled past the deserted Cavalry Barracks and turned right into Death Valley. This was a steep sided valley almost a canyon at the end of which was the road head and beyond which even the nimblest jeeps couldn't go. The enemy couldn't see into it but he knew its importance and day after day in the following weeks from various points on Snake Head Hill we watched the patterned bombardment of Death Valley. It was pock-marked with shell holes and in the light of shadows from a rising moon it looked like an eerie moonscape. 'Signals Sahibs?' It was the Subadar Major, the R.S.M. of the unit. 'Follow the track up the hill to H.Q. It's a white building, Sahib, a mile away.' We slowly climbed a zig-zag path up the stony hillside on the left, not unlike climbing Rossett Ghyll from Mickleden. The rising moon behind the clouds gave sufficient light but we made slow progress because of our heavy loads. I was carrying on my pack frame a heavy wood-encased lead acid battery weighing about thirty five pounds along with my personal gear, side pack and sleeping bag. We were also greatly handicapped by unsuitable footwear, our regulation shoes studded with flat metal protectors giving little grip on the loose slippery track. From time to time we stood aside to let returning mule trains pass by, and occasionally we passed groups of American infantrymen slithering back down the hillside. After a while the steepness of the track eased and we slanted upwards and left in the general direction of the monastery across the face of the hill which we learned later was known as the 'Snake's Head'. It was by now a brilliant moonlit night; there was no sign of our H.Q.; indeed there was no sign of anybody. One of the paradoxes of battle action from our experience was the amazing contrast from pandemonium one minute to utter stillness the next. It happened to us often at Cassino. Our track had dwindled into a diverging maze of minor trails and we were confronted with a choice of routes. The two porters patiently followed without question and presumably believed that we knew where we were going. We held to the same line, uphill and westward, moving carefully, talking little and listening hard. The little trail we were following led us across the heads of two steep gullies and proceeded towards the moonlit silhouette of a long spur. Coming round a sharp corner we stopped, petrified. The ground fell away steeply in front of us into a dark void, and high above us on the opposite side rose the monastery, its whole southern face brilliantly lit by the moon. It was beautiful, a breath-taking moment before we hastily retreated back round the corner. I can't understand why we didn't receive a hail of bullets: we must have been clearly visible to the Germans dug in round the base of the walls perhaps four hundred yards away. Anyhow we had certainly ascertained our position and taking the opposite track uphill we presently spied our goal, a battered white farmhouse on a terraced hillside. The two Indian bearers quickly doffed their packs, bid us good night and disappeared. It was about four o'clock, there was no one about and we looked around for a level sleeping place. Just below the farm on a small terrace we could dimly discern a line of sleeping figures with room to spare at the end. So we joined them, unrolled our waterproof bags, used a side valise for a pillow, and dog tired we promptly fell asleep. It was broad daylight when we were awakened by shouting and laughter. Grinning down at us from the terrace wall were three gunners, friends of ours, members of the elite fraternity of artillery observers. 'Morning, Sigs,' they shouted, 'You sleep in queer company.' We looked to our left at the recumbent forms. They were all on stretchers with blankets over their faces and with their boots sticking out uncovered. We had slept with the dead, poor fellows, American dead. We grimaced and then joined the laughter. So does war debase man and so does man hide his finer feelings in sheer self protection.

Half an hour later we were established at Command Post inside the building. Our set was in order and working well; we had briefly established contact with Brigade Control; and we were already on listening watch. It had taken three busy days to reach this salient behind Cassino and it had never been dull.

In spite of the failure to clear Point 593, Dimoline planned an attack towards Monastery Hill with four battalions on the night of 17/18 February. At midnight, 4/6th Rajputana Rifles, taking three companies of the Royal Sussex also under command, would launch another attack on Point 593 and continue to Point 444 below the west face of the monastery. On their left, two hours later, 1/9th Gurkhas would attack to capture the saddle which lay between the ridge running south-east from Point 593 and the monastery, while, at the same time, 1/2nd Gurkhas would attack the monastery itself. When that had been done, the two Gurkha battalions would thrust down the far slopes of Monastery Hill to Highway 6 to join hands, it was hoped, with the New Zealand Division. The attack was to be supported by 394 guns, 144 of the US 2nd Corps artillery including 48 8-inch howitzers; but all would be firing from the other side of the Rapido at right angles to the direction of the attack. This, combined with problems of crest clearance, meant that the shells could not land immediately in front of the advancing infantry.

Both 4/6th Rajputs and 1/9th Gurkhas met heavy fire and made little progress at heavy cost, 196 casualties in the former, 94 in the latter. Neither of the objectives which would have covered the right flank having been reached, 1/2nd Gurkhas were launched into their attack, which involved crossing a gorge before climbing up to the monastery 500 yards away. Ordered to disregard their flanks and bypass anything holding them up, they plunged into a thicket of thorn bushes, infested with anti-personnel and other mines, suffering 149 casualties, including their commanding officer. All the attacks failed at a total cost of 530 casualties, and by dawn all units were back to the positions from which they had started.

The New Zealand Division had been no more successful. Kippenberger's plan was for his 28th (Maori) Battalion to cross the Rapido, advancing along the railway embankment ahead of two field companies of his engineers, who would bridge the river and repair the breaches in the embankment so that it could be used as a route forward for the Maoris' anti-tank guns and the tanks of 19th New Zealand Armoured Regiment. This force was to secure the area of the railway station and the nearby small hill, 'the Hummocks', as the first step in the advance of the rest of the division to Highway 6 and the southern outskirts of Cassino. The leading companies of 28th Battalion set off at 8.45 p.m. on 17 February, but soon became delayed by the sodden state of the ground, the mass of engineer equipment and German mortar and artillery fire. By midnight their B Company had reached the station, but A Company, due to capture 'the Hummocks', found it protected by a deep ditch which they could not cross. The engineers completed a bridge over the Rapido by 5 a.m., five hours behind schedule, but had not filled in the breaches in the embankment by first light, after which it was impossible for them to work under enemy observation. The two companies in the area of the station were therefore without their supporting arms, as they faced the certainty of a counter-attack by the German 211th Grenadier Regiment. That came at 3.15 p.m. and forced what was left of the two companies – they had suffered 130 casualties – to withdraw across the river. The Second Battle of Cassino had come to the same sticky end as the First, at a cost of 590 casualties in the 4th Indian and 226 in the New Zealand Division. During the period of both battles von Senger's 14th Panzer Corps had suffered 4,470.

Alexander's first reaction was to call it a day and pause until a major offensive, employing larger numbers than he then had available, could be launched when the weather had improved in the spring. His chief of staff, John Harding, was already persuading him to think in those terms, which Juin had been advocating for some time, but he was persuaded to have another go for several reasons: the imminence of a strong German attack on Anzio, pressure from London and Washington, the need to secure the Cassino area before any major attempt to advance up the Liri valley could start, and Freyberg's willingness to do so. A further factor was the belief of the US Army Air Force that their overwhelming strength could so weaken the enemy that just one more push could lead to a breakthrough.

Freyberg's proposal was that the New Zealand Division should attack the town of Cassino from the north, after it had been flattened by a massive air bombardment, and that, as they did so, 4th Indian Division would attack Monastery Hill from the Castle at the north-west corner of the town on the line of the winding road which led up to the monastery. Over on the right flank, still held by 7th Indian Brigade, the New Zealand engineers were to build a rough road south from the village of Cairo to Maiola, known as Cavendish Road, and continue it along 'Death Valley' sufficiently to make it possible for tanks to be sent that way to Albaneta Farm, outflanking Point 593. Alexander gave his approval on condition that the attack should be preceded by three fine days so that the ground could dry out sufficiently for tanks to be used, especially in exploitation into the Liri valley, and that visibility on the day of the attack must be such that the bombing could be accurate. All preliminary moves and preparations had been completed by 24 February, but on the previous day a spell of fine weather came to an end and conditions remained unsuitable for the next three weeks, while the unfortunate troops were stuck in their forward positions, exposed to enemy observation and fire, swept by snow and rain, soaked to the skin and shivering with cold, waiting day after day to start the operation of which few held high hopes of success. Von Senger took advantage of the pause to replace the weary 90th Panzer Grenadier Division with Major-General Heidrich's fresh and experienced 1st Parachute Division, with its Machine-Gun Regiment defending the area of the railway station, its 3rd Regiment the town and Monastery Hill, and the 4th Regiment the area west and north of that. This was the division which had successfully held up the Canadians at Ortona in December.

Anzio

While Freyberg's troops were thus frustrated, Anzio was being strongly attacked. The rest of 56th Division had been sent there to join the one brigade, 168th, already sent. They took over the left-hand sector from the coast up to a mile west of the Via Anziate, south of the Buonriposo ridge, where they joined up with the 45th US Division, which had replaced 1st British, withdrawn into reserve. Hitler attached great importance to this next attempt to throw the Allies back into the sea, giving the operation the codename FISCHFANG (Fish-catch). Von Mackensen was in command, his Fourteenth Army having Schlemm's 1st Parachute Corps and Herr's 76th Panzer Corps. The latter would provide the main attacking force with one Panzer Division (26th), two Panzer Grenadier (3rd and 29th), one Jaeger (114th) and one Infantry (715th), while the former protected the right (western) flank with 4th Parachute and 65th Infantry Divisions. The principal thrust was to be along and to the east of the Via Anziate, and it was launched punctually on the morning of 16 February, although the forces concentrated for it had been attacked with 700 tons of bombs over the preceding seventy-two hours, intelligence having accurately alerted the Allies to its imminence. Strongly supported by artillery and air attacks – priority for the latter having been switched from support of Freyberg at Cassino – 45th US Division fought stubbornly and successfully, while the Hermann Goering Panzer Division, carrying out a diversionary attack against 3rd US Division on its right, made no headway. On 17 February von Mackensen authorized Herr to commit 26th Panzer and 29th Panzer Grenadier Divisions to a renewed attack, while Lucas, to whom Truscott had now become deputy, ordered the 1st British Division, less one brigade, to a back-stop position behind the 45th at the Flyover Bridge. On that day its commander, Major-General W. R. C. Penney, was slightly wounded in the head and Templer, commander of 56th Division, assumed responsibility for both divisions until Penney returned to duty on the 23rd. 2nd Infantry Brigade placed 6th Gordons west of the bridge and 1st Loyals east of it, with the 2nd North Staffordshires in reserve:

24th Guards Brigade occupied positions to their left rear. On the following morning the Loyals found their positions forming the front line and were fiercely attacked by troops of both 26th Panzer and 29th Panzer Grenadier Divisions. They gave no ground, and by the end of the day the line was stabilized just north of the bridge, the Germans consolidating the salient they had gained, some two miles deep and five miles wide. It was ironic that this successful defence of the beachhead, a few days before Lucas was removed, had only been made possible by his initial decision not to try and rapidly extend it in the direction of the Alban Hills. Had he done so, the force which Kesselring had assembled would certainly have had little difficulty in penetrating it and cutting its link to the coast.

Gilbert Allnutt was with the 8th Royal Fusiliers in 56th Division's 167 Brigade and describes the German attack:

On the morning of 16th February 1944 dive bombers screamed through the wadi dropping bombs and spraying gun bullets in all directions. This initial attack was followed by a prolonged bombardment by shells of all varieties – including mortars. Our heads were well and truly down. A few prayers were said that morning and I imagine that His switchboard was overloaded; my own prayer was a request that I be given strength to endure and that request, it seemed, was always granted. The War History of the Royal Fusiliers shows that this attack began at 0615 hours. As the shelling eased we heard the sound of the infantry attack that followed. During the course of the morning contact was lost with the platoons as it was obvious that disaster had struck. From time to time badly shaken Fusiliers would appear – they came with stories of heavy casualties and of their good luck in getting back and escaping death or capture. Among these men who lived to fight again were Sergeant Sutch who proved invaluable in helping Major Allison and C. S. M. Raynor organise Headquarters personnel into a front line effective unit. By 1505 hours that day the Company strength read:- 1 Officer, 1 W.O., 19 N.C.O.'s and other ranks.

Major Allison placed bren guns at each end of our section while he manned the middle. I remember laying on the top of the wadi with Fusilier Wheeler, one of the escapees, feeding the magazines as he fired the bren. We could hear the enemies' cries and shouts as they kept contact and approached our position. Because of the undergrowth they never came into view. Wheeler was a stolid

Welshman. It was no time for conversation. With his eyes still firmly fixed to the front he remarked from the corner of his mouth: 'There must be better places than this – even Newport – on a Sunday!' The noise of battle rolled on – we were well aware that we were isolated and likely to be overwhelmed – but the brens kept firing and we held our ground. Later that night Major Allison received the order to withdraw and we silently left our position and made our way back to Battalion Headquarters.

Some time during the night and before the pre-dawn stand-to, we reached Battalion Headquarters. The advance Orderly Room Sergeant, The Regimental Sergeant Major and other Headquarter personnel were in trenches on the low ground of the wadi. We were directed to our positions at the top; quite a climb at night when incessant rain made the foothold difficult. On our left were members of the Battle patrol led by Captain Fanning. We soon made ourselves at home in our new surroundings but found that life was far from comfortable. Shelling was intense and the rain fell on friend and foe alike. Quartermaster David Brown ensured a regular ration supply and this included a tot of rum. Although at that time I was virtually a teetotaller I accepted the rum ration which helped keep out the cold in those long hours. An order had been given that socks must be changed daily. In view of my experience on the Volturno it was an order I was happy to comply with for I had no wish to get trench feet and the trenches were filling with water. In the low ground of the wadi the water was getting deeper and movement could be heard from our position of men sloshing their way through the water.

As a boxing enthusiast I am inclined to see situations in boxing terms. As we settled at Battalion Headquarters I noticed a change in Major Allison. I saw him as a champion boxer, of outstanding courage and resource who had now fought one fight too many. As he sat in his slit trench he looked, to use a boxing term, 'out on his feet'. The blow that had shattered him was a mental one. For the second time, he said, he had led the Company into action and lost them. He could have endured any physical hardship – but this was too much to bear. However he was still in command and I knew it. To my amazement he told me he was promoting me to Lance Corporal although there was no stripe to give me – and so I was promoted in the field. This promotion boosted my ego at the time and shortly afterwards it received another. One morning, during a heavy bombardment, I saw the solid form of C.S.M. Raynor approaching with a young Fusilier. He told me that the youngster was going 'bomb happy' and was upsetting those around him. 'He knew', he said that the shelling did not worry me and he asked – not ordered – if I would have him in my trench and cheer him up! I knew then that it was possible to fool some of the people some of the time but the C.S.M.'s words, off the beam though they were, did also boost my ego and morale. Courage as well as fear is infectious. My daily trip to the Orderly Room to hand in the parade state usually gave me a sight of R.S.M. Murphy who, as I saw him, was courage personified. There was one particular morning in the rain and heavy shell fire that he took from me the Company return. All around us were sensible Fusiliers with their heads down. He noted that we had suffered no casualties, asked kindly after Major Allison and with the rum ration he added a bottle of 'tonic' for the Major alone. We both knew that the Major should not have been in the line. We also knew that he would not leave of his own volition.

Soon after this conversation a Fusilier in our Company was wounded. No stretcher bearers were available so a comrade and I assisted him down the wadi and along and up the other side – quite a journey – to the Regimental Aid Post. Some sort of shelter had been erected at the Post but the sight that met our eyes was staggering. There were literally bodies everywhere – we could not appraise the situation as to how many were dead, wounded or just sleeping because the Padre appeared. Looking unutterably weary he thanked us for bringing our comrade in. He had insisted, he told us, that the stretcher bearers rested. They had been working non-stop for over 48 hours. As a Padre it would appear he had two Commanding Officers and at Anzio he was inclined to obey the order 'Be not weary in well doing'. Jack Essery was in charge of the stretcher bearers and he was mentioned in despatches. Their efforts should never be forgotten.

Private S. C. Brooks arrived as a reinforcement for the 6th Cheshires in the division on 19 February. He wrote in his diary:

Feb. 24. 8 pln. come out, kicked out, 7 out of the whole platoon come in on their feet, most are carried out. All the tales they tell of the last 24 hours are terrible, it appears they have been surrounded for two days. Burgon, Fielding, Ludlow, Mr. Kerr and Cross fought their way out at 1.0 this morning, their tales are almost unbelievable and certainly unprintable, its a wonder they are alive. On one occasion Gerries trapped them in a cave by climbing on top and lobbing stick grenades in at them, they got out of that by dashing out and shot them off the top with a bren, whilst in the cave the Gerries were falling down, being engaged by the D.L.I.,* now we are putting covering fire down to get the D.L.I. out, all in poor state. We got too far into their lines. On making our way back the enemy sentries shouted 'Halta', so those were got without with a rifle, things are decidedly desperate with still a long way to go. Burgon and two more come upon two more positions dug in on a little hill, they barred the only way out so three of them crept forward until almost on top of them and then let them have it with a bren m.g. and nothing happened, the mag. was empty, they were then on their guard but a hand grenade and two rifles eventually sorted them out, another 15 minutes and they were halted by our forward troops. They came in with a week of beard, unwashed for 5 days, clothes torn ragged, blood everywhere. Burgon it seems carried Carr out on his back, he had been hit, what the position is I don't know, Burgon had to bury the two watches and all his money, so all that is lost. Planes are over early this morning but well out of range. S.M. and I go round all CCs and MDs looking for any who might have been brought in from and by another unit, we only find Sgt. Wood of the day before and Coupes, I wonder where Pongo and Dinty are now. 9 pln. go into the line, all drivers and Coy H.Q. carry for them, we set off at 6.0. and go so far on trucks then walk, we get a bit too close for my liking, veri-lights are being fired over us and it means remaining like statues, nothing is flung at us but lots of stuff is falling all round us. We get in and out O.K., but get a little lost on the way back, we arrive at a detrucking area to find everything gone but two of our trucks are there battered up, looks like they have been hit by shells. We carry on, all we can do. Get lost again, come across a Yank tank and the crew give us six tins of corn beef. We sit behind the hedge and eat up, get lifts back at 4.30 a.m., just lie on our blankets till morning, have breakfast, discover that one of 7 pln. and Hughes were hit in the trucks we found smashed, Hughes in the dock the other too late. Before going to kip for the morning I decide to put

* Durham Light Infantry.

brens higher!! I am trying to write on a stretcher in a shed on Anzio dock. Finally got a bren bullet in bottom of my guts, I have been on the table and have to pee out of a tube, I have to lie on my side.

Von Mackensen had not yet shot his bolt. He now planned to switch his main effort to the 3rd US Division's sector south-west of Cisterna, held by the Hermann Goering Panzer Division. That division was to thrust through Isola Bella while 26th Panzer Division attacked on its right, both starting at 4 a.m. without preliminary artillery preparation, the 362nd Infantry Division attacking further west an hour and a half later. As a diversionary measure, 1st Parachute Corps was to launch an attack at Buonriposo and 76th Panzer Corps another one away on the eastern flank at Sessano. The operation was to be launched on 28 February, but bad weather on the two previous days caused a twenty-four-hour postponement, although 1st Parachute Corps's attack on the positions of 56th Division's 168th Brigade started on the 28th, 2nd Sherwood Foresters and 2/6th Queens being involved. A combination of heavy rain and stubborn defence brought the German attacks to a halt on 1 March, and Kesselring gave orders for the counter-offensive to be called off after von Mackensen's Fourteenth Army had suffered 2,731 casualties over the two days.

As part of his plan for a general reorganization in preparation for a spring offensive, Alexander ordered the relief of 56th British Division by the 5th, transferred from 10th British Corps's Garigliano bridgehead, while 18th Infantry Brigade from 1st British Armoured Division replaced 24th Guards Brigade in the 1st Division. 56th Division went to Egypt and 24th Guards Brigade went to the area of Naples, to rest and refit.

Cassino

One of the principal reasons for the renewed attack at Cassino, to relieve pressure on Anzio, had therefore lost most of its justification when, the weather having improved sufficiently to meet Alexander's conditions of four clear days, it was launched on 15 March. Between 8.30 a.m. and midday a total of 455 aircraft dropped 2,223 1,000lb bombs, a weight of 992 tons of high explosive, 47 per cent of which fell within a mile of the town centre and the rest near the town and on Monastery Hill. 43 aircraft attacked other towns by mistake, killing 96 Allied soldiers and 140 civilians. Cassino, engulfed in smoke and dust, was reduced to rubble. The bombardment, during which the forward New Zealand posts on the northern edge of the town had been withdrawn 1,000 yards, was followed by an artillery programme fired by 890 guns which continued until 8 p.m., by which time nearly 200,000 rounds had been fired. In spite of this terrific bombardment, the survivors of the German 2nd Battalion of the 3rd Parachute Regiment came up from their cellars and dugouts and manned their machine guns, mortars and anti-tank weapons with fierce resolution. The attack was spearheaded by the 25th New Zealand Battalion, supported by a squadron of the 19th New Zealand Armoured Regiment. Progress was slow, 100 yards in an hour instead of in ten minutes as planned. By last light the leading companies had almost reached Route 6 as it entered the town from the east, but not as far as the Continental Hotel, where it turned south. One company (D) had succeeded in capturing the Castle. The tanks had great difficulty in making their way forward over the rubble, as did the engineers' bulldozers, which were not armoured. Night brought torrential rain, filling every crater and ditch with water.

The next stage was for 5th Indian Brigade to relieve the New Zealanders in the Castle and begin their advance to the Monastery. This started after dark, but took much longer than planned. 1/4th Essex had not completed their occupation of the Castle until after midnight, and it was 3 a.m. before they had gained their next objective, Point 165. Two companies of 1/6th Rajputs passed through them and, at 4.30 a.m., attempted to attack Point 236, the second hairpin bend, but were driven back to the Castle, while the other companies were heavily shelled and disappeared. The third battalion, 1/9th Gurkhas, marched in the rain-swept darkness all the way from the village of Cairo on crowded tracks, and reached the northern outskirts of Cassino about midnight. Their commanding officer, Lieutenant-Colonel G. Nangle, could not discover where the other battalions had got to and decided to make his own way to his objective, Hangman's Hill, at the fourth hairpin bend south of the monastery. When daylight came his battalion was still struggling up the hillside on the western outskirts of the town; but as they would be exposed in the open he stopped them there, having lost contact with Captain M. R. Dunhall's C Company, which astonishingly had made its way to Hangman's Hill, meeting and dealing with only one enemy post on its way. The next day, the 17th, was spent by both divisions in trying to struggle forward to their original objectives against increasing opposition from the German parachutists, now being reinforced from outside the town. Very little progress was made apart from the capture of the station area by the 26th New Zealand Battalion.

During the following night, 17/18 February, the rest of 1/9th Gurkhas infiltrated themselves, platoon by platoon, to join C Company at Hangman's Hill, and the only significant advance made on the 18th was by the 25th New Zealand Battalion, which, moving south from Point 165, captured Point 202, well behind the key area of the Continental Hotel and the Hôtel des Roses, which they proceeded to attack without success.

Freyberg's plan for the 19th was for 28th (Maori) Battalion, moving through the 25th at Point 202, to attack and capture the Continental Hotel and the Hôtel des Roses. The disorganized Rajputana Rifles were to relieve the Essex in the Castle, after which the latter were to join with 1/9th Gurkhas, now precariously supplied by a combination of porterage and airdrop, in an attack on the ruins of the monastery, while over in 7th Brigade's area a force of nineteen Sherman and twenty-one Stuart light tanks, drawn from 20th New Zealand Armoured Regiment, 760th US Tank Battalion and 7th Brigade's own Reconnaissance Squadron, was to move down Cavendish Road to Albaneta Farm, from which it would attack the monastery from the opposite side. Results were disappointing. The attack on the two hotels failed.

In 4th Indian Division's 5th Indian Brigade, to the right of and above the New Zealanders, 1/4th Essex, not relieved until after midnight, ran into a German counter-attack aimed at Point 165 and Castle Hill, and only seventy of them eventually joined the 1/9th Gurkhas at Hangman's Hill. Their attack on the monastery was to be dependent on the success of the tanks in reaching it from Albaneta Farm. The tanks reached the latter, but, as they tried to thread their way uphill over the rocky ground towards the monastery under a hail of small-arms fire and the occasional hand-held anti-tank weapon, six were knocked out and sixteen more damaged. At 5.30 p.m. they were withdrawn and no attack on the monastery was made.

Major Denis Beckett was commanding C Company of 1/4th Essex in this action and wrote his account of it shortly afterwards:

To begin with [on 18 March] I completed the relief of Pt 165 with the 1/6th [Rajputana Rifles] at 0330 and concentrated my company in the Castle. Frank* and I were to leave two hours later than B and D as our preparations were not so well advanced owing to the change of plan. At 0400 B and D moved from the Castle and a little before 0500 CSM COX and about six men from B Coy came running back to say that a very large number of Germans, whom they had first thought to be an Indian carrying party until noticing their helmets, were advancing on the Castle. We were in a pretty fair state of chaos. The 1/6th were supposed to have taken over the defences, but in fact most of our men were still in the sangars, and we were trying to issue rations and ammo, and sort out weapons which had been buried among the debris during the tank shoot the previous day.

However Frank gave the order 'stand-to', and everyone ran to their posts. The Indians did not quite know what to do naturally, and eventually gathered in a herd at the back of the Castle although a few fought very bravely in the courtyard and some did magnificent work as snipers. I do not make this criticism of the Indians unkindly as there was really nowhere for them to go as we had already occupied the defences and there was very little room for anyone else on the perimeter. The situation was now 1/6th in possession of 165, and 1/4 and elements of 1/6th 193.

The enemy counter-atttack opened with intense machine gun fire sweeping the Castle. I have never known anything like it. It came from every angle. This lasted for about ten minutes then they were on us. We could not use artillery D.F. [defensive fire] because we did not know how the Raj Rif or our own people were faring out in front. Our mortars had not then been registered. It had to be fought out with infantry weapons man to man. Frank went on the blower to tell Battalion whilst I did the best I could to organize the defences. The men were a bit shaken by the intensity of the fire, so, more to encourage them than anything else I got a man to spot and fired about a dozen 2″ Mortar bombs at a wave advancing under the castle wall. The first attack very nearly succeeded. One or two tried to

* Major F J. Ketteley, commanding A Company, 1/4th Essex.

penetrate the courtyard and many were stopped only a few yards from the walls. We broke them up with mills grenades, Tommy guns and Brens.

Frank now became eager to take a more active part in the battle and crawled forward to pick off a machine gunner who had been giving us trouble. He was the fellow who had wounded me twice slightly in the arm and neck a little earlier. Unfortunately the Boche got Frank first, straight through the head and he died not long after. We threw a number of Mills grenades in the direction of the machine gunner and had no trouble after this so presume we must have got him. Soon afterwards we saw a white verey light go up and the small arms fire was replaced by Artillery and Mortar fire so we assumed the first counter attack had been driven off. I took stock of the situation. It was not pretty. We had about eight 2″ Mortar HE bombs left, 12 grenades, a fair amount of Tommy gun and by good luck a lot of .303. We had lost a few good chaps in the first machine gunning among them I think Pat COGHLAN and a number were wounded trying to take up fire positions on the walls.

The lull did not last long. The enemy had taken advantage of his first push to occupy very favourable ground and this time began with a shower of stick grenades. But we too were more prepared, and I had been on to Battalion to arrange for our Vickers guns to bring enfilade fire on the Western end of the Castle. The 3″ Mortars too were used with telling effect, though the problem here was to find a place to observe from. Eventually I climbed on top of a wall exposing head and shoulders. I was a complete bloody fool to do this. Everything I had been taught since O.T.C. days ought to have warned me against it but I could see no alternative. Anyway a little runt of a Boche chucked a grenade at me and I was lucky not to get it on the head. By sheer luck we got the correction through before this happened so it was with some thrill that we heard Hugo's boys crumping down on the wicket and the tapping of their Vickers guns.

I think this pinned the Boche for a bit because we were able to reorganize a bit. Just afterwards I got a message from Robin Oswald, B.C. of 52 Bty (1st Fd RA) to say they were dreadfully thin on the ground in the courtyard and short of ammo. They had suffered heavily from Boche grenades and were in a bad way. A force was organized under Doug BEECH consisting of Ronnie ULPH and about 12 men of A Coy carrying bags of ammo to go and help out.

To get these across, we lined up the Brens on the inner wall and blazed away at the openings while the leading members of the party also shot their way across with Tommy guns. They got across without casualty as far as I can remember.

The courtyard had been the scene of the toughest fighting. Three times the Boche had penetrated. Several times they had climbed its walls only to be driven off. On the Cassino side Cpl PARKER fighting his post with inspiring coolness, broke up a wave on his own, firing the Bren until the enemy were within a few yards and then finally smashing the attack with mills grenades. Around the tower were some old arrow slits. These were manned by Bren gunners to cover the gaps in the walls. The Boche very quickly realized the nuisance value of these. I saw three of our chaps go down in succession shot through the head and a little fellow from B Coy pick up a rifle and say quietly 'I'll get him, Sir'. He waited till the man's shadow appeared on the wall and shot him dead.

A German prisoner, who had been wounded, now came in and on cross examination said 200 of them formed up for the first counter attack and 40 for the second. He said they came from the Monastery.

Battalion now warned us to expect a third counter attack and asked if we could state whether Pt 165 was clear of our own troops. Capt. JENKINS (1/6th) said he had not been in touch with his men for two hours and would assume they had been overrun. D.F. was therefore laid on very close in and as soon as the attack commenced a full blunderbuss of arty., mortars, mmg's and small arms was brought to bear. This counter attack was supported by a tank from the road bend above Pt 165 and a systematic shoot aimed at the destruction of our West wall commenced. As a result the wall collapsed burying about 10 of our men including Capt BEECH and Lieut ULPH. However, the attack was not pressed home due I think to the effectiveness of the D.F. which continued in the face of heavy enemy arty fire on our mmg's, a fact which gave great heart to the defenders. Once again the enemy withdrew under a concentration of arty and mortars and no fresh counter attacks developed.

Alexander was beginning to feel that, although there were intelligence indications that even Heidrich, the German Parachute Division's commander, was beginning to have doubts about whether he could hang on to Cassino town much longer, the time had come to call a halt; but Freyberg was for continuing, not having yet used all the troops available. On the 20th the 4th Indian Division renewed the attack between Castle Hill and Points 165 and 445 without success, defeating however a German counter-attack aimed at Castle Hill during the night 20/21 March. On that same night 21st New Zealand Battalion, with two companies of the 24th, tried to secure the area between the Continental Hotel and Point 202, in the hope of linking up with 1/9th Gurkhas, but failed, renewing their attempt the following night, again without success. Lieutenant Clem Hollies was commanding a platoon in the 21st New Zealand Battalion, involved in this attack. He wrote:

> We were taken forward by truck along Highway Six (the road to Rome) and debussed about a mile short of the town and then moved forward by foot along the road, suffering an uncanny feeling of utter nakedness, with no protection, nerves taut for the burst of expected fire or incoming shell. We were lucky, and safely reached our assembly point in a building that turned out to be the convent. Our company (D) was ordered to attack along the axis of Highway Six, 16 and 17 platoons forward and my platoon (18) in reserve. Tracer and mortar bursts lit up the night sky and gave us occasional glimpses of the devastated buildings around us. Actually, Highway Six no longer existed, being obliterated by thousands of tons of debris. However, the leading platoons kept moving forward, closely followed by us, all trying to keep direction more by instinct than anything else. It wasn't before long that the front platoons ran into trouble and converging fire forced them to take cover. The moon was now bright enough to enable us to see a track of sorts leading through some shrubbery. We were later to learn that we were moving across the Botanical Gardens of the town. We followed the track, wading through water-filled bomb craters and stumbling across a couple of creeks until we ran into fierce machine-gun fire, so we dived for shelter in the nearest building. As we waited, we could hear and momentarily see 17 platoon being attacked from the flank. We tried to help them with fire but it was no use and they were over-run, most being taken prisoner, including Jim Rabarts. The other platoon was luckier and was inspired by Sgt. Mason who took over when their platoon commander, Lt. Dewson, was wounded. For this action, Sgt. Mason was awarded a Distinguished Conduct Medal.

It was nearly dawn when my platoon was attacked but we broke up the attempt by concentrated fire from our Bren guns. When the enemy retired, we saw German stretcher parties were busy carrying in their wounded and two New Zealanders were in danger of being picked up. There were no Red Cross arm-bands available, but 'Pom' Pomeroy and I removed our steel helmets, and indicating that we were unarmed, took the risk of being shot at from the Continental Hotel about 150 yards away, and assisted them both to regain our lines. This incident of a few minutes seemed like an eternity and I had a horrible feeling of hundreds of baleful eyes watching us. On regaining our house, we collapsed and didn't stop shaking for hours afterwards.

When daylight came, the shelling increased in intensity and it was impossible to move in the open without the protection of smoke shells. Our wireless set was destroyed and our house was being blown down around us. It was a great relief when a runner brought a message from Battalion Headquarters ordering us back to the comparative safety of the Convent. In what we hoped would be a long enough lull in the firing to allow us to retire, we struggled back across the gardens and managed to make it without too much trouble. We took up defensive positions in the Convent and here we spent our time in a haze of yellow smoke and a rain of shells and mortar bombs. Smoke shells burst over us unceasingly; it was this smoke that gave us some protection from the prying eyes on Montecassino. But they were most unnerving as they swished over our heads and exploded with a loud 'plop'. You had the terrible thought that they could be filled with high explosive. It was a case of 'smoke, smoke and more smoke'. One of our men was blown out of his observation post by a rifle grenade, which the paratroop defenders used with uncanny accuracy. Our local war had reached a stalemate as far as our attack was concerned. There was still plenty of action by the Indians in the hills above us and other New Zealand units were attacking in the town. However, try as they may, the troops could make no impression and these attacks were the last efforts to clear Cassino town.

On the 23rd therefore Freyberg himself recommended that the battle should be broken off. Clem Hollies describes what the New Zealand troops were feeling like at that stage:

Our four days and nights were absolute hell; mortar bombs continued to rain down; we had a nebelwerfer rocket through our roof; and the never-ending smoke shells meant we lived in a world where there was no day. Our nerves were stretched to breaking point, hands shaking so much cigarettes were hard to light. Hot meals were impossible, as was washing and shaving. My diary notes: 'It takes all our nerve to move from our position to Company Headquarters 25 yards away.' On the night of 25 March, we were relieved by the 22 Battalion but I felt so knocked about, physically and mentally, that I couldn't even feel pleased about it. The walk out was tough, with the odd shell landing close, but we just kept stumbling along. We picked up some stretcher cases at the Regimental Aid Post and carried them with difficulty to the Bailey Bridge over the Rapido where we boarded trucks on Highway Six. We were so exhausted that some who tried to sing, fell asleep instead. On looking back at this our first time in Cassino, it amazes me that in my platoon not one man was killed, although we had our share of wounded. The odds were certainly stacked against us, but Lady Luck must have been on our side.

Back at our San Pietro billets, we slept most of the next day and then had a clean-up. Company roll-call showed that we had 22 left out of 70 odd who had gone into Cassino five days earlier. We were introduced to a new Company Commander, Major Allan Copeland who had recently returned from a tour of duty in New Zealand. (After the war, he was to be Auckland Coroner for many years.) The remnants of C and D companies were pooled and the platoons so formed were bits of C and bits of D, hence Allan Copeland took over a new company, appropriately named 'Bitza D.'

Clark and Alexander agreed to a pause, Freyberg being told to organize defences on the line he had reached. With some difficulty the troops at Hangman's Hill and Point 202 were successfully withdrawn during the night of 24/25 March before the exhausted 4th Indian Division was relieved by Major-General C. F. Keightley's 78th Division and moved back to the Adriatic coast, their casualties having been 132 killed, 792 wounded and 155 missing.

Lieutenant P. Royle, of the 17th Field Regiment Royal Artillery, describes his battery's experience as 78th Division moved into the Cassino area to relieve the Indians, quoting from the diary he wrote at the time:

General Alexander and Admiral Troubridge
coming ashore at Anzio. 22 January 1944.

Men of the 2/7th Middlesex dig in at Anzio. February 1944.

Revd Francis Dow celebrates Holy Communion with
1st Reconnaissance Regiment at Anzio. 7 February 1944.

'Grub's up!' for the Middlesex at Anzio. 21 February 1944.

Smoke from American shells hangs over the town of Cassino
while above it is the Monastery. Early February 1944.

A low aerial view of Cassino Monastery showing its complete destruction. May 1944.

Indian troops pass bomb-shattered buildings on the
outskirts of Cassino town. 16 March 1944.

New Zealand infantry in Cassino town. 8 April 1944.

Evacuating a New Zealand casualty, Cassino. 26 March 1944.

Generals Juin and Leese with General Alexander. 26 March 1944.

Mule supply train, Garigliano front. 17 February 1944.

Evacuating a casualty of the 2nd Moroccan Division by mule. 10 April 1944.

A Sherman tank crosses the River Garigliano by Royal Engineer ferry. 20 January 1944.

Machine-gunners of Cheshire Regiment near Lorenzo. 27 January 1944.

Observation Point of the 4th Parachute Battalion near Venafro. 30 April 1944.

Temporary graves near the summit of Monte Damano near Castelforte. 27 January 1944.

As soon as it got dark on the 28th [March] the battery packed up and 'moved at 11. An unpleasant journey as we were being shelled. Bad gun positions north of Cassino.' As soon as we turned right onto Highway 6 it was obvious that 'shit corner' was receiving its usual attention from the German artillery. I could see the flashes of exploding shell fire about one mile ahead every twenty seconds or so. Being shelled is always frightening, but on this particular night I had a lot of time to think about it as the column advanced slowly northwards at 8–10 m.p.h. and by the time we were a few hundred yards away I was feeling quite terrified. There was nothing I could do except go straight into the area of exploding shells and pray that we weren't hit. R.F. my armoured carrier was protection only against flying splinters, a near miss or direct hit would be the end and I felt convinced that night that we would receive a direct hit – maybe this obsession was caused by the darkness or because I couldn't hear the gun firing, only the shell exploding, but the fact remained that I was in a terrible state by the time we reached the north end of Mount Trocchio and looking back am thankful that it was dark and my O.P. crew couldn't see me. In all probability they were just as frightened as I was but that wasn't really the point – I was their leader and meant to set an example.

The only thing that saved the Battery on that march from serious damage was the fact that the shells were falling just beyond the road, 10 to 15 yards on our right, and when a shell bursts the high explosive and splinters carries forward and sideways and not much comes back. I had been crouching down alongside the driver shaking like a leaf as we went through the shelling and then we turned the corner and left the immediate danger behind. We had roughly a thousand yards more to go on Highway 6 before turning right on to the track up to San Michele and I could now see our own shells exploding ahead on Monastery Hill – continuous fire was kept up night and day. We found our turning and made our way into the hills facing Cassino, and my diary for the 29th started 'Got nearly everything bogged and didn't have the position clear until 5.30. Digging and camouflage all morning. Slept in p.m. Quite a lot of Boche shelling.'

The shelling of the previous night and the fairly continuous attention paid by the German artillery and nebelwerfers on the 29th played havoc with my nerves. Looking back now I suppose I was on the verge of a nervous breakdown – the Americans would have classified it as 'battle fatigue' – it was a mild form of shell shock but it affected my speech and I found it increasingly difficult to speak without a fairly serious stammer. I think I realised that I could not carry on my role of O.P. Officer with all its stresses and pressures. At the time I had two main worries – the all important one a real fear and my inability to control my actions and secondly the knowledge that I would disgrace myself in front of my own men. I had never been one to take unnecessary risks but up to now I had always been able to control my actions under fire and to appear outwardly calm – I felt it my duty to do this – but now this self control was no longer there – the culmination of many months of action was the cause. All I wanted to do that day was to get away from it all, to run away as far as I could from the shelling and the war in general.

Our O.P. party had a small stone building situated just in front of E and F troops but although it was tucked into the hillside and out of sight of the Monastery, it was a noisy spot as we got the full blast of our own guns during the night as well as the German fire coming back at us. The next morning we had a visit from the CRA* and after he had gone I collared Duffie on his own and told him 'my nerve had gone and I had a word with Duffie who was very nice about it. I am to take on Battery Captain in a day or so.' The mere fact of having told somebody made me feel better and it happened to coincide with two fairly quiet days due to poor weather and very low clouds which reduced visibility and suited us fine. A constant stream of HE and smoke shells were poured into the Monastery to make observation for the Germans as difficult as possible, but when the elements also came to our aid it naturally made our existence that much more bearable. But on the 1st April the weather changed and after a misty start the sun came out and midday F troop had just put the finishing touches to the gun pits and were cleaning up the troop position when 'E troop caught a packet in the afternoon and had one chap wounded. We had the odd round on the hill above us and a few splinters through the Command Post. Left at 7 with Basil for Battalion Headquarters. Some shelling on the way up passing E troop but otherwise quiet. Up there about 8 and relieved Duffie.' Enemy O.P'S had obviously spotted E troop from the Monastery and during

* Commander Royal Artillery.

the afternoon until it got dark they were subjected to a continuous bombardment some of which fell near F troop.

I had been asked by Duffie to relieve him that night at Battalion Headquarters of the Royal Irish Fusiliers who were the forward battalion in the hills behind the Monastery and Basil Austin was to man the O.P. so we set off at 7 p.m. as soon as it was dark. E troop was still receiving attention from German artillery as we passed but once we were clear we had a quiet trip but certainly a nerve racking one. After leaving San Michele, the track started descending into the valley of the Rapido twisting and turning as it went and throughout its length it was in full view of the Monastery. It was only usable in the hours of darkness and every night a mule train left San Michele as soon as it got dark, and made its slow and dangerous journey over the 7 miles to Battalion Headquarters, dropped its precious load and returned – a round trip of 14 miles. Betweeen 600 and 800 mules did this trip and the Battalion relied on this method of transport for everything – water, food, ammunition. Some nights the journey was more unpleasant than others – it depended on how accurate was the German mortaring and shelling but there were casualties every night.

The temporary New Zealand Corps was now disbanded, Lieutenant-General Sir Sidney Kirkman's 13th Corps taking over responsibility for the sector, 1st Guards Brigade, which had recently joined 46th Division from its parent 6th Armoured Division in North Africa, relieving the New Zealanders in the town. Freyberg returned to his division, replacing Brigadier G. B. Parkinson, who returned to the command of 6th New Zealand Brigade. He had been commanding the division since 2 March when Kippenberger had trodden on an anti-personnel mine and had to have both his feet amputated. The division also moved over to Eighth Army.

Future plans

While everyone had been waiting for the weather to clear, important exchanges had been going on between Alexander at 15th Army Group, Wilson at Supreme Headquarters in Algiers and the British Chiefs of Staff and their colleagues in Washington, all concerned at the slow progress towards the situation which it had been assumed would have been reached in Italy before OVERLORD, the operation to cross the Channel and land in France, was launched. The target date for this, agreed at Teheran, was May 1944. It had been assumed that, before then, 15th Army Group would have captured Rome and reached the Pisa–Rimini line, and been able to release US and French troops and the necessary amphibious shipping for Operation ANVIL, a landing in the south of France of two divisions, with ten more following up. This was to precede OVERLORD and draw German forces in France away from opposing it. But not only were Alexander's troops stuck a long way south of that line, unable to release divisions for elsewhere, but the maintenance of Anzio and the possible need for its reinforcement was tying up amphibious shipping.

On 22 February Alexander sent to Wilson a strategic assessment prepared for him by Harding. The aim was clear, and had not changed. It was to force the enemy to commit the maximum number of divisions to Italy at the time that OVERLORD was to be launched. But there were disagreements about how this should be achieved. Harding argued that neither pushing back the German line nor capturing Rome would help to achieve this aim. That must be to destroy German formations in Italy to such an extent that they had to be replaced in order to prevent a disastrous collapse. There were three requirements to achieve this: first, a three to one local superiority in infantry; second, good weather, so that the Allies could exploit their great superiority in artillery, tanks and air power; finally, time in which to rest, refit and retrain the divisions exhausted by the winter fighting. An additional seven and a half divisions would be needed. They were available within the Mediterranean and Middle East, but shipping limitations could not get them to Italy in time to take part in operations before the middle of April. This would however meet all the other criteria, including that of acting as an overture for OVERLORD.

Having considered the possibility that Alexander's armies might have advanced to either south of or even north of Rome by mid-April, and shown it to be much less likely than that the Germans would still be on the GUSTAV line then, Harding took the view that this in fact would be advantageous. If his criteria were met, there would be a good chance that an attack by three or four divisions from Anzio, combined with a major offensive up the line of the Liri valley, would stand a reasonable chance of encircling and destroying a considerable part of Kesselring's forces. The chances would be improved if operations could be developed up the Ausente valley, which led from the lower reaches of the Garigliano up towards the Liri valley, and if a diversion could be landed from the sea in the Gulf of Gaeta. The command arrangements should be changed. If Eighth Army were to continue to be restricted to east of the Apennines while Fifth Army commanded everything west of the watershed, the former would have only four and the latter twenty divisions. Mark Clark had a hotchpotch of nationalities in his army, unnecessarily complicating logistics. His army should become primarily American, including the French who were equipped by them, while British divisions, and those equipped and supplied by them, like the Poles, should preferably come under Leese. This would mean Leese becoming responsible for the Liri valley, leaving his current sector to a corps directly under Alexander, while Mark Clark was restricted to Anzio and the lower Garigliano. The navy's priorities should be to get the additional divisions to Italy as soon as possible and build up supplies at Anzio to support an attack from there. The air forces should maintain the supremacy they had established, keep up their attacks on the enemy's rail communications and be prepared both to deal with any further counter-attacks against Anzio and to attack targets which could have a significant effect on future operations.

The controversial aspect of this assessment was the conclusion that Operation ANVIL should be cancelled, as neither the troops nor the shipping could be spared, but that it should be simulated as a deception plan, the proposed landing in the Gulf of Gaeta contributing to this. For the first time since the invasion of Sicily a clear, penetrating, overall examination had been made of what the Allies were trying to do in Italy and how they should achieve their aim.

Wilson objected to this on two grounds, both of them influenced by the trouble they would cause in London and Washington. The first was the proposed cancellation of ANVIL: the other was the postponement of further offensive operations until mid-April. Not only would this disappoint Churchill, but the airmen at Algiers, mostly US Army Air Force, headed by Lieutenant-General Ira C. Eaker, with the British Air Marshal Sir John Slessor as his deputy, believed that they could bring about a German withdrawal by a combination of extensive interdiction of road and rail traffic and direct attack by massive bombardment of key positions like Cassino. Wilson also had reservations about the demands on shipping.

After an exchange of views at high level between Algiers, London and Washington, a compromise, suggested by Eisenhower in London, was agreed at the end of February. Operations in Italy should have priority over all other operations in the Mediterranean, provided that plans and preparations for a seaborne diversion to help OVERLORD continued, ANVIL being the first choice. The Mediterranean fleet of assault shipping could be retained until 20 March, when the situation would be reviewed. If it was then clear that nothing more than an assault by one division as a deception plan could be mounted, all amphibious shipping in excess of that needed for it would be transferred from the Mediterranean to be used in OVERLORD. The delay in launching the Third Battle of Cassino and its failure brought Wilson round to the view that ANVIL could not be launched before OVERLORD, in fact not until July. He wanted therefore to cancel it, and Eisenhower agreed, demanding that all the amphibious shipping earmarked for it should be transferred to OVERLORD. But the US Chiefs of Staff refused to cancel it, preferring to postpone the operation, renamed DRAGOON, until 10 July, saying that they could transfer craft from the Pacific if the British would commit themselves to a definite date. One of their motives was to ensure that after Alexander had arrived at the Pisa–Rimini line there would be no question of trying to implement the strategy he favoured, which was backed by Churchill, of turning right-handed, once the Po valley had been reached, and heading for the Ljubljana Gap in the hope of reaching Vienna before the Russians. An acrimonious exchange of views took place, the Americans insisting that if there was no guarantee of a date there would be no transfer of shipping, the temperature rising when Wilson reported that Alexander's preparations for the next major assault on the GUSTAV line, Operation DIADEM, could not be completed before 11 May, which meant that DRAGOON could not be implemented until August. The British saw no point in executing it so long after OVER-LORD, and while arguments were still going on Churchill sent a unilateral directive to Wilson, confirming that the aim of operations in the Mediterranean remained to help OVERLORD by destroying and containing as many German formations as possible. This was to be achieved by Operation DIADEM and by 'developing a threat' to southern France. The amphibious shipping left in the Mediterranean was to be used to support operations in Italy and 'to take advantage of opportunities' in southern France. The latter was not to prejudice DIADEM. The Americans did not approve, but did not actively object at that stage.

Anzio

Meanwhile static trench warfare prevailed at Anzio, both sides restricting their activity to shelling, mortaring, patrols, and air attacks, both on land and at sea, where enemy submarines were also active. Lieutenant A. C. W. Jones was the paymaster in the destroyer HMS *Laforey*, which was involved in an action at this time, which he describes:

> On 28th March 1944 an L.S.T. was torpedoed north of Sicily. We were at Naples at the time and Admiral Morse sailed us with four other British destroyers and two U.S. destroyers to find and sink the submarine. We found her on the 29th but were unable to drive her to the surface by depth charges; the water was so deep that the submarine had time to escape before the depth charges sank to its depth. Captain Armstrong therefore decided to follow the submarine keeping in contact by sonar, until it had to surface for air, and calculated that it would surface early on the 30th when the moon had set. The ship was therefore sent to Defence Stations so that some men could get some rest, and the LAFOREY and the four other British ships in line abreast swept behind this submarine, while the two U.S. ships carried out a box search on a square a few miles away in case the submarine doubled back and escaped us. The submarine

came to the surface very quickly in order to escape on the surface if possible and although we had fired starshell it had not started to burst and Captain Armstrong ordered the searchlight to be turned on it. I was then at the pom-pom mounting (I had transferred there from the Oerlikon gun) and remember feeling very naked as this very bright light shone out across the sea and picked up the submarine on the surface, stern to us. All the ships started firing at the submarine but suddenly there was a violent explosion close to me and I remember a lot of water falling on me and then being in the sea with, I think, some guard rails wrapped round my legs. I was able to struggle out of this and swam away from the ship. I could see that her back had been broken, the stern remaining afloat for a couple of minutes and there was a lot of shouting. I was wearing my life jacket, but I did not get it blown up nor did I light the little red light, but luckily I bumped into a couple of cooks holding on to some wood and I stayed with them. We got alongside the TUMULT and I remember someone saying 'Hold on, there's a third man there' and I was helped to scramble up a net and get on board. At first I was in a ship's company bathroom, not that I minded where I was, but someone recognised me and I was taken to the wardroom where I was lent some clothing, mine being rather the worse for wear. The TUMULT went on looking for survivors and then returned to Naples to land us. The submarine had been sunk and some of her company were also picked up. I had assumed that others from the LAFOREY had been picked up by other ships and was very shocked to learn that only the TUMULT had survivors. Apart from the First Lieutenant who was blown from the bridge onto the forecastle and one man who escaped from the plot (below the bridge), I believe that no one escaped from the fore part of the ship. I think I was the only survivor from the pom-pom; the other survivors (about 50 in all) must have been aft in the ship, though not everyone who was aft survived.

On land at Anzio, Major Jago had left 6th US Corps Headquarters and joined 2nd Field Regiment Royal Artillery in the 1st British Division as second-in-command. His diary records:

April 21. Woken up about 0500 to sound of air raid & shelling of Reg'l area. aircraft made direct attacks on us, & bombed us with anti-personnel & med bombs. Enemy shellfire in area simultaneous, designed to keep our Bofors quiet. Cowered in my bivvy whilst the stuff dropped all around. One small piece of A.P. entered my hole, via the mosquito net. Several fell just outside. Mess dugout hit, RHQ office tent & about four bivvies. 42 Bty had one man killed. RHQ 3 wounded, incl 2 signalmen & Cpl Thorley, the cook. Sloped [?] about in the mist in the valley collecting stretchers & putting them into ambulance. Meanwhile a U.S. ammo dump nearby had been hit, & was going off continuously until about 0700 hrs, bits of metal whizzing all around. Another raid about 0615, fighter bomber quite low. Our O.P. saw one plane crash, bearing 7 deg about 0615 hrs.

The nightingales in the valley sang hard throughout the whole time, midst bombs and shelling. The old cockerel belonging to the Sig Section also was undismayed.

Had a look around the area during the day, & found hundreds of A.P. bomb holes & also large craters. Held an M.T. inspection of Sigs vehicles at 1130, & RHQ at 1400 hrs. All much better than last time. Got two letters to-day, one from MKJ dated 13 Feb, & one from June of 5 March. Have now had all outstanding letters from MKJ. Duty officer from 2000 to 2400 hrs.

22 April. Awakened after two hours sleep to sound of shells bursting in Reg'l area. Conc of 88's and 105's between 0200 & 0230 with one break. Checked up, & no cas returned to bed. Shelling started again. Got up again & checked up. One man from 42 Bty killed, & one broken thigh. Bivvy hit & collapsed. Went to bed again: again shelling started in the area. Got up & afterwards remained fully dressed to doze fitfully until 0700 hrs. Altogether Regt shelled 8 times between 0200 & 0700 hrs. A bad night. Lucky not to have more casualties. Area covered in craters. Vehicle casualties, one m/c. Cookhouse equipment damaged. Div Comdr (Gen Penney) accompanied by Lt Col Frankie Read (Scottish Horse) acting CRA, visited Regt in the morning & went to every gun pit. RHQ spent the morning improving their bivvies protection & digging; in the p.m. all vehs & equipt were further dug in. 1400 hrs C.O. held B.C.'s confce on courses & odd points. 1500 hrs two young malaria officers looked at our marshes, & promised RE help to drain them. During this I sank deep into the mire! Spent remainder of day, until 2030, rebuilding and deepening my dugout. When all finished found bed did not fit!! More excavations required. Went to bed at 2045 hrs, very tired. Shelling started about 2100 hrs, went on intermittently until 2300 hrs. Could not sleep altho' very tired & aching after days work. Came on duty at midnight.

Gunner J. McKay of the same regiment also kept a diary of these days, but his entries were shorter:

Friday 21 April. The heavy shelling continued all night by 1 and 2 o'clock in morning it was simply 'hell' bombers and shells what a time! by day it was quiet. At about 11 o'clock it started again, what pretty close

Saturday 22. Most of the morning he shelled all round us, big, small, in fact everything he has! No bombers raid until 6.30. 4 were brought down! but what a night. Well; we certainly had a basinful with the last two nights much more of this and I'll be a wreck or something. Still never mind as long as all well.

6

Breakthrough to Rome

May to June 1944

Alexander assumed that the Germans would hold on to the GUSTAV line as long as they could, although it was known that another main defence line, the GOTHIC, was being prepared from Pisa to Rimini, and that two intermediate lines were being prepared between Cassino and Rome, the HITLER, some six miles behind the GUSTAV, and the CAESAR in the Alban Hills south of Rome. Alexander hoped that an offensive by Truscott's 6th US Corps from Anzio, coordinated with that of Fifth US and Eighth British Armies from the Garigliano bridgehead and across the Rapido up the Liri valley, would entrap both 76th and 14th Panzer Corps before they could occupy these intermediate lines.

His plan was that Clark's Fifth Army, south of the River Liri, would launch three thrusts. On the right General Alphonse Juin's French Expeditionary Corps, with the 2nd and 4th Moroccan and 3rd Algerian Divisions and the 1st French Division de Marche,* was to advance from the north end of the Garigliano bridgehead across rugged roadless mountains to Ausonia and thence up the Ausente valley to the Liri at Pontecorvo on the HITLER line. On their left, Major-General Geoffrey Keyes's 2nd US Corps, with 85th and 88th US Divisions, would push westward across the grain of the country and along the coast to Gaeta. 6th US Corps at Anzio, with 3rd, 34th, and 45th US Infantry and 1st US Armored Divisions, and 1st and 5th British Infantry Divisions, was to thrust out of the beachhead to Valmontone, east of the Alban Hills

---

* Formerly 1st French Motorized and before that 1st Free French Division, descended from Koenig's Foreign Legion Brigade which had fought at Bir Hacheim and El Alamein. Leclerc's force which had joined Eighth Army from Chad, when Montgomery reached Tripoli in January 1943, formed the French 2nd Armoured Division, which fought in Normandy.

where Route 6 from the Liri valley met the CAESAR line, at a time to decided by Alexander in the light of progress made on the main front. 36th US Division was to be held in Fifth Army reserve until Alexander decided whether it was to reinforce the 2nd or the 6th Corps.

Leese's plan for Eighth Army was for Lieutenant-General Władysław Anders's 2nd Polish Corps, with 3rd Carpathian and 5th Kresowa Divisions (Major-General Duch and Major-General Sulik), supported by 2nd Polish Armoured Brigade (Major-General Rakowski), was to cut off the Germans occupying Monastery Hill and Cassino and 'dominate' Route 6 until making contact with 13th British Corps as they advanced up the Liri valley: then to attack and capture Monastery Hill and thereafter advance to the HITLER line through the mountains north of the Liri valley. 13th Corps, with 4th and 78th British Divisions (Major-General Dudley Ward and now Major-General C. F. Keightley) and 8th Indian Infantry and 6th British Armoured Divisions (now Major-General V. Evelegh), would attack across the River Rapido below Cassino and advance sufficiently far up the Liri valley to allow Major-General E. M. Burns's 1st Canadian Corps, with 1st Canadian Infantry and 5th Canadian Armoured Divisions, to pass through them and drive up the Liri valley through the HITLER line to Valmontone. McCreery's 10th British Corps, with only the New Zealand Division under command, would advance through the mountains on the right of the Poles, once the latter had started their move towards the HITLER line. Directly under Army Group command were 6th South African Armoured Division (Major-General W. E. Poole), in general reserve, and Lieutenant-General C. W. Allfrey's 5th Corps, with 4th and 10th Indian Divisions and an Italian motorized brigade, on the Adriatic coast.

The 1st Brigade of the 3rd Carpathian Division led the Polish attack at 1 a.m. on 12 May, and, under intense fire, succeeded in capturing Points 593 and 569 at the end of Snake's Head Ridge, but German counter-attacks and the intensity of their artillery, mortar and small arms fire drove the Poles off both positions. The German defences, which had survived all the previous attacks, had been strengthened by more artillery and were still held by Major-General Heidrich's formidable paratroopers. After a day of fighting, in which much gallantry was shown and casualties were heavy, Anders withdrew all his attacking units back to their start lines. Leese approved, and ordered him not to renew his attacks, preferring to wait until 13th Corps had got nearer.

Unfortunately they were still a long way off. The right-hand brigade (10th) of 4th Division succeeded in crossing the Rapido immediately south of Cassino, but, as no bridge had been built, could not get its support weapons over and was unable to expand the narrow bridgehead its three battalions had formed. On its left, 28th Brigade's attempt to cross collapsed in chaos, as boats went all over the place and battalions got mixed up with each other, two of their commanding officers being killed. Lieutenant H. G. Harris had started the war in the ranks of a Territorial Army Searchlight Unit and had been serving in a Heavy Anti-Aircraft Regiment in Egypt when he was commissioned into the East Surrey Regiment. He had very recently joined their 1/6th Battalion in 10th Brigade and took over command of a platoon in D Company. He described his part in the battle:

In darkness on the night of May 10th we made our way up to the river, avoiding the 'Mad Mile' and using the Abbatoir as cover until we reached the river itself. Once there we extended to our right, my platoon in the lead until we reached our marking point, the bridge at the end of the Mad Mile. We were on the extreme right of the attack and I realised years later that that night I was right hand man of two armies, the 'Right Marker' to end all right markers. As a strong swimmer, I had been selected as rope man which meant swimming the river, reaching the other bank, pulling across a rope and securing it to the other side. Folding boats full of men would then float across by pulling on the rope. I was dead lucky as I found a kind of overhang with the roots of an old tree exposed. The river was less than ten yards wide at this point but very fast flowing and I chose to dive across gambling on a good dive with little splash and less noise as we would be going before the bombardment started. In the event it worked like a charm, I landed almost opposite my point of entry, slipped the rope round the exposed roots and pulled it taut, all in total silence. So quiet was it that I could hear Germans talking on the other side of the bank against which I was leaning. At this point on the river, the bank formed a sort of parapet and we knew the Germans had dug themselves in on the reverse side of the bank. The river ran so fast that it made a fair amount of noise on its own account, and this certainly covered any noise made by those crossing first, a few minutes before the bombardment was due to begin.

It was the imminence of this bombardment that made me press

so closely to the shelter of the bank and stay half in the river, despite the cold. The initial barrage was due to land ten yards beyond the river bank, but it would be a miracle if guns firing from five miles away could maintain that sort of accuracy. Each gun had been ranged individually in the days before, but in any barrage there were always 'shorts', and these would land among our own troops, a risk the generals felt to be acceptable. Luckily, when the barrage came it proved to be accurate in our sector and the assault boats lost no time in pulling themselves over. More and more men crowded the bank but no-one tried to get over it yet. I had my eye firmly on my watch. I knew that opening barrage was supposed to lift fifty yards after five minutes and we had to be over the bank and among the enemy before they realised what was happening. If they were slow, we had a chance. As the second hand of my watch completed the last few seconds, I clapped the helmet of the man next to me and went over the top of the bank in front of me in a sort of diving rolling movement. There was no dificulty in seeing as the whole area was lit up by the continual shell bursts and I spotted a dug-out about five yards to my right. I had come over the bank with a grenade in either hand, the pins already pulled as I dragged them from my webbing belt. The grenade in my right hand went into the dug-out which I thought was the source of the voices I had heard while hugging the bank and the one in my left hand went in the general direction of a machine gun pit we knew from photographs to be about fifteen yards in front of us.

As the grenades exploded, what seemed to be dozens of Spandaus opened up firing on fixed lines and raking the top of the bank behind us. Significantly, the gun in front of us remained silent. The three sections of my platoon began to fan out in accordance with the plans made before the crossing and I set the six men of my platoon headquarters to clearing the dug-out I had bombed creating a fire base to protect my sections as they began to advance. I quickly lost touch with the right hand section and as quickly realised that there would be no re-inforcements coming over as long as those guns were firing on fixed lines along the top of the bank. I tried to reach company headquarters by radio but had no luck, although I did raise battalion. From them I asked for smoke from the 3in. mortar section to be laid just in front of us. With the way the Germans were dug in it was obvious the only way to make headway was with grenades and close quarter fighting. Smoke would give us a chance. Leaving my platoon Sergeant in charge of the Headquarter section to guard our flank, I took my radio operator and one of the two remaining sections to try and make contact with the platoons that should be on our left. By daylight, I had established that of the other two platoons of our company only two sections had got over the bank. The company commander, both the other two platoon commanders, the company sergeant major and most of the Headquarters platoon were dead. Again reaching Battalion Headquarters by radio I passed this information and was told that I was in command of the Company! My orders were to pull the two sections of the other two platoons into my platoon area and try to establish as big a bridgehead as possible. It is difficult to describe conditions at that time. Continuous smoke from mortars and artillery reduced visibility to less than ten yards, even in daylight and in this gloom there was a continuous rain of high explosive. In addition, bullets were flying in all directions, mostly in large bursts from Brens (ours) and Spandaus (theirs).

That night, Battalion tried to bring over the remainder. They were just plain unlucky, being caught in mid-river by a chance flare, a fatal chance. Mortar bombs came down until the river was heaving and frothing and nothing could live in that vortex. Nothing did. The next thing I can remember for certain is a radio message from Brigade telling me I was the only Officer left in the Battalion still on his feet and I was in command! Rapid promotion indeed but not in a way anyone would like. The battle continued for seven days in all, and in that time my command managed to advance a total of three quarters of a mile to a culvert on the Cassino Rome road.

Sheltering in the culvert were the entire section I had lost on the night we made the initial crossing. They had reached there that night and had suffered neither casualties nor resistance. God knows how many grenades we used or how much ammunition. Early on we devised a system of pulling supplies over the bank packed in sand-bags, using some of the fixed ropes. It was the only way as it was impossible to show ones head on top of the bank without getting a bullet through it. We advanced simply by bombing our way from slit trench to slit trench always taking care that no-one infiltrated behind us. This was no easy task with the small number of men I had left but we managed by keeping headquarters section well in our rear. By a great stroke of luck they had both snipers alive and fit and they were able to pick off anyone who tried that game.

For the whole of the seven days it was impossible to stand upright and stay alive. We crawled rolled slithered and dragged ourselves about on our bellies, occasionally enjoying the luxury of sitting upright in a slit trench that had been dug deeper than the norm before the attack began. After that the sound or sign of any sort of digging brought down an intense bombardment of every type of high explosive device.

The southern division, 8th Indian, had been slightly more successful, although its crossing in a thick mist was confused and seriously delayed. Nevertheless a shallow bridgehead was established and two bridges completed by 9.15 a.m. on the 12th, four Canadian tanks crossing to help clear part of San Angelo. On the 13th a bridge was completed in 4th Division's sector and both divisions advanced a few miles, 12th Brigade crossing the river and pushing forward on the left of the 10th towards the Cassino–Pignataro road, as did 17th Indian Brigade on their left after clearing San Angelo. Fusilier F. R. Beacham of the 1st Royal Fusiliers was in this brigade. He was manning a Bren gun covering the initial river crossing on 11 May, which he describes:

Immediately our troops began to place their boats in the water and the first ones started to cross. The shells whined overhead incessantly and it was difficult to hear anything above the din. I saw the first of our troops start to clamber up the fairly short, but steep, bank on the far side and then the enemy replied. Large mortar bombs started to explode all around us followed, almost immediately, by heavy artillery fire. The enemy infantry opened up with his machine guns and tracer bullets whipped and whanged their way a few feet over our heads. I prepared to return the fire but found that, as our troops were now in my line of fire, I was unable to do so. I could see them reasonably clearly moving forward just across the river and all we could do was to watch as the machine gun bullets arched and swathed across the crossing point. The enemy had obviously fixed their machine guns to fire on fixed lines so as to cover this crossing point. Had I known where that particular machine gun was located, I could have returned fire if I had positioned myself to the left of the crossing point instead of to the right.

The amount of artillery being fired now by both sides was

tremendous and a gradual mist and smoke started to envelop the battlefield. Mortar bombs were continuing to fall all around us. The bullets were flying in droves about us and it was becoming increasingly apparent that I would not be able to return the enemy's machine gun fire from that position and there was the real prospect that at any moment one of the mortar bombs would find its mark smack in the middle of our backs. I suggested to Bill that we find somewhere a little bit safer and he agreed. We crawled back a relatively short distance from the bank and found a large shell hole, it still smelt strongly of cordite but on the presumption that no two shells fall in the same place, we stayed put. The shelling continued unabated and it was whilst we were in this shell hole that we heard a cry for help coming from from somewhere to our right. It was a plaintiff [sic] cry repeating over and over again 'Help me, I've been hit'. We had orders not to stop in the event of anyone getting wounded as they would be dealt with by the Red Cross stretcher bearers. We did not go to the aid of this person and it may well be that he was killed in the continuing enemy bombardment for after a few more minutes, the cries stopped.

During the night Beacham and 'Bill' were moved over the river and came to a halt, lying in an irrigation ditch, where they remained, increasingly frustrated, throughout the following two days, pinned down by enemy machine-gun fire. He picks up the story again:

On the third night at about 2 am, our Officer crawled along to us and whispered our orders for the following morning. These were that at eleven o'clock we were going to make a frontal assault on the enemy position. It was explained that the Company's two inch mortars were to fire at the enemy positions from the flanks and we were to rush the positions whilst they did so. On delivering these instructions, he crawled away again. I reflected on what I had been told and I couldn't help but wonder what good would the two inch mortars be against a well dug in and virtually unseen enemy when a barrage of a thousand guns had failed to achieve the same result and my stomach turned over at the prospect.

The night passed slowly and at about half past three, the enemy started to shell our positions with the largest calibre shells that I had heard from either side. They came in like an express train pulling into a station and erupted in a tremendous explosion. I virtually shrank into the ground in fear. My ears strained for the first sound of the next incoming shell, which wasn't long in coming. This one came in with an even louder sound, or so it seemed to me, and I felt like getting up and running like hell, but where could I go? That shell burst no more than five yards away vibrating the earth and sending clogs of earth in all directions, which fell down on us like rain. I listened for the next one and prayed 'Oh God, don't let me die yet. I promise that I will always be good if you let me live' and I really meant it. The next shell came in and went a little bit further on that time. Thank God, I thought my prayers have been answered and the shelling, as far as we were concerned, stopped. If it hadn't, I might well have died of sheer fright.

As the time approached eleven, I tried to relax my stiff muscles a little and I prepared my Bren gun and it seemed that only seconds went by before whistles sounded and as one man, we rose to our feet and began to run forward. The machine guns began to open up at once and the crack of the bullets as they sometimes passed close to my ears almost made one deaf. I had no idea what was happening on either side of me. As I ran I knew that Bill was still with me and looking ahead, I saw that the ground was flat except for these irrigation furrows which ran parallel with the river for a distance of about four hundred yards and the ground then sloped gently upwards to where the enemy was dug in. I could see no movement at all, simply heard the sound of the bullets as they ripped by us. I don't think that we had covered more than one hundred yards or so when, with no orders being given, I saw the rest of the Company dropped into another of these irrigation furrows (thank God they were there). Puffing and panting with exertion and fear, we tried to get our breath back. The enemy kept up a constant stream of machine gun fire in the general direction of our new position and because we were that much closer to him, he was able to traverse the far side of the ditch and we found ourselves on our sides pressed against the dirt on the side nearest to the enemy. There we were in a much worse position than before and wondering what to do about it when, after a few minutes, the order was whispered from man to man, that we were to make our own way, in our own time, back to our original start line. I waited with Bill until we had got our breath back and then I told him that on a count of three, we would get up and run like hell. I counted and did we run, the thought of the bullets ripping into my back made sure that I did and so did Bill. Bullets ripped by us as we ran back and it seemed to me to be longer running back than it had been going forward. The hair seemed to stand on end at the back of my neck and eventually we made it back to our original start line.

There Beacham and his comrades remained, hungry and thirsty, all through the rest of the day and the following night. After the mist had cleared next morning, some Canadian tanks succeeded in crossing the river to support them. As his platoon began to move forward, Beacham saw the dead bodies of his company commander and several of his comrades. He came across one who was badly wounded and who asked him for a drink, but his water-bottle was dry. However he collected some from a furrow and, as he placed the bottle to the man's lips, the latter said 'Thanks a lot, mate,' and died. Having tried to help another badly wounded man, he rejoined his platoon on a slight ridge further on.

Bombardier Coltman's 52nd Field Regiment Royal Artillery was still supporting 8th Indian Division. He wrote:

Progress during daylight on Friday 12th May was slight, advances being limited to a hundred yards or so, and then only after extremely bitter fighting. For over five months the enemy had been perfecting the defences of the Gustav Line. As we saw later for ourselves, good use had been made of that time. Every building was a strong point. Dug-outs and tunnels were beneath each building. Felled trees, covered with rubble several feet thick reinforced the roofs of these underground rooms. In these dug-outs the enemy was practically immune from shell fire. The barrage may have frightened and shaken the enemy; it may have caused some to be 'bomb happy'; but it is unlikely that it inflicted many casualties. With the lifting of the barrage the enemy came up from the underground shelters, manned their firing points and poured streams of deadly fire at our assaulting troops.

The Argyll and Sutherland Highlanders, of 19 Brigade, were in a tight spot. This Battalion [the 1st] had crossed the river at a point where it formed the shape of the letter V. All day, the Battalion were hemmed in this V shaped piece of ground, unable to move, the cross fire of automatic small arms pinning them to their slit trenches. They were in an impossible position to push forward and nothing could be done to relieve them during daylight. Under cover of night it was decided to withdraw the Argylls to the east bank of the river, and to push the Battalion across again higher up, at a place where the Punjabis had crossed in the initial assault the night before, and where a bridge now spanned the river. Artillery support was required to carry out the operation, to keep the enemy quiet and thus allow the Argylls to move. The battalion had only one assault boat left and the operation was, therefore, painfully slow. Nevertheless, the major portion of the Battalion regained the easterly bank. Arthur was duty 'ack'* that night and he told me that the guns were firing in support of the Argylls for most of the night. On the night of 11/12 May, the guns fired over five hundred rounds per gun to get the Battalion across the river. On this night, 12/13 May, the guns again fired over five hundred rounds per gun, but this time, it was to get the Battalion back across the river.

Private J. Carradice was with the Argylls and wrote his account:

The battle had begun. On reaching the river bank, the Battalion had sustained several casualties. Our company Commanding Officer, Major 'Jock' Hunter, had been killed. Major Sceales was severely wounded but his company managed to have him evacuated. Lieutenant McPhee had been killed but Lieutenants Smith and Scott were wounded. It was virtually impossible at that stage to estimate the number of other ranks amongst the casualties. During the barrage, the Germans had fired smoke bombs into our group making it almost impossible for us to see a hand in front of our faces.

Now things really did begin to go wrong. Our company had only managed to push eight boats to the water's edge. The other companies did not have much success either. This shortage of boats had made it necessary for many of us to wade across the swift flowing river. To add to our increasing difficulties, barbed wire had been placed on the other bank by the enemy. I was with the lucky few who had managed to find a gap in that barbed wire defence. With Lieutenant Lamard, our platoon continued advancing from the river, until, by dawn, we were well into the open valley, in full view of the enemy as they gazed down on our ready-dug trenches. The situation was serious.

B, C and D Companies were still being held up by the barbed

---

* The Assistant to the Forward Observation Officer on duty.

wire in full view of the enemy. They lay in shallow irrigation ditches and any attempt to move or organize parties to cut the wire was met with a hail of fire from the opposition. On the other side of the river, A Company and Battalion Headquarters lay in equally shallow irrigation ditches and were constantly ravaged by shellfire. Our own link with Brigade Headquarters had failed, making communication seem like a forgotten dream. The Commanding Officer decided that, until the tanks could get across the river and work round the three companies on the far side, the Battalion could only 'sit and take it'.

The enemy continued their hammering for thirty-six hours, until it forced those gallant men to withdraw across the river. Major Elder, who was in command of the withdrawal, displayed the coolness and courage, which resulted in the award of a well deserved Military Cross.

The small, successful platoon of ours, which had crossed the river and gained its objective, was still in the thick of the action and was supported by the Punjabis of our Brigade. We were still holding onto our well-earned position, which had helped to form an important bridgehead across the river. In our trenches, we were ordered to keep hold of our positions until the tanks could move towards us with those much needed reinforcements. My saturated pants were quickly becoming unbearable. So I decided to do something about them. Off they came, to be squeezed out in an attempt to make them at least bearable to wear for some time to come. At that moment, a plane flew towards my position, it had come from the direction of the enemy lines. I instinctively jumped from the trench, grabbing the bren gun, which was mounted on its tripod, and took full aim at the plane. I ignored the sounds and danger of the enemy's guns, as they fired down on us from the Monastery ahead but I allowed the wind to take the upperhand. By blowing my shirt flaps upwards, the wind revealed to enemy, in the midst of the battle, a full view of my private quarters. The laughter that this generated was tremendous and it served as a morale booster for my comrades, although for myself, when I learned that the aircraft had been one of ours, the episode did nothing at all. The plane had been on a reconnaissance flight for the Poles in their second attempt to capture Cassino.

An important part of Leese's plan was that the first tanks to move across the river and support the infantry on the far side should be ones which could exploit success and turn it into an advance up the Liri valley without the delay involved in trying to pass different ones, from the armoured divisions, through those supporting the infantry. The difficulties he had experienced when commanding 30th Corps at El Alamein were at the forefront of his mind. The solution he found was that the armoured brigades of the armoured divisions, which he hoped would lead that advance, should provide the tank support for 4th, 8th Indian and 78th Divisions. Thus 26th Armoured Brigade, from 6th Armoured Division, was supporting 4th Division. The leading regiment was the 17th/21st Lancers, in which Trooper H. Buckle was serving. Unfortunately his tank did not get very far, as he describes:

Jack Tippett urged Bob Nutland on – 'We are crossing this stream, put your foot down'. Bob did too and then we found the ground was marshy and we reversed out. Jack now looked round for another crossing and a better position from which he could support the other troops. Again the driver was ordered to advance and once more, the Sherman tank forged ahead. This crossing was no better than the last and we were being slowed down. Bob slammed his gear lever into emergency low and then into reverse as the water and mud swirled round our tracks. Suddenly we stopped and the powerful engine, though turning the tracks, could not budge us. We were well and truly stuck.

Dawn had broken by now and though a little shelling and mortaring was evident, Jack Tippett ordered Bob and myself out of the tank to dig and see if we could get out of our plight. Some uncomfortable minutes were thus spent until the job was given up as hopeless. As things turned out, we were to stay there the entire action – which lasted four days. Though the piece of ground on which we stood was not contested at close quarters, nevertheless we experienced our share of shelling and mortaring.

Water had begun to seep into the tank by now and very soon it was half way up the gearbox. To put it another way, the water came well over our ankles. The people in the turret were not affected, for they were higher up in the tank than Bob and myself. Although stuck, we were still able to use our wireless and fire the gun electrically for the Aux Jenny [auxiliary generator] was still in use. Thus the batteries were kept fully charged.

When we first arrived at this spot, the infantry, who were dug in, seemed quite cheerful. There were one or two casualties: one chap had a fractured leg and had tied his rifle to it, acting as a splint. He and a few other slightly injured soldiers were awaiting evacuation to a field hospital. Some of these eventually got there, but not the chap with his leg in a splint. He was killed later that morning by shell fire and I remember seeing him hanging over the trench with a gaping head wound and blood overflowing around the side of the slit trench. Alas, this was only the beginning and, before the day was out, there were dead everywhere. The following two days saw them being piled up behind our tank and as the sun rose and the weather became hot, the stench became almost unbearable.

Engineers. R.A.S.C. drivers, infantrymen and tank crews. All suffered at Cassino. Two 'C' Squadron men were killed that morning. Alf Wright was one, when a heavy shell landed on top of his driving hatch. The other crew members were unhurt, but they came out, for it was impossible now to fight in a tank like this. It was a ghastly day for them and I remember the wireless operator, Frank Huzinga, telling later how they had to dodge bullets and shellfire on their way out. Poor Alf: all he ever wanted to do was to go back to his milk round, his wife and family. Now it was not to be. But war is like that and is no respecter of persons. How tragically obvious this became to me as that year rolled on. A junior commander, whose name now escapes me, was killed too. He died instantly. A Scotsman this chap, who would never go back to his beloved country. Alan Langfeld was a member of this crew and he gave the sad news of the death over the air. 'Put the body in the ditch by the side of the road' – this was the Sqn. Leader talking. 'Take command yourself for the time being'. Alan did just that and proved himself most capable.

It was surprising how people from the various walks of life acted in situations like this. I've seen the 'rough' types crack up and the quiet, shy types stand up to the strain and take a terrific hammering without any sign of panic. War, it is true, brings out the best and the worst in any man.

The 17th/21st Lancers suffered fifty-seven killed and wounded in the first six days of the battle.

On 13 May Leese decided to move 78th Division through 4th Division's sector rather than 8th Indian's as he had originally intended, anxious about the vulnerability of 4th Division's left flank as a gap

developed between it and 8th Indian, its own 28th Brigade being still
hors de combat east of the river. 78th Division's progress on the 15th
was sufficient to persuade Leese on the 16th to order Anders to resume
his attack. He did so in the early hours of the 17th, which saw both 4th
and 78th Divisions, supported by 26th Armoured Brigade, finally reach
Route 6 at last light. By that time the Poles had regained Point 593 and
the Germans had decided to withdraw from the GUSTAV line. The Poles
raised their flag over the ruins of the monastery at 10.20 a.m. on the
18th.

The possibility of a rapid break-out depended critically on the
construction of bridges over the Rapido. The most promising was bridge
AMAZON in 4th Division's northern sector in which 2nd Bedfords in
10th Brigade held a bridgehead. Lieutenant F. G. Sutton was commanding their pioneer platoon and wrote of his experiences:

> All of a sudden, hell broke loose. It was 11 p.m. on May 11th 1944.
> All our guns opened up. The screaming of the shells over our heads
> was fantastic. We had never heard such terrific noise. Howling over
> us was a real curtain of rushing steel with continuous flashes from
> behind, and the crunch of explosions in front of us. There was a
> delay when we reached the river. The Surreys had started crossing,
> but most of their boats had been sunk. The Rapido is only a small
> river, though with a fast current. But at night, and under fire, it
> looked big. Our artillery barrage had raised huge clouds of dust
> which were now drifting back towards the river. There were two
> boats left and in them the battalion crossed. When I set my foot on
> the other side I was scared stiff of mines. Soon I realised the bank
> must have been cleared. We could not see much, but we marked a
> safe lane with white tape from the river to the rifle companies. The
> latter had reached 'Queen Street', a track about half a mile inside the
> enemy line. Casualties were fairly high, mainly from mortar fire, but
> also from mines.
>
> The enemy counter-attacked seven times during darkness, but
> they were beaten off each time with the help of the gun barrage, Our
> Artillery Forward Observation Officer (the F.O.O.) was just 'pulling
> the chain!', as he said, and down came the barrage at any given spot.
> The F.O.O.'s signaller was a little chap who looked more like a book-
> worm than a soldier. But he had the heart of a lion. With complete
> disregard of the stuff flying around he quietly sat in his shallow slit

and passed on the gunners fire orders over the wireless set. He called for a 'Stonk' if the target was an area, or for a 'Murder' if it was a certain spot, or for a 'Bomber' if all calibres were to join in; he gave the number of 'rounds gunfire' which George Smith, the F.O.O., had ordered as a remedy for the situation, and in between, he read a book as soon as it got light enough. Later that year I saw him wearing the ribbon of the Military Medal.

Battalion Headquarters, which Sutton's platoon was protecting, was established on the far bank of the Rapido, and when the early morning mist had cleared they realized that they were in full view of the enemy on Monastery Hill; but their supporting artillery kept the hill covered in smoke. Close to them the Royal Engineers were preparing to build AMAZON bridge and Sutton admired the courage with which the operator of the unarmoured bulldozer carried calmly on with his task under fire from machine-guns, mortars, artillery and nebelwerfers. It became possible to search for and pick up the wounded and to get supplies up to the forward companies. Eventually the bridge was completed and tanks of the 17th/21st Lancers crossed, while a continuous pall of smoke was provided by canisters, operated partly by the Engineers and partly by a Light Anti-Aircraft Battery of the Royal Artillery.

If a force of any strength was to be maintained in an advance up the Liri valley, it was essential to open up Route 6 as a major road as soon as possible. Because of the difficulties in clearing all the rubble in Cassino town, it was decided to convert the railway, which ran just south of it, into a road, to be used as the 'down route' while the cleared road through the town was the 'up'. The 139th Mechanical Equipment Company Royal Engineers was employed on this task, which involved filling in thirty large craters and building several bridges. Lieutenant A. J. W. Scopes commanded a platoon and described their part:

We stood by, having moved our transporters forward to a point just off the main road and south of Mount Trocchio where we were out of direct view from Cassino. We stayed in an olive orchard for several days waiting for the final instructions and when these eventually arrived we moved off on a very dark night. There were, of course, no lights on any of the vehicles we had already become used to moving about at night without any lights, although it was a considerable strain to try and keep on the road at about 5 miles an hour. The bulldozers, loaded on the transporters, already had their engines running because in the quiet of the night the little donkey engines, which had to be started in order to start, in turn, the larger diesel engines, made a frightful noise and could have been heard for miles away. Even the noise of the main engines seemed very loud in the quiet of the night. Cassino was only about two miles away up the road. We moved down the tracks and reached the railway at code name 'Capetown' at about 10 o'clock at night. We soon got to work and somehow got the bulldozers unloaded without accident. The drivers, of course, were absolutely super and knew their machines to the inch. The first thing that had to be done was to get the dozer blades under the lengths of railway line and sleepers which we then pulled upwards and outwards to slither down railway embankments. Craters were filled with the nearest material that could be obtained without going too far off the railway track because the whole area was full of land mines. Fortunately no mines were set off and to be honest we worked relatively peacefully until about midnight by which time we had reached code name 'Elsie's River' where there were a series of 12 ft. shell holes covering about 250 yards. We were in the middle of trying to get this lot sorted out when a terrific barrage of our own 25 pounders started up from behind us. I am sure that the El Alemein [sic] barrage was almost a minor affair compared to this barrage!! In addition it was not long before the Germans were hurling their hardware back and we seemed to be just within nice mortar range for them. Several sticks of mortar bombs fell uncomfortably close and I came to the conclusion that we could not advance any further with our activities because by this time we were just round the shoulder of Mount Trocchio and in full view from Cassino.

By the time I had decided to pull back and wait for the dawn attack we were being 'stonked' to some considerable degree but only lost one machine. Our own barrage continued for the next hour or two and was quite deafening and I realised that our infantry must have gone in so we started off again on the work and continued our task to Kimberley where Task 'B' took over from us. Our transporters had made their way in the night up to a point somewhere near code name 'Newcastle' and we managed to reassemble in some sort of order. We had no idea that Cassino had already fallen and that 'A' Task was working in the most appalling conditions on the road in the town itself. I later heard from Al Fawcett that they bulldozed every conceivable item into some of the craters including blown up tanks and motorbikes and other vehicles. It was a case of moving on at the greatest speed possible so that our tanks could get up in support of the infantry who had done such a wonderful job in the night attack.

Kesselring's approval of von Vietinghoff's decision to withdraw had been brought about, not primarily by the pressure from Eighth Army, but by the remarkable success of the Fifth, especially that of the French Corps. They had captured Monte Majo, described as 'the southern bastion of the GUSTAV line',* on 13 May. On the 14th Juin made rapid progress through the Aurunci mountains and early on the 15th took Ausonia, on the road from Cassino to Gaeta, while the 2nd US Corps made good progress along the coast. He then sent his Moroccan Goums across the mountains between the two rapidly retreating German divisions, the 71st and 94th, aiming for Pico behind the HITLER line. Their leading *groupements* were already nearing the road running south from there on the 18th, as were the leading troops of 2nd US Corps near the coast, reaching Gaeta on the 19th. By this time Juin was getting anxious about the vulnerability of his right flank as Eighth Army's forward troops lagged behind.

R. Ridgway was a conscientious objector, serving with the Hadfield-Spears Field Hospital, attached to the 1st French Division de Marche, having previously served with a Friends Ambulance Unit. His diary covers this period:

Fri. 12th May. Casualties started to come in at about 2 a.m. My first job this morning was to help John Swindale lay out a 'nig' whose right foot had been blown off. The casualties were placed on stretchers outside 'Reception'. Most of them only had slight wounds, but their clothes were ripped and they looked haggard and grimy. I handed round cigarettes and helped two French girls to give out coffee. The tents were soon filled with groaning patients, and the operating theatre was kept busy all day. I helped in one of the wards. I washed some of the patients and did some dressings. I gather that the attack was not a great success on this sector of the front. They

---

* Sir William Jackson, *The Battle for Italy* (Batsford: London, 1967), p. 234.

met with stiffer opposition than they had expected. I went to bed early and slept soundly.

1st June. I have had very little time since my last entry to do any writing. On Sat. 13th May, I was working all day in one of the wards and also on 'Resuscitation'. I went on working right through the night. I saw some dreadful cases – men with parts of their brains hanging out and their legs blown off by mines. There was one man who was waiting to go into the operating theatre to have his legs amputated. Asked how he felt, he replied: 'Well, I couldn't run a race, but I've got plenty of fight left in me, and I'm going to live.' He died after the operation. There was an American who had a piece of shrapnel in his spine, and he was paralysed from the waist downwards. He said: 'So you think I'll get over this.' I told him that he would, but the poor chap died during the operation. There were many cases like this. I felt terribly depressed. One day Michael said to me: 'When are you going to ask to be transferred back to the clinics'. One night we were just giving someone a blood transfusion when we heard the noise of a machine gun. We all instinctively ducked, except the doctor who carried on with what he was doing. We heard the drone of a plane, and then CRUMP ... CRUMP ... CRUMP. I think Jerry was after a gun which was placed near the hospital. I do not remember how long we stayed at S. Clemente – I lost count of the days. I had no time to read or write; no time even to wash. But one morning we woke to find that the guns had gone and it was very peaceful and quiet, and most of the patients had been evacuated. Then the Colonel said: 'We move forward again to-morrow. We are going to a position which at the moment is held by the Germans, but they will have left by the time we arrive.' We had a very busy day taking down tents. The Forward theatre went on ahead; and in the early hours of the morning we left S. Clemente, and crossed the Garalgiani [sic]. The road was treacherous – very muddy and narrow, and there were notices warning us not to go too near the sides because of mines. On several occasions I nearly skidded over the side of the road. We passed many roadside wooden crosses and the dead soldier's tin hats placed on top of the cross. Sometimes the air was filled with the horrible stench of decomposed bodies. Most of our trucks got stuck somewhere or other, but apart from skidding very badly at times, I was fortunate enough to get to our new site in the Liri valley without mishap. The Colonel chose the most conspicuous site for the hospital, overlooking the German lines at the foot of Mount Cairo. As soon as we arrived we put down the Red X ground flag. Then for the next few days we were very busy again, and I saw many more dreadful sights. When I was not working I slept in a ditch which I shared with Mike Rowntree and Ralph Davies. One day the hospital was shelled. I have never felt so scared in my life. Shells were bursting all round us. One fell in Maintainance, another near the girls' tents, another hit a house about 100 yds from where I was standing. I rushed over to the wards and helped to put the patients on the floor. Fortunately none of the wards was hit, and there was only one minor casualty – a piece of shrapnell hit Gaffer's leg, and he is now hobbling about on crutches.

Leese had ordered 1st Canadian Corps to pass through 8th Indian Division on the 16th and head for Pontecorvo, but progress was hampered by severe traffic congestion and some confusion of command, and their attack on the HITLER line* at Pontecorvo by 1st Canadian Division (Major-General C. Vokes) was not launched until 23 May. At the same time 78th Division threatened Aquino, five miles further north, just south of Route 6, and the Poles Piedimonte, three miles further east. Lieutenant W. H. Pope was commanding a platoon in D Company of the Royal 22e Regiment in the 1st Canadian Division's 3rd Brigade, and had been involved in the fighting leading up to this. He wrote:

In leading 'D' Company to the start line at dawn on 17 May 1944, Major Ovila Garceau temporarily took the wrong road – which proved useful to me, for along this road I found a rifle that I used that day and the next. But the immediate result was that we arrived at the start line at H-Hour in single file. I was tight up against the flank of 'A' Company and thus, at precisely H-Hour, that company's Lieutenant Fred Letarte (who had got me out of an American clink in Naples a week earlier) and I shook hands, wishing each other good luck. I was to have more than Fred, for he was dead with a bullet

---

* Now renamed by the Germans, in order not to associate the Führer with its likely loss, the SENGER line.

through his head within half an hour. But in arriving on the start line precisely at H-Hour in single file, we had no time both to get our platoons in line for the attack and to establish clearly where each platoon's objective was. However, in the early-morning mist and the smoke of our exploding shells, I saw before me a hill with farm houses on the top. Since our barrage was moving in one hundred yard steps towards this hill and since no other platoon was now in sight, I decided that no. 17 would take the hill. Placing Corporal Colas's section on one side of me and Corporal Lachance's on the other, I began to follow the moving barrage as closely as possible – that is within a hundred yards of where our shells were landing: as soon as I saw that the barrage had lifted and the shells were exploding a hundred yards closer to the enemy, I galloped forward to jump into a shell-hole made thirty seconds earlier and still warm from the explosion. Unless there were enemy shells mixed in with our own, nobody bothered us during our advance. Therefore, during the minute rests between my hundred yard dashes, I had the time to feel proud of myself leading my platoon in my first attack against the enemy. It was then that I noticed that one of my boot-laces was undone. In retying it, I felt less proud: to be killed while doing up my boot-laces had never been part of my dreams of glory.

After a few minutes, we were almost at the top of the hill, about a hundred yards from the houses, when I arrived in a shell-hole already occupied by the first German soldier I had ever seen in my life. Since he was very still, I took him for dead. To make sure, I pushed him with the muzzle of my rifle. At this, the German, very much alive, indicated he wished to surrender by presenting me with his pistol, still in its holster. I accepted the pistol, very happy to have already captured my Luger before we had even fired a shot, and indicated to my prisoner to go to the rear by crawling through my platoon. When later I had the time to open the holster, I found it contained the German equivalent of a Very (flare) pistol! The bastard!. An instant or two after I had captured my ersatz Luger, a German soldier rose fifty yards in front of me to run as fast as he could from one shelter to another. On one knee, I fired at the centre of the target and the German – apparently a sergeant and commander of the position – fell dead, a bullet in his head. At this, we completed our until then peaceful assault. There was not a German in sight: all were hiding in their dug-outs. Here was the advantage of following our barrage so closely: we were on the objective before the enemy realized it.

We had to get the Germans out of their dug-outs. So, I teamed up with Corporal Lachance. My mother being Belgian (Walloon) and having thus learnt that the Flemish for 'out' was 'uit', and thinking that 'uit' would work for Germans also, I went from dug-out to dug-out yelling 'uit'. Unfortunately, the Germans were not bilingual in Flemish, so Corporal Lachance was obliged to throw a 36 grenade into each dug-out. At one dug-out our grenade did not explode. I told the corporal to try another and we both leaned over the entrance to see how this one would work. There was an enormous explosion at our feet and I did a back somersault for the one and only time in my life. Less lucky, Corporal Lachance lay gravely wounded in his right shoulder. At the moment, I thought that a shell, coming from somewhere, had landed between us. Now, I'm not sure: it could have been our two grenades going off together. In any case, not having a stretcher, we had Corporal Lachance carried on a door by five of the prisoners we took here.

British tanks had now come up about a hundred yards or so on our left. Since it was 'A' Company and not 'D' that was supposed to have tanks in support, I said to myself: 'Here we are on the wrong objective; worse, maybe ours is ahead of where we are now'. My signaller, who had accompanied Sergeant Maurice Careau and the reserve section during the assault, had rejoined me. I therefore tried to contact Major Garceau by wireless. The fact that I was not able to do so confirmed to me that we were in the wrong place: clearly we were detached from the company. We therefore set off for another farm a few hundred yards in front, the British tanks keeping pace in more open ground on our left. We reached this second objective without incident – maybe another prisoner or two; I forget.

Pope made contact with these tanks, but failed to persuade them to cooperate, perhaps because his men had at first fired at them, mistaking them for German ones. However he succeeded in edging his platoon forward until they came up against a German defensive position, which, at his request, his company commander allowed him to attack. His account continues:

Having given an order to the 2″ mortar detachment to cover us if necessary, I advanced with Corporal Colas and five or six men of his section to where we had seen the ten or so German soldiers, who had now taken cover. About thirty yards from their bunker, we came upon a barbed-wire obstacle that, being knee-high, had been hidden from us until then by the grain of the same height. We had just crossed the obstacle without difficulty when a mortar bomb landed between Private Gaston Simard and me, gravely wounding Simard in the stomach. I turned to see what had happened. On seeing Simard, I told Corporal Colas to help him. Then, at last, I looked around me and I realized that we were in the middle of the Hitler Line, surrounded by enemy bunkers . . . and we were without any support. I then ordered Corporal Colas's section to rejoin 17 platoon in the rear, while I dropped to one knee in front of Corporal Colas and Private Simard. Once Simard was bandaged, my intention was to help Corporal Colas carry him back to our position. But after a few minutes, Corporal Colas was wounded by a bullet that broke his thigh bone.

At the same moment, 'B' Company must have appeared on the battlefield, for during the next two hours bullets and shells whistled over our heads and even lower. At a given moment, a bullet hit my helmet, stoving it in to such an extent that the steel of the helmet struck my forehead. Blood ran into my eye and for an instant I thought I was dead, but I got off with only concussion and a headache. Finally, I concluded that 'B' Company was not going to reach the Hitler Line and thus help me evacuate my two wounded. Because of the German wire, I could not carry them back one after the other in my arms: standing up, one would not have lived five seconds. So, I took off my equipment, keeping only my pistol, and, having promised Corporal Colas and Private Simard that I would come back for them, I slid on my back under the barbed wire and then crawled back to 'B' Company, which had not been able to go beyond the line where I had left my platoon before my stroll into and out of the Hitler Line.

Pope, with the approval of Major Garceau, returned with five men, four carrying two stretchers, all unarmed and having put on Red Cross armbands, Pope having removed his rank badges. Waving a Red Cross flag, they made their way safely to the German line. Simard had died and the Germans had bandaged Corporal Colas's wound, which was still bleeding. Pope went with him to a German aid post, but was not allowed to return to his own lines. A German captain correctly pointed out that, as combatant soldiers, as Pope had admitted that they were, they should not have worn Red Cross armbands and were not entitled to be treated as if they were medical personnel. He was therefore treated as a prisoner of war. When being taken to the rear on 30 May, he jumped out of the back of the truck and escaped, joining a partisan group, and was helped by them to cross back into Allied lines on 20 July. Corporal Colas survived.

After a fierce battle which lasted all day on the 23rd, in which casualties were high, the Canadians broke through, opening the way for their 5th Armoured Division to pass through next day, when 13th Corps, on their right, found Aquino and the Poles Piedimonte abandoned. 6th British Armoured Division was then ordered to pass through, adding to the traffic congestion.

By this time the break-out from Anzio had started. On 18 May Alexander had released 36th US Division to Anzio, and it took four days to ship it all there. On the 23rd Truscott launched his attack in the right-hand sector of the beachhead towards Cisterna with 3rd and 34th Infantry and 1st Armored US Divisions and their Special Service Force, while the 45th made a subsidiary attack near the Via Anziate and the two British divisions a similar one near the coast on the left. Lieutenant Harold Mitchell had been commissioned into the Oxford-shire and Buckinghamshire Light Infantry and sent to the Middle East as a reinforcement at the end of 1942, finding himself posted as a Liaison Officer with the Free French and promoted to the temporary rank of captain. Keen to see more active service, he was posted, after more training, as a lieutenant to the 1st King's Shropshire Light Infantry in the 1st Division, and joined them as a platoon commander at Anzio in May 1944. He wrote regularly home, as he did on 14 May:

This is a grand life and I am thoroughly enjoying myself. Please don't think I am saying this just to make you happier. It really is so. I've not been so happy since my early days with the Legion, and I wouldn't go back to liaising on a Div. level for anything under the sun. I had almost forgotten what a terrific satisfaction Platoon commanding is. There is no job in the Army to touch it. You are the link between the idea of the C.O., Brigadier or Army Commander, and the men who carry that idea out. As a Company Commander circumstances force you to be somewhat aloof. For one thing, the numbers in a Coy are too large for you to get to know everyone – particularly when you have casualties and constant replacements. You deal with your men largely through your Subalterns, Sergeants, C.S.M., C.Q.M.S. and so forth, and the only private soldiers you get to know well are those in Coy H.Q. – storeman, clerk and so forth. With a platoon in the line, you live with your men and share their existence. In home soldiering (how glad I am I've left that behind me!) the officer lives apart, has privileges and comforts the men don't get. This has always irked me. After four years I was getting used to it, but I still don't see the necessity of it.

In the line, all that goes by the board. You don't get the situation of the officer sleeping on a camp bed, and the men sleeping on the ground. You carry one blanket, and your only mattress is mother earth. Your kit is what you carry in your small pack – shaving tackle, a spare pair of socks and a cardigan. In the morning you will find yourself sharing a shaving mirror with your runner, or Mortarman. We are doing section cooking, using petrol fires. (Woodfires would smoke too much and give the positions away). Platoon H.Q. has an excellent cook in Edwards, who serves up M. and V. as well as he fires the 2″ Mortar, which is saying something. I have, I am told, the best Pl. runner in the company, Taffy Protheroe, a twenty-year old laddie, very small, with a great shock of tousled hair. I'm told he has never failed to get through and deliver his message, even in the hottest situation. I share my shelter with Davies, my Platoon Sergeant, who is absolutely first class. There is nothing he doesn't know about his job, and he's loyal as you make 'em. But what makes a Platoon are the rank and file, and they are terrific. For simplicity, humour, and sheer guts, the British Tommy is the salt of the earth. I know all this must sound frightfully conventional, but it's true, and its truth has never struck me so forcibly before. After having lived with these people, worked with them, yarned with them, ducked down with them when the stuff comes over low amd laughed at it afterwards – do you think I could go back to a staff job? Not on your life. They can keep that third pip and they can keep their staff pay. I'm happy right here.

One learns quickly. For the first few days in the line, your tendency is to duck every time you hear a whistling noise. And then you gradually begin to distinguish something that is coming from something that is going. You recognize that that high whine gradually falling in the pitch of its note, which sounds so terrifying at first, is surely only a shell passing high overhead, destined to shake up someone at Bn. H.Q. But the sound you do learn to listen for is the 'swish-swish' of the mortar bomb which tells you that you've got about two seconds to get under cover. (Incidentally, rather the same noise is made when you rustle a ground sheet, so that sometimes you find yourself taking cover for nothing at all). Phase II of ones education comes when you find that even when a mortar bomb goes off quite near you, making a terrific crack, it does surprisingly little harm and you may get off without a scratch. Then you get a contempt for the things and (unless they sound right on top of you) you don't even bother to duck, Phase III comes after you've been badly hit for the first time, or when you've had someone killed when sitting next to you. Then you get shaky and jumpy again, and it needs a real effort to keep calm. I am at present at Phase II, and I'm not anxious for my education to proceed any further for the moment. This is a great life. Things are pretty cushy and I promise to keep my head down' as they say.

In his letter of the 27th, he wrote:

Since I last wrote [20 May] I've been unfortunate in losing my Platoon Sgt. Davies, one of the grandest fellows you could hope to find anywhere. It was a mortar bomb and he got it in the chest and shoulder. I was a few yards away at the time and luckily escaped with a scratch – I did not even have to leave the line for a day. I've had worse scratches on wiring. The stretcher-bearer and I helped Davies to the Platoon Command Post and we dressed his wounds. Another bomb just afterwards killed a signaller and wounded another, whom we helped inside. This chap was very bad. By the time we'd finished the place looked like a surgical ward. Well, I'm very glad to say that Davies, although serious (he has been evacuated) will be OK and with any luck the war will be over by the time he's fit for duty again. My new Pl Sgt. Smith, is good, but Davies's are few and far between in any army. Smith is all right, but talks too much. He has an alarming habit of jumping from topic to topic, in his conversation, with no logical sequence, rather like Mr Price. I wonder if he comes from the same town. (Sgt. Smith is a Welshman). I'm told he did grand work in N. Africa and got recommended for the M.M. . . . .

Darkness. We move off and embuss in trucks. We crawl along the road with no headlamps on. Everything goes wrong. One truck goes into ditch and blocks road, and immediately there is a traffic jam of 20 vehicles. Jerry chooses this moment to stonk the area. The names the driver is called would scorch the paper. Finally after much pushing, we arrive at the debussing point. A long trudge along a road marked by shell-craters and lit by flashes of artillery. We meet the guides. They are complete dopes and lead us round and round and back and forth the same wood for two hours, emerging finally where we started. The troops are too tired and exasperated even to swear. We start again. This time everything goes swimmingly until we meet an outcoming Platoon in the same communication trench. In full equipment there is no room to squeeze past. Some-one must obviously get out, but no-one is disposed to. Jerry is stonking again. It ends up with the outgoing unit getting out and going over the top. They are anxious to get away – more so than we are to get in. We moved. Relief complete 4 hrs late but just in time. That is a sample relief for you.

He had written more in the same vein on 29 May and his next letter is dated 1 June:

The glorious first of June, and lovely weather with it! I've actually had a bathe today – took the company down to the beach. Nice to get a bit of fresh food – even though the meat is stringy and the potatoes taste of soap ('I do like my food clean', says TW, 'But that is taking cleanliness a bit too far.'). In the line one gets rather tired of the tins. Actually my Platoon had a bit of luck, as a shell hit the reserve dump of compo boxes, and scattered tins of every variety all over the wadi. I had a search-party out scavenging for tit-bits – salmon, marmalade, pudding, steak-and-kidney, and so on. The stores were written off as 'destroyed by enemy action', but we had them as buckshees and kept dark about what we had found.

I suppose the censor will let me say (what is in all the newspapers) that Jerry has been retreating. It was quite a novelty, being able to stand up in broad daylight in positions where previously one wriggled, crawled or crouched, to be able to stroll over and see where those posts actually were, which had been so annoying, to see what sort of field of fire his spandau had, to see just how near one had got when on patrol, and so on; to be able to stroll with impunity round

landmarks which had been notorious hot spots, all of them nicknamed with English names, some reminiscent of home . . . We found
a lot of our own boys, killed earlier on, lying where they had fallen,
unburied, in corn that is waist-high. The odd German grave with
'UNBEK. SOLDAT' on the cross. A ruined house, smashed to rubble,
with a child's pram, painted white, spick and span in the middle of
it. A dug-out that had been scooped out under a knocked out tank.
All most entertaining and instructive.

Tailpiece: After a particularly heavy stonk, the guns quieten down.
Dust and smoke are still in the air. Figures emerge tentatively from
trenches and dug-outs. A voice, querulously: 'To think my mother
wouldn't let me play Rugger because she said it was too dangerous!'

Love to all. Roll on that second front. It can't be long now, and
I dare say you'll be glad when the tension of waiting is over.

That was his last letter. He was killed by a mortar bomb soon afterwards.
As the Germans began to withdraw, the 46th Royal Tank Regiment
found themselves moving forward through the area in which they had
supported 24th Guards Brigade in the early days of the beachhead
fighting, as Signalman Lovett recorded in his diary:

30 May. Move up further in the evening – tanks have yet met no
resistance in Carroceto area. Main road choc-a-bloc with lorries nose
to tail creeping through their own dust-screen – dust which but a
few days ago would have brought a hail of shells. And here, round
about the much contested 'fly-over' bridge, was the scene of a most
amazing transformation. Literally not a square yard of ground was
without a shell-hole or bomb-crater scattered with shining jagged
shrapnel, parts of the concrete bridge were pitted and crumbled but
miraculously the bridge still stood. Every few yards the railway was
chopped as by a huge cheese-wire, steel rails were broken off and
twisted in fantastic contortions and sections of track were lifted and
hurled into the fields. Just beyond the bridge lay the house we had
lived in in January – now just a heap of bricks; all the neat orderly
fields were ragged and high with weeds, fences vanished and everywhere savage bomb-pits. For the next mile of what was once a quiet
stretch of blue tarred road, we lurched and bumped along the now
torn and shell-pitted track, marked every few yards by the burnt
wreck of an American truck or the rusting hull of a Sherman. We
passed a German Tiger tank by the roadside, a grotesque monster

with tremendously long gun and queer muzzle brake – several Mark IVs lay smashed and decrepit in the ditch and many American tank-busters and our Shermans. Every house had been pulverised – Carraceto wiped off the map and the 'factory' left a brick skeleton like a Roman ruin. Never have I seen such appalling destruction in so small an area. Turn left into the wadi country past a German tank splayed all over the road, a burnt-out British bren-carrier with the driver's blackened body leaning half out – the grisly bric-a-brac of war. Leaguer up once more in German leaguer recently evacuated – occupy their dug-outs, read the Deutsche Illustrierte Zeitung, look out for booby-traps and wondered if we're in a minefield.

At the opposite end of the chain of command, Alexander had been having trouble with Mark Clark. His intention had been that Truscott's thrust should be directed towards Valmontone on Route 6, east of the Alban Hills, hoping thus to block the withdrawal of both von Macken-sen's Fourteenth and von Vietinghoff's Tenth armies. Hitler was in fact playing into Alexander's hand by refusing to allow any withdrawal from the front facing Eighth Army. Truscott had made good progress in that direction by 25 May, on which day the leading troops of 2nd US Corps made contact with his right flank, while Kesselring's last reserve, the Hermann Goering Panzer Division, was ordered from near Rome to the Alban Hills and Valmontone. Truscott was now confident that he would be able to reach Valmontone on 27 May, and was taken aback when he received orders from Clark that he was to switch his main effort to the north-west, through the Alban Hills, directly towards Rome. Clark was determined to get there before the British, whom he suspected, in spite of the fact that the city was well within his army boundary, of trying to forestall him there, if possible before OVERLORD was launched. The excuse he gave after the war was that he thought Truscott's corps was not strong enough to reach Valmontone, once it had been reinforced, and that his orders allowed him to switch his effort along Route 7 if opposition to an advance towards Valmontone was too great. When Clark proposed to Alexander that he should take advantage of what he described as a weakness he had detected in the German defence of the Alban Hills, Alexander agreed on condition that the main effort to Valmontone was maintained. Clark's response was to leave only 3rd US Division with that task and to switch four others towards Rome. They took four days to break through the hills, allowing Clark to enter the Eternal City with much publicity on 5 June, the day before the landings in Normandy. The Germans had withdrawn from the CAESAR line during the night of 2/3 June, threatened by 6th US Corps on Route 7 and the 2nd on Route 6 at Valmontone, Eighth Army's forward troops being still some way down that route to the east. The Germans escaped from the trap Alexander had tried to set for them along both main routes and by other more difficult ones to the north in spite of the Allies' overwhelming air superiority, which however inflicted severe casualties on many of their vehicles. Sergeant L. S. Rivett was a navigator with 13 Squadron RAF which was engaged in night bombing operations. His diary records:

May 17th. Night off. Only 3 a/c took off. The rest scrubbed.

18th. On duty in Ops room – Road Frosinone–Val[montone] again at 22.30. Late take off (5 mins) as we had a terrible job taxing to the North end. It was a wizard trip – some low stratus about but it was no bother at all. Dropped 1 x 500 and 1 s.b.c. on a light and one 400lbs – scored a direct hit on it. Before this we had run up on three lights but nothing happened. I found out afterwards that my drum switch had been turned – most probably by my elbow. The second salvo (1 x 500lb and 1 s.b.c.*) aimed at a light – undershot but a medium size fire was caused (petrol dump?) which we could still see 20 miles away. The next crew in the area confirmed this. Bucked up over to-night's do – it seems worth doing when you get results like this. Trev's mad rush to the Ops room to get debriefed before anyone else.

19th. Stayed in bed until 11.30. Trev is sick with a bad back so we are not on the programme. Interview with the Wing Navigation Officer. A fine chap and very keen to want to see us. We had a general talk. He certainly appreciates the difficulties.

20th. Trev still sick. Duty crew in afternoon. Stayed on all evening. A letter from Betty's mother who was very shocked when a friend was killed, while here we have lost twelve men in less days – how callous I am getting – how dreadful it all is, but still this is war, and now we are more or less in the thick of it.

---

* Probably 'small bombs container' with incendiary bombs.

21st (Sunday). The Chaplain does not realise how Night Flying messes everything up. I wrote to the Ordinands' Secretary about difficulties out here compared with those ordinands at home; encouraging laziness, being put on a pedestal by other chaps – pride, humility. Stimulus of Toc H talks, difficulty in praying etc.

22nd. Swing a/c in afternoon.

24th. On duty in Ops room all day. Very busy.

25th. Fred went to V– for an interview with the A.O.C. re his commission. The front line has joined up with the Salerno [sic – he must have meant Anzio] bridgehead today. The Grp Captn said that now we were out to kill every German we can, taking of towns is unimportant – we are out to kill! Ops. It was a pretty awful trip – could not see much of the ground and we circled for quite a time. Saw a light shortly after entering the area and dropped two bombs but it was over before we saw anything else to bomb. Trev was getting tired of orbiting. My bigsworth [navigator's mapboard] came to pieces, the back light went u/s and my intercom plug kept pulling out. A most displeasing trip.

26th. Air test in afternoon. Fred returned. Ops – 17 a/c in two lots on Arsoli (I think we only had 18 a/c in the Sqdn). A fairly good trip. We circled the target for a long time because the illumination was late. Bombed a village just to the South – no results seen. The flares were wizard, but unfortunately there was a mist in the valley, which reflected the light back to you. Trev again very impatient circling about. Fairly pleased with the trip. A lot of chivvying in the Mess at Supper. Jack said they had flak and Willie saw green flares – all in good fun. Felt tired after it was all over. Alf talking in the tent before the trip about his number of hours and sorties etc. He is afraid of averages but would not see it that way. Fred is too. They talked about after the war. I left for the Ops room feeling how different I was to them – I was made to fight (although I hate fighting) and must live always fighting. Strange how with flying one's first few trips you think of crashes etc – then after a time you become confident – then when you do too much the fear of averages. Felt a terrific desire (or obsesssion) to write a book about the life on the squadron.

May 27th. Interview with the Grp Cptn this morning. Told just after I got up so got ready in a flurry. Went with Beb and two others. [Commissioning interview: he was commissioned in October 1944.] He was very friendly – it was like a chat. I was not terribly scared. He asked two or three tricky questions (Ortona? logarithms, cosines) but seemed satisfied. Talking about night flying most of the time. Air test in afternoon. A full symphony orchestra playing over the radio in the Ops room, which tried to take me to another world but somehow I would not go. I must not have my'soul so deeply stirred while still flying and the war. Bombed Aquila by flares. A pretty good trip. The flares were late though and we had been to the left of the track and I was not happy about things. Trev got cheesed with circling and told me to bomb the first thing I saw, but then the flares came on. They lit up the target wizardly. I aimed for the road junction to the South of the town and according to Freddie scored a bull. On the way back I noticed the fusing switches were up and so we jettisoned again. On landing we had no fusing links on. I felt terrible. Wynne did not seem to care too much at de-briefing. Trev rang me up later and said the Armaments Officer said that the bombs would have gone off in any case from that height and the second opening of the bomb doors would have sucked the links out. I felt very relieved.

28th. Ops. We did a stooge round Popoli area – not a bad trip. I bombed Popoli itself instead of the road junction just to the North. Circled Avezzano 2 or 3 times and bombed (on our own flare) a road junction. Our planet was u/s* and I was not sure when we crossed the mountains (I got a wrong pin point, I think) but Fred got a QDM [a magnetic track to Base] – his first since we started N/ F. We had a half moon and I was over estimating map reading possibilities rather.

Eighth Army's casualties since 11 May totalled 13,756 of which almost 4,000 were in the Polish Corps.

---

* Planet: a light beacon, sited within a few miles of the airfield to which they were to return, which flashed a Morse code letter, changed every day. U/s: unserviceable, i.e. not working.

7

Push on to Florence

June to August 1944

The day after Mark Clark drove into Rome, Alexander sent a signal to Wilson, who had moved his headquarters from Algiers to Caserta, that set the cat among the pigeons of the Combined Chiefs of Staff. Their attention had been focused on events in Normandy and the Americans had been satisfied with the directive Wilson had been given to study a post-OVERLORD amphibious operation using troops from Italy, for which they were prepared to contribute landing ships from the Pacific. Wilson's planners had considered a landing to seize French ports in the Bay of Biscay or operations to help Alexander's advance beyond Rome, but, to the pleasure of the Americans, they had come down in favour of DRAGOON, to be launched by 15 August. Wilson had warned Alexander that, once Rome was liberated, he would have to surrender one US corps of three experienced US and two French divisions to participate in this.

Alexander's proposal was that he should keep them and press on to Florence, which he hoped to reach in the second half of July. By 15 August he would be able from there to launch an attack on the GOTHIC line aimed at Bologna. The advantage of concentrating on a thrust in that area was that it would follow the line of the valleys through the mountains, whereas a thrust along either coast would cut across the grain of the terrain. He was relying on the skill of Juin's Moroccan troops in mountain warfare to repeat their remarkable performance in the Aurunci Mountains in DIADEM. Once over the Apennines and into the Po valley, a decision could be made whether to turn left through the Maritime Alps to France or north-east towards Austria. The Germans would be bound to reinforce Kesselring to oppose this and it would therefore help to weaken German resistance to Eisenhower's advance from Normandy better than taking those valuable US and French divisions out of action for two months and then landing them in the south of France.

His proposal revived all the old Anglo-American disagreements about strategy. Not only did the Americans think that Alexander's concept of advancing towards Vienna a pipe-dream, but, still stuck in Normandy with only Cherbourg as a port, they were anxious to secure other routes by which they could deploy the considerable reinforcements available in the United States (forty to fifty divisions); and both they and the French were keen that the French divisions, equipped by the Americans, should play a larger part in the liberation of their own country. Churchill and the British Chiefs of Staff however saw little point in going ahead with DRAGOON and supported Alexander, although Alan Brooke was sceptical about Alexander's hope of getting to Vienna before the Russians. The argument was raised to the level of an exchange between Churchill and Roosevelt, who firmly backed his own Chiefs of Staff and clinched the matter by referring to the agreement on strategy reached with the Russians at Teheran and threatening that, unless Churchill gave way, he would refer the matter to Stalin to adjudicate. That decided the issue, and on 2 July Wilson was told to launch DRAGOON with three divisions in the assault wave on or about 15 August. It was to have priority for air and naval support, and all four French divisions, as well as the US 6th Corps with the 3rd, 34th and 36th US Divisions, were to leave Italy, reducing Clark's Fifth Army to only five, the only reinforcements in prospect being the 92nd (Negro) Division in September and a Brazilian division in October. Eighth Army retained thirteen, but, since OVER-LORD, Montgomery's 21st Army Group had absolute priority for manpower, and replacements in British units in Italy had to be found within the Mediterranean theatre. As the air threat was so reduced, men from anti-aircraft units, and even some from the Royal Air Force, were converted to infantry, an unpopular move which created morale problems.

While the argument raged, Alexander's troops pressed forward towards the Pisa–Rimini line. Fifth Army, with 6th US Corps, was on Route 1 (Via Aurelia) near the coast, and 2nd Corps was on Route 2 (Via Cassia) to the west of the Tiber; Eighth Army, with 13th Corps, was to the east of the river up Route 3 (Via Flaminia) towards Terni. The latter's advance was led by 6th South African Armoured Division on the left and 6th British on the right, each having been given an extra motorized infantry brigade, 24th Guards Brigade and 61st Infantry Brigade respectively. The initial phase of the advance was described by

Lieutenant H. A. J. Stiebel with C Squadron of the 17th/21st Lancers in 6th British Armoured Division.

The next day [6 June] we reached the Tiber River at Fonti di Papa – the advance of 80 miles having taken five days against light opposition. I was attached to A Sqn as L.O. and as the leading Troop advanced up the road to the east of the river, it was fired on by Anti-tank guns from the river bank near Monte Rotundo. The leading tank was knocked out and the crew wounded. My Dingo was speedily put under cover near a Roads Dept. house. These buildings were on all major roads, painted in red and with huge Fascist emblem on them. With Armour Piercing shells flying around, the best place for a Dingo is away from it all. A Sqn were spread out along the road and the German guns were firing from the left front – the tanks quickly pulled off the road, taking whatever cover they could find. All we knew was that there were a number of guns involved. From my position I could see further to the left than those on the road. I got to the top of a small bank and suddenly saw a muzzle flash from one of the A/Tk guns. I tried to tell the A Sqn. Leader where it was over the radio but there was no obvious point of reference. So I took a Bren gun out of the car and fired a couple of bursts towards the place from which the flash had come. The Sqn. immediately fired at the point I had indicated and, with an explosion, an A/Tk gun was no more.

We had been in the lee of the Road House for a couple of hours and something prompted me to investigate whether anyone was inside. It was double-storied and the easiest way to check, without going inside, was, now that I had the Bren out, to fire a few shots through the windows and, imagine the surprise, five Germans rushed out the front door with their hands up. This was just too much for my driver who promptly went completely to pieces. He just laid down and cried which was not very helpful in the circumstances as there was no one else about to help me or drive. With our five Jerries marching in front, I drove the Dingo back to where the R.H.Q. tanks were and got a tank co-driver to join me – my driver was sent back to the Regimental Aid Post and the P.O.W.s taken care of. The next morning, the Colonel* sent me to have a look at the sites of the Anti-

---

* Lieutenant-Colonel Sir John Marling.

tank guns – the 7 R Bs (Our attached battalion – the 7th Rifle
Brigade) had passed through in the night. Casually he said that, if
there was a Leica camera, he wanted it. I drove up to the site of the
German guns and discovered that 6 of the guns had been destroyed
and their crews killed – one further gun had been withdrawn.
Looking round, I suddenly found myself face to face with a German
about 10 yards away. My thoughts went suddenly to the .38 revolver
in a holster on my belt, my total lack of cover and the probability of
his being armed. He did not move, and after the initial shock, I
realised that he was dead, standing waist high in a field of wheat,
with a telephone wire round his neck. He was actually hanging.
Investigation proved that shelling from our guns had cut the overhead wire, which had sprung back and caught him round the throat
and held him suspended there. He had been a Sergeant Major in the
Herman Goering Divisional Artillery.

Trooper Ian King was a member of a tank crew in the 3rd Hussars
in the British 9th Armoured Brigade in 6th South African Armoured
Division. He describes his experience at the same time:

Although the invasion of Europe had started and Rome had been
taken the Germans continued to put up a stubborn resistance. What
was surprising was the large number of non-Germans facing us.
There were many Poles and Ukrainians who fought fiercely and with
apparent loyalty. This must point to the excellence of German
leadership in the field. We were shelled constantly and for the most
part could not locate the guns which were troubling us, possibly
because they were self-propelled and moved about. There was one
very pleasant leaguer in a vineyard where we discovered track marks
in a lane where there was a good view of our leaguer. The vineyard
had many wooden water storage barrels and they were ideal for a
cooling bathe. When an aircraft flew low and machine-gunned the
area, my first thought was to get out of the barrel but this was not
an easy thing to do quickly. My next thought was that if I stayed
where I was and was hit, I would probably drown. I then had the
consoling thought that, unless I was hit in the head, anywhere else
would mean that the barrel was also pierced and that the water
would drain away.

In the middle of June 1944, the Regiment continued to advance
north of Rome. It was a time of intense activity in the region of

Viterbo. The Regimental War Diary records that on 13 June 1944, we took Civitola* and advanced 19 miles to become the most forward troops in Italy. For the crew of 'Careless' the date was a momentous one. In the preceding days our driver had become increasingly irritable and on edge. He was clearly under considerable stress. He argued with the commander, Harold Furby, about the choice of routes; he was critical about the firing of the gun thinking it would draw fire on us; indeed, he was more than usually unpleasant. Because of a natural diffidence and a reluctance to assert himself, Harold Furby could not cope with this insubordination. He was not really up to the job and the driver, as the other NCO in the crew, took advantage of this. In our advance we had inflicted heavy casualties on the enemy (the War Diary says there were 300 killed or wounded though I was not aware of this at the time); and we took prisoners and destroyed some 75mm guns and machine-guns. This intensity of activity brought the problem with the driver to a head. We were approaching a village, which I think was called Monte Leone, by way of a sunken road, the banks of which were level with the top of the turret. We were point tank: the road was narrow and ahead I could see what looked like an ancient gate to the village but our passage was blocked by a felled tree and we knew that this was a sure indication that either the tree, the road ahead or both, were mined. Harold Furby ordered the tank to halt. Meantime, we became aware of movement on the bank to our right. Our weapons were useless in this position because they would not traverse or elevate sufficiently to bring them to bear on the bank, but the following tanks were giving covering fire. We then edged closer to the tree trunk. Our driver was becoming highly argumentative and I thought he was near to hysteria. We then heard the Squadron Leader call us and say that our 'bottle was leaking'. This puzzled us until Harold Furby, glancing behind, noticed there was a thick trail of oil on the road. The engines were still running, but looking at the engine dials I noticed that the right-hand engine had no oil pressure. I pointed this out to the driver and told Harold Furby. At least we were not immobile and Harold Furby gave the order to reverse. At this, the driver became rigid, his eyes staring fixedly ahead and his hands tightly gripping the steering tillers. Our position was now very

* Probably Civitella d'Agliano.

dangerous. He did not respond to the order to reverse. It looked as though the Germans had anti-tank weapon close-by which had hit us though we were not aware of this when it took place. The fact that we had diesel powered tanks certainly avoided the kind of conflagration which we all dreaded had they been petrol engined. In retrospect, the oddity of the hit, as the entry hole, piercing the bottom plate, suggested that we may have been hit by one of our own side. We had to reverse to survive and to allow another tank to pass us. To do this the driver had to be removed from the driving seat to allow me to take over. Harold Furby, who for once showed remarkable decisiveness, told me to knock him out. I took a hammer and said to the driver: 'You heard that. If you do not reverse, I will hit you with this hammer.' His response was immediate. He reversed and pulled over to let a 4 Troop tank pass through. I saw its nearside track disintegrate on a mine which bent a heavy metal bogie assembly at right angles. The crew came under fierce attack and replied with personal weapons as they made their way back. Miraculously, none was hurt. I had a bottle of local spirit on the tank and we swigged some after which I wanted to pee badly. In those days we were still discreet in such matters and I started to walk along a path which ran parallel to the road and in the direction of the enemy. Finding a secluded bush I started to pee into it when I was startled by a German who jumped up, hit me a glancing blow with what I took to be an entrenching tool, and ran off. We had clearly been on like missions and the thought has since crossed my mind that he was reacting reasonably to being pissed on. I was not hurt but to say I was taken aback would be an understatement. The blow was no more than a graze, though I still have the scar, but I was very shaken and I needed a good swig of the *acqua-vit* to restore me. While I was drinking this there was a commotion among the infantry who had now caught up with us. Approaching us was a German with his hands up. It was the man who had just hit me. He came up to me and opened a First Aid satchel motioning me that he wanted to dress my wound. As he only had paper bandages, I declined. We had better dressings on the tank. However, I gave him a half a mug of my drink and he left on his merry way.

We returned to the Squadron leaguer on one engine and removed all our kit from the tank which was taken to workshop. We sat rather disconsolately among our belongings to await a replacement. The

Troop Leader joined us for a chat in which he was appreciative of the way we had extricated ourselves.

General progress initially was rapid, the first serious opposition being met between Lake Bolsena and Terni. On the left the South Africans had to deploy both their infantry brigades to attack a strong delaying position at Bagnoregio east of the lake, which they cleared on 13 June, reaching Orvieto next day.

While 13th Corps continued to press forward on that route towards Arezzo, 10th Corps was brought into action on their right, taking over command of 6th British Armoured Division to lead the advance towards Perugia. The division had a stiff fight to clear a delaying position at Narni and faced bridging problems before reaching Terni on the 14th; but thereafter had a clear run before reaching the outskirts of Perugia on 18 June. During the next two days, in heavy rain, both motor infantry brigades attacked, 61st from the west and 1st Guards from the south, the Germans withdrawing during the night of 20/21 June, having already left Assisi. The 2nd Battalion of The Rifle Brigade was in 61st Brigade: Rifleman R. L. Crimp was a signaller at its 'B' Company's HQ. He recorded his part in the attack in his diary:

20th June. Still raining.

When all's ready and zero-hour's come, the three infantry Companies move off from the start-line at intervals on foot; first 'C', then 'A', then us. As usual I'm working the 18-set. For a couple of hours we tramp along twisting lanes, avoiding the main road, HQ leading the platoons. The night's pitch dark, and the Company Commander's not at all sure of the way. Time's going fast, we've got to be on our hill by daybreak, and there seem plenty of hills, some left, some right. Eventually, however, we find one which looks like ours and begin ascending, just as the sky is starting to pale. Fortunately Jerry's not in possession – otherwise moving up in growing light would be no picnic. Reaching the summit, which is screened by trees, we start digging on the reverse slope. A heavy mist now springs up, yesterday's rain steaming out, clamping down on sight and sound. All that can be heard for half an hour is the clink of our spades on rock.

By the time we've scooped out some sort of hole, sounds of strife have become audible, down in the valley a rattatting of machine-guns, and further west a couple of explosions. I can get an idea of the general situation from the 18-set: 'A' Company have reached their objective and found it empty. 'S' Company are in their village, and have taken a few prisoners; but their Company Commander is getting a bit anxious as the hill which overlooks him hasn't yet been occupied, as scheduled, by 'C'. When the mist clears his position will be rather tricky, and he asks for instructions from Batt.HQ. The Colonel's* answer is 'S' Company must stay put.

After a while we hear twigs cracking and somebody plodding up our hill. Its a Jerry, as soon he begins calling out in German. We lie doggo, ready to put him quietly in the bag. But suddenly his voice and footfalls cease. No doubt he's got wind of us and blown the gaff.

By nine o'clock the mist has yielded to bright sunshine. Wooded hills rise all around, enclosing, behind us, a narrow valley where the road runs. Suddenly, from a hill on our left, rips the rapid, metallic 'splitting' of spandaus, abruptly breaking the silence; which settles in again, ominously expectant, at an equally sudden concerted cessation. Then there's a stillness for about an hour, save for the rustling of leaves, the creaking of trees, the singing of birds, and occasional subdued remarks between ourselves. Just as we're beginning to relax, however, the stinging clatter of spandaus, obviously reinforced, breaks out again, and from the far side of the hill mortar bombs begin sailing over: a small phut of firing, a few seconds' silence, a gently swishing, insidious descent, and tremendous, brutal crash on landing. One after another they come, with pauses only to vary flight. This lasts about ten minutes and is extremely unpleasant. The chaps in the platoons, up on the brow, have it worse than us in HQ, about thirty yards down, as they're under full observation by the spandau-gunners. The curse of it is there's not a Jerry in sight, they're so well hidden and camouflaged. They obviously know the ground to an inch and have their weapons exactly ranged over it. The mortar bombs crash around, some explode overhead on impact with branches. All we can do is lie in our holes, and smoke and sweat and hope for the best.

When a lull comes the Company Commander gets me to try reporting the situation to Rear HQ. But the battery's low (the second I've used since last night) and there's no reply. He's getting a bit

* Lieutenant-Colonel T. C. Sinclair.

worried; apparently some relief in the way of tanks or guns should have shown up by now.

About an hour later comes the next dose. The spandaus seem to have crept nearer, the mortar fire is more concentrated. The platoons have a very rough time, and get a bit restive. If only they could see something to have a pot at, retaliation would ease matters. But of Jerry in person there's not a glimpse. Its a ridiculous situation and the Company Commander is in a quandary. But he wants to hang on until he gets instructions or relief arrives. During another respite I try to contact Rear HQ, but no luck. I can still hear the other Companies, who seem to be getting it fairly quiet in their positions, and have a shot at passing through them, but my signals, on a weakening battery, aren't strong enough. Half an hour later the battery gives out and there's no spare.

After a third bash about one o'clock, in which several platoon chaps are wounded, the Company Commander decides to withdraw. A scheme is worked out for two platoons to go down first under the Sergeant-Major, taking the casualties, with the rest of the Company, including HQ, following twenty minutes later. The whole Company will re-assemble at the bottom and dig in somewhere less exposed, until further orders.

At this stage 6th Armoured Division was relieved by 10th Indian Division and transferred to 13th Corps west of Lake Trasimene.

Both corps were now up against Kesselring's intermediate ALBERT defence line. Running from the mouth of the River Ombrone, near Grosseto on the west coast, immediately south of Lake Trasimene and thence to the east coast north of Pescara, it was designed to keep the Allies away from the ports of Livorno (Leghorn) on the west and Ancona on the east coast. The German Fourteenth Army, now commanded by General Joachim Lemelsen, had von Senger's 14th Panzer Corps facing 4th US Corps (which had replaced the 6th) on the west coast and Schlemm's 1st Parachute Corps facing the French on their right. Von Vietinghoff's Tenth Army had Herr's 76th Panzer Corps facing both 13th and 10th Corps in the centre and Fuerstein's 51st Mountain Corps opposite the Polish Corps, which had replaced 5th Corps on the Adriatic coast.

4th US Corps made slow progress through this line along the west coast, reaching the River Cécina and crossing it, after some hard fighting, on 1 July, bringing them within twenty miles of Livorno. The French Corps, who had their eyes fixed on DRAGOON, were held up on the River Orcia west of Lake Trasimene until the Germans withdrew on 27 June, allowing them to enter Siena on 3 July. Eighth Army faced the strongest resistance on both sides of the lake. In 13th Corps, 78th Division, supported by 9th Armoured Brigade, fought a tough battle for Citta della Pieve on 17 June and another at San Fatucchio at the south-west corner of the lake on the 21st. In a series of further attacks, some in heavy rain, the division fought its way forward along the west shore of the lake, 4th Division advancing through the hills on their left. Meanwhile 10th Corps, with 10th Indian Division, now reinforced by the 4th Indian, was making progress to the east of the lake, and on 24 June the troops of both corps met on the north shore, as the Germans withdrew towards Arezzo.

When 78th Division reached Cortona on 4 July, it was withdrawn for rest and retraining in Egypt, while 6th British Armoured Division led the way to Arezzo. Lieutenant D. A. Main, a pre-war Territorial soldier in the London Rifle Brigade, had been commissioned towards the end of the campaign in North Africa, in which he had won the Distinguished Conduct Medal. He was now commanding a platoon in the 7th Battalion of The Rifle Brigade in the division. He describes their attack on Monte Castiglion Maggio, some ten miles south of Arezzo, in the first week of July:

At three o'clock [a.m.] I assembled my platoon with two sections forward with one behind, and passed through 'C' Company advancing towards the top of the mountain. Enemy small arms fire had ceased as the two German soldiers had been killed. I came across the two bodies when a rifle shot went off apparently caused by one of the dead Germans whose fingers had been on the trigger of his Schmeiser and a reflex action had set in.

We had now stirred a hornet's nest and the first counter-attack came over the crest of the mountain. We had no time to dig any slit trenches and I dragged one German corpse to the other, firing my rifle at the attacking enemy. This counter-attack was repulsed, and I advanced to the crest on which was a stone wall about three feet high, which was used as a sheep pen. I vaulted over the wall towards the enemies' side in the hope that I could see the enemy. I could see none in the early dawn light, when suddenly I saw a number of enemy stick grenades in the air. I immediately evacuated the sheep pen, and told my platoon to start digging in. Suddenly another counter-attack developed around the right-hand side of the sheep pen. My four sergeants and I found ourselves lying in the open on stony ground returning the enemy fire. Bullets were hitting the ground amongst us and most were ricochetting off the rocks. Unfortunately the rest of my platoon had withdrawn about fifty yards to safer ground. I was therefore compelled to allocate defensive positions just below the crest and to dig in. I was sharing a slit trench with my platoon sergeant.

Another counter-attack developed from the same sheep pen. By this time the R.H.A. O.P. officer was now with me and I asked him if his guns could fire at the top of the mountain. He said that he would try, but warned me that the fire would be too close to us and to expect the odd shell falling behind us. One shell did land behind us and wounded my platoon sergeant in the back. I told him to leave us for the R.A.P. and took his Tommy gun. By this time our small arms fire and that from the R.H.A. had stopped this counter-attack.

We had now dug in with 'C' Company on the left and 'A' Company on the right. No sooner had we dug in than another counter-attack developed. On our right flank the ground sloped steeply to a spur parallel to us and approximately five hundred feet lower. From this flank came machine gun fire from at least five Spandaus. These positions could not be seen from our positions. A fellow platoon commander, Harry Whiter, went forward on the right flank to observe for my two-inch mortar. The first shot was well short but the second made a direct hit on a Spandau. I then asked the O.P. officer if he could engage the spur. Within a few minutes ten rounds of gunfire from the Divisional Artillery covered the spur and knocked out the remaining enemy machine guns.

Another counter-attack came from the left flank and Harry Whiter and I decided to lead a joint two-platoon attack on the crest of the mountain. I asked Harry to watch his left and front whilst I would watch my right and front. We shouted 'Charge!' but enemy small arms fire was heavy and I can only assume that the platoons did not hear the order, and thus failed to advance. Harry Whiter was mortally wounded by an enemy sniper who shot him with his Spandau machine gun. I shot the German sniper and dragged Harry Whiter back to dead ground, but he was already unconscious and it was with great regret that I remembered that he was blind in the left eye, although he always disguised this. I then advanced up the mountain with my Tommy gun. On the forward wall of the sheep pen was an enemy officer looking through binoculars which obviously limited his vision as I was approaching at an angle. I gave him a burst and he collapsed. Two of the enemy appeared, and collected the officer, so I shot them as well. The counter-attack faded away as the enemy had withdrawn to the reverse side of the mountain.

In the afternoon it became quiet and we improved our slit trenches, whilst 'D' Company had been used as porters to bring up more ammunition and hand grenades. Since early morning, the Germans had been shelling the village on the lower slopes of Monte Castiglion Maggio, and clouds of red dust would be left where a shell had exploded on the red-tiled rooftops.

All was quiet when suddenly a mortar bomb landed in the middle of our positions, the significance of which we were to learn later. Our positions were now such that we could bring fire to bear on the top of the mountain but also to shoot downhill on either flank. At the same time I had arranged for two of the three company two-inch mortars to dig in in dead ground just behind me.

We had not appreciated that the moon would rise only one hour after darkness had fallen and we sent a listening post to the crest of the mountain. We heard some bursts of small arms fire and the explosion of hand grenades. Suddenly and silently a line of the enemy appeared from the top of the hill, whilst enemy small arms fire was engaging our positions from both flanks and in certain cases from the rear. I had counted the line in front of me and when it exceeded the number of our listening patrol, I realised that it was an enemy attack and gave the order to fire. I was busy firing my Tommy gun from the hip with short bursts at the enemy line. Unknown to me, as the enemy attack commenced they had fired a rifle grenade which blew the head off Sgt. Parker and another sergeant by his side was knocked unconscious by the blast. At the same time the enemy bumped into our listening patrol at the top of the mountain, and a survivor hopped back to us with his foot almost severed by a stick grenade.

Before the attack began I had put my compass and eight Tommy gun magazines, also my revolver, by my slit trench. Fire was now directed at the two two-inch mortars behind me, whilst the enemy appeared to have over-run my right section as the fire from weapons could be seen pointing towards our positions. The noise of small arms fire was considerable but I shouted out three times asking if any rifle brigade were left. When I received no answer and could see more firing from our positions on the right flank, I fired several bursts from my Tommy gun and I presumably hit the enemy as the firing from this area was silenced. I now continued to fire short bursts at the enemy. The moon had now risen and we had been fighting the latest enemy attack for two hours. By this time tracer from two enemy machine guns was passing either side of my slit trench. As I had now exhausted my Tommy gun ammunition I decided it was time to contact the Company Commander of 'C' Company, Major Larry Fife M.C. to decide what should be done. We had no O.P. officer as the relieving O.P. officer had lost his way in the dark, also I had not seen my acting Company Commander since we had attacked Monte Castiglion Maggio. My actual Company Commander, Major Shepherd-Cross M.C., a first class leader, had been wounded and was in hospital. Major Fife agreed that we should fall back and dig fresh positions lower down the mountain, and that I should arrange for our artillery fire to be brought on our positions once they had been evacuated. The necessary orders to withdraw were given and I then asked on the radio set which was tuned into Battalion Headquarters for our guns to commence firing. I then ran down the mountain side to where we were digging fresh positions. My run was uneventful until I mistook a shadow for a gorse bush and fell flat on my face a matter of six feet.

The divisional commander, Major-General Evelegh, now decided that he needed more infantry to deal with 15th Panzer Grenadier Division, blocking his way, and Leese sent the New Zealand Division, which he had hoped to keep in reserve for the attack on the GOTHIC line, to reinforce him. They did not reach the front line until 14 July. Early next morning they attacked and secured Mount Lignano, south of the city, into which the tanks of 26th Armoured Brigade drove at dawn on the 16th, while 10th Corps approached from the east with 4th Indian Division and the 10th turned eastward to capture Citta di Citello on the main road from Perugia towards Ravenna on 22 July. The Poles had entered Ancona on the 18th, the day before the Americans entered Livorno. Corporal R. I. Higgins was with the 1st Durham Light Infantry in the 10th Indian Infantry Brigade in 10th Indian Division and describes an action at this time:

I never found out exactly what happened that night, but I have always suspected that our Platoon Commander lost his way, a very easy thing to do at night in this undulating and wooded country. Anyway, we were making our way cautiously up a grassy incline with woods behind us and to our left and right. Our leading section with Platoon Headquarters had crept over the crest of the hill when, suddenly, the night was filled with unfriendly noises. Spandaus started firing at us from both flanks and grenades came lobbing in. One of our blokes on the left flank pitched a 36 grenade into a trench and, as I was now squatting on the downward slope looking towards our rear, a shadowy figure dashed past me screaming, and faded into the darkness followed by a couple of shots from my Tommy-gun, though I have no reason to suppose that they caused him any inconvenience.

By this time, a Spandau was putting bursts over our heads though, judging from the sound, not so far over at that. I also heard loud German commands being given and my thoughts dwelt briefly with the large officer we had seen in action earlier that day – or perhaps the day before. I whispered to my chaps to maintain a look-out to the rear while I tried to find out where the voice and the Spandau flashes were coming from. I judged that the range was short and that I might be able to induce some German hiccups with a burst or two from my Tommy-gun. We had obviously run into an ambush and I could visualize all manner of unpleasant things happening on top of the hill. Before I had reached my objective, I heard a loud German command and the Spandau ceased firing. In fact suddenly there was a complete and frightening silence all the way round. I waited where I was for a few minutes, keeping as close to the turf as possible so as to avoid providing a silhouette against the skyline. As nothing seemed about to happen, I decided to rejoin my section and I carefully snaked my way back to where I had left them two or three minutes before. I could then sympathize with Old Mother Hubbard in her time of stress, for when I got there, my cupboard was bare; nobody at home and I felt that I was the only living soul in Italy.

I had heard of under-populated regions on the earth's surface but felt that this was ridiculous. At one moment the air was full of voices and clamour and red hot pieces of metal and the next ... nothing. I

inched my way to the top of the hill and lightly called a few names –
I suppose an outdoor stage whisper might describe the racket I made
– to no avail and I wondered what action I should take. I apparently
had no section to command and no platoon whose rear I had to
guard. I didn't fancy trying to return the way we had come and so I
decided to continue in the direction our platoon had been going. By
doing this I hoped to be able to overhaul my comrades. Everything
remained silent as I carefully continued my evening stroll, making
myself as inconspicuous as I possibly could. I had gone perhaps thirty
or forty yards and had just reached the beginnings of a cart track
when suddenly: 'HALTE! HANDE HOCH!'

I fought back a request for a translation and hurled myself against
the cart tracks. As I did so I spotted three figures outlined against the
dark grey of the night sky. By way of introduction I gave them a
burst from my Tommy-gun, which rather upset them judging from
the sound of their comments as they also hit the turf. The next move
was a loud blast from the region of my boots; one of these inhospi-
table types had tossed a grenade which had landed quite near my
outspread legs. Fortunately, the German stick grenade was a thin-
skinned article designed to scare rather than to maim. It made a very
loud report and this one merely tipped my steel helmet over my eyes,
though it had the effect of reminding me of the two No. 36 Grenades
I had on my belt. These were 'segmented to assist in fragmentation'
and were designed to wound people in the vicinity of their explosion.
Accordingly, I unhooked my grenades, one after the other, removed
the pins and lobbed them about where I had seen the opposition a
few seconds earlier. I kept my head down and the moment the
second grenade blasted off, I did the same. I hurried along a cart rut
on my stomach, taking up as little room as, and rivalling for speed
and silence, the King Cobra moving to the attack.

Higgins managed to make his way back to his battalion, where he
found that although a few other survivors of the patrol had returned,
some wounded, most were still missing: in fact almost all, including
the whole of Higgins's section, were captured. His return by himself
was regarded by his commanding officer with some suspicion, but his
explanation was accepted.

All eyes were now on Florence. In 13th Corps, 6th British Armoured
Division led the way down the Arno valley from Arezzo, with 4th

Division moving on their left, and to the left of them the 6th South African Armoured Division advancing through the Chianti Hills. Lieutenant H. G. Harris of the 1/6th East Surreys, in 4th Division's 10th Brigade, describes his part in their advance:

Our start line coincided almost exactly with a German defence line newly occupied. We debussed in a hurry and made our way on foot to a village called Tuori, with orders to hold at all costs. The church contained two bodies, hanged partisans, executed just half an hour before we arrived and drove a German section out, killing half of them. My Company were concentrated on a farmhouse on the forward edge of the village surrounded by vineyards. Our slit trenches were dug on the terraces, steep up above the farmhouse. On the way to the farmhouse we had passed a Bren carrier left by a forward observer of the Artillery and his signaller. They had both been killed and their bodies were still kneeling beside the track. Corporal Good decided the carrier would be useful to us and went back to drive it up to the farmhouse. He must have been seen because as he parked it behind an outbuilding shells started to rain down. The first shell landed in the farmyard just as the C.S.M. opened the kitchen door to go into the yard and the blast blew him backwards across the kitchen knocking over a camp kettle in the process. He started to yell he had been hit and was covered with blood when he realised it was the hot tea from the kettle. The shell was a 110 mm, which has huge blast but hardly any shrapnel.

That night, the Germans tried to attack the tank column in the valley below us and two of our platoons were ordered to move down and provide close defence. As we did so, machine guns which must have been aimed on fixed lines in daylight began to fire laying down lines of tracer a foot above the top of our slit trenches. Once again it was the accuracy of the Spandau that saved us. We were able to roll out of our slit trenches, knowing exactly where the danger was by the tracer. Going down the hill, we had to execute the most difficult task in the book joining up with tanks in the dark. Luckily for us the tankers were old hands, not prone to fire at anything that moved. The following day we were relieved and as we marched out I proved to myself that you really can march in your sleep, only waking as you bump into the man in front of you.

After two days rest, we were back in the line again based on a farmhouse, but now on the extreme right flank of the division. On our right was the New Zealand Division, a reassuring thought.* We received orders to carry out a recce of our immediate front, this to be done in daylight unusually. It was my turn, so I decided to keep the patrol small, believing this would be the best way of avoiding attention and we set out as a party of four, myself a corporal and two privates. The men carried tommy guns and I had a revolver and a Luger. Our first task was to cross the river, the Arno. This is a large river and we had to swim for it hoping not to be seen as we believed the enemy only had small numbers of men holding the line.

After crossing the river we intended to make our way along a gully and we were doing so having travelled some one hundred yards, when there was the most enormous explosion and I was blown clean out of the gully. I had stepped on a 'Schuh' mine, half a pound of explosive packed in a wooden box, making it very difficult to detect with a mine detector as the only metal part was the detonator. I had seen no sign of mines although I had been looking for them and I found out later that there had been a heavy rain storm after they had been laid, removing any evidence of ground disturbance. As I began to recover my senses I could see the lower part of my leg was a mess. The calf muscle had been blown away and both bones broken. I had stepped right on the mine and, being light, the explosion had blown me up and out of the gully. Had I been heavier, more damage would have been done. As it was the leg was still in one piece, just.

Harris saw that his patrol was hopelessly outnumbered and ordered them to surrender. He was taken away by a German stretcher-bearer and was well cared for in a German field hospital, which was gradually moved back through the mountains. In October he was transferred to an Italian POW hospital at Imola, run by nuns, where the conditions and medical treatment were primitive. After two weeks there his leg became gangrenous. His account continues:

There was only one treatment, amputation. Within hours I was wheeled along to the operating theatre with two other poor devils due for amputation of an arm each. There were no anaesthetics

---

* In fact the New Zealand Division was well away to their left, 6th South African Armoured Division being between the 4th Division and the New Zealanders.

and operations were carried out by using four strong men to hold down the patient while the doctor went to work. The next hour is something I want to forget but have never been able to. The pain is indescribable and the only relief is to faint. Unfortunately I am not the fainting kind.

After it was all over we were wheeled into a side room and left with a nun sitting in a chair by the door. An orderly, bringing in a jug of water, told me that we were in the morgue. Expecting us to die in a short time, the nuns had decided to save work by taking us straight to the morgue instead of back to the ward and then to the morgue. This saved my life as I became so angry that I was determined not to cooperate. After two days, the other two were dead but I was still hanging on and so I was taken back to the ward.

At the time that Harris was captured, Kirkman moved the New Zealanders and 8th Indian Division, the latter supported by 1st Canadian Armoured Brigade, further over to the left to replace the French Moroccan divisions, which were withdrawn. On the night of 1/2 August the New Zealanders launched their first attack on the hills south of Florence. This was not strong enough to dislodge the Germans and was renewed next day, while 10th Corps was approaching the city from the east on the far side of the Arno. During the night the German 1st Parachute Corps withdrew to the north of the river, demolishing all the bridges except the historic Ponte Vecchio, which they blocked at both ends, and South African armoured cars entered the southern part of the city next day, the 4th. Although Kesselring declared Florence an open city, Schlemm continued to occupy the northern part of the city for another week, by which time 1st British and 1st Canadian had relieved the New Zealand and South African Divisions; and, when three platoons of the 1st Buffs of 18th Brigade in 1st British Division crossed the Arno and entered the great Piazza on the 11th, they were shelled from the north of the city.

8

First Crack at the GOTHIC

August to September 1944

On 4 August, the day his troops entered Florence, Alexander and Harding met Leese at Orvieto airfield to discuss planning for the attack on the GOTHIC line, which it was hoped would start on or about 15 August, when Kesselring might be distracted by DRAGOON. The former two envisaged Eighth Army making the main thrust to Bologna astride Route 64 from Pistoia and Route 65 from Florence, for which a logistic base was being built up south of the Arno, fed by the railway being repaired and restored to Arezzo; but Leese had other ideas. He had been persuaded by Kirkman that an attempt to thrust through fifty miles of mountain (as the crow flies) would not allow his army to use to best advantage its great superiority in numbers of tanks and artillery, and it would therefore be a slow, laborious business, expensive in infantry lives. It would be better to redeploy Eighth Army's strength back to the Adriatic coast where a break through the GOTHIC line near Rimini would lead directly into the Romagna plain of the Po valley, which he erroneously imagined would be suitable for mobile operations.

After hours of discussion, Alexander accepted this drastic change. It would have other advantages. Leese did not find it easy to cooperate with Clark, and separating the two armies would make it possible to employ Alexander's favoured strategy of alternate blows, striking with one hand when the enemy's reserves had been drawn away to meet the threat of the other. However this overlooked the fact that Kesselring would be able to transfer forces laterally on the excellent road network of the Po valley much more rapidly from one sector to another than could Alexander across the mountains; and that Leese's advance would be across the grain of the terrain as he faced ridge after ridge and river after river. With only five divisions in Fifth Army, Clark would not have the strength to strike an effective blow across the mountains, and

Alexander therefore decided to transfer Kirkman's 13th Corps, two
infantry (1st British and 8th Indian) and two armoured divisions (6th
British and 6th South African) to Clark's command, the South Africans
being transferred to 4th US Corps.

This decision placed a heavy burden on Leese's logistic, movement
and engineer resources. The only route across the Apennines was the
road from Arezzo through Perugia to Foligno, near Assisi, and thence by
two roads to the coast, one to Ancona and one to Macerata, on both of
which the Germans had carried out extensive demolitions which had not
been repaired. For reasons of secrecy, all movement would have to be by
night and many of the tanks would have to move on their own tracks as
there were not enough transporters to move them all, nor could
sufficient bridges capable of taking loaded transporters be constructed
on both routes in time. The period needed for the move would cut into
precious summer weather and allow Kesselring to recover from the
surprise of DRAGOON. Apart from the practical difficulties involved in
this plan, there was the embarrassing complication that it coincided with
the deception plan which Harding and his staff had been trying to put
into the heads of Kesselring's intelligence staff.

In spite of these difficulties Leese was ready to start his attack,
Operation OLIVE, on 25 August. Kesselring was taken completely by
surprise. He had in fact been distracted by DRAGOON, from which he
feared that Lieutenant-General Alexander M. Patch's Seventh US Army
would thrust east into Italy. He therefore sent 90th Panzer Grenadier
Division to reinforce the Italian Marshal Graziani's Army of Liguria west
of Genoa, replacing it in reserve near Bologna with 29th Panzer Grenadier Division. He had lost three veteran divisions, Hermann Goering to
the eastern front and 3rd and 15th Panzer Grenadier to von Rundstedt
in France, leaving him with two panzer divisions, 16th and 26th, both in
14th Panzer Corps in the western sector, two parachute, one with two
infantry divisions in 1st Parachute Corps north of Florence, and one,
with one mountain and two infantry divisions, under 76th Panzer Corps
on the east coast. 51st Mountain Corps had one jaeger and five infantry
divisions in the mountains between 1st Parachute and 76th Panzer
Corps.

Leese's plan was for the Polish Corps to continue its advance along
the coast to the River Metauro, eight miles south-east of Pesaro, which
would be the start line for his attack. The Poles themselves would take

Pesaro and then come into reserve, as 1st Canadian Corps, with 1st
Canadian Infantry and 5th Canadian Armoured Divisions, moving
closely on their left, would take on the advance along the coast to
Rimini. The main effort would be made by 5th Corps (now commanded
by Lieutenant-General C. F. Keightley) with 4th, 46th, 56th British and
4th Indian Infantry Divisions and 1st British Armoured (Major-General
R. A. Hull), which had not seen action since the Battle of Mareth as
Eighth Army entered Tunisia from Libya in March 1943. The corps was
to move through the hills south of the Canadians and cut the main road,
Route 9 (Via Emilia), to Bologna west of Rimini. 10th Corps, with only
10th Indian Division, was responsible for the mountainous sector
between 5th and 13th Corps, the latter under Fifth Army north and
north-east of Florence. By the time the attack started, on 25 August,
Paris was liberated, Seventh US Army had reached Grenoble in the
Maritime Alps, while General de Lattre de Tassigny's First French Army
would liberate Toulon and Marseilles within the next three days. Russia's
summer offensive was making good progress, Romania declaring war on
Germany that day, Bulgaria withdrawing from the war next day, and
Finland's Field Marshal Mannerheim having told Hitler a week before
that Finland felt free to make its own terms with Russia, which he did
shortly afterwards.

For the first four days Operation OLIVE went well, as the Germans,
taken by surprise, withdrew to the main GOTHIC line defences behind
the River Foglia inland from Pesaro. The Poles and Canadians broke
their way through these between 30 August and 3 September, by which
time the Canadians had established a bridgehead over the River Conca
five miles east of Rimini. On the right of 5th Corps, 46th Division had
kept up with the Canadians, but further into the hills on their left 56th
and 4th Indian Divisions made slow progress. Private Charles Seibert
was serving in C Company of the 2/5th Sherwood Foresters in 46th
Division's 139 Brigade in these operations. Their most important action
was the capture of the village of Monte Vecchio on the north bank of
the River Foglia on 30 August. He describes his part in it:

> On August 30th, when 'A' Company attacked Monte Vecchio, 'C'
> Company were held in reserve at Monte Fabbri. Rumours soon
> started to circulate that things were going badly for 'A' Company.
> We heard that a bayonet charge had been across a minefield resulting

in many casualties. We also heard that an attempt had been made to blow open the gates with a Bangalore Torpedo,* which had exploded prematurely killing the squad carrying it. How true these rumours were is uncertain. I do know that Frank Woolmore had a foot blown off by a 'Schu' mine, and died of gas gangrene. When night came we were told that 'A' Coy were short of 'ammo', and a party of us led by Sgt Riding set off for Monte Vecchio, each man carrying 4 bandoliers of .303s, grenades, Bren gun magazines and two cases of mortar bombs. We ran into a German patrol and another friend Fred Bowker was killed.

When morning came we were told that the situation at Monte Vecchio was critical and we must go to assist 'A' Company at once. We set off supported by 5 or 6 Sherman tanks, by the time we approached Vecchio only one tank remained. Our section was leading 'C' Company and we were sheltering by the side of the tank as far as we could. A Spandau opened fire from high in the wall and we all went to ground. The remaining tank was now out of action with a broken track. I looked back and could see the whole of 'C' Coy were lying under the cover of a small embankment, and in the middle a 'confab' was taking place. Sgt Herring came crawling back and ordered 'Fix bayonets' – 'When the whistle blows – every man to his feet and charge!' The whistle sounded and off we went. The gates of Monte Vecchio were directly in front of us hanging loosely on their hinges. They looked as if they had been blown away. 'C' Company charged through the gates, cheering and shouting. Directly in front was the side wall of a house. A number of Germans were pinned against the wall by men of 'A' Coy who were prodding them with bayonet and rifle butt. One corporal was in such a rage that I thought he would open fire at any moment on the prisoners with his Bren gun. There was a clutter of boots, and more Germans came running, chased by men of 'A' Coy. They were also pinned against the wall. All the POWs had thrown away their helmets and equipment except for one man. I was astonished at how old he seemed, perhaps sixty. He was a big man, fully dressed with helmet and equipment, he stood apart from the others, to attention, and apparently oblivious of what was going on around him! Funnily he was the only prisoner not being given a hard time. My view is that by the time 'C' Coy

* A pipe full of explosive, used for clearing wire obstacles and minefields.

arrived, 'A' Company had won the day, and were carrying out a 'mopping up' exercise. I found myself on the steps of a church. A wounded German was lying on the steps, (he turned out to be a Frenchman) I dressed his wounds, and while doing so I could hear the sounds of an organ from within the church. When I entered the church, two or three Foresters were wandering about inside. I believe the organ was located in a gallery above the altar. The organ was continually stopping and starting, as though the organist was practising. It was a familiar piece perhaps something like 'In a Monastery Garden' or such like. The village was being heavily 'stonked'. There were shell holes in the roof of the church, plaster and dust was falling everywhere. The organ stopped, and Sgt Plowright came down a small flight of stairs. I queried why he had stopped playing, and he replied that the organ was too damaged to play properly. He left the church and I went to look for my section.

Facing the Canadians and 46th Division was a low ridge, between the Rivers Conca and Marecchia, behind which lay the village of Coriano. Leese now decided that the time had come to try and push 1st Armoured Division through 46th Division, as the latter took this ridge on 4 September, expecting Hull to have to pursue a beaten enemy. Although, like the other armoured divisions, it now had two motorized infantry brigades (18th and 43rd Gurkha), its armoured brigade (2nd) was to lead and be accompanied only by its own motor battalion (1st KRRC) and an infantry one (2/6th Queens). The tanks faced a long approach march, which started on 2 September and took place over rough tracks which had to be negotiated in low gear. Many suffered from mechanical failures, breaking down or entering battle in a poor state, while the slow progress, with constant delays, had deprived the crews of sleep and the opportunity to eat and drink. Most were very tired by the time the brigade crossed the Conca at 10.30 a.m. on 4 September to find that 46th Division had not captured the ridge, while the Canadians on their right had also been stopped, von Vietinghoff having reinforced 76th Panzer Corps with 26th Panzer and 98th Infantry Divisions. Hull had to revise his plan to one in which the tanks, with little infantry support, themselves attacked; and they did not do so until 3.45 p.m., by which time the sun was in their eyes and behind those of the German tank and anti-tank gunners. The result was an expensive failure. During the night Herr's corps was reinforced by 29th Panzer Grenadier and 356th Infantry

Divisions, Leese renewing attacks on 8 and 9 September after heavy rain fell on the 6th and 7th; but little progress was made and he decided that a pause was needed in which to prepare a more set-piece affair.

On Fifth Army's front Kesselring had ordered a withdrawal into the prepared GOTHIC line defences, 13th Corps following up 715th Infantry Division of 51st Mountain Corps as it withdrew north-east from Florence, and 4th US Corps occupying Lucca on 6 September and Pistoia on the 12th. 2nd US Corps was to make the main effort initially astride Route 65 and then along the secondary road which led to Firenzuola through the Il Giogo Pass, and thence towards Imola. 13th Corps was to cooperate on the right with 1st British Division along Route 302 towards Faenza and 8th Indian along Route 67 towards Forli.

2nd US Corps faced the German 4th Parachute Division as it began its attack on 10 September with massive air support, while 13th Corps attacked the defences of 715th Division. 8th Indian Division's good progress on the right helped 1st British and 85th US Divisions turn the flank of 4th Parachute Division's position at the Il Giogo Pass on 17 September. Jim Carradice, now a corporal, was still with the 1st Argyll and Sutherland Highlanders in the 8th Indian Division. He wrote:

> That morning, as I struggled into my kit, it was the same as it had always been, yet in some way, it was so different. Suddenly, I became conscious of a very tangible difference, I felt an intense upsurge of fear. This wasn't a game of rugger. I'd often seen it happen to men before. Brave men, who could go no further. Brave men, who simply sat down where they were and cried like babies. Fear like that was no respecter of persons. It could happen to officers and battle-hardened sergeant-majors, just as easily as it did to the rank and file. Now it was happening to me.

Having described his emotional state, he went on:

> My platoon was to lead the attack and my section was to lead the platoon. I knew, just knew, that something terrible was going to happen to me that morning. It was as if I could smell that blood was in the air. A young South African Lieutenant was standing over me; freshly shaved, his map case and binoculars slung round his neck; looking for all the world as if he was in the middle of an exercise on Salisbury Plain. 'Are you alright, Carradice?' He peered down anxiously at me as I sat there. I must have looked dreadful, but I

struggled to my feet and managed to say that I was alright. 'Get your men together then. You lead off in exactly eight minutes.' It seemed a very long eight minutes before a whistle sounded and we clambered out of the trenches on to our feet, and began the long descent to the river in the bed of the valley. It was only a shallow stream and we scarcely got our feet wet as we splashed through the water. Then we began to climb upwards through the trees. There had been no sign of any enemy and I thought wildly that they had perhaps withdrawn during the night. Perhaps we were in for an easy day after all.

I was leading the section and behind me I could hear my comrades scrambling up the hillside. When the trees thinned out, day had come and we could see, stretching before us, a steeply sloping plain of knee-high grass that rose all the way to the summit; that summit was our objective. I paused for a moment, whilst the platoon, which was behind me, collected itself and they gained their breath. I remembered that we had heard the German patrols during the night, so it was certain that my hopes of an easy day were to be proved unfounded. There they were, right on the top of the hill, lying in wait for us to put our noses out of the wood.

We started off again but this time we spread ourselves out so that we wouldn't present such an easy target for our enemies. If I'm going to die, I thought, I'll die leading the British Army into a battle. I hope that they will tell the folks back home, so that they will be proud of me. Slowly, I put one foot before the other, trying desperately to make my mind a blank, as I forced myself to go forward, faster and faster, until we were right out in the open and still nothing happened. Why the hell didn't they open fire and get it over with. Anything better than this cat and mouse game.

When it did happen, it was with an appalling suddenness that was almost beyond belief. One moment there was an eerie silence, broken only by the sounds of birds singing in the trees behind us; then, the next moment, the air was filled with the vicious rattle of machine gun fire and the dull crump of the mortar bombs as they exploded amongst us. Before I could throw myself down into the long grass a bomb burst so close to me that my helmet was torn off by the blast. For what seemed like an eternity, I watched fascinated, as my own helmet twisted and turned in the sky, high above me, just like a rugby ball. Then I was down on the ground, aware of the blood which was streaming down the left side of my face and onto my chest. I was still conscious, when Jock, our bren gunner, crawled to my side. Viciously he tugged the field dressing from my pocket, then he carefully tied it over my temple in an attempt to staunch the flow of blood and brain matter that was still oozing out. 'My God, Jim you've copped it. You've really copped it', he whispered in my ear. It was something that I had already realized but his words seemed to comfort me a little. Then suddenly, I realized that Jock was gone and I could only hear the stutter of his bren as he backed slowly down the hill.

Lying there in the grass, with the sounds of battle sweeeping over me, I drifted into a semi-conscious state. I was back again as a child in dear old Wigan and living my life all over again. I had no way of knowing how long I lay there, the thoughts of my past flowing across my mind, but suddenly I became aware that those sounds of gunfire had ceased. It was much later that I learned that my comrades had never reached their objective. Badly battered, they were forced to retreat, leaving behind many dead comrades in that valley of death. They had carried with them as many wounded men as they could but somehow they missed me. I was alone, with the knowledge that my life blood was draining away into the dry Italian soil. My damaged brain suddenly began to function again as I realized that to stay where I was would lead to a slow but certain death. My one thought was of survival.

Painfully I unbuckled my equipment and started to crawl through the grass on my hands and knees. I soon became aware that this method of locomotion was too slow for me and that I would be dead long before I could reach the comparative safety of the woods. The bleeding had increased because I kept my head below the level of my feet and as a result I was rapidly losing consciousness. The only alternative seemed a poor one but I simply had to try. I must struggle to my feet and pray that the Germans either would not spot me or that they would show mercy to a man who could never fight again.

It was not a good moment. I felt as if my very brain was seeping out through that terrible gash in my head. Logic could not persuade me otherwise, indeed, logic was something that didn't seem to apply. Now on my feet, the field dressing was saturated with blood. I desperately prayed that the enemy up there on the ridge would recognize that I was a badly wounded man who needed help. If they did, perhaps they would hold their fire and give me a chance to return to my own lines. It was a vain hope. I had only taken a few unsteady steps when a spandau opened up, its bullets kicking up the turf at my feet. I dropped down once more, resting for a few moments and trying hard to think logically. It seemed odd that the German who held that gun hadn't finished me off completely. I was a sitting target for any gunner out there staggering about, yet he had missed me. Did that machine gunner have some humanity? Was he obeying orders to fire, yet deliberately trying not to hit me? Was he the answer to my prayer? Suddenly I felt I knew the answer. I was convincd that I was going to be allowed to escape.

Once more I staggered to my feet and once again the gun began to fire but the bullets were still wide. Then I knew with absolute certainty the answer. On that ridge was a man just like me. A human being with feelings who wanted me to escape and return to my own lines and find the help which I so desperately needed. I stopped; turned round and made a gesture which I hoped my unseen foe would accept as an acknowledgment of his help and consideration. It seemed the most logical thing to do at that moment. Then I concentrated my efforts on the task of keeping on my feet and reaching the cover of those inviting trees at the bottom of the hill. The gun did not fire again.

It was becoming increasingly urgent that I made some contact with my own side. Every step was an agonizing one. Could it be that my comrades had withdrawn and had left me here, in this place, to die, alone? An old memory of a nearly forgotten classroom and a nearly forgotten Bible teacher flitted across my mind. 'Eli, Eli, Lama Sabachthani.' The words came from the dark recesses of my mind. 'My God, My God, why hast thou forsaken me?'. Those ancient words from St. Matthew's Gospel seemed suddenly to be very apt. I was now in the wood but scarcely conscious of even walking. I could feel my consciousness ebbing away. Soon I would be unable to go any further. I would collapse in a crumpled heap never to rise again. It had been a long day, the longest day I could remember. My sense of direction had gone and the black clouds were rolling across my brain taking away with them even the desire to think.

What happened next was so miraculous that I couldn't believe it was really happening to me. It seemed like just another fantasy of my tortured mind. I remember the dusky face of the Indian soldier close to mine as he put his arms around me and kept me from falling.

I remember being lifted with infinite gentleness on to a stretcher, which was strapped on the back of one of those faithful mules. I remember wishing with all my heart that I could mutter a few words of gratitude but the power to speak had gone. Then I could remember no more ... When I regained consciousness, it was to a realisation that everything around me was very still and quiet. There had been a noise and now it had stopped. A door opened and there were voices: ''Ere we are matey. Let's be 'aving yer' said a cheerful one.

Further west, 6th South African Armoured Division was leading the drive of 4th US Corps into the mountains from Pistoia and Prato. On the right-hand route from Prato 24th Guards Brigade headed the advance. Lieutenant William Bell was commanding a platoon in the 3rd Welsh Guards and described their action in a letter to his parents dated 20 September:

I had the honour of leading the assault on the Gothic line in one place this week. My platoon acting as a fighting patrol was sent out up a long razor back ridge. We had 3 field, 2 medium and 1 heavy regiment of artillery on call, apart from being covered by a tp of tanks, our own HMGs and mortars, so that we were not without support. Well, we worked up the ridge from feature to feature, leapfrogging the sections forward, maintaining the principle of 'one leg on the ground' for about a mile. It was steep rough going but there was no sight of the Germans until we were within about 500 yds of our objective, when we came across one rather miserable specimen wandering about among the bushes. Asked what he was doing, he said he was blackberrying (his hands and mouth were purple) and that he had had no food for 3 days. Then he went down on his knees as usual and begged us not to kill him. Then I sent out a small recce patrol to the objective and found it held by about 50 Germans. I didn't feel inclined to tackle them, so the remainder of the coy came up and established themselves where we had got to. We spent some 3 days up there and apart from being cold at night (3000 ft up) it wasn't too bad. One very sad thing happened. Three days before a very nice new officer aged 19, fresh from reading Classics at Balliol called Keith Hamylton Jones, had joined the coy. I was immediately struck by him – very quiet and modest with an excellent sense of humour. Well, he was sent out next day on the same short patrol to see if the enemy were still there. I had an uneasy feeling before he went and even told him to be very careful and that the course of the war could not be vitally affected by his patrol and it wasn't worth taking any great risks. Well, as soon as the Spandaus opened up and the bullets came zipping over our heads, I felt very alarmed about him. Two minutes later his two companions came back without him. We have every reason to think that he is wounded and a POW, but it seemed to me that this small incident was typical of the real tragedy of war. It was all so complete and so quick. I felt very shocked and depressed by it especially since at first I was sure he had been killed. Only on one other occasion do I remember having the same premonition of disaster. One afternoon at Philippeville I went for a walk with a friend of mine in the Scots Guards called Duncan McMurtrie. It rained and we walked along the beach by a stormy sea and talked about life and death. Next day he left for Italy and he was killed within a week.

Hamylton-Jones had left the two other members of his patrol at the edge of a wood while he crawled forward. When he was thirty yards from a German trench, they saw him and fired a shot which hit him in the thigh, and then captured him. The bullet, which penetrated almost to his spine, was removed in a German military hospital, where it was presented to him. He spent the rest of the war in POW camps.

Between 4th US Corps on its left and 13th British Corps on its right, 2nd US Corps, with 34th and 91st US Divisions, forced the German parachutists to abandon the Futa Pass on Route 65, and by 21 September had driven them out of Firenzuola. Keyes now brought up his reserve division, the 88th, and pushed it down Route 610 towards Imola until it met fierce resistance on Monte Battaglia, twelve miles short of Imola, on the 27th.

While Clark's troops had been crossing the Apennine watershed towards Bologna, Leese made another attempt to break through near Rimini, supported by air attacks and naval gunfire. 1st Canadian and 5th British Corps, each led by its armoured division, cleared the Coriano ridge on 13 September, but found that the rain had made the going difficult for tanks as opposition increased. In the second phase, infantry divisions took over, while German reinforcements arrived in the form of 90th Panzer Grenadier and 20th Luftwaffe Divisions. 56th Division attacked on the right of 5th Corps, having a particularly stiff fight for the village of Croce, just over the River Conca. Corporal Charles Ferne was commanding a section in A Company of the 9th Royal Fusiliers in 56th Division's attack and described his experience, the 'Charles' referred to being himself:

> There was now a flurry of movement up front. German infantry must have come down in numbers from the village, down into the top end of the vineyard, – not vast numbers, fortunately, – maybe a couple of platoons, – might even be a whole company – hard to tell, – but in the comparative lull between the exchanges of fire, they were certainly doing a lot of shouting to one another. It didn't look like a full-scale counter-attack, but it was enough to hot things up still further. To broaden the section's field of fire he [Charles] spread them out laterally across the next two or three rows of vines to the left. They'd be better placed like that, he thought, than bunched behind one another, – each could then fire freely and unhindered. He had no time to take full stock of them, but it didn't look like ten men who thus re-deployed themselves. Some had obviously gone down. Only the occasional really, clear target was visible now, – a glimpse of field-grey changing position, – the vestige of a coal-scuttle helmet momentarily rising above the unpicked grapes, – but mostly it was the unnatural movement of the vines up there that suggested a presence. For the most part, Jerry too, was hugging the ground, – like them. 'Shoot at anything you see, or even think you see', he told them 'don't waste ammo, but keep them on the hop, wherever you think they are, – and fire low down, two, three feet above ground, – stand a better chance of hitting something.' In line abreast, they kept up a steady fire along their ridiculously small frontage, and it was sickening to him to hear a cry from one or other of them from time to time. He was thankful for the Thompson and the greater fire-power it gave him compared to their rifles, but those who were left were doing so very well. He couldn't afford to be wasteful himself, however. Tommy was a hungry gun, and he was already on his fourth magazine.

He did not know what had happened to the rest of the company, although he could hear some voices somewhere over to his left. His section had been gradually fighting its way forward for about one and three-quarter hours, and he thought they may have advanced some three hundred yards. After a lull, he was joined by Corporal King, who commanded the section on his left, and an older corporal, 'Vic' Oliver.

They had no better idea of the situation. King had not got many men left and thought that about half the company had fallen. Ferne's account continues:

> Oliver, King and he were standing close together, – stupidly standing in a huddle, as if deliberating to go for an after-dinner stroll. It was a crazy thing to be doing, but they weren't thinking, – or rather thinking only of what to do next. They hadn't realised that they were standing up above the vines, and the men had slumped to the ground for a rest, awaiting orders. Oliver had barely uttered the last words [he had suggested falling back and re-grouping] when a thin streak of scarlet appeared across the bridge of Corporal King's nose as he stood there. He brushed a hand over his face as though irritated by a fly, – and hadn't realised what had happened. Charles, who was directly facing him, stared at the faint smudge, hypnotized by it for perhaps a second, – and then shouted 'DOWN', dragging the other two to the ground. 'We've been spotted, and you've been shot at, old son' he told King. A bullet had nicked his nose, drawing forth just the faintest smear of blood, and when King twigged what had happened, he nearly passed out.
>
> The burly figure of CSM Alf Cooper, accompanied by a couple of other stray bods, loomed up and joined them. 'A right balls-up this is', he said, echoing King's earlier assessment of the situation. 'How many of you are there?'. Oliver explained their numbers [Ferne had only two men left], – the dodgy position they were in, – the considerable losses they'd had, – and the lack of any further forward impetus with only the handful left. He repeated his suggestion of falling back to re-group.

The CSM agreed, and, dodging the enemy fire among the vines, they made their way back down the hill to where they had started from.

Squadron Sergeant Major Paddy Cleere was with the 7th Hussars, from 7th Armoured Brigade, who were supporting 56th Division in the attack. He had already fought with the regiment in the North African desert and in the withdrawal from Burma, where he had won the DCM. This is his account:

> Early on the morning of the 13th September, Major Fox (the Squadron Leader) sent for me and gave me orders to take my Troop through Croche [sic] to support the infantry and pursue the enemy.

When I was almost through the village, an officer from the Queen's Regiment jumped up on the side of my tank and told me that his Troops were dug in about 100 yards ahead but they could not move on because they were being fired on by our own Troops from the rear right flank. The enemy were dug in about two or three hundred yards further on. I was held up for some time while I reported the situation to Major Fox on his wireless. Major Fox had the firing stopped and ordered me to continue the advance. I had not advanced far when my leading tank, Sergeant Aitchison, was hit and his right track was broken; the crew escaped. I continued the advance past Aitchison's tank through German infantry trenches. My second tank, coming up behind me, got bogged down, but I kept on going with my machine gun blazing at infantry popping up all over the place. As I got close to the top of the ridge just in line with the cemetery, I spotted an artillery gun position a few hundred yards further on past the cemetery. I took this gun and its crew out with 75mm shells from a standing position. I then continued to the top of the ridge between Monte Zazzano and Coriano. At this stage the enemy seemed to be surrendering all around me except for one in a trench with a bazooka.

I had now run out of machine gun ammunition and I could not depress the 75mm gun enough to shoot him, so I shot him from the top of my turret with my Thompson sub machine gun. There was a lot of confusion now as there were hundreds of German prisoners and not being able to speak the language, I could only wave them back with my gun from the top of my tank. The infantry had not kept up with the advance to collect the prisoners. I reported the situation to my Squadron Leader, Major Fox, on the wireless, who told me to come back and load up with ammunition from Sergeant Aitchison's tank and drive as many prisoners as possible in front of me to the infantry. This I did, but when I arrived at Aitchison's tank, it had been blown up, so I continued into Croche (where Regimental Headquarters were situated). Captain Williams' troop had been following my tank to the ridge so they took up my position while my crew were loading the ammunition. I was then told to report to Major Congreve who was commanding the Regiment for the battle. He informed me that Captain Williams's tank had been hit and my brother, who was the gunner, had been killed. Major Congreve told me that I need not go back, but as soon as my tank was ready to move I reported back to my Squadron Leader, Major Fox.

Since it was now getting dark the Squadron moved into a harbour area to be replenished. I continued to pursue the enemy with the Squadron for the next four days. On the fifth day I was allowed to take some voluntary crews back to the battle area with Padre Metcalfe to recover and bury the nine bodies. Luckily in those days the tank crews used to wear a webbing harness. When I got to my brother's tank, I found that his head had been blown off by an 88mm shell that went through the tank killing my brother and the operator. Captain Williams lost an arm.

I was able to recognise my brother from his broad shoulders and with the help of a friend we managed to lift his body up with the aid of the web equipment. All the bodies were wrapped up in blankets and were loaded onto three ton lorries and taken to a wood where Padre Metcalfe decided that the bodies should be buried in temporary graves. Padre Metcalfe and I lined up the bodies; my brother (a Roman Catholic) on the right. Trooper Povey, also a Roman Catholic, next then Church of England and so on. I dug my brother's grave and members of the various crews dug the others. Once all the bodies had been lowered into their respective graves, Padre Metcalfe and a Roman Catholic priest gave a combined service and the bodies were covered over. The Padre marked the area on the map for the War Graves Commission, who later moved the bodies to the military cemetery at Gradara.

46th Division had a similar experience to that of the 56th in their attack, to the latter's left rear, to clear the Gemmano ridge on the near side of the Conca. After a fierce struggle, they reached the summit of the ridge on 13 September, but were then driven off it by the German 5th Mountain Division. 4th Indian Division was then ordered to attack it next day and its 11th Brigade succeeded in driving the enemy off it by dawn on the 15th.

Leese now transferred 4th British Division to the Canadian Corps to help them cross the River Murano by taking the village of Ospedaletto during the night of 14/15 September. Keightley now tried to get 1st Armoured Division forward again to cross the next river, the Ausa. Beyond it lay the last ridge before the open Romagna plain was reached. During the night of 16/17 September 4th Division captured Cerasola on the ridge west of Ospedaletto and 56th Division crossed the Murano to take Mulazano with 167 Brigade, passing 168 through to line up with the 4th, but meeting stiff opposition in trying to do so. 21st Army Tank Brigade, equipped with Churchill tanks, was supporting 4th Division. Trooper Edmund Cook was the radio operator/loader in a tank of the 48th Royal Tank Regiment in this operation and describes his part in it:

> There was the usual rumpus of battle around us – bursting shells, gunfire and the general noise made by our tanks. I remember seeing some infantrymen going through the maize or whatever it was on our right, but it was impossible to make out who they were – even whether they were Canadians or Germans – because of the thickness of the growth. Suddenly we heard that unmistakable clang of an AP shell hitting a tank, and we halted for a moment, wondering who had been hit. It wasn't until we moved a few yards further past a brick wall, some eight to ten feet high and on the right-hand side of the lane, that we could see the tank which had taken the point position just ahead of us standing in the middle of the road. One look at it showed that it had received a direct hit: there was a body lying beside it, but no sign of the rest of the crew. The road curved slightly to the right beyond the tank and about one hundred yards or so further on stood a barn or casa. There was another clang as a shell found its mark: the tank which had taken the other arm of the lane, which we could see quite clearly from our position, swerved and came to a halt and I heard its commander report that it had received a hit in the suspension. Had we been a moment earlier up the lane, it would have been our tank on the receiving end of that shot. As it was, it just gave us time to take evasive action by pulling in behind the wall and, once there, to take stock of the situation. We turned the tank to point toward the road in case a quick getaway was required. One tank alone (the others of the Squadron were spread out under cover there was back down the lane behind us) was hardly a match for a German anti-tank gun holed-up and out of sight one hundred yards away: it would clearly have been suicidal to get on the road again as it would have picked us off without fail. The only thing to do was to remain where we were for a while to give the infantry a chance to liquidate the gun crew – that was their job in the circumstances.

There they stayed for two hours, as German mortar bombs landed on the turret every time they began to open up in order to get a better look than that they obtained through their periscopes. Cook continues:

It was when I was at my periscope that I caught sight of two Germans running from a screen of bushes away to our left; one of them was carrying a bazooka. They disappeared behind cover, but having momentarily seen them, although not having the time to put a machine-gun on them, I warned the gunner and kept a pretty good look-out as they obviously had us tanks in mind as targets. On the opposite side of the lane from where we were, and beyond the roadside ditch, was another thick clump of maize. As I watched, I saw the missile of a bazooka push out from the cover and movement behind it, although I could not see any Germans. I shouted to the gunner 'Traverse right, quickly: bazooka men other side of road by maize – on, about there, fire!' then 'Spray along that ditch'. There was no time to say anything to the tank commander, and anyway he could hear me over the Tannoy system to which we were all linked. The bazooka withdrew and a few moments later I saw one German staggering as though wounded, running across to the bushes further beyond the road. We got the machine gun on him, but he went under cover and disappeared.

1st Canadian Corps's attack the following night, that of the 17/18th, was led by 1st Canadian Division on the right and 4th British on the left, with strong air support designed to break up counter-attacks, and additional artillery support provided by the New Zealand Division, which was in army reserve. The aim of the attack was to gain the ground overlooking the Ausa in preparation for crossing it. These, and attacks the following night, were successful and led to German withdrawal from Rimini itself during the night of 20/21 September, as the Canadians gained the San Fortunato ridge south of the town.

Meanwhile 5th Corps had been struggling across the ridges further inland. On the left, 4th Indian Division crossed the Murano on the night of 17/18 September and entered the republic of San Marino at Faetano, while 56th and 46th Divisions fought their way forward between them and 4th British Division, the 56th being heavily counter-attacked by 90th Panzer Grenadier on the Ceriano ridge on the 19th.

As the prospect of 1st Armoured Division being able to break through at this stage seemed poor, its armoured brigade was brought up to help the 56th and met heavy and accurate fire, particularly from 88mm anti-tank guns, as it did so. Casualties were heavy again, the Bays (2nd Dragoon Guards) losing twenty-four Sherman tanks at a cost of 22 killed and 76 wounded.

The Germans now withdrew to the River Uso a few miles west of Rimini, in pouring rain. Eighth Army had reached the promised land of the Romagna plain to find it a waterlogged expanse intersected by waterways, the rivers being lined by raised embankments. On 22 September the New Zealand Division, under 1st Canadian Corps, led what was expected to be a pursuit along the coast road towards Ravenna, with 5th Canadian Armoured Division struggling over the sodden ground on its left, getting entangled in the vines strung up on high poles, like Kentish hops. 43rd Gurkha Brigade, leading 1st Armoured Division, did not reach Route 9 until 24 September, an event which it had been assumed would initiate a dash by the division to lead 5th Corps along it to Bologna. Both corps made steady but slow progress, succeeding in crossing the Uso on 26 September and reaching the next river, the Fiumicino, by the 29th; but four days of heavy rain forced a halt and 5th Corps, at least, was too exhausted to push on further.

Since the start of OLIVE, Eighth Army had suffered 14,000 casualties and lost 250 tanks by enemy action and 230 from other causes. All infantry battalions had to be reduced from four companies to three for the next six months. 1st Armoured Division was broken up, 43rd Gurkha Brigade going to 56th Division to replace its 168th Brigade, which was merged with the 167th, and the battalions of 18th Brigade to replace three in 46th Division. 2nd Armoured Brigade became an independent armoured brigade group, available to support any division. A pause was called for before renewing the advance, and, during it, on 1 October, Leese left to take over command of Mountbatten's land forces in South-East Asia, being replaced by McCreery, his 10th Corps Headquarters being temporarily taken out of the command chain and later sent to Greece, where a civil war between communists and their opponents had erupted when the Germans withdrew their forces from the country on 7 October. 10th Indian Division was transferred to 5th Corps.

*

At the beginning of this period, 178 Squadron Royal Air Force, equipped with Liberator bombers and based near Foggia, was involved in flying supplies to the Polish insurgents in Warsaw. Sergeant Lloyd Lyne was a bomb-aimer in one which took part in this on 13 August. He gave his account of it after the war:

Some of us might have had a bit of breakfast, others were doing their ablutions, and one or two might have been still asleep, when an air force truck came up to the tents with a chappie on board with a loud hailer, shouting: 'All aircrew to report to briefing tent'. Which was most unusual. We normally went down to headquarters and saw whether or not we were flying that day, and that would be it. So we all went down to the briefing tent, and couldn't believe what we heard. The commanding officer said: 'Get your flying gear, you're flying down to the port of Brindisi.' That was all the information we had. So we did that, got flying kit and got aboard and flew down to Brindisi. Beautiful day. I can almost see it in my mind's eye, the sea and the sky almost met as one, you could hardly tell the difference, glorious day. We went back into the bomb bay of the Liberator and opened up the beam gun apertures and enjoyed looking out of those. There was Dick Scott the mid-upper gunner and the rear gunner and myself there watching. On landing at Brindisi, not a very good start because we burst a tire. I know that an ambulance and a fire tender were there within seconds of us stopping, but everything was alright, and put it right for us before it was time to take off. I suppose it was some time after lunch that we were called in for the briefing, and in the briefing a big map on the wall showed we were going to Warsaw. Which was quite a journey, although we had auxiliary petrol tanks. We had the briefing and one or two Polish chaps who had been there before gave us a description of it, and we were told that 400 feet was the best height to be dropping supplies. I suppose except for a bit of mine-laying Doug [MacRae, the pilot] hadn't been really trained for low-level bombing. I understand that for low-level bombing of the Ruhr dams they were practising for months before they actually took off.

I suppose we took off about 8 o'clock, and of course we had to fly over enemy territory practically the whole of the way. Didn't have a lot of trouble; met up with one Messerschmitt 109 but he didn't even bother to attack, why we never found out, whether he was young and a bit scared or old and wanted to live through the war. Doug got into a cloud formation, and when we came out he was nowhere to be seen. I would put it was around about Romania, around about the oilfield area [which they had bombed previously when based in Palestine]. But it did put us on our mettle, and from then on we were dropping out masses of this 'window' stuff. We flew singly [not in formation]. There weren't more than about 20 [aircraft on the operation], and that from different squadrons, 178, 31 South African, and 148 which was a specialist squadron. They met it so badly over Warsaw – Gordon Taylor was a flight lieutenant at the time and all the flight commanders and the C.O. were killed, and he had to become C.O. and was made up to acting wing commander.

Coming back to the actual flight, Gordon [the navigator] said to me, 'There should be a river visible', and I said, 'Yes, there is,' and he said 'That's the Vistula'. Navigating that far and coming spot-bang right over the Vistula, I thought was great.

Then Doug had to turn to fly up the Vistula, those were the briefing instructions, and it wasn't more than a few minutes passed by, fairly quickly we could see what was ahead of us, and it was nothing more than a huge pall of smoke. In between you'd get red glows that were obviously fires, and that was all we could see of Warsaw. We had to fly up and pass over three bridges and turn to port after the third bridge, that was said to bring us to Pryzinski Square where Polish females fighting in the home army would be holding hurricane lamps in the form of a cross, and that's where we were supposed to drop the supplies.

The canisters were in the bomb bay, just like bombs. I think it was 12 x 500 pound canisters. At about the second bridge the anti-aircraft fire was really intensive, and this was the moment that saved my life. I'm absolutely certain of that, more certain than I can possibly ever be. Doug came over the intercom and he said, 'Lloyd, go back onto the beam guns; you'll be able to help silence the ground fire and be more advantage there than dropping the supplies. I'll get Gordon to nip down and drop the supplies when we're over the target.' So with that I got up immediately, never thinking for one minute I wasn't going to be back there again, left my parachute in the storage position, and went back onto the beam guns, opened up both starboard and port apertures, stuck the guns out and started to fire at the ground, where the flak was coming from. I can also of course hear and realise that the mid-upper gunner and rear gunner are also firing a hell of a lot down onto the ground. And I suppose it was a bit of a horrific sight, that I was on the port beam gun, and I could see that the outer port engine was on fire, and that wasn't too pleasant. But it wasn't long before the port inner was on fire as well, in fact the whole wing looked to be on fire, and the most amazing thing was, I suppose my thoughts were quite amazing, that at this particular time the anti-aircraft shells were coming through the bottom of the aircraft and going out through the top. I likened them then and I still do, to cricket balls that were on fire. They looked about the size of a cricket ball and they were glowing. The 20 millimetre stuff, I could have thought, I could virtually have put my hand out and caught them. And I thought a strange thought really, I thought well, they're not going to do us a lot of harm because they haven't got the range right and they're going up through the top of the aircraft and exploding above us.

From that moment I knew nothing. We must have been very close to the target, because it was after the second bridge so we only had a few minutes flying to get to the actual dropping zone. According to reports from witnesses that I have since met in Poland, in Warsaw, that the plane actually was on fire, flew into the dropping zone and dropped the supplies, and turned to port again and after a short while there was an explosion, then the aircraft carried on and eventually crashed into a wooded area. Now all the witnesses I have spoken to, I can't see any other way it could have happened, was that this explosion might have been a petrol tank exploding or something like that, that explosion threw me out of the beam hatch where I was operating the beam guns. I had nothing [restraining me] on at all . . . had you still been in the aircraft you would have been killed as well, because it fell at the beginning of a very large wood and it took the limbs, whole trees off from where it started in the wood until where it crashed, like an avenue. They said there was no way anybody would survive that . . . It burned. The bodies were charred. They said that that must have been what happened because I was found on a small island in a lake in Paderewski Park . . . I was picked up on this small island. The island was covered with small bushes, small under-growth, which now has grown considerably but at the time they said it was the height of four to five foot, and covered the whole of the little island. The island couldn't have been more than 80 yards by 40 yards or something like that. The area around the island as well was sort of sandy, muddy texture, and they reckoned that that sort of softened the fall as well. Whether I would have been drowned if I had gone into the lake I don't know – that's something one will never know. But I recall Germans in a rowing boat and myself being picked up and put into it. And the thought going through my mind, which I thought, well, I must be dreaming, sort of a minute or two ago I was in an aircraft with my crewmates and now I'm in a rowing boat with Germans rowing. It was just something bizarre. According to the witnesses it must have been four or five hours [after the crash]. We were shot down about midnight – they put down the operation as the 13th–14th of August, because it might have been just after midnight when we were shot down. I found out in Warsaw that daylight then started at about five o'clock, and it was just getting light when I was picked up so I had been there four or five hours. But remember nothing about it.

He regained consciousness in a German hospital two days later.

9

Winter of Discontent

October 1944 to January 1945

While Eighth Army had been battering its way through the eastern end of the GOTHIC line and the Fifth had clambered over the crests of the northern Apennines, Roosevelt, Churchill and their Chiefs of Staff had met at Quebec in the OCTAGON conference from 10 to 16 September in optimistic mood. Eisenhower's armies had liberated almost all of Belgium and, in France, Patton had reached Nancy and joined hands with General Jacob. L. Devers's 6th Army Group, which had come up the Rhône valley. The Russians had advanced into Central Europe, reaching Warsaw and the borders of Hungary. In this euphoric atmosphere, it seemed quite likely that the war against Germany would be over by the end of the year. Eisenhower had no need of further transfer of divisions from Italy: he had not yet received all the reinforcements available from the United States. The Americans were even prepared to look favourably and provide landing craft for a force to cross the northern Adriatic and land in the Istrian peninsula south of Trieste, both as an encouragement to Tito's partisans in Yugoslavia and a first step towards Alexander's favourite concept of an advance through the Ljubljana Gap to Austria. There was a general feeling that one more push in Italy would bring both of Alexander's armies into the Po valley, resulting in either the total collapse of Kesselring's forces or their withdrawal to the River Adige; and, with the cities of the valley in Allied hands, better winter quarters for the troops than the comfortless Apennine mountains. Kesselring in fact proposed to OKW a contingency plan to withdraw by stages to this line, codenamed AUTUMN MIST (*Herbstnebel*); but realizing, as turned out to be the case, that Hitler might not approve, he prepared to defend the successive lines of the rivers which ran down from the mountains to the Adriatic across the routes of Eighth Army's advance.

That army having attracted reserves to von Vietinghoff's left flank, it was now Fifth Army's turn to strike another blow in the centre. On 2 October Clark resumed the offensive with 2nd US Corps astride the main Route 65, 13th Corps taking over Route 610 to Imola, its attack led by 78th Division returned from its sojourn in Egypt. After three weeks of bitter fighting, 88th US Division took Monte Grande within five miles of the Via Emilia south-east of Bologna on 20 October, and three days later 34th US Division took Monte Belmonte nine miles south of the city centre. By this time von Vietinghoff had reinforced 1st Parachute Corps to a strength of eleven divisions, and, on 27 October, Alexander agreed that Clark should call a halt until McCreery had drawn off some of these by the renewal of Eighth Army's offensive. This was two days after von Vietinghoff had taken over from Kesselring when the latter was seriously injured in a traffic accident. Herr replaced him in command of Tenth Army.

McCreery favoured an attempt to press forward through the hills rather than the plain, and the renewed offensive began with an attack by 10th Indian Division (Major-General D. Reid) across the higher reaches of the River Fiumicino on 5 October, which made it possible for 46th Division to cross it lower down, followed nearer the coast by 56th Division and the Canadian Corps. The Polish Corps was then brought into the line to the left of the Indians, forcing the Germans back in four days of tough fighting, ending in the capture of Monte Grosso and helping 46th Division to press forward on Route 9 to take Cesena on 20 October. Major Richard O'Brien was commanding C Company of the 2/5th Leicesters in the division's 139th Brigade and took part in these operations, as he describes:

> At 1200 the telephone rang: the CO* for Major O'Brien. 'Oh God!' I thought, 'surely not another advance.' The CO was quiet – too quiet. 'Have you got your map?'. 'Yes'. 'See the bridge in Pontecello?' Pause. 'It is undamaged. Take it.' Long pause. 'Now?' 'As soon as you can.' 'Er – all right, I will make a recce then phone you my plan.' 'Thank you'.
>
> In a moment the whole company seemed to know. I summoned the platoon commanders, and set off to have a look at the bridge. Why C again? We always claimed to be superior to the others, but this seemed a dubious honour. We slunk through the vineyards and

* Lieutenant-Colonel F. L. Martin.

reached the forward house occupied by the Durham Light Infantry. There, in a dirty dark stable, we found a dirty dark company commander (odd how miserable men always chose miserable quarters), who took us up to a window to show us the ground. From this window we could see the bridge and its approaches with appalling clarity. A ridge gently sloped down towards the gully the bridge spanned, and then rose a little on the further side to the buildings the enemy occupied. The ground on our side was bare ploughland, devoid of all cover. No covered approach to the bridge existed and there was no way round. The only way to advance was in open order across the plough-land. It needed no imagination to appreciate the mortars and machine guns which would have time to annihilate us. This attack would be suicide. I foresaw C Company decimated in a few minutes without anything being achieved. The platoon commanders were visibly and justifiably dismayed. We returned full of thought.

The rest of the day was a long period of strain for all of us. I felt the lives of many of the men as well as myself hung on my efforts to prevent the attack on the bridge. That it was eventually postponed was due to the CO furthering my opinions; neither he nor the Brigadier* had seen the ground so they could not argue about it with me. Jacko was ordered to send out a patrol at last light to find out whether the bridge was prepared for demolition, and I was warned to be ready to attack the tiny village on the far side as soon as Jacko had established a small bridge-head. This plan was better but still unattractive. A night attack on a village without a proper fire plan seemed unsound; safer if it could be made in the dawn with the support of the tanks.

Darkness fell. Jacko gained the bridge, and the Company moved up to the farm from which we had first seen the ground. Here memory fails me. The intention was for Jacko to get his whole Company over and then allow us to attack through him. I had already produced my plan to the CO – a march round to our left flank held by the Poles, and a dawn attack with tanks firing from the ridge on the right; but there seemed little hope of its acceptance. How it came about that it was agreed upon I forget, sufficient that one platoon of Jacko's was left on the bridge while we withdrew

* Brigadier A. P. Block.

to our old positions. The men prepared to snatch a few hours rest and I sat down in Battalion HQ to work out another plan. Exhausted as we all felt, it was a relief to be doing something that seemed feasible.

It was a long and tiresome night. Everyone except me was anxious about Jacko's platoon which seemed so far away. I felt interested only in our coming attack, feeling for some reason that the platoon would safely hold its ground. We drank tea and talked about artillery support. For a long time we waited for the Polish Liaison Officer to arrive but he failed to show himself. Eventually we decided to start without him. The men were woken up, orders were issued, and an hour before dawn we marched away from the battalion HQ down into the valley which separated us from the Poles. The men seemed tired but not noticeably depressed. I felt confident and excited and wide awake. It would be dishonest to deny that in spite of everything, I always felt invigorated by the prospect of an attack.

We found the Poles, and, after a feverish and comic conversation in French, confirmed where we were on the map (which was where we expected to be!) and where the enemy was. The company lined up along the hedges, and as the light grew, I gave Burgh the order to move off. Battalion then came up on the wireless to say that the Divisional Commander had personally ordered the tanks to move from their ridge across the bridge into the village, so that, although we should have no supporting fire, we should find the tanks in or near the village as we approached. The news did not sound as good as it turned out to be for plans altered in the middle of a battle had a way of misfiring. But this time all went well. The company led by Burgh advanced on the village, and found the tanks just arrived there without opposition. We had a peace-time entry, and as Coy HQ moved into a half-ruin, Booth and Cyril continued up the road. I wirelessed battalion. For a moment there seemed nothing much to do – until suddenly some prisoners turned up from 13 platoon and we realised there were Germans about. Hurriedly leaving Coy HQ, I found that 13 and 15 had both gone further than I intended and were engaged in chasing Germans. Our luck was still holding for they had reached two good houses which would make good defensive positions, and had surprised the enemy. With the aid of the tanks we soon rounded up over thirty. Everyone suddenly woke up and became excited; the smallest victory always had that effect. I disposed the tanks, arranged for some anti-tank guns, and got on the radio to urge that now was the time for the promised infantry-cum-tank force to break through. The CO had explicitly stated that it was waiting behind for my word that the bridge was firmly held. This was the moment: for the first time I had seen the Germans in confusion, and would have followed them myself had circumstances allowed it. We bombastically announced that once again we had gained our objective, and turned to welcome Steele and the CSM with ammunition. They were followed by the CO, who was more than usually effusive. I again pressed for the breakthrough.

But we were not to be left in peace. 13 platoon reported on the 38 set that a German tank was behind the house in front of them. They sounded worried so I talked airily about Piats and reminded them that they had a Sherman with them. Our 'good' tank – the one with the 17 pounder – was behind so I ordered the tank officer to send it up. At that moment the shelling began. Heavy shelling is a phrase often seen in newspapers and communiques but I had never experienced what I believed it to be. Now I was to have the opportunity. Up the road the Germans must have collected a few SP guns and with deadly accuracy they rained down a hail of fire on the village and bridge. On the way to Cyril I took shelter in a house with the CO. The air was full of red dust and the house shook with the blast of the 88s. It was full of frightened tank-men, who had had their tank hit, and were lying under the tables and chairs and anything they believed would give protection. The house was hit more than once, and we decided to leave. The 'good' tank appeared and was directed on its way. I then ran back to HQ to whom I had given orders before I left to move to a better house. I found the house in ruins and no HQ, so I turned back to walk up the road to 13 platoon. Every few seconds the shells came crashing over. I was glad of the ditch at the side of the road into which I could fall flat. At this time I first saw the KRR Battalion which was supposed to move through us. One company was lying in the middle of the ditch, obviously disorganised; they were going to be of little use, but they had arrived at a bad time.

After some delay I reached Cyril. He was redder than usual and his eyes were glittering: the tank was unsettling him. The men were crouched about looking frightened and apathetic, and the two tanks round the farm were behaving with infuriating stupidity. But the danger seemed less than it appeared for if the Mark 4 left its hide-out behind the farm to come down the road, we should easily knock it out. I went upstairs and watched Pepper's heavy guns landing shells round the farm in front: for once he was doing us well. Then came the unmistakable noise of a tank's tracks on the road, some one shouted, and at once everyone realised the tank was advancing. At such a moment there is nothing to be done: the defences are disposed, and all one can do is to await events. I clambered over some furniture and out on the verandah to watch the scene. The tank came down the road and at the same time one of our tanks moved out from behind our farm to engage it. The swastika could be seen plainly on the turret as it drew level with us. The loud report of an HE gun firing, followed by another, crashed out but the tank still came on, and was in fact just beyond our house and opposite Booth's on the other side of the road, when the third shot rang forth and flames suddenly appeared from the turret. It came to halt, the crew jumped out and began to run back down the road. We shouted at the Bren Gunners to open fire. The field-grey uniforms were clearly visible as the Germans ran desperately hard back the way they had come. Aided by a ditch and some indifferent shooting, they all escaped. Only the tank was left burning in the road.

There 46th Division was relieved by the 4th, which succeeded in crossing the River Savio and building a bridge by the 24th, the Canadians having done the same lower down two days earlier. Lieutenant F. G. Sutton was still commanding the pioneer platoon of the 2nd Bedfords in the 4th Division. His task was to find and clear mines while the battalion passed through the East Surreys and attacked the twin hills of Bertinoro. He wrote:

The CO* had decided to take the Bertinoro peaks by surprise. A and D companies were ordered off the roads, during the night, under wireless silence, they scaled their way up the higher of the two hills. The enemy withdrew, but he left behind the heaviest mined and booby trapped area we had yet come across. A section of Royal Engineers of 46 Division had arrived, at dawn, at the C.O.'s command post and had started to give us a hand with mines and demolitions. When I arrived there a little later, I was told they had

* Lieutenant-Colonel B. A. Burke.

cleared the area of mines. I went into the farm and saw the C.O. He looked tired out. He told me that A and D companies had taken the highest Bertinoro hill, but had run into booby traps which had caused fairly heavy casualties. I was to take my three jeeps forward, send one section to the top of the hill to help A and D with the booby traps, and with the other two sections clear the way for B company and the tanks, to take the town of Bertinoro.

The farm was in a cul-de-sac; we turned the jeeps round and drove back the fifty yards to the crossroads we had passed before. I was in the leading jeep, Waller was in the second, and Worboys commanded the third. There were about ten yards between jeeps. I had just reached the crossroads when there was a terrific bang, and a dark cloud of smoke hung over the whole scene. I saw that Waller's jeep was all right, but the third one had blown up on a mine, over which the other two must have driven just before. All the crew of five were knocked out, more or less, but luckily none were killed. The driver had a piece of metal in his back and was shell shocked. Corporal Worboys had his left eardrum burst. Bayliss, who had sat over the left rear wheel which had been torn off, had sailed for fifteen yards through the air; he was picked up by the C.O. who had come running from the farm to help. Poor Bayliss, he looked a heap of misery, but he was the luckiest of the lot as nothing was broken in his body. Maile, who was a big chap, had been blown into the ditch. He seemed all right and even volunteered to stay, but I insisted that he should go back with the ambulance, and it turned out that he had part of his spine fractured. Paxton seemed to be the worst off. His left leg was broken in five places. When I saw him in Luton, a year later, he was just beginning to walk again. When the ambulance had taken care of the wounded we took the trailer of the third jeep and hitched it onto Old's jeep, which was now towing two full trailers. We then took the three good tyres and the spare wheel, as jeep tyres were at a premium just then. The damaged jeep was pushed into the ditch out of the way.

I told Corporal Mann to take his section and walk up the hill to A company to clear the booby traps. Waller and I started to walk up towards Bertinoro, while the jeeps followed slowly, with the remaining section thoroughly checking for mines on the road. Waller and I lifted mines as we walked along. For the first time we found some 'Riegel' mines. These mines had the form of a bar, about 4 by 5 by

30 inches, and they could not be disarmed. We had to yank them out of their hiding places in the road, and lean them against the trees on the verge, visible to all. At a blown bridge we left instructions for the section behind us to prepare a passage for the tanks. Then we reached B company, and met Graham Martin who was waiting for us to clear a way into Bertinoro for his company. A few mines were in the road just there. Waller and I thought it might be a good thing to show B company that we had the situation well under control. So we proceeded to lift these mines with the greatest of nonchalance; we lifted the lids, extracted the detonators and kicked them into the next field, and then we heaved the mines there too. B company seemed duly impressed. The Company Sergeant-Major then came along and pointed to a big wooden box. It was standing on the verge of the road and had obviously been left behind by the enemy. It would make a nice kit box and the Sergeant-Major apparently needed one. Waller lifted the lid carefully; I could just see a piece of string underneath and I yelled. Waller held the lid and I cut the string very slowly and carefully. There were no further strings or wires, so we opened the lid. The box contained about a hundred two-pounds demolition charges, all high explosives. One of them had a detonator and a pull switch. The latter was connected to the lid by the string we had cut.

Waller and I walked on; our chests were well out and B company followed, full of confidence. Before the entrance to Bertinoro the enemy had blown a dozen large trees across the road; we left instructions for the jeeps to tow them out of the way, and we went on to get B company through in single file. I was very conscious of possible trip wires in the branches of the lying trees and we both walked very slowly, advancing inch by inch. Then I saw a dead dog among the branches. I thought that it must have run through the fallen trees, tripped a wire connected to a concrete mine and been killed that way. I stopped. I looked around slowly and carefully. Suddenly I could see the wire; it was only a few inches from my legs. It was difficult to see because it had been painted green, and it led to a green concrete mine two feet away. I was too afraid to move and Waller reached forward, slowly, to cut the wire. We then disarmed the mine. There was another one, and then we were through the trees. A few more mines in the road, and we entered the town of Bertinoro.

It had been the need to reinforce his centre which had caused the German General Herr to withdraw across the River Bevano to the Ronco, covering Forli and Ravenna. The attempt by 4th Division to cross it on the night of 25/26 October met with a rebuff, but attacks by 10th Indian and the Poles in the hills led to successful crossings and penetrated as far as Grignano beyond Forli by 2 November. The Reverend T. F. Torrance was a Church of Scotland chaplain who ran a Mobile Canteen with the 10th Indian Division. He described his experience:

> The battle moved forward under fearful weather. Side by side with the Colonel and his HQ I marched under driving rain through churned up mud, and splashed through swollen rivers. But as Colonel Anderson said this is all war! All the time we had to watch out for booby traps. Sometimes the mist shielded us from spotter planes, but we did not escape enemy shelling, and suffered not a few casualties. We tramped day and night and spent nights without sleep. Then, as the battle moved swiftly ahead, the Colonel asked me to stay for a few days and bury the dead, and then push on as rapidly as possible and join them. He also asked me to round up some troops on jeeps further back, and send them on. I think they had lost their way. I myself kept very fit, but was getting rather tired. We preferred to sleep in the open rather than under a roof for the retreating Germans did their best to foul everything with stinking excrement. When we took prisoners, they were astonished at the way we took care of their wounded as well as our own. We were to find that when so many of our own wounded men who came back from hospital into the battle, the Germans not infrequently put into effect a policy of shooting up our wounded on the ground to stop that happening. That enraged us.

At an earlier stage of Operation OLIVE he had been temporarily attached to the Manchester Regiment, and tells of his time there:

> The Manchesters were operating just then in the high Apennines, which was not suitable for trucks, so that they had to make do with mules and horses to bring up supplies and ammunition. I was given a fine grey horse, at which I was delighted, but it was too conspicuous, and one day when we were heavily mortared, he broke loose and galloped over the hill into the hands of the enemy! And so I had to make do with a mule for myself, and several mules to carry the supplies. It was really great fun, for it reminded me of my days as a

boy travelling with my father on mule-back in the Min Shan mountains of Sichuan! However, we had to camouflage the mules dyeing them light brown to fit in with the colour of the trees and shrubbery! The battle area had been heavily churned up and was very muddy. It was dirty work, and I longed for a bath, and so some times when we had to wade through a mountain torrent, I wanted to tumble in and get clean again! My task was to visit troops sheltering in the bushes and wooded mountain slopes in preparation for an advance – what a welcome the Church of Scotland's mule always got!

*

On 29 October, Alexander met with McCreery and Clark to discuss future operations in the light of events since the OCTAGON conference. The euphoria had faded with Montgomery's setback at Arnhem and a general slowing down of progress, not only in Eisenhower's command, but on the Russian front in Central Europe also, although they had reached Belgrade. When Churchill, on his way to Moscow to report to Stalin the results of OCTAGON, had stopped off at Naples on 6 October, Wilson and Alexander explained to him their plan for a landing in Istria and its development towards Ljubljana as the best way of bringing about the collapse of German resistance in Italy. To make this possible they asked that three US divisions, due to reinforce Eisenhower, should be diverted within the next three weeks to Italy, releasing Eighth Army for the Istrian venture. Churchill needed no persuading and, from Moscow, sent a signal to Roosevelt requesting this. He received a closely reasoned but dusty answer, which concluded:

Diversion of any forces to Italy would withhold from France vitally needed fresh troops, while committing such forces to the high attrition of an indecisive winter campaign in Northern Italy. I appreciate the hard and difficult task which our armies in Italy have faced and will face, but we cannot withhold from the main effort forces which are needed in the Battle of Germany. From General Marshall's reports on the problem now facing General Eisenhower, I am sure that both of them agree with my conviction that no divisions should be diverted from their destination in France.

This, combined with Hitler's refusal to allow von Vietinghoff to implement AUTUMN MIST, forced Alexander to revise his ideas. Under the guise of helping Tito, whose partisans were increasing their power daily, he would develop the ports of the Dalmatian coast so that a substantial part of Eighth Army could be transferred to Yugoslavia once the Fifth Army had driven the Germans back behind the Adige. This could not be envisaged before February 1945. In order to complete all the preparations for this, both armies would have to bring their current offensives to an end by 15 November, by which time it would be important to have secured Bologna and Ravenna as winter quarters. He planned that Clark should withdraw two divisions to rest and pretend to withdraw another, giving the impression to the Germans that he had abandoned for the winter his attempt to reach Bologna. McCreery would continue his offensive, aiming to take Ravenna and to attract as many as possible of Herr's mobile reserves towards his sector. When he had done this, Clark would secretly return his divisions to the front line and resume his attempt to take Bologna.

When Alexander put these proposals to Clark and McCreery, the former pointed out that his army had suffered 20,000 casualties in recent operations and that his divisions could not be ready before 30 November. McCreery undertook to keep his offensive going until 15 December. Alexander therefore decided that Fifth Army should start its offensive on the first date and that both offensives should end on the second, by which time he hoped that Eighth Army would have reached Imola and the River Santerno.

After 10th Indian Division and the Poles had reached Grignano beyond Forli on 2 November, they were relieved by 46th Division which attacked Forli itself on the night of 7/8 November, as 4th Division joined in from the direction of the airfield and the Germans withdrew to the River Montone. Both divisions crossed this and continued to press the enemy back until they reached the River Lamone at Faenza on the 24th. There 4th Division was withdrawn, not to rest and retrain in Palestine, as had been intended, but to Greece, as was also 4th Indian Division.

Meanwhile, on the left, the Poles had pressed forward in the hills until they joined hands with 8th Indian Division in 13th Corps at Modigliana, ten miles south of Faenza. 10th Indian Division had been withdrawn from that sector and moved over to the right of 4th Division to cross the Montone and advance to the Lamone. This involved them in tough fighting against the German 365th Division, which had breached the river's floodbanks and inundated the surrounding fields.

1st Durham Light Infantry took part in this, in which R. I. Higgins was serving, now apparently reduced in rank from corporal to private since we last heard of him near Perugia. He remembered a night attack on a Lone Tree Hill.

Jerry had anticipated our move and decided to do all he could to spoil the party. He had scattered Schumines all over the place and as soon as somebody trod on one, he opened up with everything he had. There was no artillery as he had men at the foot of the hill in slit trenches just behind the stream. We got Spandau fire from the boys at the bottom and from the top of the hill, and the din was diabolical. I thought I could never survive this but could only hope for the best, pull my steel helmet down firmly, grasp my Tommy-gun in a purposeful manner and plod on, gritting my teeth and swearing softly to myself. On my immediate right, a man fell flat on his face without a sound, his weapon falling from his lifeless grip and his helmet tilting comically forward, brim wedged in the turf. I found out later that a bullet had passed through his head killing him instantly. A few more yards and there was a loud report and a frightful yell from my left as Big Bill Bowdrey trod on a mine and also fell down, but he was screaming because he had lost a foot.

From further over to the left, a flame-thrower soon opened up, hoping to singe the fellows who were making things uncomfortable with their Spandaus at the bottom of the hill. These flame-throwers were the smallest issued and were completely operated by one man. He carried a pack on his back which presumably contained the fuel which was ignited as it passed through a hand nozzle with a pistol grip and trigger control. The device was very effective in sending a gust of flame some twenty or thirty yards. It looked spectacular in the dark and was undoubtedly annoying to anybody in a slit trench in front of it. There was, however, another effect which made me thankful that I was never required to operate this grotesque cigarette lighter. In the jargon of 1977, this weapon was self-defeating in that the moment it was used on a dark night, the exact position of the operator was disclosed to all interested parties for miles around. Any of the opposition with rifles or machine-guns immediately filled the area with missiles, and a flame-thrower rarely survived long enough to enjoy a second squeeze on his trigger.

We who were still walking reached the stream and the opposing machine-gunners who had been defending that zone were silent; deceased or decamped we knew not. Our Platoon Commander had been knocked out and we who were left were now under the command of our Platoon Sergeant. He was an ex-Artilleryman and knew little about the sort of situation he now found himself in. Our Bren-gunner was out and I took over his weapon. We also found that none of the corporals was present and, in fact, our platoon, which had started out over thirty strong, was down to the sergeant and about a dozen men. As a former NCO, I became Senior Private/ Bren Gunner and the sergeant was reduced to asking my advice as to our immediate future movements. I said I thought we should carry on up the hill and try to achieve our purpose. The stream was not too wide and, by swinging the Bren a few times, I was able to get its 23 pounds to pull me over – well, almost over. I dropped slightly short and entered the water over my knees and had to drag myself and friend up the far slippery bank. Once on the hill proper, we made our way up as far as possible but soon found that Jerry was still sitting on the top and playfully lobbing his grenades amongst us.

It seemed that we were getting nowhere swiftly and as dawn would soon be upon us, I told the sergeant that I could see no useful purpose now being achieved and that I advised our withdrawal across the field before daylight made us sitting ducks. It was now comparatively quiet; a few isolated bangs and rat-a-tats persuaded us that the war was still going on. The sergeant agreed and we shuffled down again and, feeling naked and exposed, and apprehensive about the remaining mines, we re-crossed the field. As we neared our ramp, the German machine-gunner from the hill top, presumably in anticipation of the withdrawal of any survivors, had trained his gun on it. Fortunately, the Germans were so systematic that we often had cause to bless them for it and this occasion was an example. Our little party approached the ramp and awaited the next burst of fire. We noted the time and then waited for the next; this gave the frequency and, following the next burst, we pushed several fellows up the ramp, the rest of us following in appropriate rushes until we had all safely reached the farmhouse. I should perhaps add that, as Sergeant Bond eventually tried to stop something hard and hot with a hand and wanted nothing more to do with the Army – and certainly not the Infantry – Private Higgins now became acting Platoon Commander/ Platoon Sergeant. The farmhouse was now largely inhabited by men in various degrees of unfitness caused by bullets or shrapnel from mines. They were lying on straw on the stone floor while NCOs of the Medical Corps were moving around washing, bandaging and handing out nerve-stilling cigarettes and generally doing their best for morale.

When 4th Division reached the Lamone on 2 December they were relieved by the New Zealand Division. On that day 1st Canadian Division on the left and 5th Canadian Armoured on the right, which had been out of the line for a month, launched the advance of 1st Canadian Corps (now commanded by Lieutenant-General C. Foulkes) along the coast road towards Ravenna, which they entered on the 4th.

Meanwhile the Polish Corps in the hills south of the Via Emilia made good progress and succeeded in driving the Germans back across the Lamone south of Faenza and forcing their 305th and 715th Divisions back to the Senio, by which time the total Polish casualties in this Battle of the Rivers had risen to 3,516, of whom 669 were killed. 5th Corps began its attack on Faenza on the night of 3/4 December, led by 46th Division, which established a bridgehead over the Lamone four miles short of the town. Private Wray was still with the 6th York and Lancasters, who took part:

On the 6th of December B Company were ordered forward. I remember little of our final days in the area. I recall arriving at a farmhouse. One of the platoons had gone in ahead ... and ... at 19.30 hours on 7 December was surrounded in a house. An artillery officer arranged support. He talked back to his guns and ordered one gun to fire on the house, hoping that our lads would keep their heads down, and that the Germans outside would be persuaded to leave. There was tension as our officer planned to go after the Germans. With Company H.Q. and the reserve platoon, we were to go forward and winkle out the enemy attackers. Faint radio messages were received from those inside the house. A platoon 38 set worked back to Company H.Q. We heard the Bosch were surrounding the building and trying to get our blokes to surrender. The Company Commander digested this bad news and told me to go to the sections of the platoon sheltering in an outbuilding. I found them sprawled against an inside wall. There was light from a shaded oil lamp. I sought out the section leader and told him that the officer said 'Get dressed and move forward.' Morale hit rock bottom. They had come to the end. One or two enquired in worried tones 'What next?' Some were sobbing, too frightened to go out into the night. There was a lot of shelling and they said they were not going on. These men, in forward platoons over the months and years, had seen too many of their mates killed and wounded. They had gone through bouts of action in Tunisia, in Salerno, in the mountains in front of Cassino, and during the last four months of severe battles in the Gothic Line. The battalion had been reduced from four coys. to three. Some of the coys. had only two platoons not three.

I went back to the officer and told him they had had it. He was drained, his eyes strained through lack of sleep and battle weariness. He went back with me to the barn. He began to persuade the frightened men that they were about to be relieved and this would be one of the last actions. He confirmed that the division was to go out for a long rest. He spoke gently and said that mutiny would be foolish as they were coming to the end of their stint. Also he pointed out some of our blokes were under threat and could be captured and it was their job to rescue them. I expected bluster and threats of court martial from him but he handled an impossible situation with good sense. We were all shit scared, including him. We all went together. For some time we heard nothing on the 38 set from the men in the farmhouse.

Over the surrounding hills and valleys we heard shells, some of 'Ours', some of 'Theirs'. Explosions lit up the hilltops. Farmhouses were burning. Flames flickered in the haystacks. We moved forward. The officer checked his maps to find in which direction the farmhouse lay. The artificial moonlight* helped to light us on our way. There was the smell of burning ricks and the more acrid smell from cordite of the recent stonks. Reaching the crest of the hill we saw the enemy shells were hitting in front of us in the valley. As the lines of men approached the valley bottom the enemy fire lifted and hit the area we had just left. We crashed along and up towards the other crest ahead. Shells fell again in the valley we had left. We were lucky so far.

As we neared the farmhouse under attack we wondered what we would come up against. Two N.C.O.s went forward. Around the

---

* Produced by shining searchlights into clouds.

4.2in mortars in action in Operation DIADEM. 12 May 1944.

Smokescreen over the River Gari. 14 May 1944.

Winston Churchill with Generals Alexander and Anders, Commander of the Polish Corps. 26 August 1944.

Troops of the 1st Canadian Division in Pignataro. 15 May 1944.

3rd Hussars' tank in Chianti Hills. 7 July 1944.

3rd Welsh Guards near Arezzo. 18 July 1944.

Sikhs of the Frontier Force Regiment near Citta di Castello. 20 July 1944.

A 'Priest' 105mm self-propelled field gun of 11th HAC, 6th Armoured Division. 16 May 1944.

A 'Kangaroo' armoured personnel carrier, manned by 9th Lancers, carrying troops of 78th Division near Argenta. 13 April 1945.

A Churchill tank of 51st Royal Tank Regiment.

Fascine-carrying tanks and a Sherman bulldozer of 25th Army Tank Brigade in support of the New Zealand Division, River Senio. April 1945.

A 'Crocodile' flame-thrower supporting the New Zealand Division on the River Senio. 9 April 1945.

'Fantails' crossing Lake Comacchio. 11 April 1945.

DUKWs crossing the River Po in support of New Zealand Division. 24 April 1945.

The pontoon bridge over the River Po, erected by Royal Engineers of 5th Corps. 27 April 1945.

General von Vietinghoff signing the surrender document at Caserta. 29 April 1945.

buildings haystacks were burning. Clouds of smoke were swirling round the house. I could just make out the door. With shouts of reassurance to the blokes inside they let us in. Phew! The Bosch had buggered off. Defensive positions were taken up outside once more. The men had retreated into the building during the Teds attacks and held on until the rest of us had come up. One of the attacked platoon was missing. Hours later we heard that his position, in a haystack, had ignited. His body was found under burnt straw next to his weapon.

A fierce counter-attack on the 9th by 90th Panzer Grenadier Division was beaten off, but at a considerable cost to 46th Division's 138th Brigade. After this the exhausted division was sent to Greece to join its 139th Brigade already there.

Clark had cooperated to try and help McCreery by ordering 13th Corps to exert pressure higher up in the Santerno valley in the mountains. This was done by 6th Armoured Division, which pushed along Route 610 towards Imola. Its 61st Infantry Brigade was held up by German defences at the hill town of Borgo Tossignano. Rifleman Crimp, who seems to have been transferred from B Company to Battalion HQ, recorded in his diary the part played by the 2nd Rifle Brigade in the attack on that town:

12th December. The big attack is going in tonight. Archie Dukes has full griff* from his boss, the Adjutant.† Two Companies, 'B' and 'C', are moving on Tossignano at two o'clock. Before this there's going to be a softening-up from the Divisional artillery massed behind in the Santerno Valley and a creeping barrage in front of our chaps as they go in. Another town, Borgo Tossignano, adjoining our objective, is being tackled by 7th Battalion. But ours is likely to be the tougher assignment, because of its difficult situation; on the side of a hill protruding athwart the valley, flanked by mountain and precipice, with its only approach across open country, and that uphill. Nevertheless its hoped to gain an advantage from surprise, and as soon as the town is cleared, or most of it.

---

* Griff: information.
† Captain R. E. Worsley.

After describing a convivial evening with the Italian family in whose house he was billeted, he continues:

> Outside in the valley the guns have started. For fifteen minutes the night is rent by a jumbled succession of roarings and thunderings, which reverberate wrathfully against the hills. The darkness behind is torn and gashed with searing flame and high over Fontanelice shrills the demon-chorus of shells in flight. At intervals when the uproar's quieter, we can hear them crashing on Tossignano. Our chaps are going in.
>
> *13th December.* The attack appears to have been successful. Both Companies are well establshed in Tossignano. Jerry still holds part of the town, but is being dislodged in tough house-fighting. 'A' Company and parts of 'S' are going in tonight to help 'B' and 'C' clean the place up. The 7th Battalion have also taken their objective. The Adjutant went up to Forward TAC this morning and brought the news back. On his return he found a shell had landed against the house he's billeting in and covered his kit with dust and debris, as well as giving Archie Dukes, who was tidying up, a severe shaking. So there's life in the Hun yet!

After describing another convivial evening, in which there was no enemy shelling, he continues:

> *14th December.* Enemy shelling on Fontanelice has eased off. Not much news from Tossignano, but sorry to hear Cpl. Furze, with one or two others, was whacked in the opening assault. He was the chap in 'B' Company Carriers who escorted Randall to the Cairo cooler and whose section I was in for a while at Geneifa. They say our creeping barrage got him. It wasn't creeping fast enough and when it was lifted four hundred yards it was too far forward to give much help. Another casualty was Snowy White. He'd been abroad almost four years. What lousy luck after all that!
>
> The Adjutant's gone forward to the TAC again and on his return orders pack-up. At eight o'clock, after dark, we move out. At the entrance square we turn right, which is rather puzzling, and go back the way we came. There's no trouble on the road, but turning off at Carseggio its a terrific job getting the convoy up to Tambarella in the inky dark and swathes of mud. One White gets stuck (luckily the tail, so the rest aren't blocked) but we have to use headlights as a last

resort. This rouses Jerry's curiosity and several guns, which seem quite near, start a stream of shells screeching over. They land however a good way behind, somewhere near Castel del Rio. No doubt he suspects another attack's in motion and is trying to bust it on the startline. Why we're back in Tambarella is a mystery. Evidently there's been a change of plan. Perhaps the Batt., after its efforts in Tossignano, is being withdrawn.

15th December. Last night's stonk on Castel del Rio caused considerable damage. Over forty vehicles were put out of action, including several belonging to our 'A' Echelon. A troop of self-propelled guns, pushed audaciously forward did the trick. No more news of Tossignano. Senior people, normally in the know, seem oddly reticent. But it now seems our attack hasn't proved as successful as first reports hinted. Cold overcast weather. Life is a dream, compounded of a thousand petty carking [wearing] discomforts, dimly perceived through the atrabilious gloom of our cellar.

16th December. A forlorn air hangs over muddy bedraggled Tambarella as TAC returns from the hills. With them comes positive news of Tossignano. The attack has failed. Worse still, the Battalion has suffered a severe mauling. Cpl. Mac, who went forward as Rear-Link representative and spent most of his time helping Batt. Control wireless, gives us his version. The first phase, he says, the assault on the town, was accomplished more easily than expected, despite the barrage balls-up. Our fellows, in fact, got well inside before meeting any serious opposition. But after a while more resistance became stubborn and dislodging Jerry from his houses and cubby-holes, alive with every sort of booby-trap, proved a slow job. All that night passed in house-to-house clashes. Messages were coming in regularly to Batt. Control from 'B' and 'C' Companies, reporting progress. At dawn, however, the ejecting operations had to be suspended; they would have proved too costly in daylight and our chaps were needing a rest and chance to consolidate. Another day passed quietly with only occasional sniping at anyone showing his head. No support from our guns could be called as it was too confused. But Jerry was still holding a large part of Tossignano.

　　Towards evening signals from 'B 'and 'C' were getting fainter and fainter, their batteries obviously almost flat. Their spirits must have been sinking likewise as rations and ammo were also ebbing. To effect replenishment and strengthen a further attempt at expelling Jerry 'A' Company and parts of 'S' tried to get in after dark. But this time Jerry was ready. He had somehow managed to filter back into that part of the town which commanded the entrance and a curtain of fire across the threshold prevented our people from getting a toe in. Artillery support was again ruled out for fear of hitting our chaps inside. Then having sealed off thus our supplies and reinforcements and no doubt strengthened his own Jerry switched to the offensive within the town. The most effective among his large repertoire of winkling-out devices was blowing out walls with anti-tank faustpatronen, then chucking grenades and petrol bombs in through the cavities. Next morning the last message from 'B' came through. They and 'C' were still resisting, with no thought of jagging-in, though all their officers had been killed or wounded. After this no more was heard. The battteries had flopped and anything might have happened.

On the third night further attempts to relieve were made by 10th Battalion, but they couldn't get in either. Tossignano had become a fortress. All next day TAC remained in their hillside eyrie, overlooking the town, hoping to pick up news from anyone making a break for it. It was thought that when this became hopeless the order would be given: 'Every man for himself!' But getting out was as hard as getting in and only a handful of men cut loose after dark. By then the situation had become so bad that they could throw no light on the final outcome.

17th December. The Orderly Room is working overtime on the lists of missing. It looks as if almost the whole of 'B' and 'C' Companies will have to be written off – the best part of three hundred men. Never has the Battalion suffered such colossal losses in a single 'do' (in this war anyway). Previous casualties have been dribs and drabs in comparison. All the chaps I knew in 'B' Company Signals are among those unaccounted for, including Tolley, Randall, Trellis and Brown.

Eighth Army's attack was renewed by battalions from both the New Zealand and 10th Indian Divisions, who cleared Faenza on the 17th and pushed on to the Senio, where an attempt to cross failed. Further north the Canadians fought their way forward to the river also, reaching Bagnacavallo, five miles west of Ravenna, on 21 December. Apart from some attacks to clear the area between Ravenna and Lake Comacchio, ten miles up the coast from the city, these operations brought Eighth Army's winter battles to an end.

Lieutenant T. C. Dennis was a troop commander in 326 (Queen's Own Glasgow Yeomanry) Battery of the 64th Anti-Tank Regiment Royal Artillery in 78th Division. He wrote:

Christmas Eve arrived and in such bitterly cold weather it was far too cold to take off a sock to hang up in hope; even Santa Claus refused to turn up in this hostile place! A strange and eerie silence fell during the late hours of Christmas Eve, no gunfire and no crackling of small arms, and then a voice, weak and wobbly at first, but growing stronger, came from the forward enemy elements – 'Silent Night, Holy Night' – and one of our number replied with 'God rest you merry gentlemen' – and in retrospect, what a funny thing to sing!

It was late on New Year's Eve that the fun began. Our good comrade Dodger Green climbed up to our positions on Monte Grande to bring us a bottle of Scotch to toast in the New Year, an act which was especially applauded by our Glaswegian comrades. At precisely midnight, as we shook hands all round with Good New Year wishes, peace and home top of the list, the whole of the front line, as far as the eye could see, was lit up by searchlights from the German lines. The beams of light crossed over to form X's, and in some, a vertical beam up the centre of the X's formed like a white Union Jack. Then 'flaming onions', red fire balls linked together, snaked their way up in the air amid spirals of tracer bullets, obviously fired from the rotating barrels of a machine-gun. This uncanny and unexpected display prompted the general opinion that 'Gerry' had had enough and was 'packing in'. I was much more suspicious and ordered a complete 'stand to' – I'd seen Gerry's tricks before and most of them had a nasty sting in the tail! Once more there was a sort of unplanned truce. The opposing artillery units had fallen silent, the 'Moaning Minnies' – Nebelwerfers – were no longer whining their way to drop down on our lines, and small arms fire had ceased.

This uneasy silence was brought to an abrupt close when a distant gunshot was heard behind us in the British gun positions. The shell passed over our heads with a slithering whistle and cramped down on the enemy lines. The result was quite dramatic! The scintillating display from the enemy lines fizzled out in seconds, like chalk wiped off a blackboard, and then an almighty 'stonk', an artillery duel, lasting a most uncomfortable fifteen minutes or so. It's surprising what a lot of 'muck' the artiillery can poop off in a very short time! We heard later that the gentleman responsible for sparking off this blitz was a gunner who had partaken of the 'Demon Vino' in much larger quantities than was good for him, had pulled the plug on one of the guns which were laid on target and ready at a second's notice to spit fire and destruction on the said target. I wouldn't have liked to have been him later! I wonder even to this day what inspired Gerry to give that display on New Year's Eve, but one thing is for sure, he certainly scotched the rumour that he was packing in.

Conditions for forward troops were ghastly! The whole of our front line positions had become a sea of mud. We were at times literally knee deep in clinging wet mud, our only comfort when it was time to snatch a couple of hours sleep – our blankets were saturated and defied any attempt at drying them. The sappers, bless their hearts, used their ingenuity and built 'corduroy roads' – tree trunks laid crosswise, then covered in quarry waste and enabled some traffic movement to bring up supplies. Most personal supplies, food, water, etc were brought up by mule train, composed of Italian and Indian muleteers, but in this shocking weather the mules were quite frequently brought to a standstill. On one occasion, I was so incensed by the failure of the mules to bring up our supplies, I set off, clad in my white camouflage snow suit to kick them into action. It was a hazardous trip, snipers were active in certain spots, but eventually I found them just sitting there on the far side of a narrow mountain stream, about two meters wide. I jumped the stream then gave them a real 'rollicking'. This produced the reply that the mules refused to cross the stream. I grabbed the nearest mule and bellowed out a war cry, tastefully trimmed with adjectives, assuring the mule that I'd kick him over if necessary! I had spotted a clay hump in mid stream and reckoned that we could use this as a stepping stone.

Nothing daunted, bellowing wildly, I forced the surprised mule into action and headed straight for the clay bank in mid stream. The two water barrels strapped to his either flank sloshed about happily at the unexpected movement as I gauged the right moment to leap for my clay bank. I'd got a firm grip on the head harness as I raced him towards the stream, then I gave him one more yell as we leapt. My mule put his four 'anchors' down and stopped dead! By use of his head, I was cantilevered neatly over the clay bank, landing on the far edge and in mid stream. The clay bank proved to be ice which had rested on mud, and had been turned upside down by the running water. I landed on my knees in icy muddy water which came up to my armpits! I emerged struggling to get my breath on the far bank, while my mule stood with lowered head and still in the same spot from whence I had made my leap. Not to be outdone, I followed the stream for a few minutes, clad in my muddy snow suit which was by now freezing on me, and found a spot which could easily be crossed. These muleteers must have one-track minds I thought as I hopped across to the opposite bank. It didn't take many words from me to get them on their feet, and grabbing the mule which had caused my soaking, I marched him decidedly along the bank to the spot I had discovered and crossed the stream with ease. The remainder followed me like a flock of sheep to the delight of the chaps up in that hostile mountain.

*

Churchill's support of Alexander's proposal for an operation across the Adriatic faded when Roosevelt's refusal meant that it could not be implemented in 1944. It had never had the support of Alan Brooke. It was no longer realistic, if it ever had been, to think of pre-empting the Russians in Vienna, and the prospect of communism spreading under the shadow of their advancing armies caused Churchill increasing concern. Their proximity was already making Tito less inclined to welcome an Allied presence in Yugoslavia, and the defeat of the communist faction in the civil war in Greece was seen as a matter of high priority. Churchill therefore accepted the view of the Combined Chiefs of Staff, who, on 2 December, sent Wilson a new directive. Light forces could be introduced into the Balkans to harass German withdrawal, but no more. His immediate aim should be to secure the general line Ravenna–Bologna–Spezia, after which he should 'contain' the German forces, resting divisions in rotation in a general reserve capable of exploiting any favourable opportunities that might arise.

By this time Wilson, promoted Field Marshal on 3 November, had been chosen to succeed Field Marshal Sir John Dill, who died on the 5th, as the representative in Washington of the British Chiefs of Staff with their American colleagues. Alexander, also now a field marshal, took over from Wilson as Supreme Allied Commander in the Mediterranean on 12

December, handing over command of 15th Army Group to Mark Clark, after Churchill, to the annoyance of the Chiefs of Staff, whom he had not consulted, had supported a suggestion of Alexander's that he should combine both posts. Truscott was brought from command of his corps in France to replace Clark in command of Fifth Army. Soon after he had done so, Alexander decided that his army should not wait until the Eighth had reached the Santerno before renewing its attack towards Bologna, but do so as soon as the latter crossed the Senio and be at two days' notice for that from 22 December. However, not only did Eighth Army not cross the Senio, but, as that date approached, it became clear that von Senger, reinforced by 16th Panzer Division, was preparing an attack on 4th US Corps's sector in the west, aimed at Livorno, on which Fifth Army relied for its logistic support. This sector was thinly held by 92nd US (Negro) Division, and Clark ordered Truscott to send 8th Indian Division, which was in reserve, to reinforce them. They arrived there on Christmas Day, a day ahead of von Senger's attack, which they helped to halt, counter-attacking and regaining the ground lost.

After this, Alexander decided to stop all offensive operations for the winter. His potential for future operations was further diminished after the Combined Chiefs of Staff met in Malta, on the way to Yalta, at the end of January 1945, when, in the aftermath of the German attack in the Ardennes, they told Alexander to transfer five divisions to North-West Europe and two more when two could be released from Greece. At the request of the Canadian Government, 1st Canadian Corps was included in this move. In the event only their two divisions left Italy, the other three being found from elsewhere in the Mediterranean and Middle East. A further restriction on activity was a severe shortage of artillery ammunition. Production schedules in Britain and the USA had not allowed for the continued high rates of expenditure in set-piece operations in both North-West Europe and Italy, and had assumed that the war in Europe would be almost over by the end of the year.

Air operations however continued, as Flying Officer J. F. Bartle describes. He was a pilot in 37 Squadron RAF, part of 205 Strategic Bomber Group, and was based at Tortorella near Foggia:

> My first operation was on 3rd January 1945, when I acted as Second Pilot on an operation to the Salcano Railway Bridge in Northern Italy. After that introduction we were then on our own as a crew.

There then followed two operations to Northern Italy, dropping supplies to the Italian Partisans way up in the Alps, an abortive operation to Pola, which was covered by 10/10ths cloud and then two operations in Northern Yugoslavia dropping supplies to Tito's partisans, or to the Chetnicks of Michaelovitch, as both groups were able to get us back.

On these supply runs we had to drop the supplies from 600 feet. This meant that we had to lower our undercarriage and put on full flap in order to reduce quickly to the right height and speed while the aircraft literally shuddered its way across the dropping zone; it was then a case of undercarriage up and full power on so as to get out of the valley and over the inevitable mountain which, by then, was fast looming up in front. If, however, it was a daylight drop in Yugoslavia with a village near the dropping zone and no unpleasant valley to extricate ourselves from, then all the women poured out in strength to wave their huge and highly coloured skirts at us as we were racing across the snow trying to gain altitude. It was always an incredible scene of brilliant colour.

When one of our aircraft was shot down by a JU. 88, the pilot was killed but the crew managed to bale out. When they were eventually returned to Foggia they told us that whenever the RAF made a supply drop the people were told that it was their glorious Russian Allies helping the free peoples of Yugoslavia. If, however, it had been a bombing raid, then they would have been told that it was the Fascist Imperialists trying to destroy the free people of Yugoslavia. All in all, it was a strictly 'no win' situation.

Other attacks included the Marshalling Yards at Verona on two occasions, then at Padua, Treviso, Vicenza and those at Trento, also on two occasions. In addition we attacked railway bridges in Northern Italy, oil refineries at Fiume, Dockyard installations at Pola and a coal wharf in the Arsa Channel. This last operation was the first time that we had an American Fighter Escort. We also bombed Marshalling Yards in Southern Austria, once at Graz and three times at Villach. After that we returned to Yugoslavia and bombed the Marshalling Yards at Pragersko in the North. We then turned our attention to helping both the 5th and 8th Armies by attacking enemy concentrations at Bastia and at Malalberge to help the 8th Army's advance, and again at Casalecchio to help the 8th Army.

On all these operations we were flying off Masten Matting and one always had to remember the mud which spewed up through the holes in the Matting, coating the sides of the aircraft and covering the bomb doors. In fact, after take-off the Liberators looked more like flying boats than aeroplanes. As a result of the mud we had to open our bomb doors every fifteen minutes all the way to the target as, otherwise, they would have been frozen solid long before we reached our destination. I completed twenty-six operations during this period and my last raid was on 19th April 1945.

There was no N.A.A.F.I. on the Station but this was more than made up for by the presence of the Salvation Army. Come mud, ice, snow, rain or shine, there they were every time we returned to base all ready to issue us with mugs of steaming hot cocoa. They really were the most marvellous people. Each night an Oscar was awarded to the crew that had achieved the most accurate bombing on the previous night. There was much competition amongst the crews and I remember that we won an Oscar twice, thanks to an excellent bomb aimer and a superb navigator.

Returning to base could provide problems at times due to the weather and we therefore had two different ways of coming in. If the weather were good we returned through the San Severo Pass. If, however, the weather were particularly nasty, then the safest way in was through the Gulf of Manfredonia. On one occasion my Flight Commander had the very unpleasant experience of having a bomb dropped straight through his aircraft from another aircraft flying above him. He managed to return to base but his wireless operator was wounded in the incident and subsequently received the D.F.M. Luckily the bomb had not fallen far enough to arm fully and therefore went right through his aircraft without exploding. We also had a very unpleasant experience with a bomb when we were bombing the submarine pens at Pola. The bomb aimer called out 'bombs gone' quickly followed by 'Sorry, Skipper, one has hung up.' A couple of minutes later my Beam Gunner said that the bomb was fully armed and stuck at an almost impossible angle. I therefore had to ask the Mid-upper Gunner, Beam Gunner and Wireless Operator to go out on the catwalk and get rid of it. They each put a foot on it and on the word 'Go' they all pushed as hard as possible and down it went into the Adriatic which was the best place for it.

10

Patience Rewarded

April to May 1945

Alexander, backed by Clark, McCreery and Truscott, was not prepared to remain as passive as the directive issued by the Combined Chiefs of Staff from Malta envisaged. They were all determined that they should play a significant part in final victory by defeating the German forces, Army Group C, in Italy, which Kesselring returned to command in the New Year, von Vietinghoff going off to Courland in East Prussia to command the German army there. When Allied pressure slackened, OKW demanded that Kesselring should give up troops to reinforce the western and eastern fronts. He lost 16th SS Panzer and three infantry divisions, but resisted any further reduction, helped by Allied air attacks on the passes between Italy and Austria which restricted movement through them. By the end of March he still had twenty-three divisions, 26th Panzer, 29th and 90th Panzer Grenadier, two parachute, two jaeger, three mountain and thirteen infantry, the established strength of the jaeger, mountain and infantry divisions being reduced by 1,700 men each. He also had two Italian divisions in Graziani's Army of Liguria.

To face these, Clark had seventeen divisions. Nine were in Fifth Army: two armoured (1st US and 6th South African), five US Infantry, one Brazilian Infantry and the recently arrived 10th US Mountain. McCreery had eight in Eighth Army: three British (6th Armoured, 56th and 78th Infantry), two Indian (8th and 10th Infantry), two Polish (3rd and 5th) and the New Zealand Division. He was also given 2nd Commando Brigade (the renamed Special Service Brigade) and 2nd Parachute Brigade. As well as several independent armoured brigades, supporting the infantry divisions, he had a number of independent infantry brigades, one Jewish and two Italian, and other Italian combat groups which helped to man quiet sectors of the front, on the other side of which Italian partisan resistance groups were becoming more active.

Clark's initial intention was to give the major part in a spring offensive to Truscott, believing that Eighth Army was not likely to make rapid progress over all the rivers between the Senio and the Po; but Alexander and McCreery saw to it that both armies should play significant parts.

Kesselring had no illusions that his army group would be able to hold its present positions once the Allies launched an offensive. He therefore started fortifying the Adige line as the principal one, running from the southern end of Lake Garda eastward along the River Adige to its mouth, covering the cities of Verona, Padua and Venice. South of the Po, the River Reno would be developed as an intermediate line, and Allied attempts to cross all other rivers would be resisted as firmly as usual. Partly in reaction to intelligence that Alexander was making preparations for an amphibious operation in the northern Adriatic, Kesselring moved the inter-army boundary eastwards, Lemelsen's Fourteenth Army becoming responsible for the defence of Bologna and westward from there, 14th Panzer and 51st Mountain Corps changing places, the former taking over 1st Parachute Corps's sector defending Bologna. Herr's Tenth Army faced McCreery's Eighth, 1st Parachute Corps on the right between Bologna and Faenza, with 1st and 4th Parachute, 278th and 305th Infantry and 26th Panzer Divisions, and 76th Panzer Corps between them and the coast with 42nd Jaeger and 98th, 162nd (Turcoman) and 362nd Infantry Divisions. 29th and 90th Panzer Grenadier Divisions were in army group reserve in the rear of Tenth Army's sector, ready to move in any direction, including to oppose any amphibious landing on the coast, which the German army did not realize was completely unsuitable for one, due to the shallowness of the sea and the lagoons inshore.

The plan which Alexander persuaded Clark to adopt for Operation GRAPESHOT was designed to encircle as much of the German Fourteenth and Tenth Armies as possible before they could withdraw north of the Po. Fifth Army's main effort would be made further west than before, from Route 64, so that their advance would emerge from the mountains between Bologna and Modena, west of the River Reno. From there it would be directed northwards to the Po at Ostiglia, swinging right as it did so to form the left arm of a pincer movement. A thrust in that direction would avoid having to cross the Reno which flowed first northwards from the western outskirts of Bologna for twenty miles before turning south-east to skirt the southern edge of Lake Comacchio before reaching the sea. Eighth Army was to form the right arm of the pincers with two attacks, both executed by 5th Corps. On the right 56th Division, helped by 2nd Commando and 2nd Parachute Brigades, would cross Lake Comacchio, seize the bridge over the Reno at Bastia, near the south-western corner of the lake, and advance to Argenta on the road (Route 16) from Ravenna to Ferrara, thus securing the 'Argenta Gap', the stretch of dry land between the lake and the inundations which the Germans had created by breaching the river banks of the Reno, the Idice and the Sillaro. The main attack would be launched from either side of the salient formed by a bend in the Senio, midway between Ravenna and Faenza. It would be directed first to cross the Santerno at Massa Lambarda: thereafter, if the Argenta Gap had been secured, its principal effort would be made in that direction and on north-westwards to Bondeno, west of Ferrara, to close the pincers south of the Po. If the Argenta Gap had not been secured, the main thrust would continue westwards to Budrio and beyond until contact was made with Fifth Army. Further to the left, the Polish Corps would advance between the 5th and Route 9 directly towards Bologna, while 10th Corps, returned from Greece, and 13th, transferred back from Fifth Army, looked after the mountain sector.

There was considerable discussion about when to start. The rivers flowing down from the Apennines tended to be in flood from melting snow earlier than the Po, drawing its water from the Alps, and morning mists, affecting air support, tended to prevail in early spring. The ground would not dry up until late May or June. By that time it might be too late for operations in Italy to have any decisive effect on the war. The deception plan was that the main effort would be made by Eighth Army, reinforced by 2nd US Corps, along and north of Route 9 towards Bologna, accompanied by an amphibious landing north of the Po. After weighing up all the factors, 10 April was agreed on as the starting date. Clark was keen that Eighth Army should start first and cause Kesselring to commit his reserve in that direction before Truscott launched his attack in the mountains. McCreery did not much like this, but accepted that he should start a few days earlier, provided that, when he did so, he was supported by all the air effort available: this was agreed.

While the higher commanders and their staffs were busy with all this planning, many of the soldiers in both armies were manning the front line in conditions reminiscent of the First World War. Whether in the mountains or in the plain, in the front line they were in trenches or foxholes, usually wet and cold and under enemy observation in daylight, so that any movement drew fire from small arms, mortars or artillery. If just behind the line, they were lucky if they could find a building in which to shelter. Morale in both armies had reached a low ebb at the end of 1944, with psychiatric casualties running at an all-time high and desertions at an alarming rate. In the British army, in November and December, the number of soldiers listed as deserters or absent without leave stood at 1,200, and at one time there were over 5,000 soldiers serving prison sentences. The break-up of units and their reinforcement by men from other regiments, which became inevitable, was not conducive to good morale. The Poles had their own special morale problem. The deal done at Yalta over the future of Poland had come as a great shock to them. Anders had at first demanded that they cease to fight for the Allies and be treated as prisoners of war, but then calmed down. He was partly mollified by the offer of additional brigades, in the form of 7th Armoured and 43rd Gurkha Brigades, while further Polish reinforcements made possible the formation of a third brigade in each of his divisions.

When soldiers were not in or near the front line, they might be training in new equipment which was becoming available, especially for the Royal Armoured Corps and Royal Engineers. Some units of both these arms were chosen to man the specialized armoured vehicles which had been developed by Major-General P. C. S. Hobart's 79th Armoured Division and used in and after the landings in Normandy: amphibious, mine-clearing and flame-throwing tanks, ones converted as armoured personnel carriers, and AVREs (Armoured Vehicles Royal Engineers) of various kinds. For the operations of 2nd Commando Brigade and 56th Division in and on the edge of Lake Comacchio, the Americans had provided LVTs (Landing Vehicles Tracked), usually known as Buffaloes, but, on this occasion for reasons of secrecy, codenamed Fantails. McCreery did his best to see that the infantry spent as much time as possible out of the line, partly by making use of dismounted Royal Armoured Corps units to hold it in some areas. The 7th Hussars were employed in this role at Christmastime, as Lance-Corporal C. R. P. Gregg of their B Squadron described in a letter written on Boxing Day:

Being about the only person who understands the lingo, I have to attend to the needs of our 'partisans' & give them their orders. I have a certain number of these attached to my section for patrols etc., they're a pretty rough crew, but we get on famously together. You'd be amused to see them giving me a snappy salute & quite ignoring the Sgt. Major, who sometimes comes with me! We've been lucky in getting a few days rest, so managed to have a Christmas of sorts. But nothing like the affair we would have had back in our little town. Still we had 16 gallons of white wine & two bottles of beer per man, there were only about 40 of us out of the line, the others had their feed before going in. On the 23rd we had our first fall of snow, whilst up there we sleep for a few hours during the day but are up during the night. It's darned cold standing or lying in mud & water, by morning I find I've lost all feeling in my feet; I can see us getting frost bite yet!

A month later his Troop Commander, Lieutenant J. H. Harding, wrote to his father to express his sympathy with him in Gregg's death from 'a piece of shrapnel from shell fire that hit him at the base of his neck'.

At the end of March Kesselring left Italy to replace von Rundstedt on the western front, von Vietinghoff returning from Courland to resume command of Army Group C. This change had some implications for secret contacts which had been going on between Alexander's headquarters and General Wolff, who was the German representative with Mussolini's puppet government in that part of Italy occupied by German forces, and was responsible for internal security in that area. Through intermediaries in Switzerland he had initiated enquiries about terms of surrender for Army Group C. Alexander and his advisers thought that as Germany's situation deteriorated Kesselring might be prepared to act independently, but von Vietinghoff was much less likely to do so, and Alexander did not allow himself to be diverted in any way from pushing forward with preparations for GRAPESHOT. At General Herr's suggestion, von Vietinghoff made a significant proposal to OKW. He suggested that, as soon as an Allied attack appeared imminent, he should withdraw to the next river line, forcing Clark to revise his plans, as Ludendorff had done when he withdrew to the Hindenburg line in 1917, and then repeat the process on the next line; but Hitler refused to agree. The only change von Vietinghoff made to Kesselring's dispositions was to move 29th Panzer Grenadier Division north of the Po between Ferrara and

Padua to guard against an amphibious landing in that area, leaving 90th Panzer Grenadier as the only mobile reserve south of the river.

Clark now began some preliminary moves. In Fifth Army 10th US Mountain Division, supported by 1st Brazilian Division, advancing up Route 64 in a brilliantly executed operation, brought the front line on that Route level with that on Route 65, thus securing the start line for GRAPESHOT. In Eighth Army, on 1 April, 2nd Commando Brigade attacked and captured 'the Spit', the neck of land separating Lake Comacchio from the sea, throwing the German 162nd Division into confusion and capturing 900 of them. Three days later the Royal Marine Special Boat Section seized several islands in the southern part of the lake. At the other extreme of Clark's front, on 5 April, the 92nd US (Negro) Division carried out a diversionary attack towards Spezia, which forced Lemelsen to commit a regimental group from 90th Panzer Grenadier Division to save the situation there. On the 6th, 56th Division attacked and captured 'the Wedge', a promontory on the southern shore of Lake Comacchio which would serve as a launching site for the 'Fantails' in which they would be transported across the lake to capture the Bastia bridge. They took 700 prisoners from the German 42nd Division.

On 9 April, in clear, fine weather, strategic bombers dropped 175,000 fragmentation 20lb bombs on the German artillery and reserve areas on Eighth Army's front, followed by two hundred medium bombers which attacked individual gun batteries. Five hundred fighter-bombers then attacked the forward German defences, followed by five artillery bombardments, each lasting forty-two minutes, with ten-minute intervals between them, during which fighter-bombers again attacked German positions in the flood banks on the far side of the Senio. At the end of the fifth, the fighter-bombers swooped again without firing, hoping to keep the German heads down while the infantry advanced and crossed the river, supported by specialized tanks and armoured vehicles of all kinds, and night bombers attacked targets between the river and the Santerno and on that river. The artillery supporting the 5th and Polish Corps numbered 1,020 guns.

The main attack was launched by 8th Indian Division on the northern and the New Zealand Division on the southern side of the Senio salient, while 78th Division in the centre made a feint attack. Both divisions crossed successfully and by the evening of the 10th were nearing the

Santerno, having taken 1,300 prisoners. The Poles met stiffer resistance from the German parachute divisions, but they reached their planned objectives by that time, having suffered heavier casualties. 56th Division's attack across Lake Comacchio had been successful, two brigades having been transported across by 12 April, but they were meeting stiff resistance on their way to Bastia bridge. By that time the Poles and the New Zealanders had some troops across the Santerno, and on that day the latter took Massa Lambarda. McCreery now ordered 78th Division to pass through 8th Indian and attack northwards to Bastia, while 56th Division sent its third brigade across the lake and floods towards Argenta. He had hoped to use 2nd Parachute Brigade to support this, but German anti-aircraft fire in the area made this too hazardous to attempt, and 2nd Commando Brigade was told to help 56th Division in this operation in any way they could. 13th Corps (now commanded by Lieutenant-General Sir John Harding) was ordered to move round behind the 10th and Polish Corps and bring 10th Indian Division into the line to the left of the New Zealanders, who would come under Harding's command.

Fifth Army's attack was due to start on the 12th, but bad weather, limiting air support, caused a two-day postponement, with the result that von Vietinghoff was able to concentrate against McCreery, sending 29th Panzer Grenadier Division to oppose 56th and 78th Divisions in the Argenta Gap, so that, although the latter took the Bastia bridge before it could be demolished, they did not manage to reach the village beyond it, and 56th Division's third brigade met German opposition when it tried to land at the same place as the other brigades had on the western shore of the lake. Not until 17 April did the German 42nd and 362nd Divisions begin to fall back from the northern exit of the Gap, as 6th British Armoured Division came up on the left of the 78th, moving through Argenta itself on that day. 78th Division was supported by the tanks of 21st Army Tank Brigade, including 48th Royal Tank Regiment, in which Trooper Edmund Cook was still serving, as he describes:

It must have been about 0730 hrs [on 18 April] when we reached our start-line after skirting around the east of Argenta. I was on the Squadron Leader's tank (Major 'Bill' Joss) and we came to a halt at a really awful spot. Just at the side of the road was a huge crater and in it the remains of something I took to be a Bren carrier, although completely destroyed. Around it were scattered the remains of the occupants, lying in grotesque poses, burnt black with hideous charred stumps sticking out where before had been arms and hands and feet. It was a scene of Armageddon, a close-up of the frightfulness and utter indignity that war could wreak on men who were caught up in its horrors. We stayed there until I could no longer bear the sight of those poor remains that, such a short while before, had been young men: I told the driver to pull forward a few yards – at least far enough to have that behind me.

At 0800 hrs B Squadron's attack started off in support of the infantry, who had left our tanks because of the spandau fire sweeping across from the German positions. As so often happened, the occupants of a tank, with their very restricted view, could see little if anything either of the rest of the Squadron or of the infantry: we relied on features to describe our relative positions and on wireless communication to monitor each other's progress, all Troop Leaders reporting back to the Squadron Commander and receiving orders from him over the air. By 0830 hrs we had reached a farm complex known as Casale Nugaroni: from there two companies of infantry plus two troops of tanks went forward, the remainder of the infantry and tanks being kept back in support until the strength and positions of the enemy became known. Unfortunately, the infantry, with our tanks, led off in the wrong direction and soon found themselves in a position known in the trade as a 'killing ground' or 'killing zone', that is to say an area which provides no cover itself for the attacking force but which is completely in open view to the defenders who, with anti-tank guns, machine guns and mortars, are able to pick off anything that moves with frontal and enfilading fire. The result of this was that the infantry were quickly halted and, as the tanks moved in to support them, four of the five engaged were knocked out very quickly by AP shells. The other two infantry companies then took up the advance along a more north-westerly course – the correct one – accompanied by two more troops of tanks. However, the Germans were by then ready to deal with the second wave and four more tanks were lost to AP fire. It was in one of these four that my friend Eddie Moore was killed, together with others in the crew when his tank sustained a direct hit, thus fulfilling his prophecy to me of earlier in the day.

I was actually listening-in to a report from one commander when I heard the ominous clang of an AP shell striking his turret, and then silence. There was no further response to my calls to him. When Major Joss asked what was reported, I had to tell him that the other tank had just received a direct hit. Having by then lost eight tanks out of those which went forward, we were still in communication with the only one which had managed to get into a fairly safe position and was doing some useful work with its guns to back up the infantry. Our Squadron Commander was obviously extremely upset at the losses we were suffering and, obeying the order to press home the attack, he turned to me and in a really despondent voice said 'Well Ned, now it's our turn'. He hadn't addressed me by my nickname since he was my Troop Leader, a 2nd Lieutenant in C Squadron, years before. I knew what he meant – he couldn't let the rest of the Squadron go and remain behind himself.

Including our own, we had only four fighting tanks left in the Squadron. So far, we had remained near Casale Nugaroni with the 2i/c's tank behind us. But now we went ahead along a track for a short distance, having no idea where the enemy SP gun or guns were. It seemed to us that they must be somewhere to our left on the Boccaleone road (this was a village on A Squadron's line of advance, entered by them early in the day but not cleared of the enemy until the afternoon). We were coming up to two of our tanks, both knocked-out – one of which was my friend's – when we were fired on but not hit. Just as we passed them, an AP shell penetrated the left-hand rear of our tank, smashing the driving sprocket and completely immobilising us. Although the noise of the hit was unmistakable, Major Joss seemed not to realise what had happened and kept urging the driver to get going, although the latter repeatedly told him that we couldn't move. For some moments a state of confusion reigned. Why the German gunner did not put another shot into us I don't know; perhaps he thought that, seeing us come to a sudden halt, he'd scored a bull's-eye in the turret. We still could not see his position and therefore could not lay our gun on him, although we must have presented him with a sitting target. There was no point in tempting fate too long in staying in the tank for we would certainly have been on the receiving end of the next shot without being able to do anything constructive (or should I say destructive?) ourselves, so eventually the Squadron Commander decided we had no option but to bale out. As we came out of the tank one by one, a spandau opened up from somewhere but we all managed to drop to the ground safely and made our way to a casa just a few yards away to the right.

There they joined some other tank crews who had suffered the same fate, and some infantrymen who were taking shelter from enemy fire of all kinds. Major Joss decided that he must try and get back to regimental headquarters to tell them what had happened. After he had left, Cook and others in the house decided that if they stayed where they were they were unlikely to survive. Cook returned to the tank, removed his and Major Joss's belongings, which, in the latter's case, included a heavy bag full of drink, and with great difficulty made his way to a farmhouse further back, where he found Major Joss, who was annoyed with him for leaving the area of the tank. Cook commented:

> I was not all that surprised as I could see that he was obviously quite shattered by the virtual destruction of his Squadron. The attack had lasted only an hour and a half: in that short time, we had lost eleven tanks with eight men killed and seven wounded. Only one of the Squadron's tanks remained in action, as three of the last four to go forward (which included my own) were also hit by AP fire and knocked out.

When it got dark, Major Joss sent him back to guard the tank during the night, which he did until 3 a.m., by which time the enemy had withdrawn. Cook and his fellow crewmen were remounted in a replacement tank next day and on 21 April were taking part in the attack on Ferrara.

*

Further south, 13th Corps and the Poles, with heavy air and artillery support, fought their way doggedly forward against the German 1st and 4th Parachute Divisions, supported by 26th Panzer. By 17 April they were nearing the Idice, the last river line before Bologna.

On that day Fifth Army made significant gains in the mountains, its 10th US Mountain Division breaking through the German 94th Division, forcing Lemelsen to commit 90th Panzer Grenadier to hold 4th US Corps's attack and, in doing so, to lose most of its tanks in a clash with 1st US Armoured Division on the left of 10th Mountain, while Truscott committed his reserve division, the 85th, to increase the pressure. On

20 April 10th Mountain emerged from the mountains to cut Route 9 halfway between Modena and Bologna, while 88th US Infantry and 6th South African Armoured Divisions in 2nd US Corps reached the south-western outskirts of the latter. Sapper Robert J. Meredith was serving in the South African 5th Field Squadron and described his experience in a letter to his sister in Durban, dated 23 April:

> As you have probably read in the papers, things are going full swing up this way & it's a case of no rest for the wicked. Briefly this is how it goes. During the day its a succession of varying sounding bangs from the lowly rifle to the heavy calibre artillery. Come nightfall the same effects become intensified & the whole scene of the fighting area resembles some wild horrid fantasy brewed from the depths of hell. Brilliant Verey lights & parachute flares, the streaking red of tracer bullets, the vivid flash of mortar fire & the red searing glare of falling shells all combine to make a scene so macabre that not even the most ardent surrealist would imagine it in his wildest flights of fancy. While travelling yawning shell-holes await the unwary, the horrible stink of rotten flesh assails ones nostrils every now & again, dead pack mules & occasionally the corpses of Huns are evident on the road sides, gesticulating smiling Italians hurry southwards to claim what little is left of their former homes, the blinding white dust, clogging and stifling is a constant companion & thank God to relieve it all there is the beautiful green of the countryside which even war as yet has been unable to mar.

Von Vietinghoff now realized that he had no alternative but to withdraw north of the Po, and to do so as quickly as he could, if some of his forces, particularly 51st Mountain Corps, were not to be cut off. He sent a pathetically apologetic signal to Hitler, explaining his predicament, which ended:

> In a mobile strategy, however, I still see a possibility of preventing this threat from being carried out and of continuing our resistance with a chance of success. Difficult as it is for me, I consider it my duty, My Führer, to send you this report at this hour and to await your orders.

But his Führer had other things on his mind. Anglo-American forces were across the Rhine, had surrounded the Ruhr and were about to attack Bremen, while the Russians were attacking across the Oder and would soon be into the outer suburbs of Berlin. A few days later American and Russian troops were to meet on the Elbe.

Von Vietinghoff's hopes of an orderly withdrawal were threatened by 6th British Armoured Division's thrust north-west from Argenta towards Boldeno, which they reached on 22 April, cutting across the withdrawal route of 1st Parachute Corps, many of the men of both the parachute divisions surrendering to them, Heidrich himself escaping by swimming across the Po. The 17th/21st Lancers, back in their tanks, took a leading part in this thrust, as Lieutenant Stiebel relates:

> When we reached the meadow I saw a double-storeyed farmhouse ahead and movement in an upper window. The best way to clear out any enemy was to fire an H.E. shell on 'delay' – a turn on the screw on the fuse head delayed the explosion of the shell by 0.05 seconds; enough to allow the shell to penetrate the walls before exploding inside the house. My gunner fired at the floor level of the upper storey and so managed to spread the effect to both floors. He then fired Browning at the surviving Germans who speedily evacuated by the back door.
>
> From the church tower at Segni, the C.O. and Lt Col Douglas Darling of the 7 R.B.s* did a recce. In the meantime the Germans started shelling in earnest and any movement was greeted with fire – including a very heavy gun thought to be a 210mm. Beyond the meadow was a gap between two canals – code named 'Fish Gap' – and this was impassable without Engineer help. A Sqn on the right lost two tanks to German Panther tanks and the Hurribomber† – Rover David – was called in. This resulted in a direct hit one Panther and the other badly crippled.
>
> The Engineers brought up an Ark – a Churchill with turret removed and which, when driven into a ditch, made a bridge over which tanks could drive. B Sqn crossed and rushed as far as the next road crossing (Route 65) at Gallo, but lost several tanks in the process.
>
> Chris Hallett's troop reached the bridge and he defused the explosives set to blow it.

---

* 7th Battalion The Rifle Brigade.
† Hurricane fighter-bomber.

C Sqn were now ordered to pass through the gap. My troop was leading along the west side and as we reached the junction with Route 65, I was told to go left to see if the bridge over the Reno was intact. This meant getting right on top of the very high levee and from here I could see very many Germans rushing about. The main bridge had obviously been destroyed by our aircraft some time before, and I had to go a short way down a diversion to see that the replacement bridge had indeed been blown – probably very recently. We returned to the main road and awaited further orders and during this time, my troop sergeant's driver switched off his engine. I saw a Panther travelling fast but it was far away on a road beyond Gallo and there were Germans running towards the north and others taking cover in the roadside ditches.

Then I got the order to move on to Poggio Renatico – about 5–6 miles away – at full speed. My Sergeant's tank would not start right away so I took the lead and drove off (My troop corporal's tank was having the gun problem). At the turn-off to Poggio, the Germans had set up a road-block of a few carts, rails and planks. These we burst through and away we went at between 25 and 30 m.p.h. I shouted 'Tally-Ho' over the wireless which was not appreciated by James Maxwell!! Sergeant Cormack's 2nd troop was right behind me. There were Germans breaking cover all over the place and we chased them with our machine guns. The bow gunner was given 'gun control' which meant that he fired at anything he could see. On the road to my right – some 1000 yards away – I saw a German convoy of about 40 vehicles including transporters. Trying to shoot at them with the very long barrelled gun, traversed to the right, we only got one shot off before the gun started to hit telegraph poles and this swung the turret to face the rear. Concentrating our efforts to the front, we shot at every farmhouse and haystack – many burst into flame as there was fuel stored in them. A German horse-drawn convoy was seen heading towards us and was shot off the road by the bow gunner. All the tanks behind also joined in the fray and I had to ask them to stop firing ahead because, where the road went slightly to the left, I was getting machine gun fire from the rear around my ears. There was a freshly dug hole in the middle of the road and I told my driver to slow down in case it was a mine. From a house nearby a German stepped out and fired a Panzerfaust (Bazooka) at us but he hit the bank in front and showered my face and hand with grit. He only had the chance before Cormack, riding behind me, riddled him with his Browning. I saw a train over to the right and it consisted of an engine and two or three cattle trucks. In an open doorway was a man sitting with his legs hanging out and the train was moving slowly towards Poggio. I was certain that everyone behind me could have seen this but it later appeared that Maxwell had not. I could not traverse my gun to the right to engage this target because of the telegraph poles, nor could I have stopped or slowed down as the tanks behind would have all bunched up and, also, because I was very much involved with my immediate front, I left it to others to deal with.

As we approached the town of Poggio, dozens of Germans and civilians appeared with white flags but there was nothing I could do about them. The whole scene was of chaos with people running in all directions. To encourage the confusion my driver sounded the hooter continuously, which was very loud and alarming – but unfortunately not as spectacular as the sirens with which our previous tanks were equipped. Into the first house in the town, we fired a shell and, turning half-right into the main street, we fired two more rounds of H.E. straight into a mob of milling Germans, horses and vehicles. James Maxwell told me to turn left to skirt the town and that anti-tank guns were firing at the main column of our tanks from that direction. I was driving along very carefully with a high wall on my right. Beyond the end of the wall, suddenly a tracer shell passed by about 10 yards ahead of me. I reversed to the cover of the wall and could clearly see the tracer shells going off aimed at our tanks – the tracers were travelling just above the level of the road surface. Beyond the end of the wall there was an open gap before a wooden shed. I moved forward to try to see where the enemy guns were and hid my tank behind the shed. The guns were somewhere to the south of the town but there was so much dust about that I could not give an accurate position. Two other tanks joined me and we tried firing round the sides of the shed. The gunners must have seen our move because they then set about trying to demolish the shed that gave us cover, so we withdrew behind the wall. They then fired several airburst shells over us. I could see the smoke from the guns but could only guess that their position was on the Reno bank. Dick Tamplin got hold of a German who told him that there were four 88mmm Anti-aircraft guns on the Reno levee which were positioned to protect the bridge from air attack. Our F Battery of 12th R.H.A. under Major Cecil Middleton, who was riding on a tank with our R.H.Q., now engaged the 88's with every gun they could muster and must have secured a hit because there was a large explosion from that area.

Trooper Buckle was in a tank of C Squadron's Headquarters and gave his own account:

The rays of the evening sun were weakening as our tanks roared through the village [Poggio] and fanned out to meet any counter attack by the Germans. The lead tank of 3rd Troop was reported knocked out and some minutes later the crew came ambling past our tank, grimy, dirty and carrying their baling out bags. Derek Kerrison had been the driver and he looked no worse for the ordeal. 'Kerry' as most people called him was a cheerful soul, always laughing and joking. He was a serious thinker though and a good, fit sportsman. Above all, he was an excellent driver – among the best in the squadron.

Suspicious movements were reported from the upstairs room of a house quite close to us. Captain Wilson ordered Jack Pole to train his gun on this and put a shell through the window. With great relish, Jack did just this and as the tank rocked slightly from the impact of firing, there, just ahead of us, we saw the front of the room torn out. Curtains flapped in the gentle breeze and through the jagged masonry and splintered woodwork we saw the bed, the wardrobe and other fittings. It seemed unreal somehow – as though we had suddenly intruded into some family's private domain. In a way we had of course and when nothing seemed to move in there or indicate any signs of anyone having been there, we felt less elated. Indeed, later, even Jack Pole said he felt guilty of vandalism. But that is war.

Now there was not time to think, for the Germans, having recovered somewhat, began to shell and mortar the place. A bunch of German prisoners who were making their way to a hastily prepared P.O.W. compound, hands above their heads, suddenly disappeared in a wave of smoke and dust as their own shells crashed down among them. When the air cleared, few got up: those who did, moved more swiftly still, their faces a mask of petrified fear. This was war also.

There was no doubt about it, this sudden swoop by a British

crack cavalry regiment had taken the enemy completely by surprise. Transport containing rations and supplies were abandoned in one main street and I remember how surprised we all were to see this supply train. It consisted of carts drawn by horses. Perhaps the Germans were getting short of petrol as had been reported, otherwise why this mode of transport? This wasn't difficult terrain either. What impressed me most of all however was the stoicism of the horses. There was no panic, no bolting as machine guns rattled, pouring a steady stream of bullets up that very street. I cannot recall one horse moving – nor one shot, amazingly enough.

The forward patrols of 6th British met those of 6th South African Armoured Division from 2nd US Corps at the aptly named small town of Finale on the 23rd.

13th Corps now took 6th British Armoured under command and moved north to the Po, while 5th Corps moved 8th Indian to the west and north of Ferrara and then to the Po north of the town, preventing 76th Panzer Corps, with 26th Panzer and 29th Panzer Grenadier Divisions, withdrawing across the river there.

Sapper Eke's 754th Field Company Royal Engineers was supporting the New Zealand Division in 13th Corps in this move. He had served in the campaign all the way from the beaches of Sicily, and wrote:

The minor road gradually became choked with the litter of German equipment and the advancing transport of the New Zealand Division. It led to a small bridge over the Reno canal that was still being defended from concrete bunkers on the far side. The last of the brave defenders were the remnants of the German Paratroopers, and they had temporarily halted the advance of the 'Kiwis'. Two Churchill tanks moved into position just below the top of the canal bank, and sent great tongues of fire from their massive flame-throwers looping over the canal and smothering the bunkers in flames and black smoke. The liquid fire ran down the walls and into the firing slits. There was no chance of the defenders surviving the inferno, and we lay on the canal bank and watched their terrible death in silence.

The troops not involved waited beside their trucks and played cards until the order came to move forward once more. The enemy had not had time to mine the road and canal bank to delay the advance. Stick grenades were left to explode at the slightest touch, and every piece of German equipment left behind had to be treated as a potential booby-trap. We drove stakes into the verges and ran white tapes either side of the road as far as the canal.

Slowly and cautiously we picked our way along the road like beachcombers, clearing it of the lethal debris. Abandoned vehicles were pushed into the field by the bulldozer, and the mines carefully examined for booby-traps before being defused. The safest way to deal with the grenades and avoid casualties was with rifle shots. Each first time hit bringing a cheer for the marksman or derisory jokes if he missed. One grenade was wedged between the roots of a tree and impossible to hit. It was too near the road to be left, and we decided on the bulldozer. The driver would be safe in his armoured cab, but he was busy further up the road. Our problem was solved by the intervention of the sergeant from I platoon. His platoon was waiting to pass through our lines, and being impatient to move on and noticing that a few sappers working on their own appeared to be having difficulties, could not resist taking over. He was a good experienced sergeant but known to take risks in front of his men. We were quite happy for him to volunteer, and quietly walked back out of range.

His idea was to tie a long string to the handle of the grenade and give it a quick pull. I had told him I thought it was too risky as only a slight movement would set it off, and we watched dubiously at what we considered was a piece of unnecessary bravado. He gently slipped a clove hitch over the wooden handle. As he slowly tightened the knot the grenade exploded, hurtling him backwards into the roadway. We ran to him as his agitated body convulsed with shock, and his boots scraped back and forth on the roadway. His right hand and wrist was gone, the red stump of his forearm gushing blood onto the road. As he recovered his senses he strained to see his arm that had been quickly swathed in two or three field dressings. He could feel no pain as we carried him back to an ambulance, his body twitching and trembling in our arms. His voice was a hoarse whisper asking how badly he was hurt, and we told him he had been wounded but not seriously.

For him the war was now finished, and he had been maimed quite unnecessarily demonstrating his experience and fearlessness to his fellow platoon. It puzzled us why he had taken such a stupid risk after nearly two years of dealing with mines and booby-traps. Possibly his expertise had made him contemptuous of a mere hand grenade, and his one second of carelessness had cost him an arm. We walked back slowly to continue our deadly search, our insides trembling with shock. We knew now that over-confidence was now the greatest threat to our lives, and we were grimly determined that at this stage of the war we were not going to be killed by our own mistakes.

A special Po task force, consisting of bridging equipment and the Royal Engineers to erect them, had been formed under 10th Corps, but its commander, Lieutenant-General J. L. I. Hawkesworth, fell seriously ill and McCreery divided the force between 5th and 13th Corps and told them to build as many bridges as they could to cross the Po as soon as possible.

An Italian force had also been involved. Lieutenant-Colonel Brian Webb-Carter headed 51st British Liaison Unit, attached to the 'Cremona' Gruppo, one of the three division-sized formations which the Italian Army contributed to the Allied side. In a letter written after the war to the Royal Engineer officer of the Unit, Major Jack Cooke, he wrote:

> Cremona did extremely well in the final battle and for some days were the leading troops of 8th Army. Signor Generale was supposed to only do a holding role astride the Alfonsine road but petitioned corps to be allowed to attack. This was granted & they were given one Bailey Bridge. A four bn. force under General Zanussi – Force ZA (!) attacked across the Senio with great spirit – took Alfonsine and streamed ahead led by Col. Ferrara in his jeep. The crazy gang then took 18 hours to put up the Bailey! Not so good. The entire Gruppo then streamed across and went on and on crossing canal after canal and finally the Po. Here all the Genio *shone*. With NO equipment at all they produced bridge after bridge made out of old boats, packing cases, three ply and string in record time. Just the sort of job they understood – no ruddy made up bridge certain bits to fit into other bits but good old straightforward muddling along somehow. They were excellent. Ferme (C.O. of the Genio) a trifle inclined to abandon his bn, and swan off to capture prisoners but otherwise good.

Both corps of Eighth Army began to cross the Po on 24 April against no opposition, and by the 27th they were over the Adige also, advancing rapidly thereafter, reaching Venice on 29 April and Trieste on 2 May, which Tito's forces had already reached and to which they were laying claim.

Meanwhile Fifth Army had made even more rapid progress. By 25 April Truscott had five divisions over the Po, 10th US Mountain entering Verona on the 26th, after which 2nd US Corps turned eastwards, crossing the Adige to the west of and at the same time as Eighth Army. 2nd US Corps crossed Lake Garda with 'Fantails' and DD tanks to cut the road on the far side to the Brenner Pass and pushed on westward to cut all the escape routes for 51st Mountain Corps and 90th Panzer Grenadier Division, as Graziani surrendered his Army of Liguria. By then von Vietinghoff had authorized one of his staff officers, Colonel von Schweinitz, to accompany General Wolff to Alexander's headquarters at Caserta, where they arrived on 28 April, the day that Mussolini was captured near Lake Como by partisans of the Italian resistance and shot, with his mistress, as they tried to escape to Switzerland. After some discussion, terms of surrender for all German forces in Italy were agreed, to be effective from 6 p.m. on 2 May. General von Senger und Etterlin arrived at Clark's headquarters on the 4th as the German liaison officer to ensure that the terms were observed. The war in Italy was over to the great relief of all, on both sides, who had taken part in it.

11

Prisoners and Partisans

The troops on both sides were not the only ones to suffer. A great many Italians suffered as much, and many perhaps more: those who lived where the battles raged and the bombs dropped, those whose husbands, brothers and sons lost their lives fighting, whether in the ranks of the Italian forces or against the Germans and the forces of the Fascist state, both before and after the latter was reduced, after September 1943, to that part of Italy occupied by German forces. It is not easy to assess fairly the contribution made by the Italian resistance movement and its partisan groups. It was never more than marginal as far as its effect on operations was concerned; but its very existence, in both towns and the countryside, was a constant source of annoyance to the Germans and the Fascist authorities, particularly in mountainous areas, and made both nervous about their safety. The partisan groups drew recruits from sources other than Italian; from escaped Allied prisoners of war and those, of many nationalities, forced to work for the Todt organization on German defences and other construction projects; and crews of ships stranded in Italian ports. Italian participants came from all walks of life: professionals, political activists, deserters from the forces and those trying to avoid call-up by the Fascist state, and all those who resented domination and interference in their lives by Fascist bureaucrats, farmers and peasants being prominent among the last. Possibly the greatest weakness of the resistance movement was its division by political differences: all were anti-Fascist, but different groups were jockeying for political power at the end of the war, the communists being the most numerous.

One of the activities of the partisan groups, especially those which included or were led by escaped prisoners of war, was helping the compatriots of the latter, many of whom, in the case of the British, had been captured in North Africa and had escaped from their camps at the time of the Italian surrender.

The most distinguished of these was Lieutenant-General Sir Richard O'Connor, who had commanded the Western Desert Force that had totally defeated the Italian Tenth Army in Libya in February 1941. He, his successor, Lieutenant-General Sir Philip Neame, and Brigadier John Combe had all been captured early in April when Rommel, soon after his arrival, drove Neame's force back to Tobruk in confusion. With other senior officers, including Major-General Carton de Wiart and Air Vice-Marshal Boyd, both of whom had come down flying between Gibraltar and Egypt, they were incarcerated in a castle, built by an Englishman in the nineteenth century, not far from Florence. Six of them, including O'Connor, Carton de Wiart, Boyd and Combe, escaped by a tunnel they had dug through the walls in March 1943. Two New Zealand brigadiers reached Spain, but the others were all recaptured after a week trying to make their way to Switzerland. When Italy surrendered in September, the Italian General Chiappe, in command at Florence, helped them to get away to a contact he gave them at Arezzo. There they passed into the hands of monks, who put them in touch with anti-Fascist families who sheltered and helped them. After two abortive rendezvous with submarines, O'Connor, Neame, Boyd and two others, in December, found a trawler skipper at Cattolica, twelve miles east of Rimini, who was prepared to try and take them to behind the Allied lines in return for the equivalent of £800. A considerate Italian agreed to provide the money in return for an IOU. After they had spent the night in the hold of the trawler in harbour, the skipper sailed, evading inspection, and delivered the party to Termoli on 21 December. Having seen Winston Churchill, in bed with pneumonia near Tunis, they reached Prestwick from Marrakesh in Morocco on Christmas Day. Sadly many of those who had helped them were later badly treated by the Germans or the Fascists, two brothers of the Spazzoli family being brutally killed.

Also captured in North Africa was Lieutenant-Colonel Henry Lowry-Corry. He was an ex-regular gunner, a veteran of the First World War in which he had gained a Military Cross and been wounded, leaving him slightly lame. Having retired as a major in 1935, he joined the Territorial Army and was commanding 67th Medium Regiment, Royal Artillery, in Tobruk when it was surrounded by Rommel's forces in June 1942. At the time of the Italian surrender in September 1943, he was in an officers' prisoner of war camp at Veano, sixteen miles south of Piacenza, and he and others escaped on 10 September when their Italian guards left before Germans arrived to replace them. With three companions he gradually made his way southwards through the mountains, continually fed, sheltered and helped, at considerable risk to themselves, by Italian peasant farmers, until, at the end of November, they came across a partisan band led by a British major, Gordon Lett, who had escaped from the same camp. The band was based in the village of Rossano in the mountains some twenty miles north of La Spezia. Under his general supervision, Lowry-Corry spent the winter partly in a mill and partly in charcoal-burners' huts in the woods, food being supplied by friendly Italians. When the spring of 1944 came, he spent his time moving about with Lett's partisans, becoming involved in their quarrels with and suspicions of other groups, generally of political origin. In mid-May a party from a detachment in Corsica of 'A' Force, the Allied organization supporting the partisans with occasional airdrops of arms and supplies, contacted Lett with news that a motorboat from Corsica would come to the coast at Vanezza, ten miles north-west of La Spezia, on 19 May and the two following nights, to take off as many British prisoners of war as Lett could get there. On the 17th, Lett, Lowry-Corry, five other officers, fifteen soldiers, three Poles, four Italian commandos, the 'A' Force mission of three and an Italian partisan guide set off from Rossano. After an arduous journey, they reached the rendezvous on the coast, but no boat turned up and they had to struggle back exhausted to Rossano. After a pleasant period spent with an exceptionally welcoming Italian family called Cura, who owned restaurants in London, Lowry-Corry set off on another equally arduous trip to meet an 'A' Force boat on the coast on 14 July, this time in radio contact with Corsica; but the boat was intercepted and, having received a message from Corsica that no further boat trips would be arranged, they had to return to Rossano, where they received an airdrop, but also an unwelcome visit by German troops, who dispersed the partisan group, now some eighty strong. At the end of October Lowry-Corry set off, as several other parties of prisoners of war had done, to try and make his way through the opposing front lines to freedom, rejecting the official advice that those who were not young and fully fit should stay where they were until liberated by the Allied advance. With Major Fairleigh of the Indian Army, Captains de Clermont and Hedley of the 8th Hussars, and Lieutenant Edward Raeburn, Royal Artillery, he left Rossano on 28

October. They spent a week making their way over the mountains, ridges and valleys between them, covering a distance, as the crow flies, of fifty-one miles in thirty-nine hours of actual marching, climbing and clambering, testing the stamina of the fifty-seven-year-old colonel nearly to the limit, until, on 3 November, they finally crossed the lines. Lowry-Corry, who recorded on a calendar all his moves from the time he left Veano, wrote an account when he got home and this is his description of that day:

November 3rd [1944]. Isola Santa – Ruosina. 7 hours 10 Kilometres.

Up soon after three and ready by four. We had made an error and eaten all the food we had brought. But I had a small tin which I thought held four sardines but was in fact potted meat. There were one or two similar tins and a little bread which we shared but it was not possible to make tea although we had some. Baionetta [the guide] did not arrive at four as promised and after half an hour or so Edward wanted to send down to see what had happened. Restive though we all were, that was absurd, patience was necessary.

Just before quarter to five Baionetta turned up and we moved at once. He wanted to move as fast as possible to pass the village, road and river well before daylight. To avoid the village we went by small tracks and not a main path. So down we plunged with not too bad a light as there was a moon only just past full behind the heavy clouds which poured on us a pitiless rain. We passed the village and got down to the river, crossing a narrow plank from one rock to another and then another one. The sort of crossing I hate by daylight and I welcomed a helping hand.

Then we started to climb and soon came on Boya's party waiting for us. This of course cut in on our column but de Clermont firmly put them behind us and except that Bruno who had joined our party went in front with Baionetta we kept our usual order. Still on up and another large party was waiting for us, including the two men we had passed on to Lett at Rossano. This brought the total up to the monstrous figure of forty seven. However much we disapproved it was no good protesting and de Clermont again forced them into place behind us. To my great surprise there was no further attempt to cut into our party, probably due to their thinking we were in the most dangerous position in the lead.

It now became a story of mere plod, plod, plodding. Short halts occasionally when I was out of breath, but no long ones, not even ones of five or ten minutes. It rained and rained and it was too cold and windy to stand still. When daylight came we got glimpses through the clouds of other hills but my eyes were too glued to the path to pay attention. Up through the chestnuts to the beech, above the beech to tussocky grass and stones. When I thought we ought to be getting near the top de Clermont told me Baionetta had just said we were half way up. My heart sank.

We passed from rain into sleet with slushy snow on the ground where it could find a place to lie and from sleet to snow. It coated our jackets an inch deep. The wind was pretty strong but not a blizzard. About a quarter of an hour after being told we were half way we reached a ridge. Visibility was only two or three hundred yards and I could not see how we could climb more unless we first went along a knife edge. Baionetta stopped and cheered on the crowd with 'Su Ragazzi, su, su, Moriete' (Up, boys, up, up, lest you die.). They staggered up and as soon as all were up Baionetta plunged down the other side.

At first I feared this was mere loss of height which would have to be made good again, but as we went on down, it seemed we must be over the pass and a query brought confirmation. It was a horrid descent, soggy tufts and loose stones, both of which gave way under one's feet and I fell more than once. Bruno came to my rescue and gave me a hand; I had no false shame about taking it. Then we got to marble quarries where the path was so steep that even Baionetta fell and we eased ourselves down on our seats. And still it rained. Passing over another shoulder we were told to hurry as we were on the skyline and might be seen by a post, not far behind us. Then we looked down into the main valley and saw villages which were in Allied hands. Several steep bits of path where wire hand rails had been fixed and then we were in trees again. Still down and then a village after which we were on a main path. Cobbled and broad it zigzagged down and down and tried one's legs and feet badly. Hedley told me he felt all in but a tot of Grappo helped him on, a little later I had some too and so did Edward and it helped us over the last mile. At last we got down to the river bed having climbed not less than four thousand feet and come down the same. Crossing the river we got on a proper road. Order of march ceased to matter and the Italians pushed ahead.

As we neared Ruosina [seven miles south-east of Massa] we saw a soldier, a negro. We had reached the forward company of a battalion of American Negroes. We introduced ourselves to the N.C.O. of the guard who took us to Company Headquarters where we arrived just before noon, after marching seven hours. There we met white officers. We were very well received but they said they had nothing to give us to eat and no transport to take us on to Battalion, but they rang Battalion Head Quarters who said they would have coffee ready for us. I was so tired and stiff I did not dare sit down lest I could not get going again. They then did produce transport and we piled into a couple of jeeps, taking Baionetta with us, as it seemed to us he was just the man for establishing regular communications across the line.

On arriving at Battalion at Seravezza we were taken into the guardroom and the black R.S.M. said rather apologetically that he had been told to see if we could identify ourselves and whether we were armed. On my producing my identity discs and saying I could vouch for the party he expressed himself satisfied and we went over to the officers' mess.

Two other gunner officers, also captured near Tobruk in June 1942, were also helped by their Italian Commandant to walk out from their camp at Fontellanato, not far from Lowry-Corry's camp. The officers split up into groups of two or three, and one pair were Captains K. M. Goddard and E. T. Hampson of the 28th Field Regiment. They decided to make their way south along the line of the Apennines in the hope of reaching Allied lines, which then, in September 1943, were a long way away. Goddard's account reads:

Moving by day we followed a procedure of first enquiring of solitary labourers what lay ahead and if towards evening we learned that no Germans were in the next village, then we would approach an isolated farmhouse, ask for food, and an overnight stay in a barn. Such requests were sometimes met with refusal by menfolk but invariably they were overruled by the women whose maternal instincts seldom failed us. We had set ourselves the target of being home for Christmas and this simple aim kept us going when spirits flagged, weather worsened and we suffered setbacks or our stamina and nerves were overstretched. At the same time our ultimate goal was seldom in the

forefront of our daily thoughts, which were concerned with evading
the enemy, food and sleep.

After a number of adventures, by late November they had reached
the rear of the German defences of the GUSTAV line north of the Sangro,
by which time the higher mountains were covered with snow and it was
no longer possible to live off the country. Goddard's account continues:

The next morning we carried on along the hillside in sunshine,
listening to intermittent gunfire and watching vehicle movement
along the valley road. We felt like spectators of an event rather than
participants and when we saw a group of about 20 figures moving
below in our direction we did not immediately realise that we were
their target. It was not until they began shooting that we reacted
and beat a retreat into the trees where we hid in a small cave.
The Germans showed no determination to follow up and probably
assumed us to be local villagers who had been given a sufficient
fright. We discussed our next move and decided that at nightfall
we would descend at the point from which the Germans had
approached, assuming this to be the most direct way to our lines.
We followed this plan until we saw a fireglow and heard voices.
Approaching as near as we could, we watched men come and go and
considered whether we should risk walking through in the hope that
we would go unchallenged. Our nerve failed and we decided to work
our way round on the heights above. We should have realised that if
the line was the River Sangro, then the valley had to be crossed but
logical thought was often absent and wishful thinking controlled our
actions. We set off up the mountain side and at one point heard
voices close to us in what was probably a German O.P. Then we
moved higher onto ice, so hard that we could make no impression
with iron shod boots. I lost my footing and tobogganed some
distance, coming to rest in a depression. I was unhurt but an injury
could have put paid to our chances and this prompted us to return
to a lower level. It was by now approaching dawn and we were back
where we started the previous night. In the grey light we saw huts
around us similar to those near Opi and as we crouched beside one
a mule passed us, presumably going up to the O.P. It was obvious
we could not stay where we were and it was getting lighter all the
time. We got up and ran in the general direction of some rocky
outcrops we had seen the previous day and, having encountered

nobody, we paused for breath and to take stock of the situation. From almost at our feet a figure rose, giving us a tremendous shock, but he proved to be a Free Frenchman who said he had been concealed there for several days but, because the area was so closely defended, he could find no way through. His morale was low and he asked to join us. Whilst we felt little inclination to increase our risks by additional company, sympathy won, and we agreed to let him tag on, and the three of us then made for an area which appeared to offer more cover. We were brought up sharply on the edge of a gorge which dropped almost vertically several hundred feet to the river. Now in a state of exhaustion, having had no real sleep for about three days and none at all during the previous 24 hours, we decided to make the descent. Showers of stones and boulders went crashing beneath us making a tremendous noise but we were more concerned with foot and hand holds than anything else. It was no easy task tired as we were, and then we became aware of the roar of the river below us which, as we descended between the walls of the gorge, became deafening and must have completely veiled the sound of the minia-ture avalanches we were causing. We had good reason to be thankful because to our dismay we now saw a small group of figures on the far side of the river. We were too high above to make out clearly who they were but we presumed them to be enemy. Rational thought should have persuaded us to go back up, traverse to a less conspicu-ous position, or stay on the cliff face until the end of the day, but exhaustion and desperation drove us on, accepting that recapture was almost inevitable. It was not a sound or sensible course and we should have summoned up sufficient courage and will power to act differently but down we went amidst further avalanches. At the bottom there was no cover and we found ourselves separated from a party of five German soldiers by the river torrent, some 30 feet across. They were outside a hut, one chopping wood, one cleaning a rifle and the other preparing food or similar tasks. We watched them for some moments unable to believe that we had not yet been seen; then as realisation dawned, we crouched and ran along the narrow track towards a bend expecting every moment to hear shots but none came and we rounded the bend safely. To this day I believe the hand of Providence guided us that day and lowered a curtain between us and the enemy, enabling us to see them whilst they were unable to see us.

In front of us was a rock sangar, probably used by a shepherd, and on the floor were some empty tins and a small heap of husks. Although in distance we were less than 200 yards from the German hut, it was not in view, and we pushed our luck further by lighting a fire in order to have something hot to drink and eat and give a little warmth. We put the husks in water, boiled up a sort of porridge which we shared, and then slept for some hours. We awoke feeling cold with only the fire embers, but immediately discussed means of crossing the river torrent. Our plan was to strip naked, tie boots and clothing round our necks, and when across, to follow the track past the German hut in darkness and hope that this would lead us through their front positions. When darkness fell it really was black and the noise of the water seemed greater than ever. We tested the depth with long staves and found it to be about chest high. Using the staves as a link between us, Erik went first, then myself and the Frenchman last. The icy water was like an electric shock but it was the force which was more alarming. One slip and there would be no chance in the boiling stream of regaining a footing. When Erik was almost across the Frenchman slipped and grabbed me and had Erik not stood firm we might all have gone but with his help and the staves we made the far bank. We dressed where we stood, Erik and I now donning battle dress. We set off immediately, passed the German hut which was in darkness and started an uphill climb nothing like so precipitous as that which we had descended on the other side. In starlight above the gorge we crossed some open ground, then heard dogs barking after which we saw their silhouette. We flattened and froze feeling sure these would be guard dogs. The animals remained motionless and we thought they might be awaiting a move by us when, after an age, one moved slowly towards us and we saw it to be a sheep. Breathing sighs of relief we carried on until we came to a small railway station and an apparently deserted village. We stopped to listen and heard the crunch of boots and voices; then discerned a patrol column which passed a few yards from us, the last man with a cigarette glowing. It was all a patrol should not be and I hope it was not one of ours. We were still expecting to find some kind of continuous defended line so we were not prepared to treat any movement as other than German. Later we came across white tapes which we took to be night lines but again the question was – whose?

The sky had clouded and now rain began to fall and at first

light we found ourselves in wooded country and again heard voices which we thought to be English but could not believe that we were beyond the German Lines. We sat at the edge of the woods concealed by bushes and watched shell bursts on the adjoining hillside, not knowing from whose guns, when the Frenchman jumped up and shouted 'Un Soldat Anglais'. Our first impulse was to shut the Frenchman up but we then saw, across some open ground, indisputably a British soldier in battle dress with steel helmet, webbing equipment, respirator and rifle. Without more ado we careered across the field shouting and waving as we went. What we must have looked like in our unshaven and bedraggled state I can't think but we achieved surprise and the poor chap made no attempt to move or challenge us. We explained who we were and that he was the first of our countrymen on Allied soil we had spoken to for 18 months. He was a runner with the forward company of the Northamptonshires with the 5th British Division and he led us to his company HQ and the smell of breakfast cooking.

It was the morning of 1 December and we were home, if not dry.

Trooper J. W. Paterson of the 4th County of London Yeomanry had been captured in North Africa in November 1941. Before the Italian surrender in September 1943, he escaped from a canal-digging working party near Venice and was sheltered by local farmers. When he heard of the surrender, he set off south to try and cross the lines, eventually reaching the area near Anzio after the landing there in January 1944, as he describes:

Finally we realised that we were now in the front line. When the moon shone clear we could see machine guns a few feet away on either side of us and then more than this we suddenly heard someone whistling under his breath a few inches away. We were literally lying alongside a German soldier in the front line. It was now quite obvious that we could never survive the guns from this side let alone escape the guns of our own chaps if we tried to rush for it. I have seen Piccadilly less full of people than this place. I don't think a rabbit could have made it. Every now and then there were bursts of fire from one side or the other which would set everyone off. For the first time, Frank agreed by signal that we had to go back. We did exactly the same in reverse as we had done to come, only this time without hope in our hearts. By dawn we had crept back far enough for us to stand up and start walking back to the mountains which we reached with a sigh of relief. We rapidly but dejectedly climbed the mountain and got back to the charcoal burners hut by night fall.

It would have been tempting to stay here whilst we planned a new attempt at a crossing but it would have been unfair for us to have lived on such pitifully poor people. The fact that they would have been very willing to share the little they had made it even less acceptable to us. We continued next day and agreed to return as quickly as possible to our last base and re-equip ourselves for another try somewhere else, perhaps in the south. Our boots were collapsing and we badly needed food. We hurried on. Down the mountain side. Across the Appian way and then across the low hills to the area of Gennazo [Genzano?]. We found a new capanna [hut] which was the size and shape of a bell tent. It was ideal because it was in a remote place. After a long rest we looked out old friends to help us sort ourselves out again.

Almost at once one of our lesser acquaintances excitedly told us about two relations of his who had shot a German general and were being hunted and desperately needed us to help them hide. As usual it was difficult to be sure where the truth actually lay but the pressure upon us was enormous. We had been given so much help and now they wanted a little of ours, and yet we knew that it was the wrong thing to do. To the depths of our being we knew that this was a disastrous thing to do and yet eventually we agreed to let them share our capanna provided that it was very temporary indeed. Fairly instantly the pair appeared. Frank and I both took an instant dislike to them. We fully believed that they had committed some heinous crime but not that they had made a patriotic killing. They were just not the type. However, we had given our word and that was that. We took them to our place and sat and talked trying to trick them into giving away what they had really done. The next day they went off in one direction and we went another, giving them stern warnings about being careful and not mix or talk with anyone – they promised faithfully that they would not go near anyone else. We walked along the ridge that our capanna was built on and found a good spot to survey the whole area for miles around. We sat in the sun and dozed and Frank smoked his awful cigarettes. Then, around midday, a small boy came hurtling up the ridge to breathlessly tell us that there were hundreds of Germans looking for us. I suddenly remembered that it was the first of April and that the Italians also have April Fools Day. So this was it. The big joke. In spite of his protestations that it was true, we told him to go home. And then I looked down into the valley. Across the whole horizon were Germans spaced a few yards apart walking towards us. There must have been hundreds of them. We were already in their sight but fortunately a long way away. We writhed our way out of their vision, so that they wouldn't be attracted by movement, and made our way up to higher ground and towards their extreme flank. It took the rest of the day but we got round behind them on the ground that they had already searched and as they had now passed our capanna we returned to it at dusk. So did the other two.

We spent the rest of the evening discussing our problems in whispers. Next day we kept the other two with us but when it started to get dark they made some excuse of needing to go and get some things. We were against the idea but we really couldn't stop them except by force. It must have been nearly midnight before they got back and we were furious. Eventually we all settled down to sleep on the mud floor.

Sometime in the night I awoke to the mechanical click of things being done to guns – suddenly, the two Italians threw themselves through the tiny opening and down the slope outside. At the same moment automatic guns started to fire into the capanna and down the slope at the same time. There must have been twenty guns firing at once. I was petrified. The noise alone was demoralizing. Frank, who had been late waking up, just continued to lay there quietly. Suddenly the firing stopped and we waited for the next inevitable move. The German practice at this point was to give you a few seconds to come out before throwing in a hand grenade. A German voice called out in English – 'Come out English.' After a pause, Frank called out that we were coming. I was far too petrified to call out and even had difficulty in standing up to get out. This delay was attributed by Frank to courage and no amount of fervent explanation on my part could ever persuade him otherwise. However, once outside, an arrogance swept me. It was almost like a reaction to the fear that had previously completely possessed me. They tied our hands behind our backs with rope and then they started to question us. With the Germans was a Fascist officer who decided to show off on me now that I had my hands tied. Stupidly

I had answered some questions in my best Italian thinking that we might just get away with being local peasants. The Fascist, of course, jumped on this opportunity of accusing me of being an Italian spy who had to be disposed of. He now got out his gun and demanded that I admit it. The German told him he was wrong. Still he continued to shout hysterically in my face and so I insulted him in Italian. Whereupon he lifted his gun above my head and brought it down to smash my skull. As the gun came down, the German in charge stepped quickly forward and deflected his arm enough to make him miss my skull and hit my shoulder instead. That was painful enough. The German told the Italian to get out of the way, amongst other things, and we were told to march.

We were convinced that we were going to be shot, but nevertheless with a mixture of resignation, annoyance with the Italian and reaction to the earlier fear, I demanded that our bag with its few belongings be carried with us. This was done in the manner of the master requiring his servants to bring his luggage. The Germans bridled but we refused to move until eventually a soldier was instructed to pick up our belongings and we were pushed, stumbling down the slope. As we walked through one village a crowd gathered to watch. A German soldier pointed to a young woman and said that she had given us away. We then realised that our two idiot friends had done as we feared and warned, and gone to a prostitute. Not only that but told her where we were all sleeping. No wonder the Germans knew we were English even when we were still in the capanna. The Fascist found it convenient not to know. After hours of walking we got to their headquarters where it now became apparent that I had been recaptured by the same regiment that captured me in Africa. As this became known everything became jovial and friendly. Our wrists were untied and they gave us drinks. In the end it became a very jovial party.

Major A. O. ('Jock') McGinlay and other officers of the 7th Royal Tank Regiment, including the commanding officer, Lieutenant-Colonel H. R. B. Foote VC, had been taken prisoner in Tobruk when Rommel captured it in June 1942. Like Lowry-Corry, they ended up in POW Camp 29 at Veano near Piacenza, and also escaped at the time of the Italian surrender and made for the mountains, where they were befriended by an Italian family from Milan, which they had left to avoid

the Allied air raids, and by other families of the same village. They
decided against attempting to make their way south, but to try and get
to Switzerland, and the daughter of the family, Maria, was willing to
help them. McGinlay wrote this account of their adventures:

As I spoke the best Italian of the four, Maria and I went to Milan.
To do this, I was fitted out with a rough old jacket, and wearing my
tank beret pulled down at the front, my battle dress trousers dyed
black with ink, and army boots with the uppers cut off to look like
shoes, Maria and I set off. We walked over the top of the hill we
were on, and down into the next valley. There a small bus left once a
day for the plains below, and we caught this, with Maria buying the
tickets. I had picked up a book as I was leaving, so that I could
pretend to be engrossed in it and so prevent any unwanted discussion
with fellow passengers. It worked, though for no other reason than
the fact that it was early morning, and nobody felt like talking
anyway. Just as well, as it turned out that the book I had taken was a
school book belonging to Angela, aged 7. Arriving at a station, Maria
bought two tickets to Piacenza, and we sat separately on the train
which was nearly empty. Arriving at Piacenza, again two tickets were
bought to Milan. I had my ticket, but again sat separate from Maria.
There were Germans on this train, but funnily enough, I did not
mind them in the slightest. I felt more Italian than they did, and no
one bothered me.

Once in Milan, I followed Maria on to a tram, which took us to
the outskirts. It was night by this time. Again Maria got the tickets. I
stood next to German soldiers, but wasn't in the slightest bothered
about them. They seemed to be 'Foreigners', not me. It was a strange
sensation. We got off the tram, and after a short walk, reached a
block of flats. The Battaini flat was about four floors up, and there
I stayed for about ten days.

The next phase was as follows:

1. Find out if identity cards were required at the frontier.
2. Check on trains, timing and fares.
3. Buy money, if possible (This was surprisingly easy, once
   we contacted some of the many pro-allies people among
   the Battaini family acquaintance).
4. Buy clothes for the others back up in the hills.

All of this was put in hand, and took time. Maria went by train to Como, and sure enough, the Germans were very much on the alert, examining all identity cards. Then she tried Varese, with happier results. Next she contacted a business man who had several shoe shops, and was very pro-British. He promptly gave me quite a lot of money (I forget how much), solely on a promissory note, promising that the British Government would repay the sum after the war. (This was indeed repaid, as I checked after the war, by the Allied Screening Commission). With this money we were able to buy clothes and shoes, and packing them into a case, I sent the lot back up to Casella, with a covering letter. In this I gave all the details necessary to have the correct change ready when buying tickets, where the toilets were on the stations, and so on. [However] the young Italian I sent up with the clothes delivered them to some other Britishers hiding in Tornazera, the village next to Casella, and only the letter to Colonel Foote was sent on to him.

The shoe shop man was most helpful in other ways. He offered us the use of his house when we got to Varese, if we wanted to lie up till dark before attempting the crossing. 'But', he said, 'Why don't you use the services of the Contrabandieri?' That word means smugglers. Apparently there was and had been for centuries, a thriving smuggling business between Switzerland and Italy. So sure enough, a representative of this enterprising band was brought to the flat, and a real cloak and dagger scheme was worked out, whereby we would take the train to Varese, walk to an indentified cafe, sit and have a coffee watching for a man wearing some distinguishing feature, follow him out after an interval of a minute, then at a distance Etc. Etc. But then this chap said, whilst quite willing to do this for us, why did we not contact the partigiani? 'The who?', I asked. Apparently this was a group calling themselves Partisans, or Partigiani, who had already helped several escapees into Switzerland. Bring them along, I asked.

Sure enough, two days later, I was standing at the stove with an apron on, when a knock came at the door. When I opened it, the most glamorous female stood there, beautifuly dressed and promptly spoke perfect English to me. She turned out to be the wife of an Italian Colonel, held prisoner by the British in India. We talked and agreed that she should return the day after the Colonel, B.J. and Johnnie got down from the hills. This was to make the complete arrangements. Down came the other three, helped and guided by the other members of the Battaini family. It was a rotten ordeal for Johnnie especially. Being so tall, he takes size 100 at least in shoes, and of course the shoes he eventually managed to scrounge were far too small, and, to cap it they were too scared to take a tram, and walked from the station. His feet were pretty bad when at last they arrived. I had a good meal ready for them, bought with my new money. I remember it was a goose, cooked in butter.

Three of the partisans arrived, including the wife of the Italian colonel. We sat round a table, and soon had a plan organised. To do this, we promised two things. The Italian colonel was to be released and sent back to Milan (I forget how this was to be done), and to take a list of things the partisans wanted from the Allies in the way of help. We wrote down a list, which contained ammunition for guns they had; guns for ammunition they had; radios, radio frequencies; dropping areas and code signs; alternatives for them; priority bombing targets such as German ammo dumps and fuel dumps; and a tunnel which had a train-load of Tiger tanks hidden in it.

Milan half emptied itself each evening about five p.m. when most of the population finished work, and got away from the city and possible bombing. We took advantage of this and in two pairs, each with a partisan guide walking a few yards in front, we left for the station. Johnnie* and B.J.,† being the tallest, had the tallest guide. The Colonel and I had the Italian Colonel's wife. Travelling separately, each pair having been given our rail tickets which had been bought before, we boarded the train; Johnnie and B.J. at the front end, we at the rear. The train was very crowded, and each pair, looking for a seat, walked along the corridors towards each other, and finished up together in the middle. There we stood until Varese. It was dark. Our instructions were to watch for a young lady in a large hat, shining a shaded torch on her face. To follow her at a distance out of the station. This we did, and followed her round several blocks. Then she passed a man who was fiddling with the chain on his bicycle. He appeared to give up trying to sort it, and started wheeling it away. The girl disappeared; we followed the man. For some distance, until we were well clear of the town, we just kept him in sight. Then he pulled up at some large gates in a wall, obviously belonging to some

---

* Captain J. Maclean.
† Captain D. R. Burgoyne-Johnson.

big estate. He waited till we got near, and said quietly 'All right, gentlemen'.

And there we were, meeting the Marquis de la Peine. He held out his hand, and welcomed us to his home. It was a beautiful house. He took us in and gave us dinner, apologising that the dinner service was not the best, though it seemed gold plated at least, because the finest of his cutlery and plate was buried in the garden, where the Germans wouldn't find it. The servants were actually dressed in velvet knee breeches, silk stockings and so on. It would appear that he was a big wig, such an influence in the local area that he had been left very much alone. After dinner and coffee, he suggested we 'might like to go ahead with our crossing into Switzerland?' As if we had anything else on our minds! Apparently the frontier ran along the edge of his estate, and he summoned two of his groundsmen, probably game keeper types, gave them their instructions, and we were off into the night.

It was a long walk – several miles, through woods and paths. It started to snow, and we could see that our guides were a bit worried about this. We stopped for what we thought was a breather at a hut, and talked. Our guides were unwilling to go on. Our footprints would give everything away, in the snow, to the Germans who patrolled regularly. We sat for several hours, wondering what to do. We did not have much money on us, and what we had, we were hoping to keep for eventualities in Switzerland. But we pooled most of it and offered it to the guides, if they would take this extra risk. It worked. Another mile or so, and we went down a small valley to where a stream must sometime have been, but it was fairly dry at the time. A culvert with a barbed wire knife-rest contraption was pulled to one side and we were waved through. Switzerland. As we passed through, I handed one of the guides a postcard, previously written by one of the Battainis to themselves and already stamped. I asked the guide to post it. He did, and when the Battainis received it, they knew we were safe, and that the route was O.K. for any others. Some came after us, the same way.

Lieutenant K. G. Patterson of the Royal Australian Naval Volunteer Reserve was manning a folboat of the Special Boat Section, carrying out a reconnaissance of the beach approaches at Anzio on the night of 2/3rd December 1943. Having completed his task, he and fellow folboats failed to make rendezvous with their parent motor torpedo boat. He and his fellow crewman, Jock, at first started to paddle the eighty miles south to two islands off the coast near Gaeta, but soon realized that it was impracticable in the choppy sea. Waiting until dark on the following night, they paddled ashore and made contact with some Italian farmers, who passed them on to some partisans. With their help, they reached the area of Spigno behind the German lines on the Garigliano front. By this time they had, reluctantly as far as they were concerned, been joined by an American airman, whose Fortress had been shot down after bombing Cassino, and two escaped prisoners of war, a South African and a Belgian member of the French Foreign Legion. He now thought that the time had come to try and get through to the Allied lines, as he describes:

It was a hair raising trip as there were Germans everywhere and we kept tripping over phone lines but didn't cut them because we didn't want to stir up repair gangs. We felt our way quietly, diving into a ditch several times to avoid being run over by tanks. The shell bursts from 5th Army 25 pounders that were coming over the low hill ahead of us left a strange phosphorescent glow in the pitch darkness, when they exploded. We crossed a sunken road short of the crest of the hill and promptly fell into an excavation that was the retaining wall and doorway to a magazine for the 88 battery which was ahead and either side of us. I think this must have been part of the GUSTAV line, the prepared positions the Germans had laid down some time previously. We could plainly hear the German Fire Control officer giving his fire orders nearby so we vacated the pit, and seeing a haystack on the forward slope ahead and to the left, we burrowed underneath it pulling out sheaves of hay to do so. After a while it became obvious there was a gun duel going on between the 88s alongside us and Allied 25 pounders out on the plain towards Castelforte, and we heard and felt some hits close by. All of a sudden the haystack disappeared from over us in a cloud of straw and dirt and we realised it had been marked as an aiming point by 5th Army guns. We had seen a slit trench nearby when crawling to the haystack and withdrew there quickly, no sooner falling into it than we received a hit on the edge and I was hit in the shoulder, head and upper arm by shrapnel. Deciding rapidly that our position was unhealthy, while the 25 pounders were hard at it, we withdrew over the back of the rise and across the sunken road we had crossed on the way up, finally going to ground below the edge of the road in a large patch of 'Prince of Wales feathers'. I decided we would lie low for an hour or so and have another go early next evening and went to sleep with the 25 pounders bouncing off the road over our heads.

Early next morning I was dug in the ribs by a large soldier who was a member of a Hermann Goering Division patrol, who, I found, had seen the Frenchman, the American and the South African looking for oranges in the orchard below the road without consulting me, and rounded up Jock as well. We had less than 1 Km to go to reach 5th Army lines. We were all taken to Ausonia and 'booked in' and I was given a sling for my shoulder. I retained my watch as it was not discovered round my ankle. From there we went into a holding cage at Frosinone, where I said goodbye to the others including Jock. All I can remember of the cage was the difficulty in using the starting block toilets with an arm in a sling! I didn't stay long there but was whisked away with a truckload of officers to Rome, where we had our clothing de-loused at an army delousing station. I had my first shower for a couple of months, and had my shoulder wound probed and the other holes patched up. A bed in the hospital there was bliss. From Rome we were taken to a hospital at Perugia, which had been a convent, and was totally inadequate as a hospital, particularly in the plumbing department. After a couple of days there, I was picked up by a couple of German soldiers who were going home on leave and escorted by train through Bolzano and across the Alps direct to Hanover where I was locked in a station lavatory until picked up by my next couple of escorts who took me on a branch line to Tarmstet; this was a village not far from Marlag-Milag Nord at Wester Timke which was the main Naval and Merchant Navy camp in NW Germany. It was 23rd February 1944.

Captain James Hughes, Royal Artillery, was serving with the 2nd Special Air Service Regiment when they paradropped a party tasked to destroy German aircraft on an airfield near Perugia in January 1944. Not only were there few aircraft on the ground when they reached it, but Hughes was wounded when one of his explosive devices blew up. He and his colleagues were captured, but escaped from the train taking them to Germany, jumping out between Modena and Mantua. There they were picked up by partisans, who passed them on to other bands until they reached the area south of Ancona on the Adriatic coast. There they spent several weeks sheltered by Italian families not far from Porto San Giorgio, expecting the Royal Navy to send a boat to pick them up from a specified beach on a designated moonless night. But no boat came either on the night or on the next, and it was decided to abandon that plan and try somewhere else. His account, in which he refers to himself as 'Jimmy', continues:

The next night they set off south once more, climbing the hill beyond the river and passing between Fermo and the sea, they eventually joined the coast at Torre di Palme. It was now one hour to midnight. Little groups drifted into the rendezvous out of the dark night. 'Terzo' had gone ahead and made the arrangements, and now they knew that they had agreed to purchase an old fishing boat which lay high on the beach on the other side of the main road. The deal was fixed so that, if the two Italian fishermen would take them all south of the Allied lines, a reward would be paid for each person safely landed and the fishermen would be assured the safety of the seas in which to fish unhampered by enemy or allied air strikes. This was certainly something which was denied them behind the German lines. Twenty-two people were to make the voyage, plus one white rabbit to bring them luck, and now the tasks were allocated. The long and heavy mast took six hands who lifted it carefully and, waiting for a pause in the heavy German traffic on Route 16, raised it and trooped silently across the road. They were followed by another party of four who carried the sail and a large white sheet inscribed, in bold black paint, with the letters 'P.O.W.' This was a safety precaution against Allied air attacks, for it was rumoured that the last boat which made the trip had been shot at with a total loss of life.* Others carried the demi-john of water and the caged rabbit, plus the various bits and pieces which would make up the cargo for the voyage.

The night was dark, but crossing the road was not difficult and they turned south along the beach. But now the apprehension began, for the beach was a pebbly shore whose grinding stones, under the impact of twenty-two pairs of shoes and boots, threw out a series of loud crunches which seemed to echo across the hills, and would surely be heard by anyone in the vicinity. They had about one

---

* An SAS party of eleven had sailed from near Fermo on 7 March and was never heard of again.

hundred yards of beach to traverse in this noisy manner, expecting any moment to be challenged and fired upon, but, except for the footfalls, the night remained quiet and no gun broke the silence. They came upon the boat, an old clinker-built craft of considerable size, which had not been to sea for two years. The mast was erected and the stays secured. Each man took up his position around the boat, swung it easily in a big arc and slid it swiftly down the hard pebbles to the beach. The surface of the Adriatic was calm, but a heavy swell threw breakers on the beach.

It was a chilly night and late and, as the bows of the old boat pushed into the breakers, each man stopped walking out, fearful of getting his clothes drenched by the sea. The inevitable happened. The second breaker hit the bow at an angle and swung the whole boat round, so that it lay parallel to the beach. The next one swamped its gunwhales and poured into the craft. In a sort of panic most of the personnel realised that, if they were to get the boat into the water, they must soak themselves and, plunging up to their waists, they tugged and pulled until the bows came round and the boat headed into the waves. The shore shelved sharply and the water soon was deep. All climbed aboard. The oars were on the rollicks and they were pulling clear of the shore line, which slowly lost all shape and dipped into the darkness.

Soon they were well out, a couple of hundred yards, and the boat was drifting and being propelled in a southerly direction. Only then did the predicament dawn on those on board. The water level inside was as high as that of the sea outside. The ship was awash but still floating. She rolled sloppily in the heavy swell, making little headway. Each man took his trilby hat and began to bale furiously. The odds and ends of luggage and the big demi-john of water were all jettisoned overboard, but no one had the heart to sacrifice the rabbit which lay cold and half-drowned in the bows of the boat. They argued hotly about the best course of action. If the boat was going to sink it would be better to cling to the coast, but in doing so they ran the risk of being seen by German patrols. Sitting up to their waists in water, baling continuously with flimsy water-logged felt hats, they made the bold choice and headed further out to sea. The time was two o'clock in the morning and they hoisted the jib. Now the gentle breeze was filling it blowing them gently east by south on the compass. It began to look as if their luck was in and the constant baling was beginning to show results. The clinker planks of the boat were swelling in the sea water, the gaps were sealing and soon the water was no more than a slopping puddle around their feet. No one slept. They were too cold, wet and miserable for that as they baled and waited for the dawn.

After they had been going for what seemed hours, there was a sudden sharp crack in the boat and the single mast split and fell, bringing with it the jib. Its old timber had been unable to take the strain and now they cut it loose and cast it, with the sail, into the sea. Slowly the darkness gave way to a light in the east which spread evenly across the sky. It would be a day of even solid cloud and then they saw the mountains on their right – the great high massif of the Abruzzi Milose and, rising imperiously in its midst, the bulk of Monte Corno and Gran Sasso d'Italia. They were abreast of the highest peaks, but surely this was not possible. As the light improved 'Keg' took out the panorama sketch which showed the coastline and mountain ranges. They looked at it in amazement for the rough silhouette agreed with the skyline to the west. They really were abreast of the high mountains and they must have made incredible speed during the night,* catching both the wind and the tide in their favour. Keg explained that, about once a year, the sea, forced by the wind, built up towards Venice with a north-westerly current, and then backed, running down the Adriatic with the following wind from the north. It had been on just that night that they had sailed from Torre di Palme. The sea was now calm with just a gentle breeze, and then, with daylight, came the first aircraft flying high above them. It was a Spitfire. As they heard it approach they held out the big white sheet, hoping that the pilot, before taking any precipitous action, would be able to read the bold letters 'P.O.W.'. They waved it to attract his attention, but he was high and flew on unconcerned with other tasks to fulfil.

By mid-day they could see the flashes in the hills as the guns exchanged their lethal charges. Soon there was a fast motor boat heading out toward them, but, as it grew larger, it suddenly turned and made its way slowly back towards the coast. Then they could see a railway engine chugging up the coastal line, its white puffs of smoke outlined against the dark hillside. That must be the Allied lines. No

---

* Actually 120 km in fourteen hours, 8.6 km per hour (4.6 knots).

German trains were running along the coast. By three in the afternoon they were moving in amongst the little fishing fleet and could see the tiny port ahead of them – no anchorage, but a welcome stretch of friendly beach – and within the hour, the keel struck land at S. Vitoi Chietino, just south of Ortona a Mare.

If they had expected a red carpet reception they were mistaken, but a little reception committee did stand waiting to arrest them and interrogate them – two British Military Policemen and a Carabiniere. Clean, smart, with polished boots and blankoed webbing, they stood imperturbably as the sodden, weary party stepped gingerly, one by one, from the old boat which had brought them home. For Jimmy it was a homecoming and the Military [Police] Sergeant watched the drab little man struggle ashore over the hard wet pebbles. His ill-fitting clothes hung on his thin body and, with his dirty hand, he brushed his stubbly chin. He was one of an anonymous group who had got home. The Sergeant led them up the beach to a little house and each was given a cup of hot sweet tea.

Epilogue

Preceding pages reveal that the campaign which the Allies fought against the Germans in Italy from July 1943 to May 1945 was, in some ways, more reminiscent of the First World War than any other of the Second. This was brought about by a combination of the terrain, the weather in winter, the fierce and skilful resistance put up by their adversaries, and the fact that, except in the air and at sea, they enjoyed no superiority of strength over them. To the soldiers (rather more so than to the sailors and airmen) was added, at any rate from January 1944 onwards, the demoralizing influence that they were playing second fiddle to the cross-Channel invasion; that victory was not going to be won by them, and that their sacrifices and suffering were not essential to it and were not appreciated. This feeling was accentuated by the number of attacks to which they were committed which clearly had only slender chances of success, especially round Cassino and in the last winter.

Two questions must therefore be asked. Were the sacrifices and suffering justified? Did they achieve what was intended by those who directed the strategy? The verdict must be 'Yes'. The strategic aim was to force the Germans to deploy such strength in Italy which, if not held there, might tip the balance in their defence of France. They would not be forced to deploy that strength unless their hold in Italy was seriously threatened, and that could only be done by attack. Churchill, and at one time, it appears, his Chiefs of Staff also, thought that the same effect might be achieved by threatening the German position in Greece and the Balkans instead. But, apart from the American rejection of that strategy, it was probably a pious hope. It would not have been such a direct threat to Germany and her war effort, and she would have been able to withdraw gradually step by step. That the Allied forces in Italy achieved their aim, even when they had been reduced after they had reached Rome, is shown by the number of German divisions they held in Italy, in comparison to their own strength. In March 1944, at the time of the Third Battle of Cassino, twenty-one Allied divisions faced twenty-two German: on 11 May, the start of Operation DIADEM, twenty-five faced twenty-three: at the end of August, twenty faced twenty-six on the GOTHIC Line; and, when the final offensive was launched on 9 April 1945, seventeen faced twenty-three. It was, of course, events elsewhere, on the Western and Eastern fronts, that decided the issue. Unless they were under great pressure there, it was always possible for the Germans to reinforce Italy rapidly in emergency, whereas the Allies, with their long roundabout external means of access, could not.

That Alexander achieved the task he was set does not mean that he might not have done so more effectively and economically. As leader of a heterogeneous group of armies, he was a good choice. He was adept at charming and persuading, and none could doubt his personal courage and first-hand knowledge of battlefield conditions; but he lacked the single-minded decisiveness and drive of Montgomery and appears to have been inclined to accept too uncritically propositions made to him by others. Mark Clark, in any case, was not susceptible to his charm and persuasive approach. Once up against the GUSTAV Line at the end of 1943, there is no doubt that a major effort, as was eventually made in Operation DIADEM in May 1944, was required if a breakthrough was to be achieved. The successive battles at Cassino, combined with the landing at Anzio, were not on a large enough scale. Juin's and Tuker's alternative to Cassino, a thrust through the mountains further north, would not have succeeded unless a major effort had also been made elsewhere at the same time. The unfortunate Lucas was undoubtedly right not to have tried to thrust rapidly inland from Anzio before he had secured a firm and large enough beachhead. To have done so would almost certainly have led to disaster. Only a major amphibious assault, on the scale at least of that at Salerno, would have produced better results, and it would need to have been accompanied by a stronger attack against the GUSTAV Line than that made in January. But a long delay to prepare for such a major effort would have given the Germans a pause in which they could improve further their defences, suffer fewer losses and, perhaps, transfer divisions to other fronts.

When, at last, Operation DIADEM was launched in May, the opportunity to inflict a decisive defeat on Kesselring's forces was forfeited by Clark's fateful decision to go for Rome instead of Valmontone and Leese's over-insurance by cramming the Liri valley with one over-mechanized formation after another, leading to a log-jam, as his master, Montgomery, had done in the final stage of El Alamein. Had DIADEM achieved its original aim, Hitler would have had to send further reinforcements, if the GOTHIC Line was to be held, just at the time that the Allies were landing in Normandy.

When he did reach the GOTHIC Line in August, Alexander was surely wrong to give way to Leese's demand to switch Eighth Army back to the Adriatic coast. It lost him three precious weeks of summer weather, and although he had lost his best mountain troops, Juin's North African divisions, he had three good Indian ones. If he had developed the full force of Eighth and Fifth Armies directly forward then, his chances of reaching Bologna and the Po valley before winter set in were good. Pandering to Leese's dislike of having to cooperate with Clark condemned both armies to the 'Winter of Discontent' in grim conditions. If he had then got rid of Leese and appointed McCreery in his place, those slogging matches across the rivers between Ancona and Ravenna might have been avoided. When McCreery did succeed Leese, he produced more imaginative plans, his final offensive being as well conceived as it was executed by the British, Indian, New Zealand and Polish divisions involved. Alexander's alternative proposal, an amphibious operation across the northern Adriatic to land in Istria and advance through the Ljubljana Gap in the hope of reaching Vienna before the Russians, supported by Churchill, but rejected not only by the Americans but by Brooke also, was never more than a pipe-dream. The final offensive which brought the two armies into the valley of the Po, across the river, and forced the German surrender before that in Germany itself, was a fitting reward for all that they had been through. Eisenhower's much larger forces, as they drove forward from the Rhine to the Elbe, should have been grateful for the contribution the Allied forces in Italy had made to their victory.

Bibliography

Baynes, John, *The Forgotten Victor* (London: Brassey's, 1989)

Brooks, Thomas R., *The War North of Rome, June 1944–May 1945* (New York: Sarpedon, Tonbridge: Spellmount, 1996)

Carver, Michael, *Harding of Petherton* (London: Weidenfeld & Nicolson, 1978)

Churchill, Winston S., *The Second World War*, vol. IV: *The Hinge of Fate*; vol. V: *Closing the Ring*; vol. VI: *Triumph and Tragedy* (London: Cassell, 1951, 1952, 1954)

Clark, Mark, *Calculated Risk* (London: George G. Harrap & Co., 1951)

D'Este, Carlo, *Bitter Victory* (London: Collins, 1988)

——, *Patton. A Genius for War* (New York: HarperCollins Publishers, 1995; published in the UK as *A Genius for War: A Life of General George S. Patton*, HarperCollins Publishers, 1996)

Doherty, Richard, *A Noble Crusade: The History of Eighth Army 1941 to 1945* (Staplehurst: Spellmount, 1999)

Eisenhower, Dwight D., *Crusade in Europe* (London: W. Heinemann, 1948)

Ellis, John, *Cassino: The Hollow Victory* (London: A. Deutsch, 1984)

Fraser, David, *Alanbrooke* (London: Collins, 1982)

——, *And We Shall Shock Them: the British Army in the Second World War* (London: Hodder & Stoughton, 1983)

Hamilton, Nigel, *Monty: Master of the Battlefield, 1942–1944* (London: Hamilton, 1983)

Hibbert, Christopher, *Anzio: The Bid for Rome* (London: Macdonald, 1970)

Howard, Michael, *The Mediterranean Strategy in the Second World War* (London: Weidenfeld & Nicolson, 1968)

Jackson, W. G. F., *The Battle for Italy* (London: Batsford, 1967)

——, *The Battle for Rome* (London: Batsford, 1969)

——, *Alexander of Tunis: as military commander* (London: Batsford, 1969)

Lamb, Richard, *Montgomery in Europe 1943–45: Success or Failure?* (London: Buchan & Enright, 1983)

Lett, Gordon, *Rossano, An Adventure of the Italian Resistance* (London: Hodder & Stoughton, 1955)

Lewin, Ronald, *Montgomery as Military Commander* (London: Batsford, 1971)

Majdalany, F., *Cassino: Portrait of a Battle* (London: Longmans, Green, 1957)

Montgomery, Viscount, of Alamein, *The Memoirs of Field-Marshal the Viscount Montgomery of Alamein* (London: Collins, 1958)

Nicolson, Nigel, *Alex: the Life of Field Marshal Earl Alexander of Tunis* (London: Weidenfeld & Nicolson, 1973)

North, John, *The Alexander Memoirs, 1940–1945* (London: Cassel, 1962)

Official Histories of the Second World War:

——, *Grand Strategy*, vol. IV: *Aug. 1941–Sept. 1943*, Michael Howard (London: H.M. Stationery Office, 1972)

——, *Mediterranean and Middle East,*vol. V: *The campaign in Sicily 1943 and the campaign in Italy 3rd September 1943 to 31st March 1944*, C. J. C. Molony, and vol. VI, *Victory in the Mediterranean*, part I, C. J. C. Molony, parts II & III, William Jackson with T. P. Gleave, (London: H.M. Stationery Office, 1974 and 1984)

Senger und Etterlin, F. von, *Neither Fear Nor Hope: the Wartime Career of General Frido von Senger und Etterlin, defender of Cassino* (London: Macdonald, 1963)

Smith, E. D., *The Battles for Cassino* (London: Allan, 1975)

Index of Contributors

Ranks and units are given as they were at the time of the experience described, as far as could be determined. Unless other acknowledgement is made, extracts are all from papers deposited with the Department of Documents of the Imperial War Musuem. The name of the copyright holder, who has given permission, is shown in brackets, unless it is the individual him- or herself. An asterisk denotes that it has not been possible to trace the copyright holder: the Museum would be grateful for any information which might help to trace those whose identities or addresses are not known.

Index